GURDJIEFF AND ORAGE

GURDJIEFF
AND
ORAGE

Brothers in Elysium

Paul Beekman Taylor

⑨ WEISER BOOKS
York Beach, Maine, USA

For Orage's grandchildren

David, Marcus, Linnet, Carolyn, Piers, Toby,
and Peregrine

In Memory of Richard and Ann Orage

First published in 2001 by
Weiser Books
P. O. Box 612
York Beach, ME 03910-0612
www.weiserbooks.com

Library of Congress Cataloging-in-Publication Data
  Taylor, Paul Beekman.
    Brothers in Elysium / Paul Beekman Taylor
      p. cm.
    Includes bibliographical references (p.) and index.
    ISBN 1-57863-128-9 (pbk. : alk. paper)
      1. Gurdjieff, Georges Ivanovitch, 1872–1949. 2. Orage, A. R. (Alfred
    Richard), 1873–1934. 3. Gurdjieff, Georges Ivanovitch, 1872–1949—
    Friends and associates. 4. Orage, A. R. (Alfred Richard), 1873–1934—
    Friends and associates. I. Title.

B4249.G84 T39 2001
133'.092'2—dc21
[B]   00–043906

VG
Typeset in Times 10/14
Cover design by Ed Stevens
Printed in the United States of America

08 07 06 05 04 03 02 01
  8 7 6 5 4 3 2 1

Table of Contents

Prologue

Frater qui adiuvater a fratre quasi civitas firma.[1]

Gurdjieff and I are brothers under the skin.

—Orage[2]

Gurdjieff is a brother who has taken another path.

—Orage[3]

This book is a critical history of the relationship between two men in the cultural milieu of the West between the two Great Wars. That relationship constitutes an extraordinary drama played out in concert by two moral, intellectual, and spiritual brothers, each of whom knew the other's mind as well, or almost as well, as his own. The drama can be seen as a tug of values in which each participant pulled the other toward a higher sense of being. This story is also a love story concerning the love of Orage—who left behind an occupation in England—for an Institute for the Harmonious Development of Man that promised to reveal to him esoteric knowledge. His service to that Institute led him to America and a deep love for an American woman. Orage was wont to say: "I have two loves, the Institute and Jessie." Integrated with and enclosing these loves was an intellectual and moral commitment to a broad human concern that never quit his attention: an economic theory of egalitarian humanism that he believed could mediate man's moral relationships in his society and between societies. Its ultimate doctrinal manifestation for him was known as Social Credit.

All three of these impulses—esoteric, amatory, and social—marshaled a full commitment of energy on the part of Orage that was fused into one program for the betterment of self and the world about him. He explained to others that he was drawn to Gurdjieff because he thought the "work," as Gurdjieff's teaching was known, was a path toward the

---

1. A brother helped by his brother is like a fortified city (Proverbs 18:19).
2. Letter to Edith A. Taylor, March 1929.
3. Louise Welch, *Orage with Gurdjieff in America* (London: Routledge & Kegan Paul, 1982), p. 115.

moral goals of Social Credit. His love for the young American, Jessie
Dwight, tested and gave play to his personal relations with Gurdjieff,
his own teaching and writing, and his program for attaining one goal of
Gurdjieff's teaching that, for convenience, can be called simply "objective consciousness."

His mentor Gurdjieff's love for supernal truth was so engaging and
so possessive of his energies that he willed it to all others. His teaching
was dedicated to preparing the widest population capable of receiving
and making it theirs. His love for the world was no less than Christ's,
Buddha's, or Mohammed's; no less was his commitment to the transmission of the truth of the world he saw dimmed by the floating ash of
successive explosions of human error. He sought to restore the bleak
human landscape of ignorance to light and life; and he carried that light
and life in himself on his quest to impart it to others without discrimi-
nation.

Gurdjieff's whole life can be read as a series of passages on that
quest, whereas Orage—as Paul Gauguin, Sherwood Anderson, Hart
Crane, Margaret Anderson, Jane Heap, and countless others at crucial
moments in their lives—seemed to change goals midstream in life. In
effect, he gave up a career to quest for a conception of self that he felt
was being stifled in the banality of quotidian "mechanicalness," as
Gurdjieff called the current state of Western existence. Orage was the
editor and publisher of the London magazine *The New Age,* whose early
editorial purpose was to present discussions of issues of labor and man-
agement in the name of Guild Socialism.[4] More significantly for the
cultural history of England, however, the pages of *The New Age* contained countless articles on art, literature, and economy written by
Orage, and fiction and poetry written by the avantgarde of English letters, including Ezra Pound, Hilaire Belloc, Edwin Muir, Herbert Read,
G. K. Chesterton, Beatrice Hastings, Katherine Mansfield, and many
others who forged the literary metal of the day. Pound had been writing
for The New Age since 1912 over a number of pseudonyms, and he and
Orage often put out an issue all by themselves.[5]

Orage turned aside from this life and these contacts, as he said to
his secretary, Alice Marks, "to find God,"[6] and it was through Gurdjieff

---

4. Orage, like Pound, shunned the Fabian Socialism he had once espoused, and Shaw dis-
creetly distanced himself from Orage for a time. Orage's early book, *An Alphabet of Economics,*
defines the terms of Social Credit (London: T. Fisher Unwin, 1917).
5. They worked so closely together, notes Earle Davis in *Vision Fugitive: Ezra Pound and
Economics* (Lawrence, KS: University of Kansas Press, 1968), that Orage even supported
Pound financially for some time (p. 49).
6. Cited by Louise Welch, *Orage,* p. 25.

that he expected to find him. The years immediately following World War I constituted an era of risks, an age in which men and women were shaken loose by the courage of their convictions to change directions radically. It seemed to others that Orage left a half century of himself behind in England when he went to study with the Armenian-Greek teacher, Gurdjieff. Others who followed him to Paris and later to the Château du Prieuré near Fontainebleau included the psychiatrist Maurice Nicoll, the physician James Carruthers Young, and the directress of dance at the Paris Opera, Jessmin Howarth. These were shortly after followed by the editors of *The Little Review,* Margaret Anderson and Jane Heap, avant-garde American writers Waldo Frank, Gorham Munson, and the Afro-American Nathan Jean Toomer, who turned from his promising career as poet and novelist of essential American Black experience to explore broader social and philosophical contexts for his role as teacher and writer.

At the end of his felicitous passage through Gurdjieff's aura, on the evening of 5 November 1934, as much of England was more interested in fireworks than economics, Alfred Richard Orage gave a talk on BBC Radio to explain the principles of Social Credit to an entire nation. He coughed and paused once or twice during the talk, and later complained of some dizziness and pain. The talk went very well, and the next morning the mails were full of congratulatory messages. He never read any of them, because in the early hours of 6 November, Orage died in his sleep of a blood clot on the wall of his left auricle. Across the Atlantic, in a room on 57th Street, in New York City, near Child's Restaurant, at 11 A.M., in the midst of a discussion about the right translation of a crucial concept concerning man's will to suffer, Georgii Ivanovich Gurdjieff heard from London that Orage had died. He exclaimed: "This man, my brother."[7]

The timing was both tragic and foreboding. Gurdjieff's Institute for the Harmonious Development of Man at the Château du Prieuré des Basses Loges on the Avenue du Valvins at Avon near Fontainebleau had closed eighteen months earlier because of outstanding debts. Gurdjieff was now back in the United States in search of financial support, either to re-acquire the Prieuré or to establish an appropriate alternative site in the United States. The depression had taken its toll, however, and financial possibilities had faded. In May 1935, half a year after Orage's

---

7. Louise Welch, *Orage,* p. 137.

death, Gurdjieff's hopes for his work in the United States seemed also to die. A disappointed, but never discouraged, Gurdjieff returned to Paris where, in the autumn of 1935, he started teaching in his brother's Paris apartment a new curriculum with a small and select group of pupils.

Georgii Ivanovich Gurdjieff was most likely born in 1866, though various documents give 1872 and 1877 as his birth year. The event took place in Alexandropol, Armenia, known as Leninakan during the Soviet era, and now restored to Gyumri, its older Armenian name.[8] His day of birth is recorded on one of his passports as 28 December, but he always celebrated it on the Russian New Year, 13 January. His father was Greek—Ivan (some say Georgios, but Gurdjieff's patronymic favors Ivan[9]) Georgiades—and his mother Armenian. Her language was the koine of his early childhood in the household, though the young Gurdjieff grew up communicating easily in all the local languages, including Greek and Turkish. His family records contain the information that the Georgian Joseph Dzhugashvili [Stalin] lived in his family's house for a while.[10] Gurdjieff took his secondary education at Kars in Armenia, not far from Mount Ararat, under the direction of Dean Borsh in a cathedral school.

According to his semi-fictional autobiography, *Meetings with Remarkable Men*, Gurdjieff joined a group of "Seekers of the Truth," perhaps as early as 1888.[11] This group traveled widely between Greece, Egypt, and Tibet over a period of twenty-one years on the trail of esoteric knowledge. In 1911, he was teaching in Tashkent, and in 1913, he appeared in Moscow and St. Petersburg, where he gave talks on esoterism that attracted a number of notable followers, including the composer Thomas de Hartmann and the philosopher P[yotr] D[emianovich] Ouspensky, whose *Tertium Organum* was already known in the West in 1912. The 1917 Russian Revolution forced Gurdjieff and his followers to seek sanctuary in Tblisi and Essentuki in Georgia. In 1919, they

---

8. The definitive biography upon which scholars rely is James Moore's *Gurdjieff: The Anatomy of a Myth* (Boston: Element, 1991). He assesses Gurdjieff's birthdate on page 9, and reviews various pronunciations of his name. His family pronounced it as Gurd-ji-eff, with the stress on the first syllable, though most anglophones prefer Gurdjeeff, with the stress on the ultimate.
9. Martin Seymour Smith, *The 100 Most Influential Books Ever Written* (Secaucus, NJ: Carol Publishing Group, 1998), chap. 94, identifies Gurdjieff's father as Ionas, the Greek cognate form of Russian Ivan, but does not cite his sources.
10. Luba Gurdjieff, *A Memoir with Recipes* (Berkeley, CA: Ten Speed Press, 1993), p. 3. James Webb, *The Harmonious Circle: The Lives and Works of G. I. Gurdjieff, P. D. Ouspensky and Their Followers* (London: Thames & Hudson, 1980), p. 30, says that Stalin lodged with the family sometime between 1894 and 1899.
11. Trans. A. R. Orage (London: Penguin, 1963), p. 164.

moved on to Constantinople where he established his Institute for the Harmonious Development of Man. From Constantinople, he voyaged to Berlin, Hellerau, and London to scan possibilities for his school before re-opening his Institute in Paris in the summer of 1922.

A. R. Orage was born on 22 January 1873 as Alfred James Orage in Dacre, Yorkshire, near Bradford. He was the fourth child of a poverty-ridden family.[12] His family name derives, most likely, from a regional name, Horrage. It was pronounced by his family "Orridge," but Orage preferred a French pronunciation (which G. B. Shaw is reported to have suggested). Both his children, as well as the general public, assumed from the stress on the second syllable that the name had either Irish or French origins. Indeed, his mother, Sarah Anne McQuire, was Irish and, at least on one occasion, Orage signed his name on a role as O'Rage.[13] His father died soon after his birth and his mother took in washing to support the family.

When Orage was fourteen, his mother took him to a local squire named Coote to have him engaged as a laborer. Coote, whose son, Howard, was a classmate of Orage's, soon recognized his intellectual capacities and subsidized his schooling. When he was nineteen, Orage entered teacher training at Culham College, Abingdon and restyled his name to "Alfred Richard Orage." On graduation, he taught at Leylands School, Ellerby Boys, and Roundhay Road Boys in Leeds. His interests turned early toward philosophy, theosophy, and Fabian Socialism based upon Platonic ideals, rather than upon political egalitarianism. In 1894, he joined the Leeds branch of the Independent Labour Party and edited their free propaganda sheet, *Forward*. In 1895, he made his first contribution to *Labour Leader*. The next year, defying plans laid down for him by Coote, he married a London arts student, Jean Walker. Howard Coote, not happy with this sudden turn of events, refused Orage the loan that would have allowed him to work for a degree at Oxford. So Orage settled down to a plodding occupation and a childless marriage. He soon

12. For biographical material concerning Orage's early life, I have drawn upon James Webb's *The Harmonious Circle*, pp. 195–212, James Moore's *Gurdjieff and Mansfield*, pp. 79–93, and Philip Mairet's *A. R. Orage: A Memoir* (Hyde Park, NY: University Press, 1966).
13. Tom Steele, *Alfred Orage and the Leeds Art Club 1893–1923* (Aldershot: Scolar Press, 1990), p. 40. J. J. Wilhelm, *Ezra Pound: The Tragic Years 1925–1972* (University Park: The Pennsylvania State University Press, 1994), p. 91, identifies Orage as "the French Huguenot editor of *The New Age*." Mairet also suggests a Huguenot ancestry. Ezra Pound, in a letter to Wyndham Lewis, October, 1956, said that Violet [Hunt] said his "real [name] was 'Horridge' from Liverpool." Timothy Materer, ed., *Pound/Lewis: The Letters of Ezra Pound and Wyndham Lewis* (New York: New Directions, 1985), pp. 298–299.

joined the Theosophical Society, where he mingled with George Robert
Stone Mead and Annie Besant, among others.

In 1901, Orage met Holbrook Jackson, fell under the spell of
Nietzsche, and founded, with Jackson, the Leeds Art Club.[14] His per-
sonal charm and sharp intellect attracted the attention of prominent
thinkers of the period, many of whom, such as G. B. Shaw, Gilbert
Keith Chesterton, and W. B. Yeats, volunteered to lecture at the club. In
1905, an intellectually restless Orage left his employ with the Leeds
School Board. In 1906, he separated from his wife and moved to
London, where, in the spring of 1907, he and Jackson, with £500 loans
from George Bernard Shaw and Lewis A. R. Wallace, bought *The New
Age*. They produced their first issue on 2 May. Shortly after, with a
friend from Leeds, A. J. Penty, they founded the Fabian Arts Group.
That same year, Orage was joined at the magazine by Beatrice Hastings,
who became a principal contributor to the magazine, as well as Orage's
personal assistant and mistress over the next seven years. In 1913,
Beatrice left Orage for his friend Wyndham Lewis. In 1914, she in turn
left London, Orage, and Lewis for Paris and Amadeo Modigliani.[15]

Orage himself left England in 1922 for eight years, most of which
he spent in New York as Gurdjieff's agent. He returned to London in
1930 with a new wife and infant son, and, in the spring of 1932, published the first issue of a new journal, *The New English Weekly*. At the
end of his life, thirty months later, Shaw could say, with an enthusiasm
that transcended his financial interest in Orage's early career as an editor, that he was "the most brilliant editor for a century past." T. S. Eliot
echoed with the epithet "finest literary critic of his day" and "the finest
critical intelligence of our age."[16]

Orage's second wife was born Jessie Richards Dwight in Albany,
New York, on 7 February 1901. Her father was Harvey Lyman Dwight
and her mother, Bertha Richards, whose family had moved to Albany
from Albertus, Iowa. Jessie was named after an aunt, Jessie Logan. Her
mother died in September of Jessie's first year. Her father, who was a
direct descendent of Timothy Dwight, the 17th-century "Connecticut

---

14. Steele, *Alfred Orage*, pp. 106–116, discusses Orage's philosophical leanings after Nietzsche,
the major influence of which was Plato.

15. For Beatrice's brief liaison with Modigliani, see Armand Lanoux, "Les Belles du Montparno," *Les années folles,* ed. Gilbert Guilleminault (Paris: Denoël, 1956), pp. 275–276.

16. Cited by C. S. Nott, *Journey Through this World* (London: Routledge & Kegan Paul, 1969),
p. 70, and Phillip Mairet, *A. R. Orage,* pp. 121 and 123, respectively. The current use of the term
"New Age" in reference to theosophical tendencies may be partly due to Orage's journal, though
Orage had only kept the existing name of the journal he bought.

Wit," was engaged in the family's tannery business, principally owned by John Watson Dwight. He died suddenly at thirty-nine in May 1910, leaving Jessie and her older brother, Harvey A. Dwight, to the disciplined care of their grandmother, Alfilenah Chase Richards. Jessie enjoyed the status of a well-to-do young woman in Albany society. After graduating from the Albany Academy for Girls in 1921, she crossed the Atlantic to visit Venice, Rome, and Naples. After her return in mid-1923, she was given enough money to buy a limited partnership in the Sunwise Turn bookshop in the Yale Club building on 44th Street in Manhattan.

Writing about both Orage and Gurdjieff in a single text presents obvious problems for the critic and biographer. Gurdjieff was always controversial. To present a fair portrait of the man, one must take into account the fact that he both engendered and invited controversy, adoration, and rancor. He played many roles. Much that has been said and written about him has to be scrutinized in the context of the play of his character from event to event. He was not a man who wanted, or even appreciated, adulation. He would, he often said, step on people's corns. As a teacher, he came to shock, not to soothe, the human conscience, and, characteristically, he prompted negative judgments.

Orage is a more difficult topic for one who would reveal the virtues and faults of his subject objectively. His obvious faults seem but peccadilloes. He enjoyed, perhaps to excess, the appreciation and affection of others—though he disdained adoration. Such a speculative observation is, however, a weak pejorative. At the end of his active career with Gurdjieff, he admitted that one of his faults—in his mentor's eyes—was the affection he nourished for the New York Group, an affection that went beyond his appointed role as Gurdjieff's agent.[17] Only he and Gurdjieff could have made such a charge. I have found it difficult to discover and evaluate the negative objective opinions of others. There are few. Yes, he smoked too much and he pushed himself physically and emotionally to a dangerous extreme in his work. As a young man, he seemed to have a roaming eye for female charms; but he was liked and admired by all. He seemed selfless to others, in whom he searched for and drew out the best. He was a journalist, essayist,

---

17. Letter to Israel Solon, autumn, 1930, cited by Welch, *Orage,* p. 115.

philosopher, literary critic, teacher of writing, economic theorist, theosophist, and, most of all, a humanist. He performed admirably in all these roles, though the common criticism of those who knew him well before the Gurdjieff years is that he suffered fools. Few men have so influenced English literature in the 20th century. Yet, in refusing to draw attention to his influence on others, he condemned himself to remain to the public a largely unknown value.

In the pages that follow, after a brief look at the career that prepared him for his axial turn of life, I trace in considerable detail Orage's experience with Gurdjieff. Louise Welch has written an excellent account of Orage in those years from the sympathetic point of view of someone who knew him well from the spring of 1927 until the early summer of 1931. Though I spent the first three Christmases of my life with Orage and his family, and just missed a fourth by his untimely death, I knew Orage hardly at all. My only clear memory of him is from an occasion when he took my sister and myself with him and his children to see the changing of the guard at Buckingham Palace. I have a vaguely remembered sensation of his large hand on my back as I strained to see the pageantry. I imagine his smile, but that image might be of the smile that was so familiar to me over the years on the face of his son, Dick. This book does not intend, therefore, in any way to replace Welch's. It seeks rather to complement it by laying before you an accurate record of Orage's life during his Gurdjieff years. I try to minimize my own analytic commentary on that record.

I knew Gurdjieff better. I spent some hardly recalled time with him as an infant in Fontainebleau and Paris, and was in his company for scattered moments during the last year of his life. He is vivid in my mind's eye. His voice, smile, frown, and bodily gestures—particularly his manner of waving an arm to signal a verbal point or halt someone else's—are fast in my memory. Nonetheless, I try to keep a certain distance from my own experience with the man in order to hold to a stance of disinterest, though I admit I do not always succeed.

Acknowledgments

The Beinecke Rare Book and Manuscript Library at Yale University made the Toomer Collection of papers, including the correspondence between Orage and Nathan Jean Toomer, available to me. Pascale Mignon did a valuable piece of research at Yale's Sterling library on my behalf. Kay Boyle has granted permission to quote from Robert McAlmon's and her *Being Geniuses Together*.[1] Edith Taylor's papers in my custody are referred to with permission from my sister, Eve T. Chevalier. I quote excerpts from the Sherman Manchester papers with the permission of Betty Manchester of Weston, Connecticut, who holds them on behalf of her late husband Roger Manchester, Sherman's son. The Orage papers, quoted from with the permission of Anne B. Orage of Henley, Oxfordshire, are soon to be deposited in the Special Collections Library of Leeds University. They include Orage's letters and Jessie Orage's diaries.

Though I have compiled this book, much of the text is Orage's and Jessie's. I have translated their words into book form and added complementary notes. Anne B. Orage, the widow of Orage's son, Richard, has graciously allowed me to extract from Jessie Orage's diary and from Orage's letters to her when they were apart between early 1924 and late 1928. Since they were seldom away from each other after their first meetings, the story extracted from the letters she zealously preserved is thin. Orage left no autobiographical record of his life besides a few

---

1. McAlmon and Boyle, *Being Geniuses Together: 1920–1930* (Garden City, NY: Doubleday, 1968).

reflections in short essays under the rubric "An Editor's Progress." He made it a practice to discard letters that concerned his private life, including all of Jessie's letters to him. One biographer has regretted that Orage's "persistence in burning his boats down to the last laundry list has left little in the way of documentary record."[2] A rare exception is the letter he kept from Ouspensky replying on Gurdjieff's behalf to Orage's petition in the summer of 1922 to join the Institute. Many fragments of letters to him are recorded in Jessie Orage's diaries, since, in her own diary record of her life with Orage, she often reproduced passages from them that she felt were important.

Jessie's diary entries tell a discrete tale of their private life. For her pen, there was no world outside theirs and their immediate circle. One misses comments on national and international affairs in her records— reflections on Prohibition, which touched their lives considerably in New York, or on the stock market crash of October 1929, which had a marked negative effect on Orage's fund-raising efforts. Even Lindbergh's daring flight across the Atlantic did not rate a notice in her diary. On the other hand, there is almost nothing in Jessie's diaries of Orage's relations with others that did not concern her directly. Occasionally, one suspects from her entries that Jessie wrote of Orage's relations with others in a manner to align his feelings with her own. Perhaps it was just that she unwittingly attributed to her husband her own feelings about third-party relations, most particularly her anxieties concerning Orage's relations with Gurdjieff.

Though many interpretations of the record in this book are mine, the book is the Orage family's as well, because they, and particularly Orage's daughter-in-law, Anne, have inherited, nourished, and administered the threads of interest in Orage's remarkable career. Orage's own daughter, Ann, aspired to transmit that legacy, but died too young and too soon. Others whose lives were touched by Orage have helped me. I have an outstanding debt to Dushka Howarth, whose command of the history of Gurdjieff is equaled by none, and whose mother, Jessmin, wrote of Orage in her unpublished journals. I have stolen fact and opinion from the excellent biography of Orage by Philip Mairet and from the biographical sketches of him by James Webb and James Moore. There are untold brief notices of Orage in his Gurdjieff years, perhaps the most notable of which are in the works of his friends and collaborators, Edwin Muir, Hugh MacDiarmid, Waldo Frank, and Gorham Munson.

---

2. Tom Steele, *Alfred Orage and the Leeds Arts Club: 1893–1923* (Aldershot: Scolar Press, 1990), p. 2.

Betty Manchester has kindly let me see the voluminous notes her father-in-law, Sherman Manchester, carefully recorded from Orage's talks between 10 January 1927 and 14 January 1929. Other commentaries on Orage's particular teachings I have scanned include those of Daly King and Stanley Nott, as well as the unpublished notes of Blanche Grant. Walter Driscoll, bibliographer of Gurdjieff, has been generous with references. In the multiple stages of constructing this story, I have been encouraged by Bob Hohenberger of Houston, Texas and aided in my research by Hugh Witemeyer of the University of New Mexico. Walter Driscoll, Martha de Llosa, and Anne B. Orage have read earlier drafts and have made pointed criticisms and corrections. Michael Benham's careful and critical reading of the entire text has uncovered errors that I have happily corrected. Anne Orage has gone through records, photos, and journal clippings with me, and has, more than anyone, inspired this work. What errors stubbornly adhere to the text, despite the help others have provided, remain my responsibility.

Chapter One

1873–1922

THE MYSTIC OF FLEET STREET

"New Age No Wage"

He who attempts to penetrate into the Rose Garden of the Philosophers without the key resembles a man who would walk without feet.

—Atalanta Fugiens[1]

It is easily assumed by historians that Orage led a perilously divided life trying to reconcile urgent interests in esoteric lore with a journalistic career whose main thrust was to have art serve economic and political reform. I will argue in the pages that follow that there was no essential conflict between these interests in Orage's mind and, ultimately, in his varied activities. Orage sensed and promoted a collaboration between these two vectors of his energy in the service of the world in general, and England and America (as he called the United States) in particular. From the moment he began his career as an editor in London, he strove to bring art, economy, and esotericism into a public harmony. To these, eventually, he joined the private pleasure of family. Everything he did in his life up to the moment he left England in October 1922 for Paris and Gurdjieff, prepared him for this consolidation of energies. It is to demonstrate that point that I present the following review of Orage's London career.

---

1. H. M. E. DeJong, *Atalanta Fugiens: Sources of an Alchemical Book of Emblems* (Leiden, Netherlands: E. J. Brill, 1969), p. 201. To be reissued by Weiser in the spring of 2001.

The cultural atmosphere of the London to which Orage went from Leeds in 1906 is known blandly by cultural historians as "Edwardian." Although the vibrancy of the metropolis in the early days of the century belies the typical portrait of the post-Victorian monarchs, Edward VII and George V, like their reigns, their age was one of crucial shifts in artistic, social, and political change. Decadence, pre-Raphaelite aesthetics, art for art's sake, and naturalism were giving way to the impressionism, imagism and vorticism that underlie what critics now call modernism, the prevailing artistic thrust in *entre-guerre* Europe. This was an age in which American writers, profiting from a healthy growth of native impulses, brought fresh perspectives back across the Big Pond to republican France and Italy, and to their formerly alienated English cousins. Among the Americans already abroad before Orage set up editorial shop in London were William Dean Howells and Mabel Dodge who branched out from New York and Paris to Italy, Gertrude Stein and Natalie Barney, who flourished in France, and Mark Twain, James Whistler, Stephen Crane, Harold Frederic, and Henry James, whose talents enriched English soil. In the next wave came Robert Frost, T. S. Eliot, Ezra Pound, Courtenay Lemon (Djuna Barnes' ex-husband), and John Gould Fletcher. Orage played literary and philosophical guide to them all. It was Pound, in 1913, who introduced Frost to Orage, beginning an acquaintance that lasted through Orage's New York years. Not every American literary aspirant found Orage receptive. Raymond Chandler, later to become America's best-known crime writer, was working for the *Daily Express* in London when he asked Orage to consider a couple of short pieces. Orage thought they showed talent, but didn't fit *The New Age* format.

Orage's literary activities in London with *The New Age* did not include, but rather steered toward, the two grand projects that would occupy his life after World War I—Major Douglas's Social Credit and Gurdjieff's Harmonious Development. Socialism of one kind or another had been noticeably in the air since the middle of the 19th-century. In Orage's cultural milieu, the social reform conceptions of Morris and Ruskin were lively topics of discussion. The Fabian Society, named after the Roman warrior-statesman Quintus Fabius Maximus Verrucosus, was formed in 1884 to promote social reform by peaceful means, rather than through the violence of revolution that Marx had predicted. Five years after its founding on 15 February 1889, Oscar Wilde, who had been attracted to Fabian Socialism by George Bernard Shaw, wrote a review of Edward Carpenter's *Chants of Labour,* in which he quipped:

"To make men socialists is nothing, but to make socialism human is a great thing." [2]

Orage, whose Fabian sympathies had prompted his founding of the Leeds Art Club, collaborated with Arthur J. Penty to establish a Fabian Arts Society in London. Furthermore, he made it his mission later in *The New Age* to present a program of humane social egalitarianism in the service of economic and political reform. In Leeds, between 1896 and 1902, Orage wrote some seventy-five items for the weekly *Labour Leader*. Although almost all were reviews of the literary scene in Britain and the United States, there was a generous sprinkling of articles on social and philosophical questions, and one poem of his own, "Hide and Seek." [3] From 1902 until 1907, he was a regular contributor to the *Theosophical Review* (some thirty-five articles).

In the name of egalitarian justice, Orage, very soon after his arrival in London, took up the suffragette cause with Beatrice Hastings. He wrote "Women Leading On" for the *Theosophical Review* in January 1907, the same issue in which he reviewed "The Gospel of Gnosis." This was followed, in the next issue, by "In defense of Agnosticism." These three articles incited letters criticizing Orage's stance on gender and religion. Two months later, Orage drew considerable public attention, if not scorn, for being the only male arrested along with some seventy-five women who stormed the House of Commons in the spring of 1907 under the wondering gazes of Lloyd George and Herbert Gladstone. He was duly sentenced to fourteen days in jail. [4]

Early in his life, Orage read Ruskin as a sensible man committed to badly needed reforms, rather than as the poetic visionary others saw in him. [5] The *fin-du-siècle* medievalism of William Morris and the innovative forms of *art nouveau* attracted Orage toward Penty's project to restore the medieval guild system. [6] With S. G. Hobson (1868–1940),

---

2. Cited by Richard Ellman, *Oscar Wilde* (London: Hamish Hamilton, 1987), p. 274.
3. For Orage's early writings, I have depended upon Wallace Martin's *Orage as Critic* (London: Routledge & Kegan Paul, 1974).
4. E. Sylvia Pankhurst, *The Suffragette Movement* (London: Longmans, 1931), p. 256. See Orage's "Votes for Women," *NA* 4, 4 February 1909, pp. 300–301.
5. Tim Redman, *Ezra Pound and Italian Fascism* (Cambridge: Cambridge University Press, 1991), p. 23. For a broad view of Orage's intellectual influences as a critic, see Tom Gibbons, *Rooms in the Darwin Hotel: Studies in English Literature, Art, and Ideas 1880–1920* (Nedlands: University of Western Australia Press, 1973).
6. Redman, *Ezra Pound,* p. 38.

Orage reshaped Guild Socialism out of principles of Ruskin and Morris[7] to center attention on medieval "localism"—the interlocking interests of all those engaged in a single industry. Such a structure for economic exchange would repeal, they hoped, the invidious effects of modern industrialism.[8] Between 1907 and 1913, in his regular *The New Age* column, "Unedited Opinions," Orage wrote several articles on Socialism, economics, and trade unionism, which Orage called "the egg liberty laid in capitalism to destroy the wage system."[9] In his private life, he initiated exchanges with leading reformers of his day, such as the American Upton Sinclair, and H. G. Wells.[10] At this time, Orage and other far sighted social critics like Wells were recognized as imaginative activists challenging old-guard Fabians,[11] one of whom was Orage's sponsor, Shaw.[12] Articles in *The New Age* throughout 1910 and 1911 indeed suggested that a New Age was, in fact, at hand.[13]

Seven months after the first issue of *The New Age* was published, Jackson surrendered sole proprietorship of the journal to Orage, partly because Orage refused to take in advertising and partly because Shaw refused to put up more money and to contribute copy *gratis*. Not only did Shaw feel that Orage's drift away from Fabianism left *The New Age* politically powerless, but Orage had written a study of Shaw to which Mrs. Shaw took exception. Orage withdrew it from publication. Finally, in 1913, Shaw and Sidney Webbs founded *The New Statesman* to take up the cause they felt Orage had deserted.[14]

Although he never made any money from sales, Orage worked tirelessly to encourage new talent and stir up new social and critical

7. Michael Coyle, *Ezra Pound, Popular Genres and the Discourse of Culture* (University Park: The Pennsylvania State University Press, 1995), p. 9. A number of Hobson's articles in *NA* in 1911 were collected into book form under the title, *National Guilds,* edited by Orage (London: G. Bell & Sons, 1914).
8. For an overview of Orage's Guild Socialism, see Maurice B. Reckitt, *As It Happened* (London: Dent, 1941), pp. 113–117, and Wallace Martin, *The New Age Under Orage: Chapters in English Cultural History* (Manchester, University of Manchester Press, 1967), pp. 193–211.
9. Reckitt, *As It Happened,* p. 109.
10. Some of these letters are extant in the archives of libraries of the universities of Indiana and Illinois, respectively.
11. Samuel Hynes, *The Edwardian Turn of Mind* (Princeton: Princeton University Press, 1968), p. 92.
12. In a letter to Clarence Norman, chairman of *The New Age,* a company formed on 24 September 1908, Shaw complained that Orage had accused him of being a bad Fabian because he would not continue to support the magazine. Shaw reminded his old friend Norman, who earlier had been Shaw's transcriber of his public addresses, that he had given Orage £500 pounds, and had contributed over £1000 worth of copy to support the magazine for its first six months, and he was not going to give more copy. See *Bernard Shaw: Collected Letters, 1898–1910,* ed. Dan H. Laurence (London: Max Reinhardt, 1972), pp. 209–210.
13. Wallace Martin, *The New Age Under Orage,* p. 128.
14. John Gross, *The Rise and Fall of the Man of Letters* (London: Weidenfeld and Nicolson, 1969), p. 228.

issues. He introduced Katherine Mansfield to his public in 1910; Hilaire Belloc and Gilbert Keith Chesterton were early contributors. Llewelyn Powys, brother of John Cowper Powys, got his first encouragement from Orage in 1914. Orage opened his journal to almost any writer who was motivated by the good and the just. Pound, who joined Orage in 1911, observed that he demanded from his writers only "an ideograph of the good."[15] He also looked for the new, and Orage's own articles in 1918 and 1919 on Jung and Freud were among the first on psychoanalysis to appear in the British press. He had, himself, written on Nietzsche in 1908, and, in 1909, on women's suffrage. In 1912, he voiced a "New View of Women." To justify the eclectic mix of art with economic and political commentary in the pages of *The New Age,* Orage wrote in 1912: "The literature and art of today are the parallels of the economic situation of today."[16]

More than two thirds of Orage's articles were on literary subjects, many of which were collected and published as *The Art of Reading* in 1930. He was one of the few critics to take particular interest in the development of American literature and language. As early as 1916, he had reviewed H[enry] L[ewis] Mencken's critical writing on English literature, and *The Little Review* solicited a review of Henry James. His good reading command of French gave him critical access to French literature as well, and in 1916, he wrote about "Stendhal on Love." He was among the first to recognize in print the talent of the Bulgarian-born Armenian novelist Michael Arlen [Dikran Kouyouomdjian], who became a good friend. All in all, critics agreed that *The New Age* was, for its day, the most brilliant journal that has ever been written in English.

In "National Guilds," written in December 1913, Orage exposed the imbalance in British labor between goods and services and its effect on national policy. "A commodity is something that has exchange value," he wrote; "labour is priceless, and therefore, its value cannot be expressed. . . . Economic power precedes political power."[17] Orage's appreciation of Ruskin's convictions about the cultural responsibility of art allowed him to depreciate current romantic claims for the autonomy

---

15. Cited by Forest Read, '76: One World and the Cantos of Ezra Pound (Chapel Hill: University of North Carolina Press, 1981), p. 433.
16. 4 December 1913, cited by Redman, *Pound and Fascism*, p. 22. This article is not listed in Wallace Martin's bibliography, *Orage as Critic*, where he lists Orage's own contribution on National Guilds in a June 1917 issue of *NA*.
17. Cited by Coyle, *Ezra Pound*, p. 134.

of literature. He advised John Gould Fletcher, for example, to abandon the Romantics and read Walt Whitman.[18] In *The New Age,* in 1915 he made the oft-quoted statement that "art includes utility, but it also transcends utility."[19] As one critic observes: "Orage used Ruskin in his eclectic program to anesthetize socialist attempts at reform."[20]

In effect, Orage's economics had their origin in his early reading in Plato, but they were shaped by his reading of John Stuart Mill (1806–1873), whose *Essay on Some Unsettled Questions in Political Economy* (1844) discussed the influence of consumption on production and the relation between wages and profit. Even closer to Orage's eventual interests was Mill's *Principles of Political Economy* (1848), which attacked a policy of distribution of goods and monies that condemned the laboring class to penury. Like Mill, Orage developed an economic theory that involved broad humanitarian interests. Ezra Pound, writing out of Orage's thoughts near the end of the war, explained: "Fundamentally I do not care 'politically,' I care for civilization, and I do not care who collects the taxes, or who polices the thoroughfares. Humanity is a collection of individuals, not a *whole* divided into segments or units. The only things that matter are the things which make individual life more interesting."[21] Of course, for Orage, art in general and literature in particular were the primary things making life interesting, but social survival came first. He identified his own interests with the predicament of the working class and the causes of poverty. "A starving man needs food, not instruction," he wrote in 1912. A year later, in his popular column "Readers and Writers," he proclaimed that "literature affects life for better or worse."[22]

Under Orage, *The New Age* probed with intense urgency the relation of socialism to art and philosophy. Orage considered political and economic problems inseparable from the problems of culture as a whole. On 10 October 1912, he wrote: "If I were asked upon what I rely for the renaissance of England, I should say a miracle, but it does not follow that because we cannot define the cause of miracles, miracles are not therefore to be understood. They can be understood easily enough if they are regarded as works of art instead of works of logic. . . . We can

---

18. Stanley Weintraub, *The London Yankees* (New York: Harcourt Brace Jovanovich, 1979), p. 282.
19. *NA* 18 (1915), p. 761, cited by Wallace Martin, *The New Age,* p. 180, and by Coyle, "'A Profounder Didacticism': Ruskin Orage, Pound's Reception of Social Credit," *Paideuma* 17 (1988), pp. 7–28.
20. Coyle, *Ezra Pound,* p. 46.
21. William Cookson, ed., *Ezra Pound, Selected Prose 1909–1965* (New York: New Directions, 1973), pp. 199–200.
22. "Unedited Opinions," *NA* (8 Feb 1912), pp. 347–348, and *NA* (31 July 1913), p. 395.

both divine what it will be and prepare for its coming." [23] His first biographer remarks that Orage, above all else, sought "to cooperate with the purposes of life, to enlist in that noble service, the help of serious students of the new contemplative and imaginative order." [24] In 1914, Orage was known throughout London's cultural circles as a man of the highest imaginative order and taste. The gifted Augustus John cried out, when his project for Ormande Terrace was being debated, "We ought to have Orage as dictator." [25] Looking back to that time forty years later, Pound considered Orage a quintessential Englishman: "Wonder was the ANY english or if Orage (with a French spelling) was the ONLY englander cent pure." [26] For John Cowper Powys, who preferred American openness to English snobbery, Orage restored faith in his origins. "When I beguiled Mr. Orage to come to tea with me in our ramshackle alley," he wrote, "all my fancies about English snobbishness seemed to melt away. This subtle critic struck me as one who might have been wearing a friar's cord under his discreet dress." [27]

It is deceptively easy to say from all this that Orage was committed to the elevation of the public weal, as Pound recalled vividly after his death:

Orage wrote *into* a public that had been blindfolded by generations of books produced under the heel of the profit system, fouled by the mentality of decades oppressed by university and educational systems warped by the profit system, by a bureaucracy of education, the bureaucrat being a man who avoids "dangerous" knowledge, who can almost indefinitely refrain from taking, officially, cognisance of anything whatsodamnever that is likely to disturb his immediate comfort or expose him to the least convenience or ridicule. . . . There were, and are, arrears of learning for the public to make up, and against this siltage Orage battled until his last heart gripe. It was the sea of stupidities, not a clear sea, it was the bog, the mud storm, the quicksand of obfuscation.[28]

23. "The Possibility of a Cultural Renaissance in England," *NA* (10 Oct 1912), p. 569.
24. Philip Mairet, *Orage: A Memoir,* p. 41.
25. Michael Holroyd, *Augustus John* (New York: Holt Rinehart Winston, 1974), p. 453.
26. Letter from Pound to Wyndham Lewis, October, 1956, cited by Timothy Materer, *Pound / Lewis: The Letters of Ezra Pound and Wyndham Lewis* (New York: New Directions, 1985), pp. 298–299. James Moore, *Gurdjieff and Mansfield* (London: Routledge & Kegan Paul, 1980), pp. 82–83, cites a number of contemporary compliments concerning Orage's direction of *NA*.
27. Ezra Pound, *Autobiography* (London: Picador, 1967), p. 559.
28. Cookson, *Selected Prose,* p. 449. Orage would have agreed with the spirit in Oscar Wilde's view of the subjection of the people to private interests: "There is the despot who tyrannises over the body. There is the despot who tyrannises over the soul. There is the despot who tyrannizes over the soul and body alike. The first is called the *Prince*. The second is called the *Pope*. The third is called the *People*" (Ellman, *Oscar Wilde,* p. 310).

Orage's commitment to human relations was more than a public editorial principle. He manifested it in all of his personal relations. Most of the testimonies about his personal relations come from those he advanced in their careers as their reader and editor. John Gould Fletcher recalled that, as a critic, Orage was "neither contemptuous nor condescending."[29] Pound praised Orage as "that necessary and rare person, the moralist in criticism: not the inquisitor who tries to impose [his] morals upon literature, but the critic who perceives the moral *of* literature."[30] As a recent observer remarks: "Orage sought to collapse the aesthetic realm—not by undermining its claims for value—but by expanding it not only beyond the writing of literary genres but also beyond writing itself. This was the ultimate goal of Orage's journalism."[31] Though Orage habitually denigrated journalism as a form of art, he raised his own to the level of a literary genre comparable to its 18th-century status. Perhaps Pound was thinking of a basic value of *The New Age* when he said, in a letter to Scofield Thayer, the editor of *Dial,* in November, 1920: "A magazine is important in proportion to amount of good stuff it prints which wd. not be printed (or even written), if the magazine did not exist."[32]

Few profited more from Orage's "humanity" than Pound. Although *The New Age* was known to it contributors affectionately and less affectionately as "No Wage" (because Orage, instead of paying fees, promised not to censor contributions), Orage involved himself personally in the welfare of his associates. Pound includes in his draft for Canto CXI a glance at Orage's *compassione,* which identified "the extent to which Orage's humanitarianism must have stood for Pound as the antithesis to [Wyndham] Lewis's scorn for 'the herd.'"[33] Pound recalled, in a letter dated 25 October 1919 to John Quinn, that "Orage, of course, willing to do anything he can for me."[34] "Anything" consisted, for some years, in their collaboration of four guineas a month as a sort of salary—not much, but Pound managed to live on it. He wrote from Rapallo to John Drummond on 30 May 1934: "Orage's 4 guineas a month . . . was the SINEWS, by gob the sinooz."[35] He went on to say

---

29. Leon Surette, *The Birth of Modernism* (Montréal: Queen's University Press, 1993), p. 279.
30. From *Criterion,* 15 January 1935, cited by Redman, *Ezra Pound,* p. 19.
31. Michael Coyle, "'A Profounder Didacticism,'" pp. 26–27.
32. Walter, Sutton, ed., *Pound, Thayer, Watson and The Dial* (Gainesville: University of Florida Press, 1994), p. 184.
33. Wendy Stallard Flory, *The American Ezra Pound* (New Haven: Yale University Press, 1989), p. 83.
34. D. D. Paige, *Ezra Pound: Selected Letters 1907–1941* (New York: New Directions, 1971), p. 151.
35. Paige, *Letters,* p. 259.

that: "he did more to feed me than anyone else in England, and I wish anyone who esteems my existence would pay back whatever they feel is due to its stalvarrdt sustainer."[36] More significantly, Orage protected Pound from a hostile British public who resented the American's attacks on British cultural tastes. With the exception of *The New Age*, the English press was closed to Pound, but Orage remained loyal to Pound's talent, and to his editorial conscience. "Orage tried to steer him [Pound] to literary subjects," notes Leon Surette, "but Pound clung stubbornly to his platform for vituperation."[37]

In effect, as he had done for others, Orage "shaped" Pound for the brilliant career awaiting him. As a recent critic reflects: "Orage's common sense, clarity of insight, and ready criticism were crucial stabilizing influences for Pound, and once they were removed, Pound's decline into confusions and self-deception was swift. Both in introducing Pound to new intellectual interests and in opening his eyes to new dimensions of interests that they found they already held in common, Orage more than anyone else provided Pound with his real 'postgraduate education.'"[38]

Furthermore, Orage instilled in Pound a fundamental optimism about human nature and a belief in the basic decency of ordinary people, all of this despite fundamental differences in their points of view concerning literature. Orage described Pound in *The New Age* on 3 October 1918 as "one of the most gifted, slovenly, arrogant and spirited writers of our day."[39] Pound himself reflected years later: "For twenty-three years I don't think that either of us ever took the other seriously as a critic of letters, and now thinking of it in retrospect, I wonder how far the difference of view was a mere matter of the twelve years between us."[40]

The Great War, 1914–1918, changed Orage's economic views, as well as, in general, his philosophical views. He had not believed a war was possible, but when it loomed large on the horizon in August 1914, he championed England's role in it, because "England is necessary to Socialism, as Socialism is necessary to the world."[41] When the war had begun, however, he lamented that England was "compelling the poor to

---

36. Paige, *Letters*, p. 544.
37. Leon Surette, *A Light for Eleusis: A Study of Ezra Pound's Cantos* (Oxford: Clarendon Press, 1979), p. 279.
38. Flory, *The American Ezra Pound*, pp. 42, 48.
39. *NA*, 3 October 1918.
40. *Criterion*, April 1935.
41. *NA*, 6 August 1914, p. 396.

fight for the rich in war as they sweat for the rich in peace."[42] A week later, he wrote on the tension between "Civilisation and War." Orage saw that the war continued the same class struggle abroad that marked English society at home. In March 1916, he launched an attack on the wartime banking system and the Bank of England's issuing of treasury notes.[43] In April, he focused on "The Ethic of War." In a lengthy series of fifteen articles written throughout 1916 and 1917, "Notes on Economic Terms," he elaborated on the relationship between labor, war, and profits. In August 1918, he observed that, since "credit is really the dominant form of economic power," the ordinary people should have access to it, rather than industry alone.[44] As Pound cogently puts it, "he was a moralist, and then an economist."[45]

Throughout the war, Orage continued his attack on the inequality between service and sacrifice. Men, not capital, were conscripted, and, while lives were being lost in the trenches, profits were being made in industry. From the battlefield, between November 1915 and March 1916, at Orage's urging, T. E. Hulme contributed war notes to *The New Age,* before he was killed at the front. By autumn 1918, Orage noted, over 50 percent of British infantrymen in France were under 19 years of age. At home, Orage fought against a censorship of the press that limited his dialectic against social inequalities. In September 1916, he wrote: "The power of the Daily Press is the power of the rich men who own and control it," claiming that the articulation of truth is impeded if the truth threatens "interests of the privately wealthy."[46]

Orage's articulation of "truth" acquired a new ally in Major Clifford Hugh Douglas, a former engineer and a proponent of Guild Socialism who, attracted by Orage's articles on economic disparities, submitted an article to Orage in 1916. Orage, taken by Douglas's economics but numbed by his inept prose, taught him to write. In return, Douglas taught Orage a social scheme whose efficient distribution of capital would render a society less apt to go to war. He gave the label

---

42. *NA,* 3 September 1914. Cited by Coyle, *Ezra Pound,* pp. 327–328.
43. Redman, *Pound and Fascism,* p. 38, argues that Orage and his collaborators unwittingly assumed that the gold standard (limiting the amount of currency in circulation to an amount measurable in the value of gold reserves held by the Bank of England) deprives the ordinary worker of the necessary money to buy goods produced by British industry. At the same time, the profits of producers were being protected by a political system that favored accumulation of funds in banks. As economic theorists were to remark later, Orage simply did not understand the "fiction" of the ratio of money to gold until the end of the war.
44. Redman, *Pound and Fascism,* p. 43. In pp. 17–50 he offers an excellent synopsis of the Social Credit system.
45. Cookson, *Selected Prose,* p. 447.
46. *NA,* 3 September 1916.

"Social Credit" to this distribution and explained it as a process where-
by work would be rewarded, not by money passing into financial insti-
tutions where it would be susceptible to hoarding and exploitation, but
by public credit to be drawn upon by individuals. Orage introduced
Douglas to Pound in 1918 and published Douglas's first article on
2 January 1919. He then helped Douglas put his first book, *Credit
Power and Democracy*, through the press in 1920, and added a 58-page
commentary.[47] Orage's own explanation of Social Credit, foreshadowing some of the credit-card principles of the last quarter of the 20th century, described it as a system of matching consumer capacity to buy
with industry's capacity to produce. A later pupil and friend put it suc-
cinctly for the American public: "The purpose of Social Credit is to give
the community a dollar to buy every dollar's worth produced by its
industry."[48] T. S. Eliot has a character in *The Rock* denounce the finan-
ciers in Orage's terms: "It's all profit what nobody gets and nobody
knows 'ow they gets it."[49] The use of credit rather than debt as the basis
of economic exchange would obviate the weakness of the gold standard,[50] Orage believed. He explained that "the theory is at least no more
difficult to understand than a thousand and one others . . . and, in com-
parison with the theory of the Gold Standard . . . it is elementary."[51]
It was a theory involving, not the overthrow of the present economic
system, but its overhaul. After being convinced of its merit, his friend
Chesterton declared Orage to be "the most lucid exponent of economic
philosophy of our time."[52]

The marvelous mix in *The New Age* of new writing, economical
and political commentary, and cultural criticism—including an innovative look at the cinema as an art form (October 1917)—produced a journal his public appreciated as both "lively and eccentric."[53] Orage had
his doubters then, however, just as he has them now. There are three
journalistic issues on which Orage has been questioned. The first is the
anti-Semitic strain in *The New Age*. A recent critic accuses Orage's

---

47. The important distinction that Orage insisted upon in his essay is between Real Credit,
measured by the potential delivery of material and production, and Financial Credit, measured
by the delivery of money.
48. Allan R. Brown, Afterword to Elizabeth Sage Holter's *An ABC Of Social Credit* (New York:
Coward, McCann, 1934), p. 109.
49. Cited by Peter Ackroyd, *T. S. Eliot* (London: Hamish Hamilton, 1984). p. 221.
50. James Laughlin, *Pound as Wuz* (Saint Paul: Graywolf Press, 1987), pp. 153–154. Laughlin
himself was an American steel magnate who was attracted to Social Credit.
51. Orage, "The Fear of Leisure," *Social Credit and the Fear of Leisure* (Vancouver, BC:
Institute of Economic Democracy, 1977), p. 20.
52. *Criterion,* April 1935.
53. Weintraub, *The London Yankees,* p. 282.

vision of a "better world, an anti-Semitic one,"[54] and adds that Orage himself is "known for anti-Semitism" along with Yeats, Eliot, and Lawrence.[55] Another commentator replies that, while Pound and Douglas drifted toward anti-Semitism, Orage and *The New Age* stood against usury, not Jews.[56] A third explains that "the *NA* was not an anti-Semitic journal, but Orage did not censor his contributors' material, even when he objected to some of it."[57] Orage himself would have none of anti-Semitism. In the late 20s, he wrote to Pound: "After all, there are lots of Jewish Social Creditors (not Munson, except by marriage), and there's Waldo Frank."[58] More to the point, as early as 14 August 1913, he wrote an article in *The New Age* titled, "The Folly of Anti-Semitism," and followed in May 1921 with "Anti-Semitism."

Secondly, Orage has been criticized for the rapidity with which he changed ideological direction. One critic cites "Orage's changing intellectual allegiances" and his open-mindedness as the "cause of his failure to achieve any lasting goal."[59] Richard Curle records Ramiro de Maeztu's observation during the war that: "Orage knows the shape of everything and the weight of nothing, but there was something noble about the perpetual search for the harmony of nothing."[60] In his defense, I would point to Orage's strength, rather than his weakness, in a heterodoxy that consisted of a willingness to entertain a number of disparate ideas until one above the others dominated his attention. Pound stressed this aspect of his mind in his contribution, "He Pulled His Weight," in *The New Age* memorial issue in November 1934, saying: "Orage's impersonality was his greatness, and the breadth of his mind was apparent in the speed with which he threw over a cumbrous lot of superstition, and a certain number of fairly good ideas for a new set of better ones. . . . I take it that in 30 years of journalism Orage never printed a lie he didn't believe."[61] Edwin Muir recalled: "He was a born collaborator, a born midwife of ideas, and consequently, a born editor."[62] Augustus John's biographer observes that Orage, a "man of

---

54. Charles Norman, *The Case of Ezra Pound* (New York: Funk and Wagnall's, 1968), pp. 24 and 68.
55. Norman, *Case of Ezra Pound*, p. 69.
56. Flory, *The American Ezra Pound*, p. 79. Orage rarely used the term "usury." He preferred "bank charges."
57. Redman, *Ezra Pound*, p. 39.
58. Flory, *American Ezra Pound*, p. 79.
59. Redman, *Ezra Pound*, pp. 16–17.
60. *Caravansary and Conversation* (Freeport, NY: Books for Libraries Press, 1971), p. 178.
61. *NA*, memorial issue, November 1934.
62. Cited by Louise Welch, *Orage with Gurdjieff in America* (London: Routledge & Kegan Paul, 1982), p. 66.

sense," was a "brilliant wayward editor of *The New Age* who, like a Mohammed always changing his Allah, had first elected Nietzsche as god, then ousted him with the Douglas Credit Scheme which gave way before the deity of psycho-analysis, and was finally replaced in New York and Fontainebleau, by Gourdjieff's [*sic*] book of tricks—at which point John lost him. Like John, he had the mind of a disciple and the temperament of a leader, which led even this last association with Gourdjieff to break up." [63]

Orage's deity, Gurdjieff, was often cited in negative assessments of Orage's heterodoxy. His "conversion" to Gurdjieff, however, was neither startling nor new to those acquainted with him. He had been drawn to Nietzsche by Jackson in Leeds. Nietzsche and the *Baghavad Gita,* to which he had introduced Jackson, were, for Orage, matched stepping-stones on a straight path toward Gurdjieff. [64] It was, according to Orage himself in a letter to Holbrook Jackson, the inspiration of Yeats' Nietzschism in *On Baile's Strand*—performed in Leeds in 1905 with Orage's sponsoring—that prompted him to strike out for London. [65] By the time Orage arrived in London, he had a full-length study of Nietzsche ready for the press—*Nietzsche in Outline,* which was published the next year. In this work, Orage, in terms suggesting his future involvement with Social Credit and Gurdjieff, rewrote Nietzsche's definition of *virtue* as "the instinctive desire to pour out life and not to preserve or amass life: the will to spend and not to acquire, the virtue of liberality, courage, gaiety, strength, the sense of inexhaustible powers, the atmosphere of an original fount and source of life, the spirit of self-giving, of prodigality, of ecstasy, of careless rapture in action, of spontaneity." [66]

Earlier in the study, Orage aligns certain humans with lower animals who live a

. . . yet undifferentiated mode of life, in which all our faults are . . . active in a single sense. Feeling, willing, and knowing . . . form a single strand. In the human mind, on the contrary, the various threads are separated. A certain retardation is given to various aspects of the undifferentiated instinct. . . . But when the mind becomes lucid, free,

63. Holroyd, *Augustus John,* p. 474.
64. David S. Thatcher, *Nietzsche in England* (Toronto: University of Toronto Press, 1970), pp. 219–268, discusses Nietzsche's influence on Orage's thought.
65. R. F. Foster, *W. B. Yeats: A Life* (Oxford University Press, 1997), p. 347.
66. Orage, *Nietzche in Outline and Aphorism* (London: T. N. Foulis, 1907), p. 109.

ethereal, the retardation may be supposed no longer to take place. . . .
Instinct, reason, and intuition may be said to stand for unity, disinte-
gration, and renewed units of the instinctual life. These phases correspond . . . to animal, human and superman.[67]

Such categories, limited as they are, recall Gurdjieff's scale of being
from motion to sense to emotion to reason, and his triad of tramp,
lunatic, and householder, in ascending order.

Early in his career, Orage had scanned the works of Annie Besant,
Madame [Helena Petrovna] Blavatsky, and Charles Leadbeater, whose
theosophy, Orage thought, was in need of a psychosynthesis. While still
a schoolteacher in Leeds, Orage had written about things that would
occupy his literary talents much later. In 1903, for one example, he submitted an article to the *Theosophical Review* on "The Mystical Value of
Literature." Soon after his arrival in London, he joined meetings of G.
R. S. Mead's Quest Society and D. N. Dunlop's Theosophists. He lectured to the Fabian Society on esoteric doctrines, and, before long, he
assembled at 146 Harley Street his own "psycho-syntheses" group,
which included, at one time or another, Havelock Ellis, James Young,
Maurice Nicoll, J. A. M. Alcock, David Eder, and Rowland Kenney.[68]
Later, they met in Lady Rothermere's studio and at the Kensington
Quest Society rooms,[69] then settled finally at 38 Warwick gardens.
Throughout this period, he published articles of his own on theosophy
for *Theosophical Review,* and still later published articles in the
columns of the *The New Age* by "M. M. Cosmoi." Cosmoi was the
pseudonym of the Serb prophet and mystic Dmitri Mitrinovic who
espoused a doctrine of "panhumanism" that had a magnetic appeal for
Orage.

Such contacts gave Orage, now known familiarly as the "Mystic
of Fleet Street," occasion to expose his own ideas at length. The science
he preached, says one critic, was spiritual evolution, a "mystical extension of Darwin."[70] It became widely known in intellectual circles that
Orage had almost magnetic powers of voice. Gerald Cumberland writes
that "Orage, in his subtle devilishly clever way, would lead his listeners
on to the very threshold of occult knowledge and leave them there wide-

---

67. Orage, *Nietzsche,* p. 81; Timothy Materer, *Modern Alchemy: Poetry and the Occult* (Ithaca: Cornell University Press, 1995), p. 19, says that Orage gave Nietzsche a cult interpretation.
68. Demeter P. Tryphonopoulis, "'The Fourth; the Dimension of Stillness': D. P. [*sic*] Ouspensky and Fourth Dimensionalism in Canto 49," *Paideuma* 19 (1990), p. 120.
69. Lady Mary Liliane Rothermere was the wife of the newspaper magnate Howard Sidney Harmsworth, Viscount Rothermere.
70. Martin, *Orage as Critic,* p. 15.

eyed and wonder-struck."[71] Anthony Ludovici remembers how "I was struck then . . . by the intense intellectuality that radiated from every part of his being, particularly, of course, his eyes."[72] Jacob Epstein observes that "Orage was a man of extraordinary mental vigour. He had a magnetic personality. . . . His charm of voice and manner drew listeners to him and he went about like a Greek philosopher or rhetor, with a following of disciples."[73] Orage was the most distinguished of those men of influence on modern thought, remarked another, who then continued: "Orage has more than a touch of genius . . . He also has the eternal spirit of youth.[74]

Among his disciples were a countless number whose good fortune it was to have been instructed in writing by Orage. Katherine Mansfield was but one. Another was the poet and art critic Herbert Read, who read *The New Age* in the trenches on the French front, before returning to England to be hired by Orage, who then polished his prose to *The New Age* perfection. Then, there was Pound and John Gould Fletcher.

Orage's brilliance of voice, appearance, and literary judgment may have combined to heighten the attraction he held for women, an attraction he reciprocated. Mary Gawsthorpe, in recalling Orage's seductiveness, wondered at his quite deliberate testing of his sexual appeal with women, both married and single, and his open display of delight with success.[75] William Patterson speculates that Orage's "central weakness," which he never overcame, was his desire for women.[76] It would be fairer to say, however, that he preferred women's desire for him. Cumberland recalls with delight that Orage's "gospel, always preached with his tongue in cheek, that every man and woman should do precisely what he or she desires, acted like a heady wine on the gasping and enthusiastic young ladies who used to sit in rows worshipping him." Nonetheless, he regrets that "along with his gifts there went . . . a knack of gathering charlatans around him."[77] Curiously, Orage himself had spoken publicly of the danger of "popular philosophy," by which he meant a drawing of undue attention to the philosopher rather than to his

---

71. Cited by James Webb, *The Harmonious Circle: The Lives and Works of G. I. Gurdjieff, P. D. Ouspensky, and Their Followers* (London: Thames & Hudson, 1980), p. 201.
72. Webb, *The Harmonious Circle*, p. 199.
73. Jacob Epstein, *Epstein: An Autobiography* (London: Hulton Press, 1955), p. 61.
74. Gerald Cumberland, *Set Down in Malice* (London: Grant Richards, 1920), pp. 130–131.
75. Mary Gawsthorpe, *Up Hill to Holloway* (Penobscot, ME: Traversity Press, 1962), pp. 191–203.
76. William Patterson, *Ladies of the Rope* (San Francisco: Arete, 1998), p. 84.
77. Cumberland, *Set Down*, p. 131.

philosophy, as Bergson was doing in Paris.[78] James Webb suggests that: "Under Orage's successful exterior was a latent insecurity which craved applause of others, and when the trappings of success were denied him, this self-doubt came to dominate him entirely."[79] Self-doubt in Orage, however, seems to have been more a function of his constant inquiry into self and an incentive toward self-observing and exploring. Of course, there were those who cast doubt on the quality of Orage's fundamental interests in theosophy. Beatrice Hastings, in her diatribe against the The New Age and its proprietor, whose side she had quit in 1913, insisted that Orage's attraction was to sorcery, that his spiritual intimate was Aleister Crowley, and that he was under the merciless influence of Mead and his Quest Society.[80]

The turning point in Orage's theosophical quest came in November 1911, when F. S. Flint introduced him to the ideas of the 33-year-old Russian philosopher P[yotr] D[emianovich] Ouspensky. Two years later, Orage met Ouspensky, who was returning via England to Russia from a voyage to the East. A year later, Orage read parts translated for him from Ouspensky's Tertium Organum (1912), which divulged fresh views into what Orage knew of esoteric doctrine. Subsequently, he corresponded with Ouspensky, and, in late 1919, published Ouspensky's "Letters from Russia" in The New Age. Claude Bragdon, who had become a good friend of Lady Rothermere, finished his translation of Tertium Organum in 1919, and saw it through press in 1920. After he got Ouspensky's address from Bragdon, Orage sent royalties to the author, who arrived himself in London in August 1921 with other refugees from the Russian Revolution. He was soon lecturing in Lady Rothermere's studio at St. John's Wood on Gurdjieff's "system" to a fascinated, if baffled, English audience that included Orage and T. S. Eliot.[81] After hearing him the first time, Orage wrote Bragdon: "Mr. Ouspensky is the first teacher I have met who has impressed me with ever-increasing certainty that he knows and can do."[82] Ouspensky's lectures gave Orage a view of a new evolutionary stage, but one that required special education toward the Sacred Brotherhood of Higher

78. Martin, Orage as Critic, pp. 203–204.
79. Webb, Harmonious Circle, p. 208.
80. Beatrice Hastings, The Old "New Age": Orage and Others (London: Blue Moon Press, 1936), p. 19. Hastings was born Emily Alice Haigh.
81. Eliot's Four Quartets, published after World War II, have thematic elements that seem to have been inspired by Ouspensky's The Life of Ivan Osokin as well as by his London talks.
82. Claude Bragdon, More Lives Than One (New York: Knopf, 1938), p. 320.

Consciousness. Orage decided almost at once that he should take a "sabbatical" from *The New Age,* and wrote to ask one of his newest collaborators, the young and brilliant Herbert Read, whether he might consider taking over the editorial reins for a year.[83] Read was hesitant, and Orage bided his time while awaiting the promised arrival of Gurdjieff in England.

In the meantime, the war had ended, and the benefits Orage had hoped for in postwar England were a disappointment. As he wrote in 1926, looking back in "An Editor's Progress" to his separation from the world of journalism, "Art as we know it today has no power over the conscience of mankind."[84] Orage had seen the human implications of Social Credit and had supplied it with a spiritual force. As one observer notes, however, "Orage emerged from the war and the inflationary aftermath with a profound sense that a swindle had been perpetrated on the British public. . . . He was disillusioned over his lack of effect."[85]

Like Ruskin's reform ideas a half-century earlier, Orage's socialism had affiliations with theosophy, art, crafts, and psychology, but its proponent lacked the power to transmit a conviction of its necessity to contemporary England. Pound had left for Paris before the end of 1920. Now, Orage contemplated leaving England to fight his battle for social justice on foreign soil. As Pound went south to Italy, where he found Mussolini with an attractive economical political premise, Orage went west to New York in the service of a universalistic psychology.

On 23 February 1922—the same day a $2,000,000 gift from John D. Rockefeller was announced for the foundation of a London School for Hygiene, and Lloyd George's meeting with Raymond Poincaré for a continuing *entente* was set—Orage was in an audience in Kensington listening to Gurdjieff outline a "system" of work. Having heard Ouspensky's earlier introduction to the "system" and its teacher, Orage was both prepared and eager to hear Gurdjieff. Although Gurdjieff himself did not know enough English to address the audience personally, he was on the dais while his Russian interpreter spoke his words. Others in the audience recall that Gurdjieff interrupted more than once in Russian to add elaboration on one point or another, which the interpreter translated. There was an English translator as well, to transmit questions from the audience. Orage asked a couple of questions, one about the

---

83. David Thistlewood, *Herbert Read: Formlessness and Form* (London: Routledge & Kegan Paul), p. 5.
84. *Commonweal III,* 20 February 1926.
85. Redman, *Pound and Fascism,* p. 48.

possibility of changing along lines Ouspensky had suggested in his talks.[86] Orage was greatly impressed with both the talk and the response to his question, and he decided right away to follow up his earlier inclinations to take a leave of absence to become one of Gurdjieff's pupils.

What Orage hoped to find in his quest is a matter of diverse conjecture. The facts, however, seem clear enough. Gurdjieff had come to London at Ouspensky's invitation, not only to address people already following Ouspensky, but to scan the possibilities of establishing there the Institute for the Harmonious Development of Man he had thought of in Moscow in 1913 and organized briefly in Constantinople in 1919. Gurdjieff was encouraged by what he heard of possibilities in Hampstead. Despite the intervention on his behalf by Maurice Nicoll, Lady Rothermere, and Orage, however, the British foreign office was not in favor of granting Gurdjieff a visa. They suspected that he had been a tsarist agent with the name Dordjieff who had opposed British interests in Tibet a quarter of a century earlier.[87]

Shortly before his London visit, Gurdjieff had considered Berlin and Hellerau, in Germany, as possible locales for an Institute, but was attracted further west. On Bastille Day, 14 July 1922—a year to the day after Emanuel Radnitzky had arrived in Paris from New York to launch a brilliant career as a photographer under the name of Man Ray— Gurdjieff arrived in the City of Light with a blueprint for the reconstruction of man's harmonious development. He soon found a suitable temporary location for the Institute. Orage, after hearing that Gurdjieff had found a base for his teaching in Paris, put pen to paper to apply for admission. Effectively, he wrote himself into a new life.

A critical point of view has it that "his conversion . . . to the system of Gurdjieff was no 'synthesis' of socialism and spiritualism, but a leaving off of attempted combinations in order to pursue what Douglas' project was unable to accommodate."[88] Perhaps the conversion did not signal a true "synthesis," but Orage did seek to use the one as a tool to produce the other. T. S. Eliot, who met Orage personally for the first time in the summer of 1922, just before Orage quit London,[89] assumed that Orage's economics paved the way for Gurdjieff. Orage, he said in

86. J. G. Bennett, *Gurdjieff: Making a New World* (London: Turnstone, 1972), p. 133.
87. Although the identity of the historical Dordjieff with Gurdjieff has been discredited by Moore, *Gurdjieff*, *Dorje* "the daring one" is an appellation that could be appended to any notable, and *Dordjieff* would designate the son of such a person.
88. Redman, *Pound and Fascism*, p. 16.
89. Paige, *Selected Letters*, p. 550: "Have met Orage and liked him."

retrospect, "saw that any real change for the better meant a spiritual revolution; and he said that no spiritual revolution was of any use unless you had a practical economic scheme."[90] Philip Mairet, Orage's later associate at the *New English Weekly* sensed that Orage's escape from England was furthered by the sheer physical burden of putting out *The New Age* (tens of issues of the journal were produced by Orage and Pound alone).[91] He adds that Orage was "looking for an inner reality between himself and God," after he had "gone as far as he could with human nature."[92] Another reason for Orage going to Gurdjieff was to gain the power to convince England of the urgent need for economic reform along the lines of Social Credit. In his last "Editor's Progress," written for *The New Age* in 1926, he recalled that he had announced that "I am going to find God," and added: "I only wish that my motives could be as clearly conscious as that would imply."[93] Be that as it may, it remains a viable hypothesis that Orage did not leave *The New Age* definitively, and that he was quite certain at the time that he would, some day, return from his "sabbatical" to his chosen career.

Those who felt that Orage had made a fatal blunder in going to Gurdjieff were numerous and rarely charitable in their expressions. With hindsight, John Gross wondered: "How could he have fallen for such mumbo-jumbo? . . . What is the point of having the finest critical intelligence of the day, if you devote it to expounding the cosmology of *All and Everything*?" He concludes, however, that Orage demonstrated that "high literary ability can co-exist with the most dubious doctrines, and survive exposure to the most extravagant kinds of nonsense."[94]

Nonetheless, Orage's move was an act of extraordinary boldness, ill-considered or not. In his 50th year, with neither financial nor domestic security on which to fall back, he gave up all material and social considerations for an adventure of the spirit. More than this, he gave up that which is most precious to the English mentality, fame. He could not have been insensitive to his reputation in London, and must have appreciated the cultural power he wielded in an England standing at a cultural crossroad. If he had thought earlier of taking a sabbatical or vacation from his work in order to study with Ouspensky, he seemed to have consciously burned his occupational bridges behind him to go to Gurdjieff.

---

90. *Criterion,* April 1915.
91. Mairet, *Orage: A Memoir,* p. 86.
92. Mairet, *Orage: A Memoir,* p. 87.
93. *NA 22,* May 1926.
94. John Gross, *The Rise and Fall,* p. 232.

Regardless of the diverse and opposing opinions about Orage's defection from Fleet Street, a page was turned in the cultural history of England when Orage left his editorship in the autumn of 1922. In looking back over Orage's *New Age* career, Waldo Frank concluded that he "gave to English literature a prose that ranks with Shaw's and that, for pure revolutionary thought, puts Shaw in his place as the quite proper Devil of old ladies."[95] Another well-informed admirer concluded regretfully that "the whole history of Orage and his colleagues and *The New Age* must . . . be regarded so far as English literature and literary journalism is concerned, as the final brilliant flare-up of a guttering candle."[96]

---

95. Waldo Frank, *Time Exposures* (New York: Boni & Liveright, 1926), p. 153
96. Hugh MacDiarmid, *The Company I've Kept* (Berkeley: University of California Press, 1967), p. 274.

Chapter Two

1922–1923

ORAGE'S TALE OF TWO CITIES

*Thanks to the nature of life, there is an insubordinate imp in
each of us that prefers in the long run all the horrors of
freedom to all the amenities of benevolent slavery.*

—Orage[1]

*It is only when you realise life is taking you nowhere that it
begins to have meaning.*

—Ouspensky[2]

"How're you gonna keep 'em down on the farm, after they've seen
Paree?" goes the popular song celebrating the exposure of Middle
America to Europe during and shortly after World War I, as the United
States settled into a thriving cultural and economic period following
the armistice. Americans flocked to London, Rome, and Paris, and the
English to Paris, Rome, and Berlin. Orage, however, having left London
for the continent, skirted Paris to Fontainebleau, where he labored for
two years before finding his appointed place in New York in 1924.

Postwar England in 1922 was well on the road to recovery from
the devastation of the Great War. The hegemony of the Empire, however, was on the wane, and the metropolis was never again to exercise the
economic and political domination it had in the days of the Empress
Victoria. The British fleet, still the pride of the oceans, no longer dominated the seaways, and former outposts of the Empire were injecting
into the international community a fresh cultural talent to replace the
loss of its promising youth that Britain suffered between 1914 and 1919.

1. Cited by Gorham Munson, *The Awakening Twenties* (Baton Rouge: Louisiana State University, 1985), p. 239.
2. Cited by Maurice Nicoll, *Psychological Commentaries*, vol. I (London: Vincent Stuart,1952),
p. 63.

After the war, T[homas] S[tearns] Eliot and a battalion of talented young men arrived from the United States to join Ezra Pound on the sceptered isle where his monumental *Waste Land* was published in 1922. The native-born New Zealander, Katherine Mansfield, had been schooled in England and had begun her writing career under Orage's tutelage at the height of England's prestige some four years before the devastation of war eroded irredeemably British power and influence in the world's cultural, economic, and political arenas.

English and Americans went in waves to the continent, many initially to Berlin. Vladimir Nabokov arrived there from Cambridge, and Putzi Hanfstängi from Harvard, though both had continental roots. Djuna Barnes, Hartley Marsden, Harrison Dowd, and Berenice Abbott also spent time there shortly after the War,[3] Postwar Paris, however, was an even more exciting feast of pleasure and profit, particularly for the expatriate, the temporary resident, the exile, and the occasional visitor who, more often than not, was a university student celebrating the end of his first year of study by touring the cultural capital of Western civilization. The postwar ambience in the West seemed to favor French cultural values, and, in general, morale was high and relaxed. Women were wearing hair and skirts short, and were smoking unashamedly in public. Men put aside stiff collars and waistcoats and dressed airily. The loose *cravate* (from *Croat*) gained sway over the tight tie. Immigrants and refugees from Eastern Europe, particularly Russia, Hungary, and Romania, added an exotic flavor to bistro and taxicab interiors. Brancusi had brought his talent from Romania to Paris on foot, and White Russians translated their taste for piroschki, zakusky, pojarsky, galubsky, beef Stroganoff, caviar, and bilini from ornate autocratic dining halls in St. Petersburg and Moscow to crowded restaurant kitchens from the Étoile to Montmartre.

American expatriates were universal explorers, some of whom had seen Paris for the first time as members of the AEF (American Expeditionary Forces). Sylvia Beach's Shakespeare and Company bookshop was a local gathering point for writers and artists. It was there, in 1922, that Margaret Anderson and Jane Heap published Joyce's *Ulysses,* after publishing portions of it in New York in 1920 and suffering the ire of the law. Robert McAlmon founded his Contact Editions in Paris and published Gertrude Stein's *The Making of Americans* and Hemingway's first book, *Three Stories and Ten Poems.* As McAlmon remarked in his recollection of his period in Paris, *Being Geniuses Together:* "If it was

---

3. Andrew Field, *Djuna* (New York: Putnam, 1983), pp. 16–17.

not absolutely in fashion to be an artist or a genius in 1920, it certainly was so toward 1926."[4]

Nancy Cunard had the Hours Press and William Bird the Three Mountains Press which published *In Our Time* by Hemingway, who had moved to Paris in 1922. Other American writers who took up temporary residence in Paris in that decade included humorist James Thurber; novelists Sherwood Anderson, John Dos Passos, Louis Bromfield, Nathaniel West, Sinclair Lewis, Ernest Hemingway, F[rancis] Scott Fitzgerald—whose *The Great Gatsby,* set in 1922, was published in 1926—and Henry Miller; poets e[dward] e[stlin] cummings, Hart Crane, Langston Hughes, William Carlos Williams, Jean Toomer— who, in 1922, submitted to Max Eastman several of the pieces that formed *Cane* (1923)—Pound, Eliot, Charles Henri Ford, and Archibald MacLeish; biographers Alan Ross McDougall and Eugene McGowan; dramatist Thornton Wilder; critics Allen Tate, Edmund Wilson, and Gilbert Seldes—who arrived in 1922 to write *The Seven Lively Arts*— journalists Carl Zigrosser and James Laughlin (later editor of New Directions Press). Irishmen James Joyce and William Butler Yeats joined them.

1922 was an *annus mirabilis* in the arts. Kandinsky, Tchelitcheff, and Chagall had brought Eastern European trends in painting westward. Stravinsky, Scriabin, Virgil Thomson, and George Antheil, whose "Ballet méchanique" was notorious, brought innovations in music from East and West. Diaghilev and Isadora Duncan brought radical innovations in the dance. Man Ray and Berenice Abbott were making a name for American photography, Alexander Calder for American art. American expatriates Gerald and Esther Murphy opened the Mediterranean littoral as a winter playground for the idle, the bored, but, above all, for the talented and the rich. Most remarkable of all in Paris in the twenties, however, was the army of brilliant women writers, mostly American, that included permanent residents Edith Wharton (since 1909), Natalie Barney, Gertrude Stein, Solita Solano, Margaret Anderson (who left *The Little Review* behind in New York), Sylvia Beach (of the Shakespeare and Company bookshop), Janet Flanner,[5] Djuna Barnes, and the sculptress Thelma Wood. Temporary residents

---

4. McAlmon and Boyle, *Being Geniuses Together 1920–1930* (Garden City, NY: Doubleday, 1968), pp. 95–96.

5. Brenda Wineapple, *Genêt: A Biography of Janet Flanner* (New York: Ticknor & Fields, 1989), pp. 90–91, reports that Janet Flanner, who became very close to Margaret Anderson and Solita Solano in 1924, had a very positive opinion of Gurdjieff, but did not become a pupil because, as she said, she preferred skeptical rationalism, and she was wary of Gurdjieff's mystical teachings.

included Elsa Maxwell, Mabel Dodge, Jane Heap, Edna St. Vincent Millay, Leonie Adams, Katherine Anne Porter, Mina Loy, and Kay Boyle. Peggy Guggenheim was on her way to becoming a leading patroness of the arts. Josephine Baker was the hit of Montmartre glittering nightclub shows. It was indeed a heady time in France for what Gertrude Stein, in head-shaking wonder at Fitzgerald's and Hemingway's errant navigation on French roads, labeled the "Lost Generation." Almost all of these writers and artists were known by reputation, if not in person, to Orage.

It was to Georgii Ivanovich Gurdjieff, in this glittering Paris of the arts, that Orage addressed this carefully composed letter on 22 July 1922,[6] asking to become a member of the Institute Gurdjieff had founded in the dance studios of the Jacques-Dalcroze school:

Dear Mr. Gurdjieff,

I wish above anything to work in the Institute with the high hopes of being allowed to work for the Institute. I want to begin at the earliest possible moment. But, even supposing that you will accept me as a pupil in anything I, then, am tied to the following life circumstances:

1) I own and edit The New Age, *a weekly I have edited for fifteen years. It is my only source of income, about £250 per annum.*

2) I have no other capital. Consequently, if I can come to Paris, I should have to sell or otherwise dispose of The New Age.

3) I probably should not get more than £100 for it.

I am quite willing to give up the N. A. *and to chance the future. However, before doing anything final, I want to ask your advice.*

A. R. Orage

Ten days later, Orage received this response, indicating that Gurdjieff knew both who Orage was, and what his potentials in the work would be:

Paris, 1st August 1922
Rue de Lille
Hotel Solferino

Dear Mr. Orage,

Mr. Gurdjieff tells me for you all *that unfortunately the organisation of the work according to the full programme of the Institute will take more time than he expected. But at the same time the work has already began* [sic] *in a temporary building (Dalcroze School) and if someone wished*

---

6. All Gurdjieff and Orage correspondence cited in this book is from Orage's unpublished papers, and is used with the kind permission of Anne B. Orage, widow of Orage's son Richard. Further citations will not be footnoted.

*to come over to work there, he will be very glad to see them, but they shall
have to live by themselves not in the Institute.*

    *To you personally he advises to sell the N.A. The more you get for it is
certainly the better, but even 100 pounds will give you a year in the
Institute and during that time you will become capable for a more
responsible work and in that case will not have to think about your living. So arrange your plans and come if you wish.*

Yours sincerely,
(signed) P. Ouspensky

*If you leave London before I come, please give all correspondence,
addresses and everything that refers to subscription to Mr. Page or to
Walton.*

So into Orage's life came his *kairos,*[7] an extraordinary adventure of the
body, mind, and spirit that was to metamorphose his career and claim
his attention for the rest of his life. On 10 August 1922, after pondering
Ouspensky's reply, Orage appealed to Herbert Read again, saying that
his mind was made up to go to Paris for a year. He repeated his earlier
request, but in vain.[8] *The New Age,* which was on a modest upward
swing in sales during the second half of 1922, announced its editor's
departure in its pages of 28 September, for more "general work," and
reported that Major Arthur Moore would assume the editor's post. A
few weeks earlier, Mme. de Hartmann, wife of the aristocratic composer Thomas de Hartmann, who had accompanied her husband in his
attendance upon Gurdjieff from St. Petersburg during his exile's track
to the West, had located an ideal property in the countryside for a
school. On 1 October 1922, Gurdjieff moved his lodgings from a
house in Auteuil and his operations from the modest dance studio
in Paris to the château known as Le Prieuré [The Priory] in Avon
near Fontainebleau.[9]

---

7. *Kairos* is a Greek term used most often in scriptural commentary to mark the spiritual significance of a physical experience. On an early autumn day in 1922, writes Louise Welch,
Orage with Gurdjieff in New York (London: Routledge & Kegan Paul, 1982), p. 24, Ouspensky,
from the window of his flat in London saw Orage coming to see him. He knew the reason, and
said to Orage: "Go."
8. David Thistlewood, *Herbert Read Formlessness and Form* (London: Routledge & Kegan
Paul, 1984), p. 6.
9. Although Gurdjieff said that he had raised the money through restaurant operations in Paris
and the sale of rugs, Ralph Philipson, an admirer of Orage, and Lady Rothermere, who was
sponsoring Ouspensky in London, contributed heavily to the cost of acquiring the Prieuré. It
was rumored at the time that the French Prime Minister, Raymond Poincaré, intervened to
arrange Gurdjieff's living permit. At first, the Château was leased with an option to buy, and
later bought for some 700,000 francs. Then, Gurdjieff borrowed on the Prieuré to have enough
funds to refurbish it, the other buildings, and the grounds.

Katherine Mansfield, dying of tuberculosis, had met Ouspensky through Orage in mid-September and on 3 October, on Orage's recommendation, she consulted with Dr. James Carruthers Young in Paris, who gave her permission to apply to the Institute.[10] Reportedly, she saw Gurdjieff in Paris a day or so later and, though he told her that a vacation in the south of France might do more for her, he said she would be welcome at the Institute.[11] On 17 October, she moved to the Prieuré to a room prepared for her, and later, in order to profit from the animal vibrations of the place, to a room above the cowshed where she was to die in early January 1923. Wyndham Lewis spoke for most of Katherine's circle when the news of her move reached England, exclaiming bitterly that Gurdjieff was "a psychic shock."[12] Murry's brief note in the 1927 edition of her *Journal* reads: "She entered a kind of spiritual brotherhood at Fontainebleau." Others in England were less sanguine about Gurdjieff's Institute. Vivian Eliot wrote on 2 November 1922 to Ezra Pound in Paris in reply to his request to know the whereabouts of Lady Rothermere: "She is now in that asylum for the insane called La [*sic*] Prieuré where she does religious dances naked with Katherine Mansfield."[13]

"Bea" (as she was known to her close friends) Rothermere had stayed just two days there, long enough to tour the gardens. Orage, who had arrived in Paris on 13 October and moved to the Prieuré near the end of the month, missed her. He talked with Pound in Paris about Gurdjieff and, at the Institute, spoke regularly with Katherine Mansfield until her last day. Besides Dr. Young, the former British Intelligence officer Frank Pindar, the Jungian psychoanalyst Maurice Nicoll, and Orage, Gurdjieff's entourage consisted of some twenty followers, mostly Russian refugees from the revolution, all working urgently at refurbishing the château and the grounds during the day, and preparing during the evenings the exhibitions Gurdjieff intended to give in Paris. Often, Orage found himself alone with Russians who spoke not a word of English. Luckily, the de Hartmanns, Lily Galumnian, and Elizaveta de Stjernvall knew some English, and the Ouspenskys were often there.

---

10. John Middleton Murry, ed., *Journal of Katherine Mansfield* (New York: Knopf, 1927), p. 218. Young was the Chairman of The Medical Society of Individual Psychology, and editor of its proceedings. The honorary President of the Society was Dr. Alfred Adler. Young was well known for his advocacy of holistic medicine, and it was this interest that drew him to Gurdjieff.
11. For a full account of Mansfield's relations with Gurdjieff, see James Moore, *Mansfield and Gurdjieff* (London: Routledge & Kegan Paul), 1980.
12. Cited by Claire Tomalin, *Katherine Mansfield: A Secret Life* (London: Viking Penguin, 1987), p. 229. Tomalin's oblique view of Gurdjieff, p. 231, is that "he was not an ascetic, but a gross drinker, eater and fornicator."
13. D. D. Paige, *Ezra Pound: Selected Letters, 1907–1941* (New York: New Directions, 1971), p. 588.

None of Gurdjieff's close family, however, spoke either English or French. Gurdjieff was often in Paris negotiating operations of cafés and restaurants he had invested in with other Russians who had fled to Paris during the war, and he spent many nights there, while Orage and others labored at constructions on the property. Orage and Pound did have the occasion once to sample Gurdjieff's cuisine in Paris together. Pound was impressed enough by Gurdjieff's cooking to record his experience imaginatively under the rubric "Le Voyage Gastronomique is a French paideuma," in which he reported that "Brancusi ed. cook on occasion and G made Persian soup. . . . If he had more of that sort of thing in his repertoire he ed. had he supposed it, or desired it, have worked on toward at least one further conversion"[14] Gurdjieff invited Pound to visit him at the Prieuré, and Pound did with interest. By this time, if not before, Gurdjieff knew something of Pound's fame as a writer from Orage. They seemed to have gotten along well in the mix of languages between them, and Gurdjieff asked jokingly if Pound might not join him as a translator. Pound smiled knowingly. Gurdjieff's exotic cuisine was not enough of an incentive for conversion.[15]

Orage's friend and former associate, Philip Mairet, in his biography of Orage, describes something of Orage's two years training at the Prieuré, and records how Orage found himself being transformed from what he had been to something closer to his being-essence by labors nonhabitual. He was among the first wave of workers on the grounds who refurbished an old hanger into the ornate Study House, tilled the soil for gardens behind the main house, dug irrigation ditches, walled the baths, and remained late at night in talk, listening to music and training in the sacred dances and the obligatory "movements." When friends visited, they were shocked at first by his thinned frame and his callused hands, but they found Orage's eyes were bright and his mood exalted.[16] "No other pupil, I am persuaded—or none anything like his caliber—

---

14. *Guide to Kultur* (New York: New Directions, 1938), p. 112. Noel Stock, *The Life of Ezra Pound* (New York: Pantheon, 1970), p. 255, reports that "Gurdjieff made Persian soup, bright yellow in colour, far more delicate—you might say Piero dela Francesca in tone, as compared to a Bortch (tinted Rembrandt)." James Moore sets this meeting in the summer of 1923 (*Gurdjieff: Anatomy of a Myth*, p. 191); Neither mention Brancusi.
15. Leon Surette, *The Birth of Modernism* (Montreal: Queen's University Press), p. 224, says Pound visited Prieuré; J. J. Wilhelm, *Ezra Pound: London and Paris 1908–1925* (University Park: The Pennsylvania State University Press, 1990), p. 334, says that Pound did not go to the Prieuré, but saw Gurdjieff "earlier." Gurdjieff's offer to Pound was related to me by Jessie Orage.
16. Anthony Storr is not quite accurate when he says, *Feet Of Clay: Saints, Sinners, and Madmen* (New York: Free Press, 1996), p. 38, that "Gurdjieff, like many other gurus, was unashamedly elitist and authoritarian," for anyone might be found at the Prieuré, whether rich or poor, high or low in estate, learned or uninstructed.

served Gurdjieff with a more implicit spiritual obedience than Orage
. . . . The rigours Orage endured included the kind of psychological bul-
lying undergone by a monk in certain monastic disciplines, or by the
chela of an Indian guru."[17] His old friend, Rowland Kenney, visited
Orage there and saw in him "outward signs of . . . inward grace," a man
"thinner, harder, and more virile in appearance."[18] John Middleton
Murry, seeing him for the first time after several years when he visited
his wife, Katherine Mansfield, there in January 1923, remarked that he
found Orage "much gentler and sweeter" than he had been before.[19]
Orage himself confided to friends that he was happier than he could
remember ever being.

Gurdjieff himself, besides his business activities in Paris, took part
in the strenuous labors of the Institute. He not only directed work, but
made himself an example for the manner of accomplishing it. A sympathetic biographer of Mansfield concludes that Gurdjieff was not a fraud.
"A man who lays bricks and planes wood, cuts out dress materials and
printing stencils, designs all the decorations of a 'holy place,' mends
oriental carpets, and picks up a little shredded cabbage in the kitchen, is
something else."[20] A pupil who spent several years there with Gurdjieff,
dismissed the stories of marvels and miracles performed at the Institute,
and said: "The most sensational aspect of his work was a sort of sub-
lime commonsense."[21]

As Orage explained to Jean Toomer about what he had learned that
first year: "Work done after desire ends produces internal results, for at
these times 'automatic activity slows down' and the opportunity for
'voluntary, non-habitual action' increases;" and, the aim of the work is
to become "free from attachment to results."[22] The fact that Gurdjieff,
an inveterate heavy smoker himself, had ordered Orage to give up his
strong smoking habit at the Prieuré certainly contributed to his new
health. Nonetheless, Orage's English friends could not turn their minds
from the fact that "the most notable English editor of his time had
become a mysterious exile owing allegiance to an Armenian magus."[23]

---

17. Philip Mairet, *Autobiographical and Other Papers* (Manchester: Carcanet Press, 1982),
p. 192.
18. Mairet, *Orage*, p. 92. Louise Welch, *Orage with Gurdjieff in America* (London: Routledge
& Kegan Paul, 1982), pp. 28–29, offers an over-view of Orage at the Prieuré in 1922 and 1923.
19. Cited by John Carswell, *Lives and Letters* (London: Faber and Faber, 1978), p. 192. Jeffrey
Meyers *D. H. Lawrence: A Biography* (New York: Knopf, 1990), p. 136, says: "Murry's weakness and betrayal led her to the mysticism of Gurdjieff and hastened her death."
20. Antony Alpers, *The Life of Katherine Mansfield* (London: Jonathan Cape, 1980), p. 378.
21. "The Strange Cult of Gurdjieff," by Armagnac, *Psychology Today*, Dec. 1936, p. 31.
22. Cited by Rudolph Byrd, *Toomer's Years with Gurdjieff* (Athens: University of Georgia Press,
1989), p. 63.
23. Carswell, *Lives and Letters*, p. 213.

It should be recognized that, in Gurdjieff, Orage had found a soul brother. Gurdjieff would come up to him at work and say, "enough work, come coffee drink," and they would sit together on the terrace, or go to the Café Henri IV nearby and talk. Orage confided to Gurdjieff his interest in Douglas Social Credit, and asked for advice on how to pursue it in England. Gurdjieff advised him to work on his own will, saying that, if he perfected that, he could translate it into others.[24] Gurdjieff read Orage's ambition to be one of the "elder brothers of the human race," and he advised him, if he would achieve his goal, he must "learn how to give, then you make other people free."[25]

Since Gurdjieff himself said that he knew not a word of any Western European language at the time, and some assume that Orage knew not a word of Russian, one wonders how they communicated in the beginning. Frank Pindar and Ouspensky were handy occasional interpreters, but there is little doubt that Orage and Gurdjieff communicated in their own ways very well by themselves. Both Orage and Gurdjieff had uncanny capacities to understand foreign languages through understanding the speaker. They were friends, as Gurdjieff would say, "in the skin," by a sort of osmosis of spirit. Most importantly, they genuinely liked each other.[26] Stanley Nott recalls that "Gurdjieff liked to have Orage near him, for few knew better how to joke and have fun with him without exceeding the bounds between master and pupil. Orage's mind was more nimble than Gurdjieff's; and to be with those two was better than a play."[27] It is probable that Orage never had such a "complete" friend, one who seemed to know his mind even as he himself did not know it. Gurdjieff doted on Orage, his "super-idiot." He enjoyed his commitment to the work, but more than that, he admired Orage's mind, wit, and ability to understand quickly the "work," the psycho-philosophical principles at stake in every aspect of life at the Prieuré. In a letter addressed years later to Jean Toomer, Fred Leighton quoted Betty Hare on the relationship between the two: "Gurdjieff needed Orage just as Orage needed Gurdjieff: Gurdjieff was the great intellect, Orage the great formulator."[28]

---

24. Mairet, *Orage,* pp. 88–89.
25. Mairet, *Orage,* p. 115.
26. James Webb, *The Harmonious Circle: The Lives and Works of G. I. Gurdjieff, P. D. Ouspensky, and Their Followers* (London: Thames & Hudson, 1980), pp. 261–262, assumes that Gurdjieff had genuine affection for Orage.
27. C. S. Nott, *Teachings of Gurdjieff: Journal of a Pupil* (London: Routledge & Keegan Paul, 1961; and New York: Samuel Weiser, 1962), p. 121.
28. Toomer Collection, Beineke Rare Book and Manuscript Library, Yale University, Box 4, Folder 138.

Gurdjieff must have felt in Orage something like Gorham Munson's wife, Elizabeth Delza, felt after she first met him: "something always in motion but not hurried, not tense, not forced—an easy swiftness which could change its course deftly and resume the original direction with perfect sureness. Quick intelligence, quick feeling and understanding, and an extraordinary speed of perception—a sort of lightening functioning."[29] Not without parabolic significance, Alexandre de Salzmann depicted Orage in the "Jungle Scene" on the wall of the cowshed where Katherine Mansfield spent her last day, as an elephant, a pictorial allusion to the son and guardian of the goddess Parvati, Ganesha, who is a Hindu god of wisdom, keeper of thresholds, lord of Buddhi (intelligence) and of Siddhi (achievement). Elephants, in Indian mythology, are the caryatids of the universe. Above that figure, on the ceiling, was inscribed the "Enneagram," the geometric emblem of Gurdjieff's Laws of Three and Seven.

What Orage must have felt in Gurdjieff, and what most people felt in his presence, is summed up nicely by John Carswell: "What he possessed, and in abnormal measure, were energy, self-confidence and control over his passions. . . . He had the power of controlled fury which commands instant obedience."[30] Orage must have realized when he first heard him in London that there was an earthy strength and vigor in Gurdjieff that Ouspensky, with his cool and confident reliance on intellect, lacked. Pure power emanated from Gurdjieff. When Orage was subjected to Gurdjieff's fury, he drew consolation from a story Gurdjieff had told him about his own earlier life when he had been a servant to a Russian-Greek duke on a two-month voyage to Egypt. He had to carry his food to him, and stand by while it was eaten. Most of the time, it was not eaten, but just thrown back in his face, spiced with insults. When the voyage was finished, Gurdjieff was capable of serving anyone. Incidentally, Gurdjieff added, he had been very eager to make the trip, for he wanted to get to Cairo.[31]

Gurdjieff told him another story to illustrate the necessity of persevering despite obstacles. When he was 21 years old, he read the works of Madame Blavatsky and took her indications seriously. He traveled to every place she mentioned in *The Secret Doctrine,* but he found that nine out of ten of her references were false. This cost him years of effort and suffering. He then took a job as collector of monastic dues for the

29. Munson, *The Roaring Twenties*, p. 253.
30. Carswell, *Lives and Letters,* p. 195.
31. Cited by Sherman Manchester from a conversation with Orage on 2 April 1928 (Manchester Papers, p. 145).

Dalai Lama, and that gave him access to every monastery in Tibet. "I will truthfully say," Gurdjieff told Orage, "that it is true I discovered extraordinary developments. I did not discover one single being with universal development, only monsters. A particular variety of the monstrous, but with no attainment of objective reason, no more than in the West, only different. I finally arrived in India, at its center of development. I would gladly spare any human being the fruitless efforts I have gone through."[32]

When Orage asked him once about his father, Gurdjieff said he was an amateur *ashokh,* or teller of tales. He was illiterate, but had a remarkable memory. About Kars there were competitions in song and in answering questions on the meaning of folk songs, but he preferred to chant his song stories at home. When he sang stories, he invariably ended with one from the Arabian Nights. A friend of his father spent whole nights analyzing his old stories. One night after the twenty-first song, Gurdjieff's father stopped to fill his pipe, and said he had just told a story of the Sumerians that was later incorporated into the Jewish and Christian bibles. This was the old song of the Deluge preserved on marble stones in Babylon.[33]

On another occasion, to illustrate aspects of essence, Gurdjieff told Orage that human beings are *essential* at birth and then become social. He offered an illustrative anecdote. When some self-appointed aristocratic Russian friends of Gurdjieff flattered themselves that they were "naturally" polite, Gurdjieff offered to reduce them to such a state that he would need a pistol to keep order. He got them to fight over meal portions, priority of service, serving times, etc. Only the one who would not push, shove, and argue had essence, he said. He then observed that "the East is wrong because it does not realize the value of personality; the West is wrong because it does not realize the value of essence. Self-observation will develop essence."[34] Gurdjieff figured essence in a number of parables. One is of the horse, carriage, and passenger. The carriage is the physical body, the horse is emotion, and the passenger is the essential "I," without which the three centers have no purpose. Orage's favorite Gurdjieff parable of essence is the figure of the exiled prince whose three centers have usurped control of his being-kingdom.

---

32. Cited by Manchester (Manchester Papers, pp. 154–155).
33. Manchester Papers, p. 163. This account of his father is reproduced in the opening pages of *Meeting with Remarkable Men.* The song is of Gilgamesh, and Gurdjieff quotes opening lines that correspond closely to the extant Babylonian cuneiform texts published by the University of Chicago Press.
34. Manchester Papers, p. 137, for 17 May 1927. I am reminded that St. Augustine said that the "self" is an abyss. The Buddhist is taught not to say "I am," but "there is an existent."

When will the prince awaken to the situation and re-assume control? Only when a Merlin is at hand.[35]

It is improbable that language problems inhibited either the exchange of stories or the development of a strong bond between Orage and Gurdjieff. There is little reason to think that Orage did not, after a short period, understand enough of the "work Russian" of the Institute. Even the young Fritz Peters picked it up in a summer, and all the English speakers who worked closely with Gurdjieff for any length of time soon understood simple directions given in Russian for speed and intensity, as well as basic Russian words for foods, drinks, and dance movements. There was, at the Prieuré, a *lingua franca* of quotidian existence that was a macaronic mix of Turkish, Armenian, Russian, English, and French. Both Orage and Gurdjieff reveled in word play in and through languages. What Orage and many others could not share, however, were the private bathhouse jokes, the endless reminiscences of the Caucuses and Constantinople, and the discreet domestic communications between family members in Armenian and Russian.

Orage, notwithstanding, fought a constant battle with himself at the Institute. He was to remark later that he had often said to himself: "My God, I awake in a lunatic asylum! I must get out. So when I found this happening again and again, I wrote a declaration: 'I have been logically convinced that self-observation and non-identification are the methods, therefore lose no time in this attitude but get to work.'"[36] Later, Orage's commentator and apologist, Daly King, remarked that Orage had experienced a state of awareness on many occasions after arriving at the Institute, but he was not, as Gurdjieff was, permanently in it.[37]

Soon, Orage, as Gurdjieff's public relations executive, was getting glimpses of technical Russian when, with the help of de Hartmann, he translated Gurdjieff's Russian texts for public announcements and for the first Institute brochure.[38] After Katherine Mansfield died and visitors started to appear to see where she suffered at the hands of this "Russian mystic," Orage was delegated to handle the wanted or un-

---

35. C. Daly King, *The Oragean Version* (New York: privately published), p. 63. In his later teaching, Gurdjieff referred to the awakening magician as an alarm clock. Ouspensky, in *The Strange Life of Ivan Osokin* (London: Penguin, 1960), identifies the magician as the means by which the hero can escape from his prison of repeated lives.
36. Letter to Jessie from Orage papers.
37. C. Daly King, *The States of Human Consciousness* (New Hyde Park, NY: University Books, 1963), p. 101.
38. For the complete text of the brochure, see Paul Beekman Taylor, *Shadows of Heaven: Gurdjieff and Toomer* (York Beach: Samuel Weiser, 1998), pp. 73–75.

wanted publicity. A month after her death, the Institute was featured on the front page of *Excelsior,* a Parisian photogravure newspaper. The page, dated Wednesday, 21 February 1923, had six photos of "un temple mystique en pleine forêt de Fontainebleau." Five were of activities in the Study House, and the last was of "des adeptes travaillant dans le parc de domaine." The text reads, in rough translation, "In the midst of the forest of Fontainbleau, and in a magnificent property, pupils practice a new method of physical and spiritual life. In an oriental temple are held evening reunions, after physical work by the pupils of Mr. G. S. (?). Gurdjieff, who has founded an Institute for the Harmonious Development of Man."[39]

Earlier in the month, Gurdjieff's institute was the subject of a four-part series of articles in the London *Daily News,* written by E. C. Bowyer, who had been guided about the Prieuré by Orage. "In a quiet lane near Avon," Bowyer writes, "I met A. R. Orage, until recently editor of *The New Age* and now a member of the colony. He was in rough corduroys and wore no collar, and a first glance at his hands told at once that he had changed the pen for the spade."[40] Bowyer then cites Orage's careful exposition of the ideas of Ouspensky and Gurdjieff.

Two weeks later, *The New Statesman* began a two-part exposé of the Institute by Clifford Sharpe, entitled "The Forest Philosophers," consisting of a scholarly and even-handed exposition. It compares Gurdjieff's colony favorably with American Utopian colonies of the 19th century, as well as with the classical Pythagorean schools. Sharpe remarks that the psychology of the teaching is less a science than an art of self-study, and compares the effect of Gurdjieff's teaching with the religious ecstasy in the scientific psychology of William James. The second part of the series concludes with announcement of an exposition of the system in a book by Ouspensky soon to appear.

That spring, Kay Boyle was sitting at a café terrace when she overheard a conversation at a table next to her. She turned and recognized Harold Loeb with a handsome young man who was telling him about another man who sat alone a few tables away "with a cream-colored turban on his head." The young man, who she learned later was the writer and publisher Robert McAlmon, identified the turbaned man to Loeb as a disciple of Ouspensky, who had opened a school of his philosophy at Fontainebleau. McAlmon explained to a fascinated Loeb and the eavesdropper Boyle, who later reported the scene:

---

39. *Excelsior,* 21 February 1923.
40. Cited in "The Study House," *Gurdjieff International Review* I:4 (1998), p. 1.

The cult has been spreading among people I thought were more or less sensible. . . . Jane Heap got involved out there, and Margaret Anderson, and Georgette Leblanc, and Isadora Duncan was also ready to join the bandwagon, I suppose, out of her despair with life. . . . It's a mass hypnotism of some kind. . . . Gurdjieff started some years back in the East as a hypnotist, they tell me, but nobody knows very much about his background. Anyway, out there in Fontainebleau he gets people of various nationalities—Dutch, French, Spanish, Chinese, Hebrew—to repeat numbers and words in their own language, to repeat them over and over, and after ten minutes he asks other people, sitting in a circle, to speak in time with them, repeating "twilight," or "dawn," or "tragedy," or "labor," or "love," over and over, in their different languages. This in itself hypnotizes, of course, and they all sway as they speak; but in the middle of the circle are placed bottles of armagnac, and the master is disturbed if these bottles are not emptied, and this adds to the hypnotism. It sounds pretty much like what we do every night in Montparnesse."

The young man was laughing now, and he called the waiter for another drink. I sat sipping nervously at my milky Pernod and looking across the tables at Gurdjieff.

"Who pays for the armagnac in Fontainebleau?" Harold asked.

"Oh Harold, Harold, be not so sordid!" the young man said. "The spirit provides! Each bottle is purchased by devoted service. You build houses in the forest, and you chop wood, and you subsist on bread and soup, and you live in fear that you will be turned away. There is one boy, . . . a kid in blue jeans who has been two years there. He says when he has stayed fifteen years he'll be admitted to the inner fold. But by that time, I tell him, he'll be dead, or mad, or uncaring, for in their state of half-starvation and overwork, they don't dare to think or feel on their own. They live on their hallucinations. . . . This kid . . . he told a friend of mine that he's miserably unhappy but that he is at peace, for he is one with the mysticism of the master. And it could be that Gurdjieff's regime is no more rigid and bleak than the routine of many a monastery or nunnery. They are all serving some master for a future that is nebulous."[41]

Such accounts were legion in Paris in the spring of 1923, and everyone tried to best one another with extraordinary stories of this kind. Cafés like the Dôme, Flore, Deux Magots, Select, Dingo, Rotunde, and La Coupole buzzed with such talk about a man already "un homme

---

41. Robert McAlmon and Kay Boyle, *Being Geniuses Together,* pp. 95–96.

célèbre" among the many exotic arrivals from Eastern Europe after the war, though he had been in Paris for only six months.

In November, barely a year after the Institute opened at the Prieuré, Gurdjieff got *The Echo of the Champs-Élysées*—the English-language version of a French journal—to dedicate an entire number to an announcement of "Demonstrations of G. Gurdjieff's Institute for the Harmonious Development of Man" at the Théâtre of the Champs-Élysées between 13 December and Christmas Day. Orage translated the program for the *Echo* just before leaving for the United States, where Gurdjieff sent him to prepare the ground for a number of similar demonstrations in New York and elsewhere. The three-part program announced a panoply of the Gurdjieffian work. Part 1 opened with a presentation of the Gurdjieffian work, followed by a presentation of gymnastic exercises identified with an esoteric school in Kafistan on the heights of Kidjera, and then by the piece known as "The Initiation of the Princess." It concluded with the famous "stop exercise" accompanied by explanations of its function.

Part 2 offered the "movements," derived from the Kisiljan monastery in Chinese Turkestan, followed by movements from Afghanistan. Then there were movements from a monastery in Khavar in Kafiristan, devotional exercises identified with Kashkar, a Dervish funeral ceremony, ritual prayer movements from Sari in Tibet, movements from a Christian monastery in Transcausasia, and, finally, movements of the Whirling Dervishes. Part 3 offered a variety of dances and concluded with a ceremony, according to the program notes, that Gurdjieff had witnessed himself in the Hudankr Sanctuary in Chitral. A supplemental page announced future demonstrations of "The Art of the Ancient East," grouped under three programs: movements, music, and religious phenomena. Philip Mairet, who was in Paris for the show, wrote that, on the basis of the Paris demonstrations, "the prestige of the Institute rose to its highest level."[42]

Before leaving for the United States as Gurdjieff's front man, Orage, through his publishing contacts, succeeded in getting news of the Institute into the *New York World* in an article written by Ernest Brennecke, entitled "Behind the Scenes at Gurdjieff's Weird Château of Mysteries." I imagine that neither Brennecke nor Orage approved of the headline, but it was shaped to attract attention to the man who would soon be demonstrating his work in New York:

---

42. *A. R. Orage: A Memoir* (New Hyde Park, NY: University Press, 1966), p. 94.

At Fontainebleau, near Paris, there is a curious colony of people who claim to be on the road to learning the true way to live, to be delving with success into the hidden secrets of existence and of ultimate happiness, and to be evolving powers which an outsider would term miraculous.

They are guided by a . . . powerful figure, an adept in Eastern "magic," to whom they submit themselves in everything they do or think.

The Institut [sic] Gurdjieff represents the first organized effort to bring to the Western world those peculiar exercises and practices developed in India and Thibet, through which the individual attains a consciousness and knowledge beyond that which is derived by the agency of his physical senses. Assuming the spirit as a principle of higher nature and power than the body in which it is embedded, the theory is that the quality of the atoms of the body may be so reorganized that it becomes a finer instrument for the spirit to function within. When through intense physical labor, fasting and elaborate exercises the physical machine is made perfectly obedient and responsible to the will, the individual becomes possessed of faculties far exceeding those of the average man. Clairvoyance, ability to see at a distance, power to know what another is thinking, capacity to telephone one's thoughts to another's mind without wires or words—these are some of the accomplishments, together with a larger vision of the universe.[43]

Brennecke had been shown about by Major Pindar, and he described in the continuation of the article his favorable impression of the beautiful grounds, the outdoor work, and the piano played outside for dance exercises. Then he met the man:

Gurdjieff, I was told, had been born and christened by his Greek parents as George S. Georgiades in the Transcaucasian town of Alexandrople some fifty years ago.[44] As a boy he had wandered through Russia, had run away to sea, had then traveled all through the East, especially through Outer Mongolia and Thibet, where he had become saturate in the mystic religions and magic practices of Lamas, Sufis and Persian dervishes.

---

43. Brennecke, Ernest. "Behind the Scenes at Gurdjieff's Weird Château of Mysteries," in *New York World*, 25 November 1923.
44. William Seabrook uses this name form in his writings, but I have not been able to identify what name the middle initial here stands for. It does not stand for a known patronymic.

Next came a description of the "movements" on the lawn under Gurdjieff's direction:

> incomparably the most amazing dancing I had ever seen. In comparison the best of the Russian ballet seemed child's play. Don't imagine there was anything sensual about it, because there was no suggestiveness whatsoever."

The article continues with a description of the Study House and the dances performed there, and then he describes Gurdjieff himself:

> He was a rather tall,[45] powerfully built man, carelessly dressed in a gray lounge suit, walking with a slouching gait. The hair of his head was cropped short, displaying a large spherical skull. Slightly squinting eyes, full, wide nostrils and a mouth hidden by a dropping mustache betrayed little or no emotion, except, perhaps, a species of cold amusement. Perhaps, also, more than a faint trace of cruelty.

The article concludes with an explanation that the work done there was intended to break habits and force one out of the usual life-style. The pupils, Brennecke wrote, are to learn indifference to the friction and all reactions met in ordinary life.

In New York, working hard to provide publicity for Gurdjieff before his arrival, Orage persuaded Maud Hoffman, whom he had met at the Institute in the summer of 1923, to get a two-column article entitled "Taking the Life Cure in Gurdjieff's School," in an issue of *The New York Times* Arts section. The article which describes her visit gives an exaggeratedly glowing account of how well one is received and treated at the Institute. About the Study House, she wrote:

> The pupils sit around this square space on goatskins and cushions in the Oriental fashion. . . . The demonstrations are unique in their presentation. They consist of movements which include the sacred gymnastics of the esoteric schools, the religious ceremonies of the antique Orient and the ritual movements of monks and dervishes— besides the folk dances of many a remote community. . . .
>
> You may or may not know about the philosophy which lies at the back of all the activities of this unique community. The American newspapers have called them the "Forest Philosophers" and you lis-

---

45. I cannot understand "tall" fitting any description of Gurdjieff. To my eye's measure, he could not have been any taller than 5' 7". Gorham Munson, *The Awakening Twenties,* p. 266, describes him as "medium" in height.

ten carefully to catch any of the teaching. But the nearest that you get
to philosophy for many days is to make the acquaintance of a good-
natured but not well-pointed, fox terrier, with a large body and a
small head, named "Philos." You venture to ask if there are any lectures or classes. Quietly you are told, without further comment, that
there are none. After this you think a while and observe the people
around you. They are all English and Americans. Where then are the
Russians—that little band of people whom Gurdjieff led safely out of
Russia when the revolution broke out?

...You soon begin to suspect that this place may be an outer court
of one of those old mystery schools about which you have read.[46]

The article goes on to describe the floor called the "Ritz" because of its
lavish furnishings, and the quaint and comfortable "beautiful 'Monks'
corridor." Everyone there "pays according to their means," and many
cannot pay at all, so they are supported by those who can pay more. The
meals are described as simple for lunch—bread and soup—and modest
teas, but there are sumptuous suppers before the evening music and
dancing.

The Gurdjieff system aims at an all-around and harmonious development of man. It is a place when every one can be an artist or an arti-
san, and the material with which he works are his own mental,
emotional and instinctive energies. . . . The claim made by the
Gurdjieff Institute is that, by the reactionary effect of harmonious
movements on the psyche, man can regain control over his being.

It is a place where man may hope to progress to that balanced
development which had been arrested by the cramping of an unnatu-
ral and mechanical civilization.

It is a place where habits are changed, fixed ideas are broken up,
mechanical routines do not exist, and adaptability to ever-changing
forms and modes of life is practiced. So "sonnez fort" and wait. Some
one passing within may open for you. It is really the kitchen boy's
duty. There is a different kitchen boy each day and it is the most
onerous job in the place. He may not be able to drop what he is doing
at once . . . He may be anyone, the editor of a London paper, a Harley
Street specialist, a court musician or a Russian lawyer.

When you enter, Mr. Gurdjieff greets you and makes you welcome, with a smile that has both sweetness and spirituality. You get a

---

46. *NYT,* February 10, 1924, p. 12.

first impression of a nature of great kindness and sensitiveness. Later you learn that in him is combined strength and delicacy, simplicity and subtlety. That he is more awake than anyone you have ever known.

At the Gurdjieff Institute an attempt can be made to fill in deficiencies, correct heredity and habit and to balance knowledge and being. Incidentally and as a by-product of these efforts you renew your energies and your youth and make yourself more efficient for life.[47]

If, a year later, a number of Americans arrived at the Prieuré with expectations to be received, lodged, boarded, and entertained in this fashion, they were reasonably certain of disappointment, and many were later to express a certain deception as well as bewilderment.

When, across the Atlantic, Mabel Dodge Luhan heard of Gurdjieff, she asked her friend Lorenzo (D. H. Lawrence) to give her his opinion. He replied virulently: "I have heard enough about that place . . . to know that it is a rotten, false, self-conscious place of people playing a sickly stunt."[48] Neither Gurdjieff nor his pupils and devotees were playing a stunt. The work was mortally serious, and there was no short course at the Institute for a quick reharmonizing of spirits and renewal of youthful energies. For Gurdjieff there were no calendar semesters in his classroom of life,[49] and no day of graduation to anticipate and commemorate.

It is worth speculating why Gurdjieff, after initial successes in Paris, shifted his attention to the United States in 1923, barely a year after the Institute opened. One can assume that the debts he incurred on the buildings and grounds of the Prieuré, added to the supporting of a large entourage, could not be covered by his business interests in Paris. Since Ouspensky had a following in England, "rich" America seemed the most likely place to raise money and spread his doctrine. What, however, did Gurdjieff know about the United States? On what information and with what expectations did he make his decision? Who ever knew what exactly was on Gurdjieff's mind? He was sure of himself, however, and of his decision. He knew something about America that others could not glean. For Ouspensky, who opposed the projected voyage,

---

47. Hoffman, "Taking the Life Cure," p. 12.
48. Emily Hahn, *Mabel: A Biography of Mabel Dodge Luhan* (Boston: Houghton-Mifflin, 1977), p. 177. Moore, traces Lawrence's knowledge about the Institute in *Mansfield and Gurdjieff* pp. 200-203. Lawrence did extract some profit from his knowledge of the Institute by writing a short story, "Mother and Daughter," about a lecherous old Turk who seduces young English girls.
49. After Gurdjieff's death, John G. Bennett did conduct a ten-month work course leading to a "diploma" in Objective Consciousness and, although he suffered the scorn of many who followed Gurdjieff, he had a limited success, at least, in introducing students to the rigors of the work.

Gurdjieff's departure for America was the occasion for their complete break of relations.

Orage sailed for the New World on 15 December 1923 and arrived in New York on Santa Lucia's Day. He and Dr. de Stjernvall consulted and went their separate ways to different quarters of New York to make contacts. If Orage was there simply to act as the doctor's interpreter, as Gurdjieff was to say in 1930 and 1931 to the New York Group, it is difficult to imagine exactly what de Stjernvall was expected to do. The doctor did make contact with a number of Russians on the lower East side, where a refugee colony was establishing itself—which apparently came to nothing—while Orage went straight from his hotel to the offices of *The Little Review* on 28th Street to consult with Margaret Anderson and Jane Heap, who had published Orage's article on Henry James in 1918.[50] Having stirred their interest in the January arrival of Gurdjieff and his troupe of some forty persons, he called Claude Bragdon and Herbert Croly, editor of *The New Republic*. Both confirmed what Heap and Anderson had said: The Sunwise Turn bookshop, a favorite haunt of writers and intellectuals, was the place to advertise. He called and made an appointment to come by on the day after New Year's Day 1924.

---

50. "Henry James and the Ghostly," *The Little Review* 5 (Aug 1918), pp. 41–43.

Chapter Three

1924

NEW YORK CITY:
THE LAND MADE ABUNDANT

*If only I had come to America years ago! I should have been
wealthy and famous. But that error must be corrected in
another life!*

—Orage[1]

[Gurdjieff] is an organic man.
—Olgivanna Lloyd Wright[2]

New York City at the beginning of 1924 seems to have fit the description Gurdjieff gave it shortly after he arrived in mid-January—
"Babylon." It was a thriving, bustling, and gaudy place, not unlike F.
Scott Fitzgerald's description of it in 1922 in *The Great Gatsby*. Things
had not quieted down a bit; in fact, the pace was even more hectic, as it
was in other major cities like Boston, Philadelphia, and Chicago. The
watchword of the day was "profit and pleasure," though neither had
clear precedence over the other. Postwar prosperity was at its height.
The Volstead act of 1919 came into force on 16 January 1920, adding
an eighteenth amendment to the Constitution of the United States that
prohibited the sale and serving of alcoholic beverages. Prohibition,
however, hardly dampened the spirits of those who could afford to frequent speakeasies, buy bootleg liquor, or distill their own in bathtubs
and basement sinks. As sociologists saw clearly in retrospect, the pleasure of indulgence in alcohol was only increased by the surreptitious
pleasures of a nationwide conspiracy against the Volstead Act. A

---

1. Letter to Jessie, 10 August, 1924 (Orage papers).
2. Interview in *The Capital Times,* 26 August, 1934.

frustrated, extenuated Congress repealed the act with the twenty-first amendment on 20 February 1933, and alcohol again flowed (legally) on 5 December of that year.

Tamany Hall ran the democrats, who ran City Hall in New York City, which ran New York State. The flamboyant Irish son of the city, Jimmy Walker, bon vivant, handsome and dapper, was on his way to being elected mayor. Al Smith was governor of the state—a post he would occupy until Franklin Delano Roosevelt succeeded him in 1929—and a leading candidate for the democratic nomination for the presidency. Despite a general devil-may-care attitude that followed the moral depression swirling large and wide in the wake of the Great War, however, and despite the growth of big-gang crime proliferating and profiting from Prohibition, the American public was being awakened from a cultural and political isolationism and lethargy to the flowering of new and exciting literary and artistic movements in Europe. And so they streamed—writers, artists, show-people, philosophers, and students—to imbibe the intoxication of a Paris that, after the war, took on a new and vibrant character that combined the fin-de-siècle spirit of its cafés and boulevards with the new industrial tools of the age: the automobile, telephone, telegraph, and radio. This emerging milieu was most notably marked by a new conception of self-importance among women, who called for a grudging respect from most men.[3]

Paris was, to those who had the money and the desire, what New York was to those who had less money and more will. The city rose as an apogee of American cultural achievement. When Orage arrived in America at the end of 1923, the cinema was in its silent heyday. The radio was sounding Irving Berlin's "Everybody Step and Pick Up Your Sins," sharing airtime with the Gershwins, Jerome Kern, George M. Cohan, Cole Porter, and Victor Herbert. Eugene O'Neill's *Emperor Jones* was a resounding success, and his *All God's Chillun Got Wings* was in rehearsal for its New York opening in February. Back in Paris, Gurdjieff and his troupe were performing, while Orage was negotiating with the Sunwise Turn bookshop in the Yale Club building for a series of talks in January to attract an audience for Gurdjieff later that month. A week later—on the afternoon after New Year's Day 1924, when the Naval Academy and the University of Washington played to a 14–14 tie in the Rose Bowl, when the United States of Mexico once again readjusted its debt, and when Saks Fifth Avenue offered for $63 a replica

---

3. A broad view of an artistic life in New York City at this time that did not include Orage's circle is given by Edmund Wilson, *The Twenties* (New York: Farrar Strauss & Giroux, 1975).

of the Prince of Wales' guardcoat—Orage arrived at the shop on the corner of Vanderbilt Avenue at 51 East 44th Street, across from Grand Central Station. As he made preparations for his talk, the 22-year-old part-owner Jessie Dwight noticed him, and asked an associate, Louise, who the attractive Englishman could be.[4] Louise didn't know, but said everyone was excited about him and about the lecture he was going to give about Gurdjieff at the Sunwise Turn a week later. Stanley Nott, an English employee of the shop, recognized Orage and decided that he would attend his lecture.[5]

GURDJIEFF'S FIRST DESCENT

On 9 January, Orage gave his first talk. Jessie and the audience in general were enthralled by both his matter and manner. He spoke with confident conviction and learning. He opened with a brief synopsis of the text in the descriptive brochure for the Institute, comprising the history of the Seekers of the Truth. He then outlined the major lines of Gurdjieff's thoughts, emphasizing the conception that contemporary individuals have little control over their own intellectual, emotional, and physical possibilities, and so live largely in a state of sleep. Gurdjieff's teaching, he explained, is dedicated to waking them and guiding them toward self-consciousness through exercises in self-observation and self-remembering. "The work of the Institute is to make such a change in oneself that nothing can occur that does not agree with one's qualities."[6] Orage's poise and intelligence made him, one later member of his group said, "the best talker I ever listened to."[7]

After the lecture, Jessie managed to speak to Orage before he left with several members of the audience whom he knew. In the course of the conversation, she offered to organize future talks at the Sunwise Turn, and to act as his unofficial secretary. In a second talk at the Neighborhood Playhouse a few nights later, Orage spoke of the ancient

---

4. From the diary of Jessie Orage, courtesy of Anne B. Orage for the estate of Jessie Dwight Orage. The other partners were Mary Mobray-Clarke, Madge Jenison, Harold Loeb, and his wife Marjorie Content Loeb.
5. In *The Teachings of Gurdjieff, Journey of a Pupil* (London: Routledge & Kegan Paul, 1961), pp. 1–6, Nott records the scene and gives a word-for-word account of Orage's first talk. Daly King, who was persuaded by Jessie Dwight to attend Orage's lectures, compiled a record of Orage's teaching in *On Oragean Version* (New York: privately published, 1951).
6. Cited by Manchester (Manchester Papers, p. 39).
7. Gorham Munson, *The Awakening Twenties* (Baton Rouge: Louisiana University Press, 1985), p. 258. Malcolm Cowley, *Exile's Return* (New York: Penguin, 1976), p. 61, claims that Orage's converts were "among older members of the Greenwich Village set."

sacred dance, describing it as "not only a medium for an aesthetic experience, but a book, as it were, or script, containing a definite piece of knowledge. But it is a book which not everyone who would can read."[8] After a third talk, Orage asked Jessie if she enjoyed the lecture. "No, not at all," she said in her characteristic blunt fashion.[9]

Gurdjieff sailed from France aboard the Paris on 5 January, leaving behind Jeanne de Salzmann and her son, Michel, born a scant week earlier. On the evening of the 12th, Gurdjieff and his troupe gave a special exhibition for the first-class gala evening, and disembarked the next day in New York City. Orage was at the pier to greet him, but the city was more interested that day in the chess exhibition Alekhine performed at the Newspaper Club of New York, pitting himself against all comers. Thanks to Orage, however, Gurdjieff was awaited by almost as large an audience as those who marveled at Alekhine. In his memoirs, Llewelyn Powys recalled that "the famous prophet and magician Gurdjieff appeared in New York accompanied by Mr. Orage, who was acting for him as a kind of Saint Paul."[10] Gorham Munson saw him rather as a kind of Peter, a "fisher of men."[11]

In two weeks, Orage had attracted a core of followers already curious to see his master. Many of these were at the Lenox Theater on East 78th Street on 24 January to hear Orage introduce Gurdjieff, but the master did not appear and the audience had to be content with another final introductory lecture to his work. At the close of the evening, Jessie and Orage walked through the city as snowflakes coated the pavement. In front of the fire in Jessie's flat at 150 East 54th Street, Orage kissed her for the first time. If everything in Orage's background had, in specific ways, prepared him for Gurdjieff and for the mission assigned him, nothing had quite prepared him for Jessie—for any other woman, perhaps, for Orage was attracted to women, but not for Jessie Dwight. The deep love that he was forming for her was a new force for him to reckon with. She was intelligent, strong-willed, and sure of her desires. She brooked no nonsense from anyone. Her major fault, perhaps, was an

8. Cited by Munson, *Twenties*, p. 254.
9. Philip Mairet, *A. R. Orage: A Memoir* (New Hyde Park, NY: University Press, 1966), p. 97. Patterson, *Struggle of the Magicians* (San Francisco: Arete, 1995), p. 115, seems to be following a mistaken retrospective view of those who did not know Jessie when he describes her as tall and blonde. She had brown hair and was short, 5'5" at most.
10. Cited by Claude Bragdon, *More Lives than One* (New York: Knopf, 1938), p. 323.
11. Cited Michael Coyle, "'A Profounder Didacticism': Ruskin, Orage and Pound's Reception of Social Credit." *Paideuma* 17 (1988), p. 258.

unreasoned recklessness. That trait was intensified when she drank, and from her late teens, she had been enjoying alcoholic beverages. In a matter of days, however, they were already strongly and inextricably attracted to each other and spent many of their waking moments together, Orage was discrete and cautious. First of all, he was still in an unhappy and childless marriage with Jean Walker—though separated for some years from her. Moreover, he felt firmly committed to his present task of presenting Gurdjieff's work without amatory distraction. He had also experienced a difficult separation a few years earlier from Beatrice Hastings, with whom he had had a long relationship. Most of all, it was Orage's character to be "sensible," and one thing that worried him above all others at the moment was the incompatibility of Gurdjieff's "work" with a sexual relationship. Could one live with a woman and avoid "teaching" to her the ideas one believes to be essential for mutual self-growth?

On the day of Gurdjieff's first public appearance, 26 January 1924, an article based on an interview with Orage appeared under the name of Raymond G. Carroll in the *New York Evening Post,* with the headline: "Gurdjieff Heads the Newest Cult, Which Harks Back to Ancient Days." Carroll noted that Gurdjieff spoke very little English, but "his mouthpiece is Alfred Richard Orage, an Irishman. . . . Orage said that [Gurdjieff] had tapped all the sources of knowledge and truth." Then Carroll repeated Orage's lecture theme of man's need "of using more of one's physical and mental capacities." He concluded with a non-Oragean assertion that, to join the movement, one must give Gurdjieff all one's worldly goods.[12]

Many of those at Orage's last lecture, as well as many others, including clients of Sunwise Turn who had seen the posted circulars advertising his appearance or who had heard about Gurdjieff by word of mouth, listened to Orage's introduction to him and his work a couple of evenings later. That same evening, Gurdjieff himself spoke to them in Russian. His personal interpreter, Boris Feropintov, translated his words into English, though Gurdjieff often interrupted and offered alternative expressions. It is no exaggeration to say that Gurdjieff's appearance and his voice stunned the audience. Claude Bragdon was disappointed, however, that "Gurdjieff spoke English badly and understood it scarcely at all."[13] Certainly, Gurdjieff was like nothing any of them had ever seen

---

12. Raymond G. Carroll, "Gurdjieff Heads Newest Cult, Which Harks Back to Ancient Days," *New York Evening Post* (26 January 1924).
13. Bragdon, *More Lives Than One,* p. 327.

or imagined. The penetration of his eyes could be felt from the back row, and when he looked across the audience, every person felt that his gaze rested heavily and directly upon them. Gurdjieff's aspect was a text in itself, and it was not hard to imagine that his look had the power to shape the demeanor of others.

When the first demonstration was performed on 2 February at the Neighborhood Playhouse on Grand Street, Gurdjieff seemed to Jean Toomer "like a monk in a tuxedo."[14] T. S. Matthews, pupil of Orage's, brother of Peggy Matthews [Flinsch], and later editor of *Time,* recalls his first view of Gurdjieff in 1924: "He was a massive, bald, heavily mustachioed man . . . with liquid, bull-like eyes."[15] Gorham Munson recalled Orage's introduction to the demonstration:

> Sacred dances and posture and movements in series have always been one of the vital subjects taught in esoteric schools in the East. They have a double aim: to convey a certain kind of knowledge and to be a means of acquiring an harmonious state of being. The farthest limits of one's endurance are reached through the combination of non-natural and non-habitual movements, and by perfecting them, a new quality of sensing is obtained, a new quality of concentration and attention and a new direction of the mind—all for a certain definite aim . . . . In ancient times the dance was a branch of real art, and served the purposes of higher knowledge and religion.[16]

The house was packed and the audience stunned by the spectacle. In the audience were a number of notables, including John O'Hara, Theodore Dreiser, Gloria Swanson, Rebecca West, Fanny Hurst, William Seabrook, John O'Hara Cosgrave, Elinor Wylie, and Zona Gale.[17] Hart Crane, who sat next to Margaret Anderson and Georgette Leblanc, wrote to his mother as soon as he got home that evening to proclaim that

14. Toomer Collection, Box 46, Folder 953.
15. T. S. Matthews, *Name and Address* (New York: Simon & Schuster, 1960), p. 207. He continues in a less complimentary vein: "His woman followers obviously adored him, and some of those who found favor in his sight had visible mementos: swarthy and liquid-eyed children."
16. Munson, *Awakening Twenties,* pp 208–209. Munson adds a description of the demonstration and its impact on the audience. Carl E. Bechhofer-Roberts wrote a description of the demonstration for the Spring, 1924 issue of *The Century.* Nott, *Teachings of Gurdjieff,* pp. 6–18, describes the demonstrations and reproduces Gurdjieff's talk verbatim. James Moore, *Gurdjieff: The Anatomy of a Myth* (Element, 1991) p. 175, says that Gurdjieff gave sixteen lectures in all between the middle of February and the middle of March. In a letter to Jean Paulhan written on 1 May 1937, René Daumal exposes Jeanne de Salzmann's explanation of the relation between the movements and acquisition of essential knowledge [René Daumal, *Correspondence III, 1933–1944* (Paris: Gallimard, 1996), pp. 98–103].
17. Meryle Secrest, *Frank Lloyd Wright* (New York: Knopf, 1992), p. 310.

"things were done by amateurs that would stump the Russian ballet."[18] To some, it seemed as if Gurdjieff were controlling the movements on the stage through the kinetic force of his brown eyes. Others thought that the expressionless faces of the dancers indicated that they were hypnotized. In the days following, further demonstrations took place at Lesley Hall, Webster Hall, and Carnegie Hall. At one of these demonstrations, as the dancers raced toward the front of the stage, Gurdjieff turned his head and lit up a cigarette. After the dancers fell pell-mell into the orchestra pit, Gurdjieff turned and called out "Stop!" Miraculously, no one was hurt, and, as they got up to resume their places on the stage, the audience applauded loudly.[19]

In the *New York Times* Sunday supplement on the arts on 10 February, Maud Hoffman's two-column panegyric on the Institute appeared, and this attracted a larger number of New Yorkers to subsequent demonstrations, as well as to Orage's lectures on the work. Apart from the demonstrations, Gurdjieff gave talks and movement exercises at the Rosetta O'Neill Studio on upper Madison Avenue, and Orage lectured apart on what he called Gurdjieff's "method." In a *New Yorker* profile on Orage entitled "Mystery in a Sack Suit," Waldo Frank, writing under the pseudonym "Searchlight," asserted: "What it [the Method] *does*—or claims to do—is nothing less than the whole and utter overturning of everything you live by."[20] It was the dances, however, rather than the lectures, that caused a sensation in New York. As a later commentator wrote: "[Gurdjieff] lived in a world of physical movement, and the organisation of dancing was at the centre—not the periphery—of his life. . . . He was a choreographer who had stumbled on mysticism for his *mise en scène*."[21]

Meanwhile, back across the water in France, D. H. Lawrence wrote Mabel Dodge Luhan, who had asked him what he knew of Gurdjieff, that he had visited "that Ouspensky place at Fontainebleau," though he hadn't. Then, after his own "stunt" to Fontainebleau in Gurdjieff's absence, he wrote again on 9 of January 1924 to remark flippantly: "One doesn't wonder about it *at all*, one knows."[22] To Lady

---

18. Cited by Munson, *Awakening Twenties*, p. 109.
19. Louise Welch, *Orage with Gurdjieff in America* (London: Routledge & Kegan Paul, 1982), pp. 5–6; and Secrest, *Frank Lloyd Wright*, p. 310.
20. Cited by Munson, *Awakening Twenties*, p. 262.
21. John Carswell, *Lives and Letters* (London: Faber, 1978), p. 185. Lisa Delza, Gorham Munson's future wife, herself a choreographer and dancer, joined Orage's group after seeing a demonstration.
22. David Ellis, *D. H. Lawrence; Dying Game 1922–1930* (Cambridge: Cambridge University Press, 1998), pp. 159–160.

Dorothy Brett on 4 February of the same year, he wrote vaguely: "seems a rotten place to me."[23] On the next day, Ezra Pound wrote to his parents from Paris to say that: "After 2 yrs at Fontainebleau, Orage has gone to US with the Gurdjieff 'gang' to continue his theosophic 'kink.'"[24]

As Woodrow Wilson's death on 3 February was being mourned by those who disdained his project to have the United States join the rest of the world in a League of Nations, Gurdjieff consulted with Orage to organize a tour for his dance group. Satisfied with the success he had anticipated in New York, he scanned possibilities—from information or intuition no one knew of—in Philadelphia, Washington, Boston, and Chicago, the major cities within convenient reach. Gurdjieff decided on Boston to begin with, and Chicago to follow, before further assessment.[25] Orage was dispatched to the land of the Cabots, Lodges, baked beans, black bread, and cod. When he concluded his preparations for the trip, Orage cabled Jessie on Monday, 18 February, from his small apartment on 240 West 73rd Street: "Beloved, Off to Boston on Tuesday, will stay at Arlington Hotel." Once he had arrived, settled in, and made a few telephone calls, one to a cousin of Jessie's with Harvard connections, he wrote the first of his letters to the woman with whom he had fallen in love.[26] He confirmed that Jessie's cousin promised to send some Harvard students to listen to his opening lecture, and would try to book the Liberal Club for the event. The conversation was not entirely reassuring to Orage, and he told Jessie that "I am in two minds about recommending G to come. However, I've put out, properly baited, several lines, and by Friday I should know the worst."[27]

---

23. Ellis, *op. cit.,* p. 160.
24. J. J. Wilhelm, *Ezra Pound: London and Paris 1908–1925* (University Park: Penn State University Press, 1990), p. 334.
25. Many, including James Moore, *Gurdjieff and Mansfield* (London: Rutledge & Kegan Paul, 1980), p. 203, Welch, *Orage,* p. 9, and Bennett, *Making a New World* (London: Turnstone Books, 1962), p. 160, assert flatly that Gurdjieff did visit Philadelphia at this time. They are misled by Gurdjieff's statement in *Life Is Real* that Philadelphia was a necessary visit.
26. Orage wrote often and voluminously in the periods he was separated from Jessie, but there is no sign of what could be called "love letters" among the collection Jessie kept. Addresses of endearment headed and terminated letters to her, but the content of his letters was always informative and opinionative, governed by carefully structured order, with only occasional humor. All of his letters are signed "Orage." Letters to others would invariably be signed either "O" or more formally "ARO." As Claire Tomalin affirms of his writing and his personal correspondence, *Katherine Mansfield: A Secret Life* (London: Viking-Penguin, 1987), p. 82: "Although he felt passionately about many issues and some people, the tone [of his writing] is dry and detached." The foremost quality many saw in him was disinterestedness.
27. All letters from Orage to Jessie Dwight, later Jessie Orage, are found among the Orage papers. Dates are indicated in the text.

Orage found Boston, compared to New York, xenophobic and enveloped by a social chill that matched the frigid season, as his letter the next day made painfully clear:

> *After kicking my heels about for these two days doing nothing, I've begun to receive invitations to interviews, talks and lectures. These will keep me busy over the week-end. . . . I shall not stay here long in any case: probably not after next Monday or Tuesday. Boston may be the hub, but it scarcely knows of the existence of the rest of the wheel—I never felt a more provincial town—no, not in England! I've been very much alone so far. Where is Stanley [Nott]? Did he expect me to bring him as luggage? . . . Fact is, I wish I had Jessie here! And now, in all probability I shall not see her for another two weeks—if, that is, I am to go to Chicago.*

Late the next night, despite setting a meeting with some Harvard boys arranged with the help of the writer-scholar S. Foster Damon, a close friend of the poet e. e. cummings, who had written him earlier that he knew of Gurdjieff in Paris, Orage wrote in a despairing tone:

> *It's doubly dull here; first because it isn't NY, and second because it is Boston. Boston will have to change very rapidly and completely to produce a pleasant going away impression upon me! . . . In a word, I miss you in Boston: so Boston must be blamed.*
>
> *I declare I have no choice but only follow chance; and it may be that this will prove the end by which to approach Boston. Stanley also turned up and threatens to be useful . . . When I think of the trouble these ideas have given me—going to France and living as a navvy, etc—I wonder if these young men can get 'em for nothing! I hope they can: but it is just possible that the difficulty of getting them is one of the means of understanding them: in which case. . . . Were you at the meeting on Wed. evening? I should like to hear an assessment of it and particularly of anything G said in reply to questions. People don't ask him nearly enough: and really they should think that it may be their last chance. Once an accepted pupil and questions are over he never gives pupils an opportunity for asking questions. But he will tell prospective pupils anything they want to know.*[28]

Orage's mood brightened after his modest meeting. On Saturday, the 23rd, he wrote:

> *Boston is beginning to improve in my eyes, but not so much that I do not wish we were back in New York. Things did, however, take a turn for the*

---

better yesterday. Auslander appeared and soon brought to the hotel a few friends who may be useful. I am to have tea with a party today which is to include some influential persons. We'll see what comes of it: perhaps a committee to arrange the Demonstration while I go to Chicago.

Last evening . . . I talked with some students at Cambridge. It was very heavy going. . . . [Edwin] Wolfe turned up with a young boy, Chase, dressed like an Esquinaux fitted out at Jaeger's. They were going to the country, though Lord knows Boston itself is country enough.

Oh yes, I forgot that I had an interview with the Boston Post yesterday. He came as a reporter and left as a pupil: that is to say he was more personally than professionally interested. But we'll see what he prints.

The evening following, Sunday the 24th: "I am gratified that Jessie talks up G. We are bound for a new life with many new joys." And later:

I don't in the least know when I shall be on my way to Chicago but it cannot be long now. I've so far drawn a blank in Boston; and I only give Boston one more chance. Tomorrow (Monday) I lunch at Cambridge with a litter of professors; and in the evening I attend a meeting for an informal lecture. If nothing comes of either, I shall ask G. to let me go: to stay would mean to stay a month—I mean, to do anything serious. You may be sure, darling, that I shall telegraph to you in time for you to recover [from her cold] and meet me in Albany. . . .

My, but Boston is a mixed pickle!

Orage accepted an invitation to tea in the city, but the conversation between sips was so trivial in its topics and puerile in its considerations that he wondered if Boston was capable of cultural discourse. As he remarked to Jessie in his letter of the 25th, it was "like a civil war in an encyclopaedia." He told her that he noted some interest there in economics; and, when he mentioned some of his own views, he was invited to offer a lecture. When he mentioned the Institute, there was no response at all, and interest in a talk on economics dissolved in the teatime atmosphere like a wisp of vapor. He continued:

I have not heard from G yet when I am to go to Chicago. In fact, I have not heard from headquarters since I left N.Y. a week ago. But it cannot be much longer now, since if I stay here another week not only Boston but Chicago will be unready for a Demonstration.

All the same, I think Harvard very good ground: and I should like a commission to stay here and cultivate it for a month or two.

Harvard turned out to be good ground. Members of a poetry society that included cummings, Damon, and John Dos Passos were drawn to

Orage's wit and manner, and became, over the next few years, followers of his New York career. Dos Passos, back from a voyage early that spring, moved to Brooklyn, where Hart Crane gave him an account of Gurdjieff's doings. Dos Passos soon became another fan of Orage's. Wallace Stevens, another Harvard graduate who kept company with Alfred Kreymborg and W. C. Williams, heard of Orage's talks, but was not of a temper to be converted to Gurdjieff.

The next day, Orage wrote that he assumed that he should move on to Chicago, having heard absolutely nothing from Gurdjieff despite his own daily reports. In fact, he wondered if there would be any order to go. As he remarked in despair: "G has been dead dog since I left N.Y, and I have had no word from him even in sleep." That same evening, however, he finally heard from headquarters: and wrote Jessie joyfully the next morning:

> *Now all is bustle and excitement. G has wired me to make arrangements for a demonstration here; & I have just engaged the Fine Arts Theatre for next <u>Wed</u>. evening (Mar 5)[29] and given the order for tickets. All with fear and trembling, 'cos I don't know in the least how the thing will come off. However, it's an adventure . . .*
>
> *I hope to God the Carnegie Hall affair will go off all right. And don't worry in listening to G. One <u>must</u> pay a price for the gospel! Chicago is now, I imagine, quite doubtful.*

On the 29th, he continued:

> *An article appeared today in the* Boston Post *today about the Institute. It is quite good—as it ought to be: I had the man here for about 6 hours, & he wanted to come to the Institute himself. All the same, if 30 people attend the demonstration I shall be surprised. Boston being in my experience the nearest approach to heaven (in the worst sense) of any place I know except Nottingham and Letchford. . . . Not a <u>word</u> from G or any of his entourage about Chicago, ditto! God alone knows what is happening . . .*
>
> *P.S. I was at Cambridge to dinner last evening with bishops & doctors: but I became so bored that I only did a small amount of business. They all wanted free tickets for the demonstration; & the party broke up when I said they must pay. IS BOSTON MEAN?*

The same day, he received a letter from Jessie containing the news that one of her associates reported all kinds of rumors and gossip that were

---

29. Welch, *Orage*, p. 6, says the demonstration took place in Judson Hall.

circulating in New York among those interested in going to the Institute. They centered mainly on reports of the "sordid" conditions at the Prieuré: the hygiene, plumbing, food, and so forth. Orage replied in letters on 1 and 2 March:

> I'm much interested in your discoveries of the intrigue atmosphere engendered about the Institute; also in the stories of vermin. They are absurdly untrue, of course, and Mary should be warned against such gossip.[30] I never heard of a "creature" at Fontainebleau and even if I had, one doesn't die of 'em!
>
> . . . All the chatter of the gangs in N.Y. is just chatter, like the babble of monkeys as they go roost or rest in the tree-tops. As a matter of fact, they are the monkey-calls of the Organic Kingdom & their function is to ebullate [?] in chatter. The real aim of this work is to evolve a few humans out of the multitude of apes. But self-observation is of much more service to this end than nature-observation. While monkeys can affect you, we are still one of them. Only when they only amuse is one safe from them. But it's a difficult job, darling: & there's not much laughing until we get out of the wood. Still, it is easier to laugh with your hand in my overcoat pocket than when I am alone! . . . the damned tickets are not yet delivered. However, it's all part of the dream. I don't think G intends me to stay here, & I cannot see any use of going to Chicago at the short notice that remains. But it might be for my discipline or something!

On Monday, the 3rd, Orage continued his attack on the rumor-mongers after reporting that he had sent out all the printed circulars for the demonstration, a thousand in all, and was having tickets printed. "For once in my life I've got some people to work!" he exclaimed. "Only G hasn't sent any money yet! I shall send him a wire in a minute or two." To a rumor circulating in New York that Gurdjieff felt Orage was too successful at his task, in the sense that he was drawing more attention to himself than to Gurdjieff, Orage felt it necessary to respond:

> These stories of Mary's etc. are really too funny for words. I only wish that G could be "jealous" of my "popularity," or anything that belongs to me. It argues such a miserably inadequate estimate of G to attribute the bare possibility of such a feeling to him. Of course, too, G has never sent me in this sense either to N.Y. or here. He always asks "would I like to go, for my own sake?" And as I realise that work for the Institute is always the best work for myself, I jump at any such chance. And

30. Mary Mowbray-Clarke, part-owner of the Sunwise Turn.

> *that is the explanation of my "terror" of G. He provides me with great opportunities.*

On Tuesday the 4th he gave Jessie a running account of the preparations for the demonstration:

> *The situation here is amusing in the xth degree. We've created so much expectation that if the Demonstration is not held, everybody who believes in us will be scoffed at in the future, I mean here in Boston. The others will simply say: "I told you so! This G is a fishy person."[31] At the same time, I'm pretty sure the demonstration will not be a financial success. Boston is a mean city. So, in this plight, I am wiring G that there is no guarantee of financial success, yet the demonstration must in my opinion be given. I'll leave him to decide.*
>
> *So the Carnegie was not a success? Personally, I scarcely heard a word over the phone this morning, the traffic outside being as noisy as hell. But Mrs. P presumably heard something. . . . The situation is all the more amusing here because I've spent all the money G gave me; and Mrs. Hartmann has not sent me any more. I have not enough to pay the hotel or return to N.Y.! I shall pawn my watch presently unless something miraculous happens!*

The miracle came in the form of money wired right away by Jessie, which Orage happily acknowledged on the 5th:

> *She is an absolute darling and G will love her. He loves "all or nothing" people, and that disposition, apart from the question of fact, is the first condition of everything "good." Actually he doesn't really care if people give all their money, etc. or not. In any case, he always accepts it, if at all, as a loan. But the willingness to do so is a sine qua non, though few people realise it.*
>
> *Yes they arrived. After going to bed last night in doubt if they were coming, Miss Gordon rang me up this morning at 8:30 to say the party had arrived by boat. And Mme H had breakfast here. G is coming by train, arriving at 4:20. The prospects for the Demonstration are, of course, doubtful: and now it has begun to pour with rain. But I am still content to have advised G to come. He is to dine at the Harvard Club with McDougall before the Demonstration; and for that cachet alone the trip will be worth the expense for the kudos it brings. Dining with McD is for an educationalist what dining with the President is for a politician. Also*

---

31. Beatrice Hastings had called the Institute a "mystical fishshop."

> *there will certainly be a few other people if not at the Demonstration.*
> *Mme H does not know yet about Chicago; but G will tell me. The party*
> *will stay here overnight and return by boat Thursday.*
> *I'm now living on ticket money!*

Orage met with a few professors from Harvard to relay a request from
Gurdjieff for certain materials he wished to use to produce phenomena
never before produced. The professors looked at Orage with incredulity and said they would attend the demonstration, but shied away from
contributing material for it. Nonetheless, it was a relieved Orage who
wrote a report to Jessie the next day:

> *The Demonstration has been just the kind of success I told G it would be,*
> *financially not good, but influentially excellent.*[32] *Enclosed is the evi-*
> *dence; and, of course, you can show it about! G had dinner at the*
> *Harvard Club with McDougall and five other swell Harvard professors*
> *who afterwards came to the Demonstration and were much impressed. So*
> *great, in fact, was the enthusiasm and regret for the poor attendance*
> *(only about 200 people) that the audience volunteered to bring friends to*
> *the next, and G promptly closed with his offer, so the Demonstration will*
> *be repeated this evening.*
>
> *G hasn't apparently decided about Chicago yet, but spoke of it as still*
> *a possibility. He suggested going himself with me which I do not like!*
> *He would be on my hands and neither of us would do anything, I fear.*
> *However, we shall see. He also said that things were difficult only for the*
> *immediate present, the prospects were good, and the people today who*
> *had and would get over the difficulties would profit first and most in the*
> *future.*

Still awake at 3 A.M. Friday morning, Orage added a postscript to his letter:

> *I believe I'm off to Chicago tomorrow (Friday), but even now it is not set-*
> *tled. The alternative was to come back to N.Y. for one day and wait for*
> *G; but in spite of the chance of meeting you, I prefer if possible to go to*
> *Chicago alone at first. My always address there will be c/o Professor*
> *Crane, 1823 Wesley Ave., Evanston, Ill; but I will send you my own*
> *address later. Crane is getting rooms for me in Chicago proper.*
>
> *The Demonstration tonight was really—considering—a great success;*
> *nearly 300 people, and as many more dollars (this latter between our-*

---

32. The concert pianist, Carol Robinson, who was performing with the Boston Symphony
Orchestra, attended the demonstration, as did Ananda Coomaraswamy, associated then with the
Boston Fine Arts Museum. Robinson became a life-long follower of Gurdjieff from that
moment onward.

selves). Boston has certainly been turned over in its sleep, and I should think that a later Demonstration here would be highly successful. The papers will publish many photographs on Sunday, I believe.

He saw Gurdjieff's party off at the dock as they boarded the boat on a sea-lane established a century earlier by Cornelius Vanderbilt, who had made his fortune in both railroads and the maritime trade along the northeast coast when travel by road was long and uncomfortable. Orage then returned to his hotel to pack for his trip to Chicago. After arriving in Chicago on Saturday, he settled into his quarters in the Hotel New Southern, where his room set him back $1.50 per day. He wrote Jessie on Monday, 10 March:

Saturday, after arriving in Chicago at 3, I dined with Crane and spent the night with another college friend, Kay. Sunday here and then a series of visits and interviews lasting until 1 this morning. I've seen several people who may be of use, and am in the way of seeing, through them, many more; but my general impression is that Chicago is too big and scattered a city for a Demonstration at short and largely private notice. It would take me a fortnight at least to <u>see</u> the people on my list, to say nothing of <u>their</u> friends, and the ignorance of most of them as regards the Institute etc. is absolute. I have already had to begin from A with most of the people I have met. Chicago is also well under snow, and it is still snowing, so, altogether, the conditions are wraggle-taggle gypsy enough to satisfy the severest taste. . . .

I wonder if G understands your suggestion re an "official position"? Mme Hartmann is the woman to speak with, since she can be depended upon to report to G anything told her in <u>confidence</u>. I always <u>confide</u> to her what I want G to know without <u>my</u> having to tell him. Her indiscretion never fails. Try this experiment! Mary's serial fiction about me must be very amusing, and I imagine she must lie awake nights inventing it. But, je m'en fiche. . . . G said again that he proposed to leave me in N.Y. for some months, and I do think that I shall have earned the delight of seeing you after my travels in these distant parts. But in any case you remember our agreement: either I stay in N.Y. or we return to Fontainebleau together.

Then Tuesday the 11th after an informal lecture to a number of faculty from Northwestern University and the University of Chicago, he wrote:

A very pleasant evening with twenty professors. It's surprising what a splash a little Gurdjieff makes when it drops into a university pool. It was very late before I could escape from the tidal wave that followed my "lecture," but of course the tumult will have died down by now, and the professors will forget their nightmare. Whether the <u>means</u> will be forthcoming for the costly trip from N.Y. I am still very uncertain. I give myself

until Friday to decide. Of course, I <u>hint</u> at the subject—not very origi-
nally; and I know that it <u>is</u> under discussion. But how deeply buried in
talk I cannot (or will not try) to estimate.

Orage continued to be amazed at Jessie's reports of rumors among the
New York followers, this time of Gurdjieff's failure in Boston, as well
as more gossip in New York about the Institute. "You are the very
source and fount of rumours," he wrote Jessie on Thursday the 13th:

They are an excellent test of one's balance, and already, it seems, N.Y. is
in the thick of them. My way to deal with them is to believe nothing I do
not know; and even then to be doubtful about it until it has happened.
About Boston, for example, I hear that G is pleased, but I know no evi-
dence whatever; and I shall only believe it when he proves it to my satis-
faction, and I don't think he will.
*   . . . Today I've been to Evanston [the home of Northwestern*
University] again and really managed this time a Committee to advertise
the Demonstration if it should take place. Sunday evening I am invited to
the <u>other</u> university at Chicago; and the reporters are at last beginning
to nibble at the bait. Zona Gale arrives tomorrow (Fri) morning en pas-
sant home. I expect to see her and hear her views and news. Tomorrow
also is the great Reception; there is a passage in the Society column of
the Tribune and I am getting a purple suit and lavender gloves. With no
reason, I begin today to think there <u>will</u> be a Demonstration here.
Perhaps after tomorrow I shall know otherwise.

After the reception, which lasted well into the evening, Orage wrote
Jessie at midnight from his hotel:

I left the hotel for the "great" meeting. . . . For the first time for weeks I
felt quite nervous. Such accounts had been given me of the swell and
momentous character of this assembly that I could not decide on <u>what</u>
line to take, and I was confused by a series of contradictory suggestions.
Seventy or eighty people showed up and all were introduced to me with
all their titles and offices, and I felt more and more swamped as they
poured in to tea. However, I started off with a cigarette and in a conver-
sational tone, and in a few minutes I was as much at ease as I am likely
to be in Chicago. Once again I'm at a loss for judgment of the <u>result</u> of
the meeting. A committee was formed with the French Consul as the
chairman, and 8 boxes at 50 dollars were immediately sold in anticipa-
tion. Also all sorts of offers of publicity were received, and perhaps the
result will become solid. But really, I'm at a loss, and I wouldn't bet one
way or the other. We phoned Mme H and heard that G was ill with a cold,
and we promised to wire after tomorrow (Sat's) committee meeting. So
delay again. My <u>impression</u> is that if G would come, company and all,

the return expenses would be raised, but I don't like to urge it because if
it did turn out wrong, I couldn't find the money. I'd risk my own money,
if I had any, on it, but not anybody else's.

. . . I don't see any reason yet to think I shall be sent back to France at
once. Somebody will be necessary in America, if only to advise intending
emigrants to Fontainebleau, and who else knows them?

The next morning, Saturday the 15th, Jessie wrote that she would lend
Gurdjieff and his troupe the necessary funds for the trip, and, with
thanks to Jessie, Gurdjieff was sending Madame de Hartmann to over-
see the arrangements. Orage replied immediately with some anxiety:

You suggested that Mme H might be coming here at once. But last night
(Fri) we rang her up, and she said nothing whatever of coming . . . How's
that? If your darling gypsy self has lent G the passage-money here, I
don't see why he should not come. We have a very strong committee that
will not only do all the advertising of the Demonstration, but will (I judge
confidently) ensure the money for G's return. In fact, I think he may now
come with safety. More will be done by this committee, I think, than was
done in Boston, and most of the clerical work will be undertaken by peo-
ple here. As I told you a few hours ago, the committee is meeting at 3:30
today, and we shall officially decide the fate of the Demonstration. I shall
wire S [de Salzmann], I hope, at once. Mrs. R[umlee] and I met Zona
Gale this morning on her way through to Portage. Zona is still very
ardent, and will help in the Chicago Demonstration. She has many
friends here and is thought much of. Also (entre nous absolument) she has
told me that, at a pinch, she could lend G the money to take him back to
N.Y. if the Demonstration were not a success. But I shall keep that fact
very very dark. I've heard no rumours of yesterday's meeting, but am now
preparing press notices to be ready if the Demonstration is dated today.
It would be next Friday if at all, the 21st.

Then, on Sunday, 16 March:

I wired to G last evening (Sat) at about 6:30 to say that prospects were
encouraging and we had <u>*booked*</u> *the hall for Friday evening next. The*
Committee turned out to be excellent and I really think there will be very
little for us to do. They will see to the printing, distribution, advertise-
ment, and even the press publicity. It is a great change after Boston, etc.
and I am very much relieved. My work now consists of keeping the
Committee itself up to concert pitch and undertaking to attend all tea and
the other parties where they think I can be of use. The hall is immense—
nearly 3000—but for the expenses incurred a small hall would be useless,
unless the tickets were very highly priced. We have fixed prices low—
from 50¢ to 3 dollars, with boxes of $50 and of the latter we have sold 13

out of the 23. I think G should come with the party on Tuesday (i.e. start-
ing on Tuesday) and perhaps he could give a small private demonstration
to the Committee and the press on Thurs evening so that the press would
advertise with photos on Friday morning. I'll write to G to that effect
now, but you can help to translate it darling. Also I should like a small
orchestra, and if Mr. Hartmann could come at once, he could easily pick
up a few musicians . . . I'm off just now to Evanston to organise a local
committee there for ticket selling, and this evening I have a similar
errand at the other end of this huge town, at Chicago University.

You and you alone have made possible G's coming here, and between
us we shall make possible his return. And G won't be unaware of it.
Things are interesting.

Not only did Gurdjieff send Olga and Thomas de Hartmann as an
advance party, Jessie came as well, as their guide and, of course, to be
with Orage. The demonstration went well before a large and interested
audience, and Gurdjieff stayed on a few days following, granting interviews and giving talks. On Wednesday the 26th, Jessie and the de
Hartmanns took the train back to New York, Jessie seizing the occasion
to stop off in Albany to see her family. On Thursday, still in Chicago
with Gurdjieff and members of the troupe, Orage gave more lectures,
was interviewed on the radio, and recruited potential members for the
Institute, while the others held one more demonstration.[33] Orage next
wrote to Jessie in Albany:

There is no news about the future, so I presume that the plan of N.Y. still
holds. My heart drops, however, when I think of the uncertainty inherent
in G's plans which change literally every hour. But McCormick has done,
and Chicago seems to offer nothing really golden, and there is talk—by
Mme H—of a farewell demonstration in N.Y. It must be all to the good to
be boiled in oil for a period, to come out brown and crisp for some god's
table. We have to be eaten, and better cooked for the sun than raw for the
moon. Life in the big sense is as terrible as it is beautiful.

. . . The radio went all right and I went to the meeting to find only seven
Chicagoans there, the rest being pupils, and Mrs. R[umlee] who leaves
for N.Y. tomorrow, was one of the seven.[34] G concluded that he had not
the "draw" of a popular lecturer and at the end he suggested . . . that I
go before him [to New York] and re-collect the original people again. He

---

33. Gurdjieff lost one member of the troupe, Olga Ivanova (Olgivanna) Lazovich Hintzenberg,
when she stayed on with her daughter Svetlana (b. 1917) in Chicago where she met Frank Lloyd
Wright and became his wife in 1928.
34. Mrs. Rumlee, who hosted a few meetings at her apartment at 242 East 49th Street, was
authorized by Orage to sign certificates for prospective Institute pupils.

would come later, but only to answer such questions as people desired to put to him. Also, he definitely said that he proposed to leave me in NY— with Feropintov to translate from the Russian for me, and Mme Galumnian to teach exercises. So that's all right! And now I am all in haste to start for NY at once, but I'm afraid it still must be a day or two because I have that swagger lunch at the Cordon Club on Monday. However, we shall see.

On Saturday, he sent a brief message to Jessie that he would be leaving Chicago on the Monday-night train and arrive at Grand Central at 8 A.M. Tuesday, while Gurdjieff was staying on without any fixed date for his departure. Orage added, in a postscript, that he had shown Gurdjieff Jessie's plan for a lecture room at the Institute, and "he is very pleased you had so soon got to work." His next letter, on Monday, was written on the train, still addressed to Jessie in Albany:

At 1 this morning, on taking leave of G, I wished him goodbye, and told him my train for NYC was due out at 8 this evening. He said, "I think you stay here in Chicago a little longer; perhaps we go back to NY together after the Demonstration."... G is a little lonely here, I think, without me, and perhaps a little at sea. It is possible that only one Demonstration will be given here, and certain if the first—tomorrow—is a failure. In that case, the whole party will return to NY on Wed, arriving on Thursday sometime.

... The lecture at the Cordon Club went off extremely well today. It was a very large and hushed audience. Chicago will wake up some weeks after we have left, and perhaps next year the virgins will have their lamps filled. I have much to learn about economy of time, however, and perhaps on another such mission I shall waste less time on this. I've been a fool, spending too much time with the wrong people, and I see it when it is too late.

We have [had] meetings every evening at Bolins or Miss Hickock's studio. There have been 30 or 40 people on each occasion, but except for certain faithfuls—Misses Dupré, Calhoun, Kinsolving, and a man or two—seldom the same persons twice. Tho' G has been very interesting indeed for me, he has failed to make himself intelligible to newcomers, and some of them have gone off in a huff. Well, let 'em. The price of eso- teric knowledge is always high, and patience is the cheapest of the tokens. If they cannot listen to the doctrine, still less can they make it their own. That is much more difficult—and as easy.

G, by the way, spoke last evening of possibly sending me to India next year. America has been too easy for me; I have had to <u>do</u> very little. But a different race... would try my resolution, and I'm afraid for the result. But it would be interesting.

> *. . . Mme Hartmann has written and telegraphed to McPhee. . . . The party cannot sail together, for the simple reason that G has not the passage money for everybody. They must go as the money comes, and Lord knows where it will come from. However, I'm not "considering internally" about it, but at the same time it is necessary not to leave a stone unturned in to find the money. That is when I blame myself for not having concentrated on people with both interest in the work and money to spend, here in Chicago.*

When Gurdjieff returned from Chicago and Jessie came back from Albany, the hectic routine in New York was renewed. Orage had indeed "re-collected" as many of the original people as he could and organized a number of work groups with them. In June, he formed one group at Mary Gawthorpe's in Westchester County. He had another operating in Pelham. In Manhattan he had a number of groups, one of which met at Lawrence Hare's, another at Jane Heap's. Jessie served as general secretary of the whole operation. She was also Orage's personal secretary, though she still worked at the Sunwise Turn two or three days a week. As part-owner of the shop, she could set her own work schedule without much difficulty. Gurdjieff continued to see people and direct movements throughout April and May. After the return from Chicago, despite the relative success of the demonstrations, he still lacked sufficient funds to pay the return fares to France for his entire entourage. Orage hit upon the expedient of having people "pay in advance" for intended stays at the Institute. This had a limited success, and Orage turned to the "original people" for necessary support, and eventually got it.[35] Gurdjieff did his part to encourage financial participation by hosting a dinner on 8 April to inaugurate the official opening of the New York branch of the Institute.

In mid-April, as the newspapers in America seemed more concerned with George Herman [the "Babe"] Ruth's abdominal surgery for gastronomic excesses, and the general public held in thrall by news of the trial of playboy Harry B. Thaw for the murder eighteen years earlier of the noted architect, Stanford White, over the affections of Evelyn Nesbit, the "girl on the velvet swing," Jessie returned to Albany to settle family problems. From her flat back at 150 East 54th Street (until their marriage they did not share an apartment), Orage wrote on Saturday the 19th:

---

35. Bennett, *Gurdjieff: Making a New World,* p. 160, says that the tour was a financial success, and raised enough to pay off the Prieuré debt, but this was clearly not the case. In fact, the money Jessie put forward for the Chicago trip was not repaid her.

*I intend in a moment to begin collecting my material for the K.M.
[Katherine Mansfield] article. . . . I've been planning, too, the chapters
of a possible series of Recollections. Why stop at K. M. when there are so
many others of equal public, if not private, interest? So my suggested title
now is: "Recollections of a London Editor" and I shall try it on the dog
on Monday. If I am to receive at least some money in advance, I'm afraid
I must also write a chapter or two in advance, and that will delay what I
wish to do, namely give G. $500 at once.*

Orage was also trying to convince Jessie to return to France with
Gurdjieff to spend the summer at the Institute. Orage spent hours with
her, describing the Prieuré and the work done there, and outlined the
principles behind the Gurdjieffian methods. After she complained once
that Orage held forth on Gurdjieff to an exaggerated degree, he sent her
a note downtown to the Sunwise Turn, to say: "How I should <u>love</u> to
hear <u>her</u> 'hold forth' on G and the Institute."

Among those who had listened to Orage's lectures and witnessed
the demonstrations, there were many who set their sights on the
Institute. Direct applications to Gurdjieff were answered with a curt:
"See Orage," and so Orage became an information center and travel
agent throughout May.[36] He also continued a lecture series that found a
larger audience, and that success led him to decide, with Gurdjieff's
encouragement, to announce classes for the fall. Orage had become
Gurdjieff's voice for Americans, his interpreter and organic correlative
of an exciting adventure in ideas. As a later commentator put it:
"Gurdjieff's initial success in the West was not brought about by the
impact of the man himself, not by the forbidding intellect of Ouspensky,
but by the personal magnetism of Orage."[37] Claude Bragdon, who
judged that Gurdjieff's mission was far from successful, notes that
Orage was left behind with Gurdjieff's debts and a confused American
public: "It was Orage," he writes, "the perfect disciple, the Plato to this
Socrates, who was responsible for most of the success which attended
the movement in America. His charming manner and brilliant mind did
much to counteract the bewilderment in which Gurdjieff so often left his
auditors."[38] Jean Toomer, after talking at length with Orage, decided

---

36. In Nott's account of this period in *Journey Through the World* (London: Routledge & Kegan
Paul, 1969), p. 74, he says he sailed for France in April, went straight to the Prieuré where,
through much of the spring and summer he had lengthy conversations with Gurdjieff.
37. James Webb, *The Harmonious Circle: The Lives and Works of G. I. Gurdjieff, P. D.
Ouspensky, and Their Followers* (London: Thames & Hudson, 1980), p. 195.
38. Bragdon, *More Lives*, p. 324.

that he, too, would go to see Gurdjieff in France. Later he wrote: "Orage's groups and the life that grew out of them became my life." Through him, "a method, a means of *doing something about it* was promised. It was no wonder that I went heart and soul into the Gurdjieff work."[39] In effect, Orage had given Toomer a sense of being and purpose on a path toward self-development.

Orage's relationship with Jessie had grown in intensity for them both, and Orage persuaded her that, if she wanted to be with him thereafter, she must at least test the terrain at the Institute for the summer. Gurdjieff not only approved the proposal, but insisted that she come, not only for his sake, but for her own.

---

39. Nathan Jean Toomer, *The Wayward and the Seeking,* Darwin T. Turner, ed. (Washington DC: Howard University Press, 1980), p. 131.

Chapter Four

1924

JESSIE DWIGHT
AT CHÂTEAU GURDJIEFF

*Modern Man . . . is to reconcile himself with his
own nature—how he is to love the enemy in his
heart and call the wolf his brother.*

—Jung[1]

*A teacher is one who brings tools and enables
us to use them.*

—Toomer[2]

After Gurdjieff's long stay in New York and his whirlwind tour of
Boston and Chicago—all arranged by his steward, Orage, who planted
notices in local newspapers and charmed local academic and artistic
dignitaries who were, mostly, either professors whose names had been
given him in New York and Boston or writers with whom he had had
previous literary contacts—Gurdjieff asked Orage to remain behind
in New York to recruit and screen new members for the Institute. It
was quite clear to Gurdjieff that "America," as he preferred to call the
United States, was fertile ground for raising money as well as interest
in his ideas, though the priority might well have been the other way
around.

Orage and Jessie saw Gurdjieff off on the boat in mid-June. Jessie
did not sail with the group accompanying him because, she said, she had
to clear up her business at the Sunwise Turn first. It is probable that she
was uneasy about the prospect of finding herself alone with Gurdjieff

1. John Bartlett, *Familiar Quotations* (Garden City, NJ: Permabooks, 1983). Found under heading "Brother."
2. Nathan Jean Toomer, *The Wayward and the Seeking,* Darwin T. Turner, ed. (Washington DC: Howard University Press, 1980), p. 438.

and his intimate entourage whose languages she did not share, so she had booked passage on a boat leaving a few days later. From Le Havre, where she landed early in the morning of 29 June she took the boat-train to the Gare Saint Lazare in Paris, then a taxi to the Gare du Lyon, where she boarded another train for Fontainebleau, and finally a fiacre, or horse-drawn carriage, to the Prieuré.[3]

Years later, she wrote an account of her arrival and stay at the Institute, prefaced with a brief explanation of her circumstances:

These are articles written about my stay in Gurdjieff's institute for the Harmonious Development of Man, in Fontainebleau. That I should go—that there was any need for such a drastic step—appeared to me incredible. After all these years it still seems incredible. "You come now," said Gurdjieff on the New York dock, "very important." "Not now," I said on the verge of tears—"not now. September I come with Orage." "No, now," Gurdjieff said—"very important—now—no Institute maybe in September." All very serious—very intense. "I hate you," I said—why do I not know unless I realized go I must.

Then he sailed, having grown a beard and wearing a grey soft hat which covered his shaven head. He looked handsome and dashing—an adventurer. He leant over the rail and made signals to his disciples on the pier. With shining eyes they gazed—semaphored an answer—dashing along beside the outgoing ship—rapt by some message they thought they understood. Perhaps they did. I only know I too was impressed as the ship drew slowly away. Somehow Gurdjieff attained a mystery and an aloneness—a figure isolated and because of his position far above. "I should not wish," I said to myself, "never to see him again, but why should I go to Fontainebleau?"

And then when the Prophet had sailed from the land of his Abundance or from the land which Orage had made abundant for him, I found that I in truth must go. Orage said so—he did not wish it—he said it had to be done. "Must I?" I said, "Why should I do anything I do not want to do? Why?"

"You see," he said, "I am dedicated to this. I have given up everything for this. You must go now without me. I will come in September."
And so I went.

3. Though C. S. Nott, *Teachings of Gurdjieff: Journal of a Pupil* (London: Routledge & Kegan Paul, 1961), is rarely reliable with dates, it is difficult to understand his account, pp. 42–43, that he sailed for France in April 1924 and went straight to the Prieuré, where he was told that Gurdjieff had awaited him for three weeks. He records long conversations with Gurdjieff and Orage and mentions that Madame de Salzmann's young son was six months old, though Michel would have been less than four months old at the time. He recounts working with Olgivanna in the autumn of 1924, but, according to other evidence, Olgivanna had remained in Chicago.

—————————————— *The Prieuré* ——————————————

A wall—a long French wall at the end of an avenue. A gate—a sign "Sonnez très fort." I did and the gate was opened by a Russian ex-cavalry officer in working clothes. The gate opened on an oval court-yard with the concierge's lodge to the left, a fountain in the middle and straight ahead the main door of the château. It was a lovely place. If I had wished to be there I might have found it beautiful.

"Mr. Gurdjieff," said the Russian (Georgian I found out later) offi-cer, "is in the garden. I will take you to him."

We passed through the chateau and walked down a garden—very long—very formal—to a little log summerhouse. There was Gurdjieff.

He questioned me about New York, about Orage, expressed his pleasure at my company, shouted for tea—for coffee—for anything desired.

The conversation was a bit stilted. Gurdjieff's English being more easily understood by intuition than anything else. After the ceremoni-al tea or coffee drinking, he took me out to show me the grounds. He stopped before a large building which I knew because Orage had told me it had been at one time an airplane hangar, and had been erected and decorated by the pupils of the Institute. The windows were cucum-ber frames painted by Saltzmann [sic]—the floor was strewn with rugs, the pupils' seats down each side covered with wolfskins (but this description came after my entry).

"This," said Gurdjieff impressively, "is the Study House." I duti-fully admired the wooden exterior. "I hestitated," he went on, "to take you in." That I had after all come to Fontainebleau was apparently the Open Sesame. He took me in. It is a place I was afterwards fre-quently told, quite sacred and only entered with baited breath, and to smile or laugh was blasphemy (a few years later I laughed so much the rafters resounded, but that is another story, blasphemous certain-ly, but in Gurdjieff's own ribald tradition). Certainly it was impres-sive; the cucumber frames were beautifully painted in Persian designs, the fountain before the stage played and was turning into fan-tasy by colored electric bulbs. The effect on me was nothing so much. I said nothing, not an adjective for or against. I stood. That seemed to be enough. I was led on and shown to my room in the château.

It was an enormous room with a huge bed, another small bed and a dressing room attached. I had the small bed. Two other pupils shared the huge one.

I unpacked and wandered down to the terrace where I sat and lit a cigarette. This was, I was emphatically told at supper, not done. Women could only smoke in their rooms.

Supper was served in the garden outside the kitchen. The food was passed through a window. The men came straight from work and with a Russian disregard, unwashed. I blush to say that first meal make me actively sick. Never again but that one did. After that I could scoop flies from my soup, flick them over my shoulder into the shrubbery, endure the different smells of cow stable and unwashed workers and still eat with an appetite—if there was anything eatable—occasionally there wasn't.

Supper over, everyone went down to the Study House. Gurdjieff went too and oversaw the exercises. He had a special place to sit in (the "royal box" describes it) hung with furs—I don't remember what kind but certainly not plain wolf. I seldom saw him in his box—he usually prowled up and down or threw himself in a pupil's seat and from there thundered orders to his pupils.

His roars no longer affected me. Once in New York when we were learning a new dance, I made a mistake and went left instead of right or right instead of left—Gurdjieff swore at me as I imagine the traditional serjeant-major swears. And I reacted. I felt I was back again in school and a culprit. Yet I knew in intent I was right. The next morning when the bull's bellow was directed at us again I said "Don't pick on me—I know what I am doing." Never again did Gurdjieff yell at me. Subtle was his technique after that, so blatantly subtle—so like an elephant trying to be a snake. So snakelike without the elephant wisdom.

Work was the Prieuré motto—work—work—work. Do things unaccustomed—break habits—but as far as I could see—and after all how could one tell—everyone was working because he must and then only when Gurdjieff was there. No one appeared to be working for what as Orage explained to me was a necessary thing for one's conscious development—to do inhabitual things—to take a reservoir of unused energy—to get beyond a mechanical doing—beyond physical fatigue onto another plane of conscious effort and to observe oneself objectively while doing it. I saw no evidence of that in others, but again, how can one tell. And what should that matter to me anyway. I was there to try and do what Orage said was the reason for the Prieuré— a place where one could experiment. So I tried but it was rather surprising when I was scullery maid and happened to be visiting friends two miles away and caught a tram which landed me at the gate at 5 A.M. to be greeted with the question "Why did you come back so early?" This from one of the pupils, right hand to Gurdjieff. "Because it's my day in the kitchen," said I and was met with a look of utter incredulity. "Then you're a damn fool" the look said. And so are you I said to myself because if you think I came back out of a sense of duty or for fear of Gurdjieff you're a bigger fool than I am.

I was fated to offend. Not only smoking but I had gone out to work in trousers. They came to me and snickered, "Do you know what Gurdjieff said?": "She dress like a man—she do man's work, Hawhaw!" "That would be easy," I said and wished I knew Russian to tell them that after all I worked not because I wanted to, not because I had to, but because I was doing something which at least I thought was worth doing and I wasn't working like a demon because Gurdjieff was watching and smoking behind a tree when he wasn't.

It was all very difficult. Unless one had a reason—some knowledge of what the Institute was for—why be there at all? I didn't want to be there—God knows. I could have walked out at any moment, sometimes I hoped I'd be kicked out, but I had to know why the place existed at all. I had to know. Orage expected me to find out. He hoped that I too would find it necessary. Many of the Russian pupils were there because it was a refuge—they worked—they danced—they said they knew why they were doing it—they flaunted their superiority because they could understand Gurdjieff's Russian. They trembled in fear at his frowns. I wondered.

When Gurdjieff was nearly killed—when he drove into a tree in the forest and was three weeks unconscious, what went on at the Prieuré? Practically nothing. This I know—I was there. A form of madness went on. I thought for a time I must be mad too. Surely I couldn't be the only rational being when there were fifty others all behaving so oddly. "He hasn't been hurt," they whispered. "He did it on purpose—he even showed the doctors what to do. He's not unconscious—he knows everything"; and then the resident doctor went in and out of Gurdjieff's room and never omitted to slam the door and Gurdjieff was supposed to have concussions.

"Wonderful," said an English woman inmate who took the cow for a walk each day, fanning away the flies with a leafy branch, "wonderful he is asleep and yet he directs the doctor where to massage!"

"I'm mad," I said to myself. "I'm mad" I wrote to Orage. What shall I do?

In spite of slammed doors, of animated Russian discussion about his bed, Gurdjieff recovered and that almost makes me believe him a superman. Then a great white and gold chair was carried out to the forest and Gurdjieff sat in it all day and watched while we felled trees and burned them in an enormous fire—tree after tree, day after day. The trees groaned—fell and bled. This is right I felt. He gets back strength and life from the trees' death. I believe he did.

Then one day, walking with him down the garden, he said "You hear from Orage?" "Yes," I said. The next day a notice was posted. All outgoing letters must be put in a special box—all incoming letters must be signed for and names of correspondents given. I was very angry—all my Americanism rose. I walked down the garden with Gurdjieff. I spluttered with rage. "What do you mean—how dare you?—my letters, I?" "I not understand," he said. His English never failed to desert him in someone else's need.

From then on I posted my letters outside the gate and regularly robbed the box in the concierge. I took Orage's letters—the others I noted dutifully in the book. I started with the President of the United States, his wife and family and went on to the Governor of New York State. Al Smith and the Smith family lasted for the remainder of my stay until Orage came.[4]

After Jessie had left for France on the Volendam, Orage, having strained in vain at the railing of the Staten Island ferry to catch a last glimpse of his beloved, moved into her New York apartment on 54th Street. There he settled down to write for American magazines and to outline his fall classes. His social life consisted largely of expanding his New York acquaintances in order to advertise the Institute. Orage had come up with the idea of selling "certificates" that would entitle the holder to entry into the Institute.[5] These he intended to advertise by direct mailing, but the printer he engaged was more concerned with other commissions, and Orage was left waiting. The afternoon after Jessie's departure, he posted a letter to her at the Institute, saying:

Among the letters I've had to reply to are several from would-be visitors to Fontainebleau. I've recommended them all to come at once, and partly with the calculation that the more the better for you. . . . Try to wallow in life there, forget about everything you were, America and all, and live as if you were just imported fresh from another world. There isn't any "Jessie" at Fontainebleau, but only an "I" that wishes to see what Jessie is in novel circumstances.

---

4. Anne B. Orage, the widow of Orage's son Richard has graciously allowed me to extract this and all following diary entries from Jessie Orage's diary.
5. The circulars were advertisements for "certificates" entitling holders to admittance at the Institute. The cost of the certificates was $120 apiece. They read: "The bearer of this, a member of the GURDJIEFF INSTITUTE, has the following privileges: First, residence, with all rights of permanent members, at the chief centre of the Institute at Fontainebleau, as well as the Insitute's boarding houses at other places; Free attendance at all classes, lectures and conferences wherever held under the auspices of the Institute, except those lectures, etc. specifically held for personal members; Free subscription to the Institute's journal and all the literature issued by the Institute. The right of enquiry and reply concerning the ideas of the Institute, any member may, if he or she wish, use any of the sanatoria or hotels of the Institute for him or herself, and family, at one-half the regular rates." The certificates bore the name of Gurdjieff over the signature of Orage.

The next day, he continued: "I saw Miss Nessa Cohen this morning and sold her a certificate. She may be coming to Fontainebleau, but is full of 'difficulties.' She is practising the exercises, however, and is very enthusiastic about them. . . . It doesn't look as if it would be easy to dispose of 100 certificates in a month or two—but we'll see. . . . I paid the Gurdjieff account."

And, on Tuesday: "Last evening I saw Miss Walker and her people invited me to a week-end in the country—everything arranged for my convenience. . . . There are still no replies to our 600 circulars. . . . It's funny, isn't it, that not one of the 600 appears to have been delivered? . . . You are still on board, of course, but my fancy sees you already in the Institute." On Thursday, after a report of long conversations with Lawrence Hare, he remarked that he had seen Marjorie Content (the future wife of Jean Toomer) at the Sunwise Turn and collected some of the gossip circulating about Jessie and himself. Toomer visited Orage twice in June, the first time to ask Orage's permission to go to the Prieuré in July. Orage granted him a certificate on credit, numbered 619, valid for a calendar year from 6 January 1924. The certificate number seems curious, since only 600 circulars were sent out. Orage probably had the printer start the numbers high—possibly even as high as 600—to make prospective visitors think that there had already been many takers before them. It is likely that Toomer was, in fact, among the first dozen American holders. In the second week of July, he visited Orage once again, this time for more practical information, and reported to him that he had tried without success to convince Waldo Frank and Gorham Munson to accompany him to France.[6]

On Friday the 20th, Orage sent Jessie some advice that he hoped would put Jessie in good stead at the Institute:

I think you should see G as soon as possible and tell him just how you stand. He perhaps thinks you have an income for life, or a family to live upon. You should let him understand how completely you have burned your boats.[7] Jane Heap is in the same situation, only rather worse because she has not even a brother. She has just rung up to say she is sailing on the S.S. Berengaria with the two boys [Fritz and Tom Peters] next

---

6. With his own regrets, Waldo sent Toomer word that he thought it appropriate for Toomer to get introduced to the ease of French culture, as if the Prieuré participated in or represented anything typical of Gallic life.
7. Jessie's family was well off, but she had no inheritance in hand. What her inheritance had given her at the age of twenty-one was enough to buy a share in the Sunwise Turn. Her brother had been given a stake in a business in Albany.

Wednesday the 25th.[8] I am so glad you will soon have her for company. She knows Paris, of course, quite well, and has many friends there. You should use her as a guide, since it is always useful to have known Paris! I'm sorry I don't know it better myself, but I've never found it very congenial, for some reason or other.[9]

Salzmann has just been in and we arranged to meet occasionally. He proposes to stay here until the end of September, but not I! My plan is to collect sufficient money for my passage and for our holiday in France, and then to return with no further delay. But I've heard nothing further of the circulars yet [the brochure Orage edited and distributed describing the Institute, which vaunted that there were some five thousand members in all countries],[10] and so far there is little doing about certificates. I lose no opportunity, but it is necessary to make opportunities.

On Saturday, 21 June, a week after Jessie sailed, he sent a letter off to her in Fontainebleau, lamenting: "No news of the circulars . . . no sale of certificates, no money. . . . Quite a number of new people but, of course, nothing more. All the same, I think several will eventually come to Fontainebleau." The next day he wrote that he had lunched with Mrs Rumlee and Ford Maddox Ford, and then expressed his wonder at the kinds of people he had encountered that intended to go to the Prieuré: "If this is the Institute and these the people undergoing repair, then anything to escape from such a crazy place and people. I write them down here, but in my experience they have been felt as flame. Perspiration pours off me as I think of them. The worst of it is that I cannot regard them as inherently ridiculous. They contain the facts."

Orage had always regretted the disparity between those who had sought out Gurdjieff to obtain a measure of the esoteric lore behind his teaching and those who sought out Gurdjieff to cure some psychological or pathological malady. He understood and supported the latter in their quests, but thought them a waste of time if the medicine did not include the message. He had been heartened that Katherine Mansfield, in the very short time she spent at the Institute, had come to a fuller realization of herself as an artist and of the value of her art. On the other hand, he discouraged members of his group in New York from going to

---

8. At the opening of *Boyhood with Gurdjieff* (London: Victor Gollancz, 1964), Peters says that he arrived at the Institute in June, but this is clearly not possible, having sailed on the 25th of June from New York City.

9. The free-spirited atmosphere of postwar Paris was certainly not suited to Orage's tight temperment. Then again, Beatrice Hastings, who had left Orage in a huff just before the war, was still in Paris, where she had been the mistress of Amadeo Modigliani, who died in 1920.

10. For the full text of the brochure, see Paul Beekman Taylor, *Shadows of Heaven: Gurdjieff and Toomer* (York Beach, ME: Samuel Weiser, 1998), pp. 73–75.

the Prieuré if they sought relief from alcoholism, divorce anxieties, homosexual tendencies, and so forth. Gurdjieff understood this, and had authorized Orage, as his agent, to screen applicants according to his own standards. Yet, Orage was reluctant to refuse certificates to anyone sincere, no matter the expectations or hopes, because those in pain "contain the facts." He drew the line before those he considered a threat to the routine functioning of the Institute. Gurdjieff, on the other hand, rarely drew lines. He was generous to a fault with what he had to offer, but a physical and moral price had to be paid by someone.

In New York at the beginning of summer, Orage found himself down to a single dollar for his sustenance, but confident of his status "in the arms of Jesus" (and he meant, as well, "Jess[i]e" from whose tree Jesus sprang). He spent a good deal of time organizing the New York group into a body politic that could function independent of his strictly pedagogical function. He encouraged the group to elect a president, secretary, and treasurer, and bound himself to their direction. He would rather be duty-bound to a group than have a group depend entirely upon him. In late June, he attended organizational meetings of the group and outlined to them his plans for lectures and classes the following autumn. Obviously, he had hopes that Jessie could also serve his work by being his "ambassador" or agent at the court of Gurdjieff. How valuable it would be if one of them on each side of the Atlantic could represent the interests of the other on the opposing shore. In such terms, he wrote Jessie with the expectation that she had arrived in Fontainebleau: "She is to see if she can find in the Institute idea a career for herself. From my point of view, after a few years of work, the Institute will be rich in possibilities of the most varied kind, and G as a big brother will certainly never grudge ample pay for services rendered. I owe you already to the Institute." Little could he have imagined that Jessie, by now, regretted her status as *commercium* in the trade between Orage and Gurdjieff.

A day later, on Tuesday the 24th of June, Orage received a cable from Jessie announcing her arrival, and he sat down and wrote a hasty note of acknowledgment, along with his New York news:

I have just seen and had a long talk with Jane [Heap], and am to see her again for dinner this evening, before she sails on the Berengaria tomorrow. I wish now that I had been more positive about her before, for she has gotten into a rather negative state. She is all right, and will ultimately be all right; but, for the moment, she is not clear as to means and object. I'm afraid that in only this day I cannot affect her very much, but I should like her to throw herself (as well as the boys!) into the life at Fontainebleau.

In his daily letter the next day, he wrote that he had not received a single word concerning the six hundred circulars he had sent out advertising the Institute, and blamed the situation on the U.S. postal service. Then, continuing his personal report, he wrote:

> *I saw Jane at dinner until 2 A.M. I wish more than ever that I had seen her before; she would have paid for attention, but, as it is, she has had to grope too much in the dark, and graze her shins. I think I have given her material for change of attitude, and it is possible that she will stay at Fontainebleau for at least a while. But you will see her yourself very soon, as she sails today and will come straight to the Institute. She did not, of course, mention you and me together, but she certainly likes you. Also she is not quite as deceived about Olga de Hartmann as I feared she was!*[11] *. . . I am seeing Muriel [Draper] this afternoon at Mrs. Rumlee's; wonder whether she is coming to Fontainebleau!*

He reported the tenor of his meeting in his next letter, and made it the occasion for some heart-felt advice:

> *I saw Muriel Draper at Mrs. Rumlee's yesterday.*[12] *She does not appear to have the least notion of "what it is all about." G interests her in a sort of way as a rare personality, but as for his aims or her own she has no idea. The strange thing is that G should, in these circumstances, appear to be so desirous of having her come to the Institute. Do try to find out, darling, what the object is. You can take yourself as an example. Why did he advise you to go? What advantage did he (so to say) promise you? For myself, as you know, I think I have the answer; but I do not like to hear people like Muriel feeling themselves irresistibly drawn to a thing they don't question. I should try to be absolutely commonsense. "Well, Mr. G, you have advised me to come. . . . What for? What am I to do? To what advantage?"*

The questions are pertinent. Did Gurdjieff have a program that included Muriel and Jessie? Both were strong-willed women with considerable intelligence, but Muriel was older and far more worldly and experienced, far more likely to know what she wanted out of the Institute, even if Orage was in doubt concerning her motives. I rather

---

11. With good reason or not, Olga de Hartmann had made herself unpopular with a number of women in the United States because of her apparent defensive, or protective stance concerning Gurdjieff. Some thought of her as an informer, or worse, a sower of discord.

12. Muriel Draper had a distinguished musical career behind her. She had lived some years in London and Italy, where she became friendly with notable musicians, including Arthur Rubenstein. After returning to New York, she became a music and arts critic.

think that Gurdjieff, in his typical manner, was testing their potential in the "work." It has been indicated in biographical studies of Gurdjieff and Orage that Gurdjieff wished to keep Jessie from compromising his own relations with Orage.[13] I am not so sure. Gurdjieff never seemed to make snap judgments of people. He preferred to watch them reveal their qualities and potentials over a period of time, even if he had to create the conditions under which they would do so.

In letters that followed, Orage reported that he had seen a lawyer in New York about divorce laws, but found they were even stricter than English laws. As in England, adultery was the only practical grounds for divorce, and so, even in uncontested cases, photographers and "models" were needed to provide the necessary proof. In New York State, the waiting period for final dissolution of marriage after judgment was three years. Orage worried that, under these circumstances and time limits, Jessie might change her ideas concerning their future together. He kept his spirits up in Jessie's absence by writing.[14] On occasional weekends he enjoyed the leisure of exploring with friends the country-side on the periphery of the city. He had no automobile himself. He had never learned to drive. He was astonished by the grace and luxury of residences along the Long Island and Connecticut shorelines that made English scenery, as he remarked, "a mere sketch."

Orage was endowed with an impeccable taste for all the arts and an insatiable curiosity about the cultural life of New York City, which seemed to contain something of the entire world. He had already discovered that Jessie, on the other hand, was attracted more to spectacle. When they were together during the previous spring, it was Orage who led the way to exhibitions, art galleries, and the theater, while Jessie took him to the films. Neither of them were devotees of the concert hall. On the last day of June, Orage amused himself by attending the second day of the Democratic National Convention at Madison Square Garden in New York, in the company of 13,000 others. He watched the ballot tallies put William G. McAdoo ahead of Al Smith 479 to 305. "When I was at Fontainebleau I forgot almost that there

---

13. Fritz Peters, *Boyhood with Gurdjieff* (London: Victor Gollancz, 1969), p. 31, tells the story of Gurdjieff's raging at Orage in the summer of 1925, and it has been generally assumed that the issue was the presence of Jessie in Orage's life. James Webb, *The Harmonious Circle: Lives and Works of G. I. Gurdjieff, P. D. Ouspensky, and Their Followers* (London: Thames & Hudson, 1980), James Moore, *Anatomy of a Myth* (Boston: Element, 1991), and William Patterson, *Struggle of the Magicians* (Fairfax, CA: Arete, 1999). There is no evidence produced at all that confirms this.
14. Waldo Frank had offered him $500 for an article on Katherine Mansfield for *The Century*.

was a world outside," he quipped in his nightly letter to Jessie, " . . . Well, there isn't much of a world." He regretted that, though circulars were finally distributed through the mails, because of the convention there seemed to be no interest at the moment. The moment endured for almost two weeks before John William Davis defeated Smith on the 103rd ballot, and Charles W. Bryan was chosen as his running mate for the vice-presidency.

On Wednesday, 2 July, the letters Jessie had written on board arrived together, all postmarked from Avon. Orage took up his pen at once with impatience: "You are now at the Institute, and I am still without news of that. . . . When I said that I am an Institute, it was to be understood that you will always be at the institute with me, whether at Fontainebleau or elsewhere." Calmed and somewhat satisfied , he wrote the next day to recall his own activities:

> The group meeting last night was rather lively; in fact, one of the best ever held. Rosemary [Lillard] was there, and a Dr. Ella Barker, author of works on Mysticism, etc. She nearly jumped off her chair with delight as some idea suddenly clarified a dark corner. . . . This Group, I think, will continue. They all hold certificates, but none, alas, can pay the full amount at once, so I must still carry on upon installments (in other words, I haven't yet been able to buy new clothes).

All alone on the 4th of July, while Central Park was being festooned and preparations for firework exhibits were being made, Orage lamented his loneliness:

> No letter yet from you at the Institute, and I've found the day hard to bear. Lucy Calhoun wrote a long letter to Mrs. R[umlee] speaking in the most enthusiastic terms of her impressions of the Institute. . . . This evening I was at Mrs. R's for dinner. She still intends to come to Fontainebleau this summer. . . . Mr. [Lawrence] Hare will be coming to Paris and to see G shortly, and Mrs. [Elizabeth Meredith Sage] Hare will probably follow him. Do you see visitors? Has Jane [Heap] arrived?

Two days later, Orage received the first letter Jessie wrote from the Institute. It contained a long list of complaints about general conditions, to which he replied with Gurdjieffian advice:

> I go with you in all your experiences at the institute. . . . It is difficult beyond belief at times, and chiefly because one has no belief. Yet I do not regret my entrance on this path. A thousand times no! And I absolutely believe that it is the only path from the infancy of adults. The theory is quite simple: to change effectively, one's old moulds of habits must be broken up. One can no more do this for oneself, or by one's own inclina-

tion, than one can *"Stop!"* oneself. It must be <u>done for us.</u>[15] *The institute is just a "Stop!" exercise for all one's former habits and preoccupations of oneself; and it enables us to see ourselves in a new light. The shock may be alarming or depressing, or it may be immediately stimulating. As you know, I didn't myself find it immediately but only long afterwards stimulating. At the same time, since I felt it was not killing me, but, on the contrary, I felt better and better, I hung on, and I have had my reward. I feel centuries older, years younger and infinitely stronger; and I do not despair of one day being real and really human.*[16]*. . . Even Mme Ouspensky will not succumb, I think, but you will see. You don't mention Miss Merston, Miss Gordon, etc. but they are good eggs too. I haven't the slightest idea what Lucy [Calhoun] meant by my "attacks," probably they were lame excuses for refusing engagements.*

. . . This complete stoppage of old habits and initiation of new ones has the effect of stripping one down to essence. And <u>then,</u> if the essence is really good and alive, one begins to grow <u>in oneself.</u>

Two days later, with another letter from Jessie in hand, he continued his *apologia pro scola Gurdjievensis:*

I've just been thinking that the Institute is like one of the "tirthas" described in the "Mahabharata," places where you forget what you had been and become something different. I wonder if you have remembered what I experienced there, the sense of being out of <u>time,</u> and almost <u>space</u> as well. I used to forget the day, the month, the year, my own age and everything. Also at times I forgot that I was in France or out of England. The isolation was so complete at times. Then the different occupations and roles one played! I remember once, after a week's continuous work at the Turkish bath, being almost persuaded that I was a workman. "Orage" was a dream-figure, but the workman was real. Such experiences of metamorphosis are very good, I think, and they are lucky who have them. But to make them complete it is necessary to think as little as possible about either the past or the future. One has to say: the past is a dream, the future is unknowable, only the present is real!

---

15. P. D. Ouspensky, *In Search of the Miraculous* (New York: Harcourtt Brace and World, 1949), pp. 351–352, quotes Gurdjieff's experiences with the exercise. For the author's own experience, see Taylor, *Shadows of Heaven*, p. 179.
16. In his autobiographical writings—*Collected Writings of Frank Lloyd Wright*, Bruce Brooks Pfeiffer, ed. (New York: Rizzoli International Publications, vol. 3, 1993), p. 205—Frank Lloyd Wright explains that "the Institute took unrhythmical neurotic human beings in all the social states, took them apart, and put them together again better correlated, happier, more alive and useful to themselves and others."

In a more banal vein, but one crucial to the real presence of his love for Jessie, after posting his letter, Orage went to see a specialist on divorce laws in other states. The various options, including different residence requirements, as well as variable grounds for divorce, made French law and Paris seem the most convenient course for Orage. The spanner in the works was the fact that Jean Walker seemed perfectly content with the status quo, and had not made the least concession to Orage's wishes conveyed through his London solicitor. On the other side of the ledger, Jessie wasn't interested in the divorce question for the moment. Her immediate concern was survival in her purgatorial position at the Institute. Complaint followed complaint about living conditions in her letters, and to these were added expressions of loneliness without him. Letter after letter from Orage assured her that he would join her later in the summer when the two of them would take a long vacation together somewhere in France. He asked how she could be lonely, since the Prieuré was filling up with acquaintances from New York:

> *Long before this, not only Stanley [Nott] but Jane [Heap] will have been there, and you have doubtless been in Paris.*
>
> *Yesterday I had lunch with Muriel Draper. She still raves about the Institute and G, but when it comes down to tacks she is not prepared to come and still less to send her boys; and possibly she is waiting for Jane's report. She is all over the shop on the ideas as well, and worse still, she thinks she has no need to hear more. However, I did persuade her that she was not a good advt. of the Inst. in her present chaos, and she has asked to see me more often.*
>
> *. . . The rest of the Group disperses after next week for the holidays. In the evening I saw Jean Toomer, and I must tell you something of him. He is a young litterateur who has also dabbled in psycho-analysis etc. He came to several of the demonstrations and was deeply impressed. Lately he has been out of NY trying out his last hope of a personal solution, [17] and now he is ready for Fontainebleau. As things stand, he will sail on the 19th and come straight to the Institute. I'm interested in him and I hope he will find his feet there.*

Financially, Orage's status looked more promising when he was offered $1000 per month until Christmas for a series of literary lectures. In

---

17. Toomer had left New York for Chicago where he was considering taking up residence. Rudolph Byrd, *Toomer's Years With Gurdjieff* (Athens: University of Georgia Press, 1989), p. 63 observes that Toomer's personal difficulty at this time was a sense of incomplete self-unification. He felt he needed to be more of a *man* in order to be more of a writer, and he didn't want himself stereotyped as a Negro.

sending the good news to Jessie, he seemed pleased, but reticent: "The offer was a little tempting for the reason that I could pay off G's debts, and leave America really free in mind." Predictably, he turned down the offer to leave himself free to join Jessie. At least he found some consolation in the fact that the certificate sales were increasing. So, he wrote confidently on 12 July, when, across the ocean, Gurdjieff was, to all appearances, fighting for his life due to his automobile accident in the early hours of Saturday, 5 July:[18]

> *Saturday is also the demonstration day at the Institute, and I am sure you will never like them. I hated them and so much else there. But it is a wonderful experience to have the strength to do what is disagreeable. You have felt the pleasure of "muscles" after heaving stones. There is a similar but more intense pleasure in being able to defy one's inclinations. I'm certain that the pleasure "I" shall get when "Orage" is my obedient servant will be godlike. As [Saint] Paul said to his Institute members: "I tell you ye shall be gods." . . . Saw Salzmann at tea. He's <u>possibly</u> getting a job to develop a theatre, but the plan is too colossal to be probably, a 4 million dollar theatre! If he should succeed, the inst. will be justified by his success! And all America will know of it.*
>
> *. . . I don't dream of your wanting only the Institute for the rest of your life! Lillie [Galumnian] or Olga [de Hartmann] leave when they have some positive wish outside. Besides, the Inst. is for a purpose, i.e. acquiring skill, and when you have enough for your purpose . . .*

There are inscriptions in the Study House, he consoled her, whose English translation reads: "Here one cultivates a correct attitude towards life."[19]

His next letter was replete with seemingly good news about himself. First, Mrs. R should show up at the Institute any day now, and would carry news of New York. Second, Orage was making plans to leave New York in mid-August, dreadfully hot at this time, for England, where he would attend to business in London for a few days before

---

18. Like so many events in Gurdjieff's life, there is considerable uncertainty over dates. In *Our Life with Gurdjieff* (London: Penguin, 1972), Thomas and Olga de Hartmann give Saturday 5 July at 5 P.M. as the time of the accident. Webb, *Harmonious Circle,* p. 289, has the same date and 4:30 as the hour. Olgivanna Lloyd Wright has the same date (Meryle Seacrest, *Frank Lloyd Wright* [New York: Knopf, 1992]). John Bennett, in *Gurdjieff: Making a New World* (London: Turnstone Books,1962), p. 160, and in other writings, is confident with the date of July 6th. In personal communications, James Moore, citing the "definitive" de Hartmann text, p. 268, tells me that Tuesday the 8th is almost certainly the correct date.
19. All the coded inscriptions in the Study House are translated in the appendix to *Views from the Real World.*

speeding to Paris to meet Jessie on the first of September. From there, in utter abandon and disregard for the Institute, they would indulge in the pleasures of a few days' vacation in the French countryside, perhaps even lease a cottage. He proposed, as an alternative, Bellagio, in northern Italy. Orage's brightened mood was also sustained by a new lecture tour offer for January through March 1925 that would bring him between four and five thousand dollars. He hadn't committed himself yet, he wrote, but with the vacation and the lecture tour in mind, he continued his report:

> *I'll write to G after your next letter saying how affairs stand and asking if I can return here about Xmas or early New Year. . . . [I'm] preparing to stay at the institute until Xmas, but there is so much to be done in America that I should like to return here as soon as possible. G may have other plans, but it appears to me that America is much the most promising field for his present propaganda, and that I am indispensable!*
>
> *I'm seeing Rosemary [Lillard, later married to Stanley Nott] on Wed, and she will decide my final arrangements. Salzmann, whom I saw yesterday, has this prospect of a very big job, designing a new theatre, but it sounds too good. He will stay here until Xmas.*

He was also writing letters to contacts in Philadelphia to prepare for a visit there to organize a group or two, but the lack of response made him realize that everyone must be on summer vacation. Suddenly, when he heard on 16 July of Gurdjieff's automobile accident, it appeared to Orage that all plans would have to be suspended. He wrote right away to Jessie for confirmation of Gurdjieff's condition:

> *This morning, early, two cables from Hartmann saying G had been injured in a motor accident. My wretched imagination went off in all directions on a mad gallop, but I reined it in, and am now quietly awaiting news. In such circumstances, if you think I should know something at once, do cable me.[20] Remember I am a living branch of the Institute, and nothing concerning it or G . . . can be told me soon enough. I am very anxious about G, and his accident disturbs me. It shows how very precarious is our perch upon the work, for if he went, I do not see how we could carry on.*
>
> *Jane's remark that you are playing "heroics" and your agreement with her are both wrong, I think. . . . Most of my London friends, all but one, prophesied that I should be out of the Institute in 6 months. But I am*

---

20. Cabling to or from the Institute was rarely a suitable option for Orage or Jessie, since any cable message would be a public, rather than private, communication. As far as I can ascertain, there was a single telephone at the Prieuré at that time, with the number 59 07. It would not have been impossible to cable from the post office in Avon, or perhaps from the Café Henry IV.

still there after 2 years, and more than ever. The creation of the Institute (for it is barely begun yet) is the work of a life. I know nothing better worth working for and fitting oneself to create. We shall never become completely human until we need to be, by trying to create a great human-ising institution. As we create the Institute we become human ourselves, and by no other means is this possible. To aim at happiness—what is it? Everybody so aims, and hits or misses according to chance. But such happiness as we are in any case capable of is a by-product of trying to create an institute, and it increases as the institute grows. I speak from experience, for as you know, I have been happier than I had dared to hope. This is a solid fact in my life, and you . . . will be able to confirm it more and more as time goes on. Jane has horse-sense enough, but horse-sense is not the whole truth of things. What's a few years given to this work, if the final result is enhanced capacity for life? Lots of people devote years to art, pleasure, business, travel—God knows what—and end up dead at middle-age. A few years of voluntary self-discipline now, and you will be secured in youth for life. You won't feel like leaving like so and so. I don't regard so and so as being in the Institute at all—so and so has no alternative! It is faute de mieux, and I should better believe their loyalty if it had been tried by the opportunity of getting out . . . All the same, I see Jane's influence strong upon you, and I hope you will try it. "Try all things, hold fast to that which is good."

. . . There are no wealthy people left in NY and the certificates just will not sell on the vague chances that classes will be opened in September. Nobody believes it. If G intended to create incredibility regarding Institute promises, he has succeeded perfectly.

His own plans, he continued, were to leave New York on 17 August, after disposing of Jessie's flat, and then take a vacation with Jessie in France before spending a few days of consultation with Gurdjieff. No matter what, they would be back together in New York in January, at the latest, "if Gurdjieff is so disposed," Orage added as an afterthought. He was still waiting to hear details about Gurdjieff's condition, however, and on 21 July, he received a telephone call from de Hartmann, who assured him that the panic generated by the news was unfounded. Hartmann complained about the stupidity of people at the Institute for spreading rumors, and wanted Orage to have a balanced account, above all to know that Gurdjieff did not plot his own accident, and that he was resting and recovering quickly. Although he was unconscious for a

---

21. Gurdjieff's "autobiographical" account of his accident in *Life Is Real: Only Then, When "I AM "* (New York: Dutton for Triangle Editions, 1975), pp. 9–93, has him bedridden for six months, and without memory for three, but those who were at the Prieuré, including Fritz Peters, Jessie and Jean Toomer, all remember him up and about in August.

time, he suffered neither concussion nor serious injuries, just shock.[21] With this information in mind, Orage wrote right away to Jessie to reassure her of his plans and, as far as Gurdjieff was concerned, to calm anxious spirits at the Institute, as well as to bolster her own:

> As for G's accident, it is absurd to suppose it self-directed.[22] What the devil next? Or that he uses any supernatural powers with which to direct Dr. S[tjernvall] etc. S[alzmann] and the rest are such "diplomats" that they would say anything, but don't you believe anything you cannot verify with your own senses. Isn't the atmosphere of mystery strange? . . . G's accident is not going to be fatal, I'm sure, but it is certainly unfortunate in the sense that everything will be indefinitely delayed. The hardest thing to bear is "waiting" for something to happen that never does, and this work is full of it. Sometimes I think G has an unfortunate destiny against which he fights as lesser people try to fight against circumstances. Nothing appears to go right for the Institute of its own accord, it makes no progress, and its pupils seem to stand still. Judged by results, in fact, it seems a failure, and yet, I suppose, if only it can keep its footing, it will one day become what G means it to be. It is like building a bridge in a torrent. Much is washed down before the foundation is really laid, but in the end there is something to build upon.
>
> I understand of course the irksomeness of the boarding-school rules, etc, and personally I used to keep or break them at my own discretion. The thing to do is to ask oneself why they are devised: perhaps just to challenge one's self-examination, perhaps for someone else, and so on. Anyhow, they did not trouble me. If I understood them, I followed them; if I didn't, I openly or secretly ignored or evaded them, as appeared politic.
>
> . . . I am writing to G today to put the situation here plainly before him. As arranged, I shall return [there] early in September, and you and I will have our blessed holiday. . . . But I have qualms about the work in America. In the first place, there are the debts of $2000 still unpaid, though due on G's own signature. . . . In the second place, there is the announcement that the classes will re-open in September, and I feel responsible for that. Thirdly, there are so many people just beginning to be interested whose interest will drop if not immediately sustained. I should like to see G personally whether, if I come over now, I can promise to return here at Xmas, or if I should stay here now and continuously until he sends someone else. . . . Well, we'll see. Probably I shall write and G will not reply, in which case I shall return as arranged. Maybe everything will be in the soup again owing to his accident. I shouldn't be

---

22. Nott, *Teachings,* p. 100, says that many years later Gurdjieff revealed that the accident was caused by his reaching out of the automobile window to pick an apple from a tree.

surprised if he asked you to go with him on a convalescent holiday, for instance, to the Alps or to Egypt. He will certainly need a long rest. In fact, I think his accident is the effect of long-continued over-strain, and he will see it as such and take a long vacation. I only wish I could raise the money here to ensure the work in his absence.

. . . Jane has written nothing. Lucy wrote that she is intensely interested. Jane has so many queer ideas about me that I wish she would commit herself to paper . . . but she won't!

As Gurdjieff lay recovering from his accident and planning the book he would shortly begin composing, the planet Mars moved in its orbit closer to Earth than it had been in over a hundred years. This cosmic event is just one of many curious coincidences that marked certain associations throughout his life, for Gurdjieff sets the long-term residence of the hero of his forthcoming book, Beelzebub, on the close red planet.

Appropriately, as emanations might be reaching Gurdjieff from outer space, Orage was writing Jessie about the law of accident:

The law of accident is not so very easy to understand, but it does not mean that such accidents—even fatal ones—cannot happen! All it means is that we suffer own individual "karma" but no collective karma. When a man is in partnership with others, he sinks or swims with them. His own exertions may be little or great, but his return will be the average of the collective business, that is, it does not depend solely upon himself, but on the "accident" of his associates. On the other hand, if he is in business on his own, anything may still happen to him, but it will not be "accident" (in this sense) but his own karma. G is always taking risks. They would not be risks if he were insured against the possibility of injury. But he does feel sure—probably from astronomy or some similar calculations—that he will not die before he has finished his task. And within that field he can not only take risks, but undertake to extract advantage from one result or another. How a thing turns out is all the same if one way such and such a course is possible, if another way, another course. "Who keeps one end in view makes all things serve."

Just got a cable from Hartmann saying "much better, soon at work." That's all right, and it confirms your feeling that G couldn't have been as bad as "they thought" or, certainly, he wouldn't have been moved so soon. But the Russians are children—presumably very near essence. Don't be too disgusted with them. . . . When many of our adults are stripped of their education etc. they will look very unfledged lambkins. . . . I'm hoping now that G is better, that he will advise me what I am to do. I hate leaving America with Gerard and Mrs. London unpaid. It will leave a bad impression of the institute and G. And I hate to leave without being able to assure people that either some instructor or I myself will come again very soon.

On Wednesday, 23 July, after driving out to the Connecticut countryside and attending a group meeting in Wilton, Orage wrote to Jessie: "My faith is in the <u>method</u>. Just as surely as I know that by walking towards California I <u>can</u> ultimately arrive there, so sure am I that by self-observation and self-identification one can arrive at self-consciousness. <u>Whether</u> we shall or not depends upon ourselves."

On Friday, 25 July, Orage struggled once again to console a Jessie distraught by the routine at the Institute:

> *Upon G's reply—if he replies—will depend my future arrangements. But I have plans for one alternative at least . . . Mrs. R is still away and I doubt if she will leave "Nature" to come to Fontainebleau this summer. Most of the rest are similarly under an inertia . . . It doesn't matter to me if you <u>don't</u> like the Institute life. I hated it too, and hate the idea of returning. All the same, from having made Orage do what he hated, I have found some strength to do what I wish, and doing what I like is presumably the reward of doing what O does <u>not</u> like.[23]*
>
> *. . . What is it that makes me so apprehensive and anxious? I wonder! Is it fear that you will not <u>see</u> the Institute as I see it? . . . To stay there at all is about enough in the way of exercises in patience, fortitude, etc. One of these days you may <u>will</u> to stay there of your own volition and choice, as <u>I</u>, for instance, now propose deliberately to return, <u>because</u> I am so damned displeased with "Orage." He lets me down on so many occasions and so badly that I could cheerfully strangle him, and the Institute and its trials are the best he deserves. . . . I don't like Orage, though I hope to make something of him in time. . . .The Institute is not home or life, but school.*
>
> *I'm awfully glad you have told Jane all about us, but I wonder what her thoughts really are. . . . She has a good deal of intelligence and I like her, so I'm glad she knows.*
>
> *. . . I think of you there in the Institute. God knows I pity you. . . . I feel about you as I used to about myself—under a curse in that fate has brought you there as it brought me there. But that is one side. That is what <u>one</u> of the three Orages says—the <u>feeling</u> Orage who in so many respects is still a spoiled infant. And just as every child thinks every feeling— happy or otherwise—will last forever (for feelings have no time-sense) so I can never <u>feel</u> that there will ever be an end to our Institute school-days. The <u>thinking</u> Orage, however, has more sense of fact and of time, and <u>he</u>*

---

23. For Orage, the triangle within the Enneagram represented the "I," and the circle the "it," corresponding to the Hindu and Buddhist conceptions of a central and essential "I" and a peripheral "it." Gurdjieff's insistent lesson is: "Like what it does not like." St. Augustine taught that the self is an abyss.

> assures me that a few years of the institute is not the whole of my life, and that the very best investment of a few youthful years may be just the voluntary suffering which the Institute invites. I unfortunately did not go to the Institute in my youth, but the investment of a single year there has yielded me a handsome profit in renewed health, in courage, in self-confidence, and in the capacity and the astonishing good fortune to fall so divinely in love. . . . I should never have known what love is if I had not sloughed off several skins of Orage in the Institute. . . . I swear on my faith . . . that one day and in this very life, you will thank God for your voluntary sacrifice.

For Orage, the conscious love-motive is manifested in the lover's wish that the beloved should arrive at his or her own native perfection, regardless of the consequences to the other. Conscious love exhibits the lover's ability to take hold and let go.[24]

Meanwhile, Orage was having little success with the sale of certificates. In fact, he had sold, altogether, only twelve, and since none of these were fully paid for, he hadn't enough money on hand to pay for the printing and postal costs. He borrowed from friends for that, but he still felt responsible for the $2000 dollars owed Gurdjieff by his New York group in signed pledges, for the Institute had already gone further in debt on the promise of those funds. Nonetheless, with advances for articles yet to write, Orage had saved enough for his voyage to Europe in August, and had booked passage on the 20th. One wonders how he was able to keep roller coasting from debt to bare sustenance for so long. Living in Jessie's flat, at least, kept a roof over his head. He had refused to ask for subscriptions to fall classes, however, because he had no intention of being in New York again until the end of the year. With this in mind, he wrote Jessie: "I've written G again today appealing for assurance regarding the re-opening of classes. I hate to leave the people here either without assurance or with assurances I don't believe myself. It doesn't seem fair, and it certainly reflects badly on the Institute—which may be G's intention. I confess I don't understand the idea. We shall see if he will cable or write."

On Tuesday, 29 July, after bringing Jessie up to date on gossip concerning members of the New York group who were still asking whether they could go to the Institute for the rest of the summer, Orage wrote about terrifying visions he had seen, in a waking state, of an unlived past. The phantasms were so intense that they caused him physical

---

24. Cited by Margaret C. Anderson, *The Strange Necessities* (New York: Horizon, 1970), p. 131.

discomfort.[25] Then, as if to shake himself loose from his morbid reflections, he commented on Jessie's news from the Institute:

> *I'm interested in <u>Jane's</u> attitude. She appears to be making a kind of investigation into the Institute—preparatory, presumably, to entering or not, and is collecting evidence, drawing conclusions, and using all her faculties and commonsense. Well, it is a commonsense procedure, but in my opinion, not of much value. The <u>only</u> value of the institute is for self-observation and self-experiment <u>under supervision.</u> No amount of objective observation and acute comments on others, etc is of the slightest use. <u>Any</u> new condition would provide such material, a boat of passengers, a Cook's tour, a big hotel . . . .The only unique feature of the Institute is the obligation to observe oneself and try experiments in self-direction. I say obligation not because one is <u>obliged</u>, but because, otherwise, one is not <u>in</u> the Institute but only living there. And I believe G would let me live there indefinitely, but always in the hope that sooner or later one would wake up and treat the rest as in a dream, and begin to observe oneself, and try stunts of self-management. I like Jane very much. I fell for her at our first meeting at Muriel Draper's. She will go along all right. But I <u>do</u> think she over-values her gift of commonsense. No, I don't mean over-values it: it cannot be over-valued, but I do mean that without self-observation and stunts it will not carry one very far.*

Out of keeping with his normally brief valedictions, Orage closed with a rare display of epistolary affection: "My darling, dearest, beloved Jessie. I am still speechless with love of you. You are in the secretest place in my heart, and nobody—perhaps not even you—will ever know how blood of my blood, heart of my heart, you are. I think of you as of my life. Let me not fear death."

Orage continued to suffer, however, from Jessie's expressions of discontent and of outright anger at the way her life was proceeding at the Institute. Once more, he put pen to paper to persuade to her adopt a more positive attitude toward herself there. If she could not do that, she should take her courage in her hands and just leave. At worst, she could announce that she needed a holiday, but anything would be better than to remain there chained to negative thoughts:

> *Naturally you will associate your experience there with me, and conclude that I am a brute or insane, and no wonder! I counted on G's invitation as his intuition that you would find in the institute what you saw in the*

---

25. Henry James' "The House on Jolly Corner," tells the story of a man who returns to a place in New York City he had left years before, and is pursued by the ghost of what he would have been had he stayed.

dances. I would never have let you go but for that and your attitude
towards him. But it seems that events and accidents have turned out oth-
erwise, and you now feel the place a prison to which you have been sen-
tenced for a term to prove your love for me!

He wrote again soon after to urge her to leave if she must, but not to hate
him for having insisted she go there! He tried to lift her spirits again
with news that friends of theirs from New York were soon to arrive,
including Gorham and Elizabeth Delza Munson. Then he asked: "How
is Toomer doing? I hope you will like him despite the touch of colour.[26]
He appears to me to be very sincere—and desperate, but perhaps his
desperation is not deep. It may find an easy solace. I don't know."

The length of time surface mail took to be carried between New
York and Fontainebleau meant that Orage was responding to letters
written ten days earlier by Jessie, who was responding to letters he had
written some ten days before that. All in all, an interval of some three
weeks between a message and its reply was usual. After reading another saddening letter from Jessie, he wrote:

Suppose the Institute is a sort of mixed prison-school-hospital, etc., there
is no reason why, because we choose to go there, we should remain
longer at a time than one feels necessary. . . .The whole incident in regard
to Gabo is frightfully interesting to me, naturally.[27] I am sure you did not
flirt in the ordinary sense, but you should realise that a "frightfully seri-
ous" talk in the woods at night, under "forbidden" circumstances, is the
very atmosphere of which romance is made.

Though Jessie was more apt to express her jealousy over the many manifestations of affection proffered Orage in New York, Orage let the
green monster creep beneath his skin more than once after Jessie had
written about her talks with other men. On this occasion, Orage leapt to
the conclusion that Gabo had fallen in love with Jessie. Then, changing
his tactics altogether, with her complaints about life at the Prieuré
plaguing him, he suggested that Jessie assume some occupational role
on Gurdjieff's behalf. She would not only ingratiate herself with him,
but would develop a direct and personal interest in the future of the

---

26. On the complexities of "color" in Jean Toomer's life, see his own *A Fiction and Some Facts*
[Doylestown: privately published, n.d. (1938?)], and Cynthia Earle Kerman and Richard
Eldridge, *The Many Lives of Jean Toomer* (Baton Rouge: Louisiana State University Press,
1987).
27. A gadfly Russian friend to the end of Gurdjieff's life, Gabo's surname seems not to have
been known by anyone. In *Daddy Gurdjieff,* Nikolai de Stjernvall describes with humor his
bizarre relationship to Gurdjieff (Genève: Georg, 1977), p. 87. When I knew him in 1949, he
acted as Gurdjieff's *starost,* overseer or personal supervisor.

Institute. Whatever Gurdjieff's plans might be, he prodded, they should include her. As for himself, he looked forward now to working together with her in the gardens at the Institute.

Orage had not yet received, however, any further report on Gurdjieff's condition. By this time, Gurdjieff had made his first post-trauma appearance to his pupils on the lawn in front of the Prieuré, and declared that the Institute was closed. Orage had heard nothing of this, and was still advising potential visitors. He therefore wrote Jessie, on Wednesday, 6 August to express his concern: "No word from G though I begged Mme H to cable. I wonder how he is, and how soon he will be well, and whether he is permanently hurt. So much for me depends upon him that I cannot feel clearly in the absence of reliable and current news of him. And as for the Sept. classes here . . . I'm just baffled by the seeming gratuitousness of the lies."

Orage had all the more to complain of from his own point of view. At his request, Jane Heap had consulted a lawyer in Paris about French divorce laws, and discovered that they had been recently changed, and now required long-term residence or French nationality. Even then, a contested divorce could drag out for a long period and incur huge notary-public fees. Orage was resolved, therefore, to try once again in England, though he knew a divorce in England would require Jean Walker's agreement. All the more frustrated was Orage when he received a long letter from Olga de Hartmann that contained little but domestic news and comments about the Prieuré. She reported that Gurdjieff had not received, or had not read, Orage's letter with its explicit questions, so he remained completely in the fog regarding Gurdjieff's intentions for the continuation of work in the United States. "Such things always happen in Institute affairs, and patience becomes compulsory," he lamented in conclusion.

He wrote to Jessie the next day, to the effect that they may as well make plans independent of the Institute. Why not go to California, where he had been offered a lecture series at the end of the year? They could spend Christmas there together before returning to New York. He added that he was pleased with the organization of the New York group, adding: "I'm meeting Rosemary for lunch today and to arrange for her to 'take over' the Institute archives." That evening, at dinner with Waldo Frank and Gorham Munson, Munson announced his decision to join Jean Toomer at the Institute as soon as possible. Frank was hostile to the idea, and made some disparaging remarks about Gudjieff. Orage took up the defense for both Munson and Gurdjieff and wrote to Jessie the next morning: "I think I've given W. F. something to think about, but of course my chief concern was to justify Munson's decision to come to

F[ontainebleau]. After Toomer, Munson was a little nervous of Frank's opinion, Frank being much the dominant, but I don't think he feels nervous any longer."

Without clear directions from Gurdjieff, Orage continued to look at possibilities other than a lecture tour in California. From publishers in New York, with whom he had talked about a tentative career in the United States, he received proposals for establishing an American *New Age*. "I'm in love with America!" he exclaimed. No matter what directions might come from France, Orage, from the very beginning of his mission in New York saw no necessary conflict of interests between his work for Gurdjieff and the continuation of his own teaching and writing. Indeed, he had to make money to live on, and most of the money he did earn with lectures and essays was marked for the Institute. At the same time, he had ideas about the expansion of his own teaching along psychological lines he had devised before going to Gurdjieff. He was in demand as a teacher of writing as well, and he proposed to Jessie that they might gather enough interesting people together and "build an Academy of real people."

On 11 August, he wrote Jessie that his work for the Institute seemed to have come to a dead end for the time being. No one was interested in buying certificates unless classes were guaranteed for September, but he could not do that, since he still planned to be with Jessie at the Prieuré. "I've just written Miss Merston asking her to save for me the far garden," he wrote. "G will have to offer me a good thing to divert me from that."

How is everything going with everybody? Lucy has given up writing to me. I haven't heard from Toomer, and I don't know how G is within the last fortnight. It's good for self-observation. . . . I wish Jane [Heap] had written to me. I think she might have once at least. She's such a devil to think behind her words. What is she making of it all? . . . No news, of course, from G, though he must long ago have got my list of questions. . . . The programme remains as arranged [for my trip].

Orage was still planning to spend two or three days in England, not only to see his solicitor, but to visit his two sisters whom he hadn't seen in years. Waldo Frank was pleased to take over the lease on Jessie's flat at 150 East 54th Street, so that, when they returned, they'd have to find new living quarters. Vexed by the lack of any news from Gurdjieff, Orage wrote Jessie on 14 August to say:

In six days I shall be sailing and not all the cables from G will stop me. . . . Mrs. R. is still in the country, but she talks of coming to F[ontainebleau] before October. If G should take a holiday, I shall have *to cable her not to make the journey for nothing. I don't understand in the least what is happening <u>really</u> in the institute. Lucy C[alhoun] never says a word about you. . . . By the way, shall I not be embarrassed by Metz's jealousy of me!!! Observations of others are not a scrap of good, really. They are natural and inevitable, but they are <u>not</u> this game. . . . Except for the prospect of work in the garden, I'm <u>not</u> crazy to return to the Institute. In fact, unless G has some real attraction to offer, we won't stay there long. . . . We shall soon learn the facts. I must write G exactly when I shall arrive.*

Finally, late the next day, Orage received a cablegram from Gurdjieff that read: "May come September but necessary to return October with others . . ." The news was welcome, but the phrase "return October with others" made Orage wonder if Gurdjieff intended either to send a troupe to New York or to send back all the American pupils. A letter from Stanley Nott arrived the same day that gave Orage all the more reason to wonder. Nott, who had met Jessie in New York in late 1923, wrote that she had changed since arriving at the Prieuré, and left his opinion at that. Poor Orage had no idea in what sense she had changed in Nott's eyes. Putting aside his worries, he wrote to Jessie, saying he would cable from Paris as soon as he arrived, and asked:

*Is my room ready? And did Pindar leave my trunk of working clothes in a safe place? Miss Merston should know . . . 'cos I still have a fancy for a spell of manual work. . . . It may be at Metz's pace. . . . The whole truth, during our school days in the Institute . . . is that you should do what you please <u>or</u> what does not please—whichever should be the hardest.
. . . Really I care only for two things now: the institute and J.*

Three days before he sailed, he wrote again:

*I feel aware of the significance of the institute as a constructive goal, in pursuit of which, as of the Kingdom of Heaven, all other things will be added. . . . Did I tell you I had a letter from Mme H.? . . . She said I could stay in America if I liked or return to Europe for a few weeks, and I was to please myself. That was her view, but G's telegram is more precise. But I shall be glad to see G again, especially after his illness. If only I had some money to bring him! That <u>would</u> give me joy.
I've told <u>nobody</u> here that I may be returning in October. I've said that classes would be resumed, but <u>not</u> that I should be returning. I've still to make sure what the idea is, and what you and G propose, and I'm not committing myself before I see <u>you</u>. I'm certainly an "Institute-man," but I'm feeling (today!) a more free agent as to means than I've felt before.*

The next day, Orage heard through the New York grapevine that Gurdjieff had announced the closing of the Institute. The news did not seem to surprise him, as he indicated in his next letter to Jessie:

> *I'm so glad you kept your sense of humour and feet during the recent manoeuvre. G's motive is a little obscure, but, in general, when he wants to get rid of one or two people he usually makes a sweep or, at least, the gesture of a sweep. He cannot "liquidate," I think, and really has no intention of doing so. He may be fed up with the personnel of the Institute temporarily, but as you rightly say, he cannot give up his life's work at the very moment that he has actually paid for the estate of the parent school. I see no reason for returning sooner than we arranged. Mme H has my letter by this time saying that I should be back [there] on Sept 7 after some days in London, and G will not expect me before then. Nor do I see at present any reason for changing my plan of returning to America early in October. My impression is that, in the absence of London pupils as recruits for F[ontainebleau], F must depend on America, and as they cannot be recruited until I return there, the institute at F will be in the meantime rather dull. His speech was, in fact, a notice that nothing would be doing in F for some months, and hence the students might leave if they liked. But it will certainly remain in being and readiness for the American contingent that we should send over next Spring. That's my impression at present, but you will know more by Sunday.*

Orage sailed on the Mauretania on 20 August, arriving on the 27th in Cherbourg. The next day, he met Jessie and Jean Toomer in Fontainebleau. Toomer had left New York on 17 July, the day after Orage had received a telegram from Thomas de Hartmann announcing Gurdjieff's accident on 8 July, but Orage had thought it inappropriate to tell Toomer at this stage in the latter's plans. When Toomer arrived at the Prieuré, he found himself barely noticed by the population, and he wandered about the grounds for a month without any tasks to perform or instruction to follow. He was befriended finally by Bernard Metz, Gurdjieff's unofficial valet, and took part in the daily meals and observed the work going on, but had no assignment himself. After Orage arrived, Toomer felt more useful, and he and Orage planned a mutual collaboration for group work in the fall. Gurdjieff called Orage to him right away and the two spent long periods together, drinking, laughing, and discussing Orage's continuing mission in New York. A month later, he and Jessie sailed back to New York.

Chapter Five

1924–1926

THE BOOK OF LIFE

Snatch the torch before it is cold
　　　　　　—Orage[1]

Arrive at the truth through the painstaking
reconstruction of a false text.
　　　　　　—Umberto Eco[2]

I am Beelzebub traveling the solar system, telling my
grandson the history of all the countries we pass. We begin
with Atlantis and end with a picture of the America of the
future.

　　　　　　—Gurdjieff[3]

While Jessie went straight from New York to Albany after their arrival in late October 1924, Orage moved into her new flat on East 56th Street, where he lost no time in setting up his lectures and group meetings. On 27 October, he sent out 300 postcards advertising his first lecture for the evening of 2 November at the Lenox Theater, East 78th Street. He planned to speak on "The Past, Present and Future of the Gurdjieff Institute." He got in touch with Toomer who, despite his disappointment in not having exchanged a word with Gurdjieff during the summer, was eager to teach the Gurdjieff "system" that he had learned second-hand through Orage the spring before. Orage had him start a group in Harlem, where his clientele included Dorothy Peterson, Aaron Douglas, Nella Larsen, Wallace Thurman, Melvin B. Tolson, and Langston Hughes,

---

1. "Religion in America," *New Republic,* Dec 31, 1924, p. 142.
2. Umberto Eco, *Foucault's Pendulum,* Rodney Needham, trans. (Chicago: University of Chicago Press, 1963), p. 383.
3. Gurdjieff to Isabel Rose, *New York Herald Tribune,* 28 January 1931, p. 15.

who remembered Toomer as "this handsome olive-skinned bearer of Gurdjieff's message to upper Manhattan."[4] Hughes brought Zora Neale Hurston to a meeting at which Orage was present, but the Gurdjieff teaching was not enough to her taste to make her a convert, though she was very much impressed by Toomer's artistry as a teacher, as she was with his literary artistry.

Toomer put behind him his disappointment that the New York Yankees were, uncharacteristically, losing the American League pennant to the Washington Senators, and applied himself to his task with extraordinary energy. Back from Albany, where she and her brother were engaged in a discussion of their father's inheritance, which was in probate, Jessie resumed her old job at the Sunwise Turn, and each evening, at Orage's suggestion, she made entries of her activities in a diary. Once a week, she attended Orage's meetings, usually serving at the door as cashier. Jessmin Howarth—who had worked on the sacred dances with Gurdjieff in Paris—gave birth in September to a daughter she called Dushka, "darling" (the affectionate Russian epithet Gurdjieff had used for her). She made herself available to help Orage and Toomer with their "movements" classes whenever she was in New York.

After Gurdjieff fled St. Petersburg and Moscow in 1917, he made the sacred dances and movements an integral part of, if not the core of, his systematic instruction.[5] Fortunately, in 1919, when he founded his Institute for the Harmonious Development of Man, he had on hand to assist him a number of experienced dancing instructors, such as the Montenegran Olgivanna [Olga Ivanova] Lazovich Hintzenberg and Jeanne [Allemand] de Salzmann, who had studied with Jacques-Dalcroze in Switzerland. Both had been retrained by Gurdjieff during his exile in Tblisi and Constantinople. In Paris, in July 1922, after he had rented the Jacques-Dalcroze school studio, he met and engaged Jessmin Howarth, who was, at the time, a dancing instructor at the Paris Opera. When work shifted to the Prieuré in October, the stop exercise, the "movements" and the sacred dances were the central physical exercises in the work.[6] Orage had spent over a year in the movement

4. Langston Hughes, in *The Big Sea: An Autobiography* (New York: Hill and Wang, 1963), p. 241.
5. In Beelzebub's *Tales to His Grandson* published in *All and Everything* (London: Routledge & Kegan Paul, 1950), p. 51. The sacred dances are mentioned as a "Legominism"—or written codes—surviving into modern times. In *Meetings with Remarkable Men*, A. R. Orage, trans. (London: Penguin, 1963), p. 163, Gurdjieff says that he discovered at the Sarmoung monastery dances that serve to record historical events.
6. For a concise description of the movements, see Pauline Dampierre, "Les mouvements" in *Panafieu*, pp.129–134.

exercises, but Toomer had no more than seen exhibitions put on by Gurdjieff's entourage in the winter and spring of 1924. Orage, therefore, invited him to attend thrice-weekly classes along with his own pupils, and reminded him that Gurdjieff used to say, "one must listen to learn to listen."[7] On one occasion, in a class directed by Rosemary Lillard (later married to Stanley Nott), Toomer made a mistake in the movement exercises, and Rosemary so severely chastised him that Orage had to intervene to make peace.[8] He frequently attended Toomer's group meetings in Harlem as an observer, but was careful not to intervene.

Orage admired Toomer's intellect and command of the Gurdjieff material, and the two soon became trusted friends, though Orage remarked to Jessie that he sometimes found Toomer remote and detached. The Broadway actress Rita Romilly, also an excellent dancer, was a faithful pupil of Orage's by this time, and soon became a friend. The photographer Alfred Steiglitz was exhibiting his photography in New York that winter, and was so impressed by Orage's lectures that he attended with his wife, Georgia O'Keeffe. As the year drew to a close, despite Gurdjieff's accident and pronouncement that the Institute was closed, the work was proceeding at a good pace in New York. With Gurdjieff's encouragement, Orage was screening pupils to find those he felt confident could profit from a stay at the Institute in the summer of 1925.

In November, Orage had a large group before him to address. It grew over time to include the short-story writer Israel Solon, the literary critic Van Wyck Brooks, businessmen Stanley Speidelberg and Sherman Manchester, detective-novel writer and psychologist C. Daly King, music reviewer Muriel Draper, actor Edwin Wolfe, architects Claude Bragdon and Hugh Ferris, five-and-dime heiress Blanche Rossette Grant, writer T. S. Matthews and his sister Peggy (son and daughter of the Bishop of New Jersey), writer Lawrence S. Hare and his art-patron wife Betty Meredith Sage, poets Melville Cane and Edna Kenton, painter Boardman Robinson, Claire Mann, writer-publisher C. Stanley Nott, writers Waldo Frank, Carl Bechhofer Roberts, Gorham Munson, and Scuyler Jackson, editor of *Modern School* Carl Zigrosser, editor of *The New Republic* Herbert Croly, literary editor of the *New York World* John Cosgrove O'Hara, concert pianists Carol Robinson and Rosemary Lillard, Doctor Louis Berman (the instigator of Gurdjieff's "The Material Question" at the conclusion of *Meetings with Remarkable Men*), Helen Westley of the Theater Guild, the historical

---

7. Toomer papers, Beineke Library, Yale University, Box 6, Folder 205.
8. Jessie's diary entry for 19 December.

novelist Mary Johnston, mathematician and short-story writer John Riordan, editor of *The Little Review* Jane Heap, and, of course, the author of *Cane,* Jean Toomer. These were joined by occasional visitors, including novelist Zona Gale, poet Hart Crane,[9] editor of the *Double-Dealer* John McLure, poetess Mavis McIntosh, and, most significantly, patroness of the arts Mabel Dodge Luhan. Over the next few years, regulars included the fashion editor and lovelorn columnist Louise Michel,[10] the painter and writer Walter Inglis Anderson, impresario Lincoln Kirstein, and Swiss consul in New York Robert Schwartzenbach and his wife Marguerite. Katie Powys dragged her brother Llewelyn to hear Orage, and before long, John Cowper Powys, who had regretted Orage's quitting *The New Age,* became interested in Orage's new ideas. Before the end of the year, as many as two hundred people had joined his groups, the fee for which was ten dollars per month. Besides these, there were any number of guests, curious to see and hear Orage. Zona Gale's protegee, the novelist Margery Latimer—later married to Jean Toomer—attended at least one meeting with Kenneth Fearing that winter. The main group met that fall in Jane Heap's and Margaret Anderson's apartment at 24 East 11th Street.

The adulation Orage received caused one of his close English friends, the sculptor Jacob Epstein, to express consternation. He lamented that, when Orage "went to America as a fisher of men, as it were—and also women—in all cases, wealthy men and women for [Gurdjieff's] establishment . . . I noticed there, around Orage, cranks of all sorts."[11] Another friend and former associate at *The New Age,* Edwin Muir, echoed Epstein's criticism of the company Orage kept, saying, in a letter to Van Wyck Brooks in January 1924, that "I have never been able to sympathise very much with the wild goose chase he periodically goes away upon. . . . Orage is really too big a man to be drawn into a circle of cranks like that."[12]

---

9. In a letter to his family dated November 9th, 1924, Crane says that he attended a lecture of Orage's with Jean Toomer, and was stimulated by the conversation following *(Letters of Hart Crane and His Family,* Thomas S. W. Lewis, ed. [New York: Columbia University Press, 1974]).
10. Louise Michel married William J. Welch in 1941, and published her memoirs of Orage with Gurdjieff under her married name. Born in 1905, she was twenty-two when she joined Orage's group in 1927. After studying at Alfred University, she wrote for the *Rochester Democrat* and then the *New York American.*
11. Jacob Epstein, *An Autobiography* (London: Halton Press, 1955), p. 62.
12. *Selected Letters,* P. H. Butter, ed. (London: Hogarth Press, 1974), pp. 31–32.

Orage's influence touched not only buyers in the mystical fish shop. A professor of economics at Columbia University and acquaintance of Herbert Croly of *The New Republic*, Alvin Johnson, was lecturing on labor exploitation and, having read *The New Age*, attended at least one lecture to see Orage and hear him discuss economic theory.[13] When Munson met Orage for lunch one day in November to ask if he could join his group, he admitted that he had never had a "revelation." "You are lucky," Orage replied, "such experiences are pathological: Peeping-Tom glimpses of the universe through a smutted window. The first thing to do is clean the window pane."[14] The first lecture Munson attended that fall concerned philosophical and moral reality. Orage argued that contemporary psychology treats only *actual* reality, not the *potential*, and the real potential for men is "that they may become men"[15] As Orage explained, personality is actual, but essence is a potential that shapes the actual.

Daly King, after hearing Orage for the first time, was deeply impressed by the "utter *rationality* of what I heard."[16] Another of Orage's early pupils, the writer Waldo Frank, with tongue in cheek, expressed wonder at Orage's hypnotic power over his audiences:

Here were true intellectuals who despise Greenwich Village. Here were socially elect who looked down on Park Avenue as a gilded slum. . . . And now if you looked still closer, you saw that they were listening with passionate concern to a man they call Orage . . . and that Orage was most intempestuously sitting in an upholstered armchair, smoking a cigarette and cavalierly smiling. . . . He knows all the scriptures from the Mahabharata to Hart Crane, and he is detached from them all. . . . He despises the world so well that he is at peace with it wholly. . . . His master Gurgieff [*sic*] is the Greek with a Polish wife and a Russian name who was once Prime Minister of Tibet, who had practiced all the professions from Highway robbery to selling carpets, who trains his neophytes in the Sacred Western Dances with a brutal

---

13. In the swing of postwar recovery, many artists seemed indifferent to, if not contemptuous of, economics. Edmund Wilson, for one, *The Twenties* (New York: Farrar Straus & Giroux, 1975), pp. 72–73, scorned Johnson as the "laughing economist." The opening chapter of F. Scott Fitzgerald's *The Great Gatsby* suggests a certain frivolity about the financial professions. Malcolm Cowley, *Exile's Return* (New York: Penguin, 1976), p. 61, says: "When Orage was in New York he gained a great many converts chiefly among older members of the Greenwich Village set."
14. Cited by Munson *American People* (New York: Creative Age Press, 1945), p. 211.
15. Cited by Munson *Aladdin's Lamp*, p. 259.
16. C. Daly King, *The Oragean Version* (New York: privately published, 1951), p. 4.

perfection that makes Diaghileff a tyro and who—according to several men whom the world call great—is the greatest man in the world.[17]

Orage had said to his audiences in New York that he no longer cared to write since he started study with Gurdjieff, but that he had gotten a glimpse of what objective writing would be. Though it was assumed back in England that he had taken French leave from serious writing during his Gurdjieff years, Orage was in great demand as a writer in New York. What he wrote usually did much to serve the Gurdjieff cause, not only as a means of making money that would serve the Institute, but as propaganda for Gurdjieff's ideas.[18] In all, Orage published more widely in America than he had in England, where he had written almost exclusively for journals in which he had a personal stake. In the summer of 1924, Croly printed in *The New Republic* two articles of his on American literature.[19] That fall, Orage saw his "Talks with Katherine Mansfield" in print in *Century*.[20] On the same day Calvin Coolidge was elected president of the United States and Al Smith Governor of New York over Franklin Delano Roosevelt, Orage sent off an article, "Unedited Opinions: Religion in America," to *The New Republic*, where it was published on 31 December. In his essay, Orage spoke of a need in America for a divination of man, and of a duty to expunge from the American people their faith in the radical suggestion that "goodness will lead to godliness, humanity to divinity, reformation to transformation. And you hold this faith," he charged Americans, "because it is easy and pleasant . . . The alternative to this easy and sterile neighborliness," he continued, is "the development of relatively divine qualities and, particularly, of a relatively transcendent and divine state of consciousness." He concluded that, despite these conditions, America is fertile soil for such an effort, for "Europe is rapidly losing what America has never had. The only question is whether America can snatch the torch before it is cold."[21] In December, his essay "On Love," which he had written at the Prieuré, probably in the summer of 1923, appeared in The New Republic with the subtitled note: "Translated from the Tibetan."[22]

17. Waldo Frank, *Time Exposures* (New York: Boni and Liveright, 1926), pp. 151–155.
18. Wallace Martin, *Orage as Critic* (London: Routledge & Kegan Paul, 1974), lists Orage's New York writings.
19. "Literature in America," *New Republic*, 39 (6 Aug 1924), pp. 299–300; and "American Literature" (20 Aug. 1924), pp. 357–358, both under the rubric "Unedited Opinions."
20. *Century* 109 (Nov. 1924), pp. 36–40.
21. "Unedited Opinions of America," *The New Republic*, December, 1934.
22. 3 Dec. 1924, pp. 36–39, reprinted in *Essays of 1925*, Odel Shepard, ed. (Hartford, CT: Edwin Valentine Mitchell, 1926).

Two months later, he published an article in *The Atlantic Monthly*—"New Standards in Art and Literature"[23]—which anticipates Gurdjieff's attack on contemporary art in *Beelzebub's Tales*. Orage's argument was that the culture of the West had lost a conscious pursuit of "impossible aims." He insisted on the American artist's need to define aims of art that critics and the "theologians of art" ignore in their works, they who block quests to re-infuse art with the necessary impossible aims that have ceased to exist in the minds of artists. Contemporary art, he noted, reflects "a virtue of which the original possessor has lost the secret." To redefine aims for art, he offered, one can look to the new: to cubism and Joyceism. The surest way, however, is to travel back to Western culture's oldest racial ancestor, India, and its sacred literature. As an example, he cites the *Mahabharata*, which, like Western scripture, is literature in pursuit of an impossible aim. In short, Orage argued here what he had argued years earlier for social reform: a conscientious pursuit of lost values that could re-enforce a traditional harmony between the arts and man's mundane occupations. Retrieval of this lost harmony is what Orage was confident Gurdjieff was preaching as well. "Real Art is knowledge and not talent," Gurdjieff had told him.[24] Often Orage would remind his pupils that an inscription on the Study House wall read, in English translation, "Never try to create or observe art with feeling."[25]

1924 was a banner year for journals featuring cultural criticism. The first issue of Henry Louis Mencken's *American Mercury* appeared early in the year, and, in August, Mencken asked Orage if he would join him as a regular contributor. Orage replied that he would consider the offer. Meanwhile, to a new self-improvement magazine he sent several articles, the last of which extolled the harmonious relationship between intellectual and physical exercises. One unfortunate ramification of Orage's appearance in the popular press, Gorham Munson regretted—though he had commissioned the articles—was that Orage attracted the gullible and the enthusiasts, while the skeptics tended to stay away, not realizing that skepticism was the intellectual stance Orage urged his pupils to adopt. Orage was fond of recalling that an inscription in the Study House at the Prieuré read: "You cannot be too skeptical." To students' questioning what Orage had found in Gurdjieff's ideas, Orage

---

23. February, 1925, pp. 204–207.
24. Kenneth Walker, *A Study of Gurdjieff's Teaching*, cited in *Gurdjieff Home Page I*: 1, 1977, p. 3.
25. Manchester Papers, p. 31 on a talk given on March 29th, 1926.

replied: "I had found some of the ideas earlier. They were beads, and some of them pearls. But before I met Gurdjieff I had no string to hang them on. Gurdjieff gave me the string."[26]

1925: GOD'S WORD SPOKEN THROUGH ANGELS (Hebrews 2:1)

Throughout the winter, Orage met with his old group regularly, and spent many of his free evenings attending Toomer's group meetings in Harlem. Since Toomer lacked an affluent following, Orage found it necessary, occasionally, to lend him small amounts of money. Toomer was writing as well, but not earning very much from his publications, and he found it impossible to send more than token amounts of money to the Institute. Nonetheless, he insisted on keeping separate accounts with Gurdjieff, while Orage sent monthly amounts to the Prieuré through the treasurer of the New York group, who was now Gorham Munson. Soon Orage was addressing Toomer affectionately as "colleague," and Toomer was becoming more and more convinced of the "science" of Orage's program. In early January, after a particularly impressive Wednesday meeting of Orage's group, Jean sent him a note saying: "I would like to learn from you, to work with you."[27]

Gurdjieff had asked for assurances that money would continue to arrive from the United States to repay the debt on the purchase of the Prieuré and to provide for future construction. He was so confident of funds forthcoming for the maintenance of the Prieuré that he foresaw renovations to the grounds. Metz wrote enthusiastically to both Toomer and Orage of plans to construct a swimming pool. Orage was skeptical, while Toomer was more enthusiastic about the New York Yankees' new first baseman, Lou Gehrig, who played his first game for Toomer's favorite team on 31 May. Meanwhile, Orage was getting into print certain ideas he had nurtured since his early interest in psychological training. Throughout the year, his articles, "Fifteen Exercises in Practical Psychology," appeared in the magazine *Psychology*, the last of which was entitled "Life as Gymnastics."[28]

26. Louise Welch, *Orage with Gurdjieff in America* (London: Routledge & Kegan Paul, 1982), pp. 42–43. Orage is comparing Gurdjieff to Vishnu as he describes himself in the *Bhagavad-Gita*.
27. Toomer Collection, Box 6, Folder 205.
28. Later collected in *The Active Mind: Adventures in Awareness* (New York: Hermitage House, 1954).

The illustrator Rockwell Kent briefly joined Orage's group in early January. Jessie started attending the group regularly and tried applying self-observation to her daily life. On one occasion, she felt that this exercise helped her at the dentist's, but it did little to control her inclinations toward jealousy. She was furious when she dropped in on Orage unexpectedly in mid-January to find the actress Rita Romilly in his apartment.

At the end of January, she joined her brother, Harvey, in Albany to sue the estate of Emily Watson for the $6,000,000 left in her will to the "children of Harvey Lyman Watson." The probating of the will was complicated by the fact that their father had predeceased the legatee, and the last will of Emily failed to mention the names of the children. While awaiting a judicial decision, Jessie returned to New York and plunged back into her work at the bookshop, taking every opportunity to steer interested people—among whom were Michael Arlen, Sherwood Anderson, Alfred Kreymborg, and Zona Gale—toward Orage's talks. At the same time, Orage set out a curriculum of reading for her, including works of William James and John B. Watson, famous for his Behaviorism.

In mid-July, while the Scopes "Monkey Trial" was in course in Tennessee, the Hares moved to Santa Fe, where, with Orage's blessing, they soon started a modest group. On the 21st of the month, Scopes was found guilty of teaching contrary to the Bible and was fined $100, but the winner of the trial was, in effect, Clarence Darrow, Scopes' defense attorney, who made a laughing stock of William Jennings Bryant, attorney for the prosecution. By the end of July, Orage and Jessie decided to return to the Prieuré to report on the state of the work in New York. They sailed from New York on 22 August for Le Havre on the S.S. Muiukahda, and arrived in Boulogne on the 31st. They spent the night in Paris before arriving on the morning of 1 September at the Prieuré, where they were directed to return to Paris where Gurdjieff had been awaiting them. The Cosgroves, Jane Heap, Margaret Anderson, and Stanley Nott were in attendance at the Institute at the time, but Gurdjieff, despite this wealth of editorial talent at hand, was eager to discuss the book with Orage. On the morning of the 5th, Orage and Jessie began intensive work. Gurdjieff enjoyed putting both ill at ease with the reading of his chapter "America" on the evening of the 8th.

The next day, Margaret Naumberg, Waldo Frank's wife and Jean Toomer's mistress at the time, arrived. Three days later, Orage received a letter from his wife, Jean Walker, saying that he must come to her in person to negotiate the terms of divorce. Before Orage could make plans to do so, Gurdjieff took them on a trip to Geneva on the 13th. The trip was a complete folly. The automobile kept breaking down, and before reaching their goal, they turned back to Cluny to await repairs. They proceeded back to Paris in starts and stops. First, the gearbox stuck in first gear, then the springs broke, and each problem meant unwanted waits at garages. They did not get home until the 19th. On the 23rd, after Gurdjieff had given Orage the first work drafts of the bulk of his book with instructions to put it into publishable English, the Orages left in good spirits from the Institute. Jessie was particularly touched by the friendly sentiments of the entire population who saw them off.[29]

From Paris, they went to London, where they spent ten days awaiting passage to New York on the Mauretania, Orage's preferred steamship. They consulted with Mitrinovic and Augustus John, who took photos of Orage for a portrait, and on their last evening in London, they saw Paul Robeson in Eugene O'Neill's *Emperor Jones,* and talked with him backstage.[30] They sailed for New York on 3 October, arriving in almost Blue Ribbon time on the 8th. Jessie left five days later for Albany to attend hearings on her lawsuit. Orage wrote to her at her family home, from her flat at 19 East 56th Street to record his first encounter with "Beelzebub":

> *I've been going on with MS all day, and it is still some job. Nobody has any idea of the labour involved, but I've no doubt whatever that the result of it will be an enormous improvement on the aboriginal. It is highly possible that G will spit at it, but that doesn't trouble me. I have an infallible conscience about English if about nothing else, and nothing will persuade me that my final text is not better than the Hartmann-Metz abortion. At the same time, such is my attitude that having now made the revision to my greater or less satisfaction, what text, if any, G chooses to print will not concern me. I shall fight for mine, but I shall still play if I lose. There's much more to be done yet, but I'm steadily getting through with it. . . .*

---

29. Following Fritz Peters' account of Gurdjieff screaming in rage at Orage that summer, it has been assumed by Moore, *Anatomy of a Myth* (Boston: Element, 1991), and Patterson, *Struggle of the Magicians* (Fairfax, CA: Arete, 1995), that the reason was Gurdjieff's displeasure at the presence of Jessie Dwight in Orage's life. I can find no evidence of this in Orage documents I have seen. What is clear from all documents is the fact that Gurdjieff expressed a great deal of affection for Jessie, though he "insulted" her on occasion, just as he insulted almost everyone else as a psychological strategy. Only his brother, Dmitri, was immune from such outbreaks. Some time later, according to Louise Welch, *Orage*, p. 49, Orage confided to his New York group that Gurdjieff "regarded me as someone who had . . . come with him from another planet with a task to carry out. But, I had fallen in love with a native, and this interfered with his aim."

30. Both Robeson and O'Neill received death threats because a scene in *All God's Chillun* has a white woman kiss his hand.

*Miss [Rita] Romilly rang me up to say there was a studio for let for
evenings in Carnegie Hall, so I popped along to see it and the propri-
etress, a Miss Bentley who teaches dancing, is a Christian Scientist,
attended G's demonstration and has heard a great and favourable deal
of our groups . . . and to cut the story short, I've arranged to take it from
the first week in November the three nights of the week it is free,
Monday, Tuesday and Wednesday.*

Three days later, Orage began intensive work on the crude first draft of
an English translation of *Beelzebub's Tales*,[31] having agreed not only to
edit the work for English publication, but also to arrange the financing
of eventual publication through his New York group. Orage was on the
lookout for patrons and he found one in Blanche Grant, heir to the Grant
five-and-dime stores, who had a large apartment in midtown Manhattan
where she hosted many meetings for Orage's group. Another was Daly
King who had independent, but not lavish, means. Rita Romilly, actress
and teacher of acting, and Betty [Elizabeth Sage Meredith] Hare, who
divided her time between New York and Santa Fe, New Mexico, later
friend of Ezra Pound, were others. In general, most of Orage's New
York groups were willing and able to support the activities of the work,
and they pledged on behalf of the group sufficient money to subsidize
an early publication of *Beelzebub's Tales*.

Orage wrote Jessie: "Yesterday afternoon I had a long visit with
Mrs. Grant at her Waylin Hotel apartment, and we are to dine tomorrow
evening with some people who may be useful to her. . . . Am lunching
with Daly King tomorrow." Meanwhile, Betty Hare had invited Jessie
to stay with her in New Mexico, but there were problems in Albany

---

31. The de Hartmann account in *Our Life* (London: Penguin, 1972) suggests that Gurdjieff
began dictating the book from his sick bed in August. When Edith Taylor and Jane Heap visited him in late August, he told them he was in the process of writing a book. James Moore says
that Gurdjieff started dictating on December 16th at his apartment in Paris, 27, Bd Pereire; and
Gurdjieff himself, in *Life Is Real* (New York: Dutton for Triangle Editions, 1975), says that he
began on 1 January, 1925. The prevalent opinion on the complex process of putting Gurdjieff's
book into publishable form in English is that Gurdjieff dictated the early text in Armenian to
Mme. Chaverdiian who turned it into Russian. Gurdjieff reviewed the Russian text and then
passed it to Thomas de Hartmann, who, with the help of Bernard Metz, turned it into as literal
English as they could. Then Orage revised the "artless" English. He was assisted often by other
English speakers at the Prieuré who, in Orage's absence, would revise the Hartmann-Metz text.
These included Payson Loomis, Nick Putnam, and Edith Taylor. With Orage's text in hand,
Gurdjieff dictated changes that he discussed with Orage and others. It is no wonder that it took
almost eight years to produce the first "finished" text of *Beelzebub's Tales to his Grandson*.
Some of Orage's translation notes are extant among the Orage papers in Henley. Orage recognized that the curious title of the work—*Beelzebub* "Lord of Flies"—is not meant to allude to
the Hebrew insult—"Lord of the Privy"—but to the god of Canaan who was revered as a builder
and maintainer of health; that is, a "controller" of the deleterious effects of flies.

probating the will, and Jessie found herself obliged to stay until the settlement of the inheritance was agreeable to all parties. In New York, Orage was busy on the translation when he wasn't holding classes or cultivating patronage for the Institute. After an afternoon with King and Blanche Grant, he wrote Jessie: "The rest of the day till now I have been revising the MS. Two more chapters done, but what a labour! You are right about King; he has some money at any rate. And I have therefore invited him to attend the private group for the hearing of the book, the first meeting of which will take place at Croly's the first Monday in November." The next day, after meeting again with Blanche, he wrote Jessie:

> "I've arranged for a new group for an afternoon in her apartment at the Waylin. . . . Today I . . . shall just get on with the MS. Metz has committed several follies, damn him. I must write for them."

He stayed up until 2 a.m. Saturday morning working on the text, and the moment he got up the next morning, he went back to it. Fatigue was evident in the composition of his daily letter:

> "I have such changes of feeling about it, now despair of never ever getting it right, now irritation with Gurdjieff, now enthusiasm and so on. I want to finish it for the simple reason that I can't settle down until it is done."

Orage was seeing Daly King almost every day now, and King proposed to hold small groups meetings in his New York flat. Orage agreed, but he felt burdened by administering the logistics of his now scattered groups. He was attending many of Toomer's Harlem meetings as well, and he was so occupied with the translation revision that he even missed writing Jessie on occasion. On Wednesday the 22nd, Stanley Nott asked him to join him for tea and talk about his own plans to return to the Institute, and Blanche Grant called with an invitation for a weekend in the country. He excused himself from both offers, but agreed to a quick dinner, before rushing back to his apartment where he worked late into the night on the manuscript. Before going to bed, he wrote Jessie: "The typist has sent the earlier chapters and they read quite well. I've nearly finished my little lot now."

Meanwhile, things had gone badly for Jessie and her brother Harvey. They lost their suit to recover their inheritance, mostly due to the inadequate tactics of their lawyer, a retired friend of the family. They immediately filed an appeal, and were told that the appeal process risked taking considerable time and money. On 24 October, Jessie returned to New York, where she quickly found an apartment for Orage on East 55th Street, close to hers. The day before, Orage had had a long meeting with Daly that concluded with Orage's authorizing him to start a group at his home in Orange, New Jersey. Besides the responsibilities of his own group, with its movements classes, meetings with Toomer, and revising the translation, Orage was preoccupied with finding the time to earn enough to support himself. He scanned a number of offers for articles and reviews from his unofficial agent, Boyd, but left things hanging until Jessie should return from Albany where the will of her aunt was being contested again in court.

After a lunch with Toomer on the 29th, he decided to ask his own group to expand their structure beyond officers. "If I'm to carry on groups in NY I must have a committee to help me," he wrote Jessie that evening. After Jessie returned to New York, she joined Orage often in his frequent meetings with Jean Toomer, whose Harlem group seemed to be thriving, but was not bringing in much money. Toomer was a victim of his own success. So popular were his classes that many of his pupils were taking time off from their jobs to attend the after-movements classes and lectures, and so found themselves unable to pay their leader. Orage attended his classes frequently, and was satisfied with his teaching. Toomer was often at Orage's "movements" classes, directed by Jessmin Howarth whenever she was in New York. Toomer was happy with the quality of his pupils, but realized that few, if any, of them had the leisure and the means to spend a summer at the Institute. He suggested to Orage that he might either take over direction of one of Orage's mid-town groups, or go to Chicago to set up a group there.

In November, Orage and Toomer lunched twice with Mabel Dodge Luhan, who was attracted to both Orage and Toomer, and was thinking of making a contribution to the work. Mabel had some notoriety for the literary salon she had hosted in Paris before the war, and for her hospitality at her Italian Villa after that. Now she had taken a fancy to New Mexico. So she left France and her good friend Gertrude Stein,[32] and

---

32. *The Harmonious Circle: The Lives and Works of G. I. Gurdjieff, P. D. Ouspensky, and Their Followers* (London: Thames & Hudson, 1980), p. 338. Gertrude Stein heard much about Gurdjieff from Paris friends over the years. It is not recorded that she ever visited him, but Webb, p. 338, supposes she practiced some of his exercises.

Italy and her friend Natalie Barney, to build a house in Taos, where she married the Tiwa Pueblo Indian Tony Luhan. She also kept a house in Croton-on-Hudson and an apartment in New York City, and, when in town, she and Tony were faithful attendees of Orage's classes. T. S. Matthews, an early regular introduced to Orage by Schuyler Jackson, noted that Tony, who usually wrapped an Indian blanket over his shoulders, served as a "barometer" for the others: "If it was an interesting evening, he sat erect and watchful; if not, his head sagged and he slept, quietly and solidly as a weathered rock."[33] Claude Bragdon saw Tony and Orage in the same company as "primitive man and civilized man in dramatic juxtaposition."[34] From the other side of the Atlantic, in England, AE [George Russell] wrote Edward Boyd that he had been following Orage's American career, and remarked that "Orage is at his best preaching big ideas to a little clan."[35]

At lunch on 1 December, Mabel invited Orage and Toomer to visit her in Taos over the Christmas holidays, and Toomer, with Orage's encouragement, accepted. The plan was for Toomer first to spend a few days in Chicago to look over the terrain there, and then to go to Taos. Orage felt too committed to New York at the time, and Jessie still spent time in the Sunwise Turn. Good news came to Orage four days later when he received a cable from his solicitor in England announcing that Jean Walker had agreed to a divorce if Orage would pay all the alimony due, some $5,000. And so Orage and Jessie settled down among good friends and in good spirits for the holiday. On the last day of the year, Orage made a New Year's resolution to raise $20,000 for Gurdjieff.

1926: "THE BOOK IS AN EPIC DIALOGUE"[36]

It was no surprise to Orage when Toomer, having passed the holidays with Mabel Luhan in Taos, wrote, in early January 1926, to say that Mabel was making Taos available to Gurdjieff with a donation of $14,000 as incentive. She added for Toomer a personal gift (which she later considered a "loan") of $1,000 to seal the arrangement. From Chicago, Toomer sent a check for $3,000. Orage and Jessie assumed, at first, that this amount represented an "investment" in the Institute, so

---

33. *Name and Address* (New York: Simon and Schuster, 1960), p. 205.
34. *More Lives Than One* (New York: Knopf, 1938), p. 325.
35. March 15, 1926, *Letters From AE*, Alan Denson, ed. (London: Abelard Schuman, 1961), p. 171.
36. Orage to his pupils, February 10th, 1927 (Manchester Papers, p. 100).

Orage wrote back to Toomer to say that he would place $2,000 in the New York publication fund, and have the group treasurer hold $1,000 for Toomer's use whenever he wished. Orage made the happy calculation that, in all, the $950 he had collected in New York before the end of the year, the pledges from his pupils that he could collect before the coming summer, together with Mabel's donation, would allow Gurdjieff to count on a grand total of $20,000 for maintenance of the Institute. The New Year's resolution had already come to pass! Toomer was back in New York on 15 January and lunched with Jessie and Orage to share the details of his visit. Jessie was ecstatic, and Orage complimented his friend on his charm.

After speaking with Orage, Toomer wrote Gurdjieff the news, enclosing a check for $1000, a description of the Taos property, and an assessment of Mabel's strong character that was bound to discourage Gurdjieff. Indeed, Gurdjieff had Elizabeth Chaverdian write a letter to Mabel acknowledging the money, but turning down the offer of her Taos house on the grounds that it was unsuitable, and that he would be unable to liquidate the Prieuré. On Gurdjieff's behalf, Olga de Hartmann wrote a brief note to Mr. "Tunmer," saying Gurdjieff was aware of the offer, but too busy to write himself. She added that the remaining $14,000 should be reserved exclusively for Mr. Gurdjieff's needs, since he was in the process of liquidating the Institute.

When Orage became aware of these communications, he realized that Toomer had allowed financial misunderstandings to arise, since there was only $11,000 available for the Institute's needs. Further, he thought it incautious of Toomer to have written a largely negative appraisal of both the place and Mabel. Orage preferred caution and patience, concerned that Gurdjieff would take the money without accepting the use of Mabel's ranch that the money was meant to secure. An exact accounting to the satisfaction of everyone involved, including Gurdjieff, never came to light, and Toomer was to suffer the suspicion of others for a decade to come that he had mishandled Mabel's gift.[37] Meanwhile, Mabel, continuing her correspondence with Lawrence, wrote him about Toomer's talks about the Gurdjieff method. He replied testily: "I do believe in self-discipline. And I don't believe in self-control. . . . But the fact that your I is not your own makes necessary a

---

37. Mabel Luhan's biographer, Lois Palken Rudnick in, *Mabel Dodge Luhan: New Woman, New Worlds* (Albuquerque: University of New Mexico Press, 1984), p. 229, says: "By the end of 1926 Toomer began to feel differently about having a center in Taos, and for the next six years he worked to convince Gurdjieff to move to America." Then, p. 230, G "had not only misappropriated Mabel's money, but was drinking and philandering with women."

discipline more patient and flexible and long-lasting than any [of] Gurdjieff's."[38]

Meanwhile, Gurdjieff had written to Orage to say that he would not publish the first book until the other two were completed.[39] In the summer of 1925, Gurdjieff had outlined the contents of the second series, later known as *Meetings with Remarkable Men,* but he gave no indication to Orage of what the third series would consist. On 4 January, the chapter entitled "The Holy Planet Purgatory" arrived and Orage set to work. For the rest of January, Orage revised translations as they arrived and read each new chapter to his group as basis for discussion. On the 26th, Daly King read the description of the application of the Law of Seven to sound, light, and color to general admiration and approval.

Orage did not neglect his social life, though Jessie wished he would spend more time with her than with the "book." They entertained Elinor Wylie and Paul Robeson, fresh from his London stage success. Mabel Dodge Luhan hosted a birthday party for Jessie on 7 February at her home in Croton-on-Hudson whose highlight was Tony Luhan's singing and playing a drum. Brancusi attended an Orage meeting two weeks later. Later that winter, they watched Lacoste play against Richards and Borotra against Tilden in the Davis Cup tennis match between the United States and France. They explored New York together, visiting galleries and making acquaintances in the artistic world. On 1 March, visiting Jessie at work at the Sunrise Turn, Orage was introduced to Ilonka Karacz, a painter and illustrator who would soon be known widely for her *New Yorker* covers, and her needlework-artist sister, Mariska. Ilonka introduced Orage to her husband, Wim Nyland, and all three soon became regulars at Orage's group meetings, now held in Muriel Draper's spacious apartment at 24 East 40th Street.[40]

On 17 January, Orage began a series of talks on the book. He began:

---

38. 12 April, 1926, cited by David Ellis, David. *D. H. Lawrence: Dying Game 1922–1930* (Cambridge: Cambridge University Press, 1998), p. 297.

39. *Beelzebub's Tales to His Grandson* was announced by Gurdjieff as a work in three books, but was ultimately published in two. The First Series was originally titled *Beelzebub*. Just as the mystic way in Catholic theology consists of three steps—purgation, illumination and union—Gurdjieff set his writings into three series in *All and Everything* (London: Routledge & Kegan Paul, 1950), to 1) destroy the beliefs about everything, 2) present material for a new creation, and 3) assist the understanding of the real world.

40. Munson, *The Awakening Twenties,* p. 260, says that Orage attracted the *intelligentsia,* and lists some thirty-five people prominent in the art world—writers, architects, editors, illustrators, etc.—among the 75 to 100 who were members of Orage's main group. Beginners were assigned to other groups. After Gurdjieff's death, Wim [Willem] Nyland became a prominent teacher in the Gurdjieff work.

Gurdjieff proposes in the book to show the steps by which he has recovered his own reason. Experiences have made him different. His Beelzebub is understanding, just as his Christ is love, and there is wisdom in each. In referring to his own odyssey on the track of truth, Gurdjieff said "I would gladly spare any human being the fruitless efforts I have gone through." Hassein is that part of you that is open to the suggestions of another part of you not yet actualized. Tuluth [Hassein's father], Beelzebub's favorite son, is an emanation of Gurdjieff himself, and so I am Tuluth to you. Remember, Philosophy means not only love of wisdom, but wisdom of love.[41]

In February, Croly published, in *The New Republic,* Orage's article, "On Religion,"[42] a transparent tribute to Gurdjieff's book, though it mentions neither Gurdjieff nor *Beelzebub's Tales to His Grandson.* The essay comprises a criticism of the short-sightedness of modern science that, so far as the knowledge of the existence of an intelligent God, "is completely and indifferently ignorant." Orage argues, on the basis of discussions with Gurdjieff that later found form in the chapter entitled "The Holy Planet Purgatory," that, contrary to scientific opinion, "the Universe is an intelligent and therefore intelligible cosmos. . . . The highest aim of Man is to understand and cooperate with the intelligent laws that govern it."[43] To accomplish this, "a special way of life or technique is necessary, and this technique consists primarily in a method of 'divinizing,' that is to say, of raising to a higher consciousness Man's present state of being." The appropriate technique to generate this raising is self-observation, a new field and method of psychological research. But, he continues, there are difficulties in observing nature in oneself that influenced the dogmas of ancient religions: "They had tried to meet themselves, Nature and God, face to face!"[44]

Perhaps more significant was the short article published in the winter edition of *The Little Review.* The issue was devoted to the theater, and Orage's three-page contribution was titled "A Theatre for Us." In a Joseph Conrad sort of setting—a group of friends in a

---

41. 17 January, 1926 (Manchester Papers, p. 93).
42. Feb. 10, 1926.
43. Anthony Storr, *Feet of Clay: Saints, Sinners, and Madmen* (New York: The Free Press, 1996), p. 171, says that "it is indeed grandiose to create one's own cosmogony in total disregard of accepted scientific opinion. Both Gurdjieff and [Rudolf] Steiner did this. . . . They are narcissistic, isolated, and arrogant." The Old Testament would, then, come under this charge. But Gurdjieff did not "create his own cosmogony." First of all, he does not take credit for inventing the material that he says was received in the course of his wanderings. Secondly, Gurdjieff's prefatory instruction to his reader invites a figurative reading of his book.
44. "Unedited Opinions III: Religion in America," *New Republic,* 31 December 1924, pp. 141–142.

drawing-room discussion of the current stage convention of love triangles, and triangles of all dramatic shapes—Orage offers a vision of a
novel triangle for the theater. He suggests a three-storied structure
above the stage, each consisting of an open room containing a single
character who remains there throughout the play. The top story contains
the mind, the second emotion, and the lower instinct, or physical
appetite. On the stage itself is a single character who is resultant of the
conflicting advice given him by the three players on the platforms
above representing his own three voices.[45] He has no will of his own,
but his behavior is dictated by the relative strength of the three players
within himself. "I do not, of course, undertake to construct a play adapted to this method of presentation," Orage the character concludes, "but
as one whose interest is centered in human psychology, I do undertake
to see such a play attempted." As he finishes and looks about him, he
finds all his friends asleep but one, "and she had not listened to a word.
It is at her request that I repeat myself thus." What a vivid demonstration of Gurdjieffian teaching such a play would present![46]

On 29 March, Orage spoke to his group on negative emotions.
Negative emotions are waste energies, he said; and waste, he noted that
Ouspensky had argued appropriately, is sin. Hate wastes the forces of
the emotional center and propagates other waste emotions, while love
generates positive emotions. The emotional center must be coordinated
with the other centers. When the intellectual center is a function of the
emotional center (i.e., under its influence or control), thought is
expressed as rationalizing; and when the emotional center is a function
of the intellectual, thought is expressed as reason. "Sin is identification
with the mechanism," rather than with its controlling force. Machines
are tools that have their potential actualized by human control, but we
must avoid "mechanicalness" in our self. Orage emphasized the effort
of Nature to "puff and blow" in order that the human machine may be
made to work, adding that Gurdjieff emphasized the important function
plants and animals have in the economy of the earth.[47]

In a series of sketches of people important to the New York scene,
appearing under the name "Search-Light" that spring, Waldo Frank

---

45. Gurdjieff's conception of humans as three-brained beings has traditional Christian ante-
cedents. St. Augustine, in *De Trinitate XI*, describes man's mind as *memoria, intelligentia,* and
voluntas (will). In *Itinerarium mentis in Deum,* St. Bonaventura describes the mind composed
of apprehensio, or perception (sense), *oblectatio*, or meditation, and *diiudicio,* or upward con-
templation.
46. *The Little Review* (Winter 1926), pp. 30–32.
47. Kenneth Walker, *The Making of Man* (London: Routledge & Kegan Paul, 1963), p. 154.

described Orage's extraordinary appeal to his notable pupils: "Here were socially elect who looked down upon Park Avenue as a gilded slum . . . listening with passionate concern to a man they call Orage (pronounce it precisely like the French for *storm*). . . . He believes in literally nothing. *Nothing that is*, I mean. This is what makes him so detached."[48] What Orage did believe in was the power of the will to make change. He explained to his group that the universe was created out of the power of will, a doctrine that, he explained, was known as Voluntarism in the 14th century. In Latin, *voluntas* and *voluptas* are doublets, and the relation between will and sexual generation is essential. Gurdjieff had told him that being, for God, was not a compulsion. His mind was not compelled to follow his emotions. Being is not a choice under necessity, but a potential exercise of will. Gurdjieff had a precept that, to escape a prison such as modern-day consciousness, we need to know, first, that we are in a prison. Then we need a tool for unlocking the doors, and finally, someone who has done it before to tell us the way to escape. To these, Orage said that there was a necessary fourth condition: to have the will to do it.[49]

Throughout the month, Orage and Jessie breakfasted with Jean Toomer and discussed whatever new chapters of the book were arriving from Fontainebleau. Toomer became a sort of assistant editor for Orage, and they shared the revision duties and scanned each other's efforts. Waldo Frank occasionally joined them, and, at one memorable dinner with I. A. Richards on 17 April, Orage suggested that he take a look at the book. Richards demurred. Another writer, Zona Gale, was becoming interested in the Gurdjieff work, and exchanged ideas with Orage by letter. Muriel Draper, whose son, Paul, was to become a renowned dancer, offered her apartment for readings and group meetings, so Orage now had Blanche Grant's and Muriel's apartment at his disposition, as well as Daly King's studio, though Daly was now busy with his own group in Orange.[50] Jean Toomer joined Orage and Jessie often in the company of Muriel, who knew and admired Jean's work. Orage and

---

48. Cited by Webb, *Harmonious Circle*, pp. 280 and 304. These were collected, accompanied by portraits, in Frank's *Time Exposures*.
49. The Norwegian Josten Gaarder's recent novel, *Solitaire Mystery* (London: Phoenix, 1977), is a pure Gurdjieffian exposition of the question: "How does one climb out of the prison of consciousness?" in a world which has become a habit (see pp. 219, 255).
50. William J. Welch, who joined one of his groups shortly after Orage returned to England, gives a sympathetic portrait of King in *What Happened in Between* (New York: Braziller, 1972), pp. 48–49.

Jessie also became good friends at this time with the art dealer Betty Parsons, well-known later for her gallery on 57th Street.

One problem Orage had to endure with Jessie was her immoderate drinking. He was never known to blame her for it, nor did he ever make a public scene over her almost chronic intemperance. Nonetheless, Jessie was painfully aware of her own problem and its potential danger to her relations with Orage. At a group meeting on 12 April, during which Orage revealed Gurdjieff's view of drugs and alcohol as conducive to "insanity"—which Gurdjieff identified as a form of fantasy— Jessie intervened and gave a lengthy interpretation of insanity that set several others ill at ease.[51] In her diary entries, Jessie chastised herself for such behavior under the influence of drink. After dinner with the Nylands on 13 May, the Orages went to a party where, as her diary records, "I got really drunk . . . when I got home I was going to kill myself, but Orage grabbed the gun. . . . I am frightened." Orage would talk calmly with her about her problem, but he felt it was a situation she had to deal with herself, and he set self-control as an exercise for her. On the other side of the coin, however, Orage himself drank, and had reverted back to the heavy smoking he had renounced during his stay at the Prieuré. His pupils rarely saw him without a cigarette in his hand or between his lips.

For Orage, late spring meant screening and preparing pupils for summer sessions at the Institute. In mid-May, he and Jessie saw Betty Parsons and Edith Taylor off on a boat to France. Betty was headed to Paris on art business, and Edith was going to the Institute with promises to Orage to cable or write of circumstances there. Orage wanted Jessie to go as well, to ameliorate her earlier impressions, and he thought Edith would be a good companion for her. Jean Toomer was also determined to be there, and on 20 May, Orage met with him to plan a strategy to convince Gurdjieff that all was being done in New York to support the Institute financially. He cautioned Toomer against making any promises for funds, and saw him off on the 24th with a personal letter of recommendation to Gurdjieff.

Five days later, on 29 May, Jessie sailed from New York on the Ryndam, arriving in Plymouth on 7 June. The next afternoon, she reached Boulogne, from where she took the boat train to Paris. By 10 o'clock that night, she was at the Institute, in time for the music in the Study House and reading in Gurdjieff's room. Shortly after, Orage

---

51. Manchester's notes for April 12, 1926 (Manchester Papers), p. 36.

sailed for England, where he hoped to settle the divorce terms with Jean Walker's lawyer, and to settle other personal matters, before joining Jessie at the Prieuré. On 9 June he arrived in England, where he met a number of people who had just returned from the Institute with good reports. After seeing lawyers, he wrote Jessie that he would arrive in Fontainebleau on the 18th or 19th. Jean Walker's lawyer called immediately for full alimony payments due and a cash settlement, but Orage felt he could not raise even the alimony due. He wrote Jessie on Monday the 14th to say that his wife's solicitor was demanding double payment since no alimony had been paid for twenty years. Orage responded to the lawyer that he could not find more than £1,000, and they finally agreed on $5,500.

Orage then set himself to the task of hiring a witness for Jean who would testify to his adultery. Once this was done, he would have to wait for a summons to be served before he was free to move on to the continent. Nonetheless, impatient, he decided to go to Paris first to meet Jessie, and then return to London the following week. Friends encouraged Orage to see Ouspensky as long as he was in London, but Orage replied that he would await Ouspensky's first move, which never came. He did meet with Major Douglas, however, who urged him to stay longer in England and join him in a new campaign for Social Credit.

Meanwhile, Jessie was one of a threesome at the Institute with Edith Taylor and Jean Toomer, who were rumored to be continuing an affair that had started in mid-spring in New York City. Edith had an apartment in Paris, and drove down almost every day to the Institute in a little Dion she had borrowed from an American friend who had gone back to the United States for the summer. Jessie and Jean had been assigned gardening jobs, and Edith, since she had an automobile, was employed as a driver for errands to Fontainebleau and Paris, and to provide a taxi service for Gurdjieff or members of his entourage to and from Paris and Fontainebleau.[52]

On 17 June, Jean Toomer and Jessie took the train into Paris together to meet Orage at the Gare du Nord. That evening, Gurdjieff welcomed Orage warmly and, although Gurdjieff's wife, Julia Ostrovska, was suffering in the terminal phases of a cancer, the Institute was animated with activities. In the days following, Orage consulted

---

52. Jessmin Howarth, "Wise Woman," *A Journal of Our Time* (Toronto: Traditional Studies Press, 1979), pp. 29–31, offers a brief view from a woman's perspective of practical work at the Prieuré.

daily with Gurdjieff about the book. On 26 June at 4 A.M., Mme. Ostrovska died. Later that same morning, Gurdjieff told Jessie to move into her room. When she told Orage that she did not feel comfortable being assigned the room so soon after Mme. Ostrovska's death, Orage told her that she would understand soon enough why Gurdjieff insisted. That evening, Gurdjieff had the Study House decked out for a vodka party and two new pupils who had arrived that day thought that a party was being held in their honor.

Hearing the news in Paris of Julia's death, Jane Heap and Mme. Ouspensky arrived the next day in time for the funeral, which took place on the 28th. Meanwhile, on the days before and after the funeral, Gurdjieff had long private conversations with Orage. At least one topic of their conversation was Gurdjieff's suggestion that Orage remain at the Prieuré until the book was completed. Since Orage's arrival, Jessie had been designated typist for Orage's revisions, and she was working all day long. Orage was also talking with Jane Heap, apparently with Gurdjieff's approval, about the possibility of establishing a woman's group in Paris with Edith Taylor and Margaret Anderson.

On 7 July, Gurdjieff announced that he would take a trip the next day, but wished to have a feast that night. He allowed Jessie and Edith to plan the menu and do the necessary shopping in Fontainebleau. The next morning, just after 9 A.M., Dmitri Gurdjieff, Dr. de Stjernvall, Mme. de Hartmann, Orage, and Jessie crowded into Gurdjieff's car and set off for Orléans. After two days there, the crowded vehicle, with Gurdjieff at the wheel, headed south. Jessie complained continually to Orage about Gurdjieff's driving, but the others were inured to Gurdjieff's style on the road and sat passively, if not comfortably. Near Bordeaux, they stopped for the habitual picnic by the side of the road. Included in the fare was caviar of dubious age and quality, and by the time the group arrived in Biarritz for the night, Orage was violently sick. He joked to Jessie that his physical constitution was so sturdy that should he ever get *really* ill, he would probably die. Jessie did not appreciate the humor. For two full days, Orage remained sick, but recovered enough not to hold up the next move toward Vichy. On 18 July, after the usual picnic lunch, Gurdjieff asked Jessie to drive because, he said, the armagnac had made him too tired. Jessie took over the unfamiliar vehicle and promptly sideswiped a fiacre. The car was damaged enough to require repairs, and the carriage was almost totally destroyed, though the horse was only slightly shaken physically. Gurdjieff was unruffled by the incident and did not berate Jessie, but went to work his psychological wizardry on the driver of the fiacre, whom he finally paid off with a thousand francs. They left Vichy after two days of taking the waters and awaiting the repair of the automobile. The group arrived back at the Prieuré on 22 July. Jessie was still smarting from Orage's gastronomical ordeal which she blamed on Gurdjieff's intentional feeding of his group with spoiled caviar. When, two evenings later, Gurdjieff made fun of Orage's "American" stomach, Jessie was furious. After dinner, slightly drunk, she went to Edith's room, "borrowed" a pearl-handled Browning revolver and stormed down the hall toward Gurdjieff's room.[53] Edith intercepted her and Jessie broke into tears and let Edith lead her back to her room. Orage never learned, or let on that he knew, of his wife's intention.

That same day, Margaret Anderson, Jane Heap, and Georgette Leblanc arrived from Paris to continue the discussion about setting up a group in Paris. Orage, as Gurdjieff's interlocutor, said that such a group could be established only after Gurdjieff was satisfied that they knew enough of the work, and the group would have to be completely under Gurdjieff's own control. He suggested that they include Elizabeth Gordon among their number, as liaison. Years later, this group would be formally sanctioned by Gurdjieff as the "Rope," a counterpart to the mothers in Gurdjieff's entourage whom he called "cows," each of which was "like a cow going round a new gate without being able to find the way in."[54]

On 1 August, with Jessie encouraged by Orage's good mood, Gurdjieff set off for Sens with them, the de Hartmanns, Dmitri, and Mme de Salzmann. After visiting the Cathedral, which Gurdjieff particularly liked—one of the oldest Gothic cathedrals in France, designed by Villard de Honcourt, and the home church of Saint Thomas à Becket—they drove on, but the car broke down a few kilometers further. Luckily, they found a mechanic nearby who was able to repair it in time for the party to reach Auxerre for the next night's stay. From there, they drove to the Col de la Faucille in the Jura above Lac Léman, where they stopped. This was one of Gurdjieff's favorite sites, and he reposed on a bench with a splendid view over the lake basin, with Geneva to the left and Mont Blanc across the Rhône valley. Gurdjieff told the others that

---

53. Edith, as well as Jessie, had been assigned rooms on the floor known as the "Ritz." Gurdjieff would not allow Orage to share her quarters, and had him assigned a room on the third floor known as the "Monks' Corridor."
54. So Gurdjieff characterized Ouspensky in St. Petersburg, according to Anna Butkovsky-Hewitt, *With Gurdjieff in St. Petersburg and Paris* (London: Routledge & Kegan Paul, 1978), p. 79.

he intended to buy a chalet there soon. The next day, they drove through Geneva and on to Chamonix in the French Haute Savoie, where they stayed for two days. Jessie complained bitterly about Orage's patience and tolerance of Gurdjieff's manners on the road and in public houses. Orage remained not only imperturbable, but insisted that Gurdjieff could not be understood as an ordinary man. They returned to the Prieuré on the 7th, in time to join the others for music and reading from *Beelzebub's Tales*.

The next day, Jane Heap came down from Paris with Edith Taylor and talked with Orage about the proposed Paris group. Orage promised to tutor the whole group for the rest of his stay. Jessie, however, was not pleased with Orage's commitment to interests of the Institute that excluded her. They argued often, and more than once, when Orage went down to dinner, she stayed in her room. Jessie's jealousy became aggravated even more when she found what seemed to her a love letter from one of Orage's New York female admirers.

On 15 August, Gurdjieff took Jessie and Orage on another trip, this time to Epernay, where they spent the night, before proceeding to Neufchâteau the next day. There were further stops at Contrexville (famous for its mineral waters) and Bar-sur-Aube, before returning to the Prieuré. Four days later, Gurdjieff took Orage and Jessie on a three-day trip to Nevers, a trip marred for Orage by Jessie's harping on his subservience to Gurdjieff. For two nights, they lost sleep arguing, but Gurdjieff ignored the obvious tension. When they returned to the Institute on the 28 August, Gurdjieff invited Jessie to sit by him at the evening reading. On the 31st, Gurdjieff was off again with them to Nantes and then Rouen, where they visited the cathedral. They returned the next day to the Prieuré. To make her feel more involved in his interests, Orage tried to get Jessie interested in the projected women's group in Paris, suggesting that she might herself form a similar group in New York. Jessie did not take to the idea, since she was not getting along particularly well with Jane Heap, whom she felt Orage esteemed excessively. On 4 September, to bolster her own spirits, Jessie joined Edith Taylor to give a party in the ironing room for all the women at the Prieuré. Jessie, well experienced in the craft, mixed cocktails for everyone. Gurdjieff roared with pleasure when he heard of the party, though Jessie and Edith had meant it as a gesture of defiance to his view that women are secondary: "If you are first, your wife is second" was one of Gurdjieff's aphorisms that irritated Jessie.[55]

---

55. Webb, *Harmonious Circle*, p. 221, without identifying his source, says that Gurdjieff interrupted the party and denounced the two women.

Gurdjieff was planning another trip to the United States, and many of his discussions with Orage concerned the logistics involved, especially if Gurdjieff planned on bringing over a troupe with him for demonstrations. There was not nearly enough money available to bring over a group the size of which accompanied Gurdjieff in 1924, so Gurdjieff decided to go with a smaller entourage, principally to observe the operations of the New York group and to plan the establishment of groups throughout the United States. For this, he depended on Orage's considered opinion. Chicago and Washington DC were obvious choices. Orage's negative opinion of Boston ruled that city out for the time being. Orage wrote letters to members of his New York group inquiring about the possibility of raising enough money there to pay travel expenses for Gurdjieff and a small number of others.

By the 10 September, no word had come back from New York. Worse, Jessie told Orage that she would not return to New York if Gurdjieff were there. Actually, Orage was thinking seriously of remaining at the Institute for another long period under Gurdjieff's guidance. For Gurdjieff, this was not practicable until someone else, Toomer for example, could assume direction of the New York group. Gurdjieff had been impressed by Toomer's enthusiasm and command of work methods and materials, and in Orage's absence, throughout September and the first half of October, Toomer revised the Hartmann translation.[56] Orage, too, thought Toomer was ready to assume a larger responsibility, both in translating the book and in directing groups in the United States. At Jessie's insistence, Orage compromised and proposed to Gurdjieff to stay at the Institute no longer than another two months. To Jessie, he promised not to go back to New York if Gurdjieff went.

Of course, a compelling reason for Orage to remain in Europe for a while longer was his impending divorce proceeding. On 13 September, he and Jessie crossed the Channel for a month-long stay, during which Orage consulted solicitors. Jean Walker was not, apparently, in a conciliatory mood, and the divorce proceeding did not advance. Orage profited from their stay, however, to renew contacts in the publishing world, and to introduce his friends to Jessie, who enjoyed London life.

---

56. On 5 October, 1926, he wrote to Edith Taylor: "Today I practically finished my revision of the translation of the third descent. . . . Metz is back and is out of sorts with me, not only because I am doing the translation, which he more than hoped to <u>fall</u> into" (Taylor papers).

They didn't return to the Institute until 13 October, when they heard that Gurdjieff had postponed his plans for an immediate American voyage. Orage then consulted with Gurdjieff about the organization of the New York group and the setting up of a group in Washington under Toomer's direction. In discussions, Toomer convinced Gurdjieff that Chicago would be a better location to raise financial aid for the Institute. So, it was Orage back to New York and Toomer right away to Chicago. Toomer left the next day for Paris and sailed for New York on the 16th. As for Jessie, she expressed an ambivalent mood in her diary after the return from London: "I am most depressed to be back, and hate the idea of going or staying. . . . What a day! God how I hate this place." As if to exasperate her all the more, Gurdjieff served Orage and Jessie dog meat the next evening.

Orage booked passage for Jessie alone on the Majestic for 20 October, along with Miss Gordon and Jane Heap. He told her he would follow as soon as the organization of the American groups was set to Gurdjieff's satisfaction. As he saw Jessie off from the Institute, Gurdjieff said to her: "You leave half of you here!" On the evening she sailed, Orage wrote her from "You know where!"

We returned at mid-day after you went away to learn on our arrival what scarcely surprised me, that G had telephoned at 7 in the morning to say he would be back [from Paris] for lunch. And sure enough, about half an hour after we got here he arrived. Then all was bustle and excitement! It seems he had found driving in an open car too cold, and, in fact, he doubts whether he will use that car all the winter. On the other hand, he asks me to tell you that unless he gets a new big car from America or England within a month he will ruin their financial systems! So perhaps you can scare Pierre Jay [Morgan] with saving the Federal Reserve for this trifling amount of a car. He asked how you had gone off and how I should exist without my "angel." Incidentally, the doctor, Salzmann and Hartmann all had profound apologies to make. Salzmann had been told that the train left at 10, and was there with your three bottles. He didn't, as is usual, blame the absent, but me! Though the Lord knows I never told him 10 or any time. We "men" sat and drank G into a state of sleep (Mme H said he didn't sleep a wink the two days he was away); and in the meanwhile H and I translated; and you'll be as surprised as pleased to know that we've finished the 3rd descent.

After G woke—at about 7—there was, of course, nothing to be done, and we went coffee-drink and afterwards sat in his room until about 1 A.M. After that, I worked for an hour in bed on the book until I couldn't keep awake to worry about my darling at sea.

By the way, [Donald] Whitcomb had arrived and last evening asked
G to let him come into the Russian reading. G let him drink a little only,
and was otherwise quite pleased with him.

This morning at 9 I started work again and got on well with my revi-
sion for typing. At 12, away to coffee-drink where G did nothing but talk.
After lunch we went to his room and he played and composed. And now,
just after dinner, he has gone to Paris. I'm to work with H. later this night.

Other scraps. Tom [Peters] has been officially appointed to look after
me, and I have now a very cheerful fire. Also a new stove is to be put in
tomorrow. G out of the blue told Mme H last evening to get me six apples
a day! That really is funny, especially as I've already got my first day's
rations. G spoke today of finishing the first volume in 1 month and enu-
merated the chapters to be included. He reminded H and me today of his
promise to give us "something" if we should finish 3 and 4 this week.
Miss Merston is settled in Miss Gordon's room very comfortably, it
seems. She also plunged into work for oblivion. Metz had a fight with
Valia [Valentin Anastavieff] while we were all away, and G won't have
either in his room. It seems they really quarrelled about that very thing—
Metz much wishing to return to his buttons!

G speculated what you would all do in NY and laughed when I told
him what Jane had said about her indiscreet multiplication by five. But I
didn't give him any hope that you would be able to do what he pretends
to expect.

I haven't said anything to him about Xmas yet, but Mme H must have
done so, because he said that he must finish before I have to be his "min-
ister" in America again. However, that is my business even more than his,
and, as I've said, I'm not going to dawdle over my part of it.

A day later he posted another report on events:

G has been away all day and H and Mme S and I have been working the
whole time. I've nearly finished the rough translation of the 3rd
Descent—and about one-third of the revision. G left word that it was to
be hurried, because Miss Merston was to send copies at once to you and
[to Toomer in] Chicago. He doesn't know! But, all the same, the revised
version is a great improvement.

Just before G went to Paris we went to coffee-drink. "We" now usu-
ally—Dr. H and I. G seemed to be very pleased because I told him the
theme of "noo moosic" he had made the evening before, and he said it
was an exact translation of the Russian text he had given it! He spoke
again of America sending him a car—from which I judge he is buying one
and preparing me for it.

It's 8 now, and G is expected back at any moment. We've worked so much in his absence that Mme S was constrained to say she hoped G would not come back until the bath! Nobody new here except of course Whitcomb. He has brought such working-clothes as Meredith might envy! Tom has been officially appointed my housekeeper, and he has begun well. I've got a stove in and it works! Both Tom and Fritz [Margaret Anderson's nephews], by the way, seem to be very keen and happy. G remarked on it.

Sat It is 2 A.M. and they are just beginning to begin a Russian reading in G's room. I've slipped out! But let's begin at the beginning. G came home last (Fri) evening at about 8. We all went to Fontainebleau and he did some work, and so did H and I. Returned—music in salon. Later, all in G's room. A funny incident occurred. I should say that Whitcomb came down on Thursday evening in his very swell dressing gown. G said nothing, but when he came into G's room last evening, G bawled out "Who invited you here? This my room and nobody come if I not invite them." Whitcomb was going, but G made him sit down, and Whitcomb fumed all the rest of the evening. Today the poor boy is in a turmoil—but he came into the room this evening and nothing more was said. G told me this morning that he had meant to call him down, as he had been very "American," and referred to the dressing gown. However, it's all right for the present, but Whitcomb certainly was in a stew of a rage. We sat up till about 2. G up early and way to coffee-drink, I worked up there, and again with Mme S and H this afternoon. More Fontainebleau and then the bath—at which there were 4 visitors—all Russian and French. It's been a hell of an evening! However, I've got one or two very good things from G today, including a pathological definition of Kundabuffer! Psychic action by association, i.e. not originating in essence.[57] *Also some other ideas that I have absorbed.*

Oh yes, Salzmann turned up tonight a cripple, so to speak. He'd been knocked down by a taxi in Paris, and had a lame shoulder, arm and leg. Michel [de Salzmann] has a fever but is better. We occasionally work in Mme S's [de Salzmann] room and Michel's behaviour is angelic. The Dr

---

57. As if alluding to kundabuffer, in "Burnt Norton," the first poem in *Four Quartets*, T. S. Eliot—who had listened intensively to Ouspensky in London and had discussed Gurdjieff's teaching with Orage—remarks that "human kind / Cannot stand very much reality" (lines 42–43). The apparent source of Kundabuffer is the Hindu "kundalini," long known in esoteric circles, which Umberto Eco, *Foucault's Pendulum*, p.89, explains as a serpent cosmic force "that dwells at the base of the spinal column, in the sexual glands. Once weakened, Kundalini rises to the pineal gland. . . . A third eye is then supposed to open up in the brow, the eye that lets you see directly into time and space." Krishnamurti's ascension to higher being is generally interpreted as an achievement of kundalini. For Gurdjieff's view of Kundalini, see *Tales*, p. 250. For the standard psychological view, see C. G. Jung, *The Psychology of Kundalini Yoga*, Sonu Shamdasani, ed. (Princeton: Princeton University Press, 1999). In Gurdjieff's system, the opposite of kundabuffer is *kemespai*, that which does not permit one to live in peace.

always asks about you; he apparently thinks you are already in America. And, by the way, Michel is always asking 'Where Miss Jessie?' Miss Merston is next to me now, and works "on book" all day. She certainly has given herself no time to worry, and I equally think she is not disenjoying herself.

You can little guess how irked I get at being delayed in finishing the translation. But "patience" is an essence; it is how one eats dog, I suppose, and-though you may not think it—I'm feeling—inside—the benefit of the diet.

G told me, by the way, this evening, that he wanted one of three things—good titillators, people very skilful at <u>something</u>, people ready to hang themselves, or "men" i.e. individuals, people without soul, with only the conception of a soul, and with soul, so I imagine he meant.

On Sunday the 23rd, he continued:

G has been here all day and in a very musical state. Hours have passed at the café, and tonight we did not leave his room until 2. But with a fire always in my room I can always write a little before going to bed.

Monday. This morning bright and early—pouring with rain—G got up and proposed instead of Fontainebleau, Paris! Mme H was sent off by train and the Dr, H, Salzmann, G and I set off. No adventures or even coffee en route, and when I proposed a sandwich before going to the Paix café, G took us all to some restaurant, and we had a plentiful lunch. Afterwards we drove to his flat where he slept and I worked with H, and after that again we went to meet a Russian professor (who didn't turn up) and to dinner. Back to G's rooms after dinner where we sat and drank until H and I barely caught the last train back.

Orage worked all day on the translation. Gurdjieff had not yet returned from Paris, where he continued writing notes at the Café de la Paix. Curiously, Gurdjieff concentrated best when he was most liable to be disturbed by the distractions of public venues: the cacophonous counterpoint of fragmented conversation, the sweep of waiters' aprons across table tops, the street-traffic noises and the shrill cries of hawkers selling everything from samovars to Algerian rugs. After Gurdjieff returned the next day, Orage continued his report to Jessie:

Wed. G came back a few minutes after I wrote yesterday and in half an hour we were at the café [Henri IV]. Later when he went to his salon I did not go, but worked with Miss Merston, and after the salon G must have gone to bed—anyhow I continued working until about 1:30 A.M. and really got a lot done. In fact, I'm within sight of catching up G—in a rough translation anyhow. Two or three long days more, and it's done.

Lily [Chaverdian] is expected soon, and I expect to have work for her. Nothing more about the book! Miss Merston is certainly working hard, she said she felt lonely for the first time in her life—but she is trying to "suffer" intentionally. Tell Jane [Heap] the boys are well, but Tom continues to complain of Fritz—or would if I would let him! Whitcomb seems to be making a bad impression all round. He seldom gets up until lunch, he usually goes to Font. taking the ever-willing B, he works very little and very seldom, grumbles about the food, and told Miss Merston that he didn't see any sense in economising (tools etc) when G was getting $5000 from America. Altogether his essence is having a showdown! H[artmann] said S[alzmann] was going to ask G to send Whitcomb off!

Thur. G didn't go to Paris yesterday, but I again spent most of the evening working alone. I've really finished now the first translation with H of all that is ready, and now we are on G's heels.

We went early to coffee this morning and G worked there until nearly 2. He really stuck to it. This afternoon he went to Paris, and I've finished my summary of the book up to date. I'm beginning to perceive some of the remote cosmic formations, I think, but everything still keeps on eluding me.

Fri I've been working without a break all day making my own notes on the later chapters. G was in Paris but came back early and all went to the café. This night he composed—and got Mr. H's goat for once! Fortunately the three of us were alone in G's room, and H very very quickly recovered when G laughed.

I've had several "glimpses" of cosmic formations reading the book this intensely. It's really a "Bible," for the "Bible" is also a parable with "history" as its material, and the Biblical history is much less plausible than G's. I told this to G tonight, and he said he had purposely made it fit history when he could—which was a broad hint. I hope to get hold eventually of some of its "keys," but so far I am still baffled.

G said again this evening that the first volume will be finished in a few weeks. Certainly I'll give him credit for working.

By the way, NY group is $650 short on its 1st quarterly payment. Toomer's doesn't count, of course.

Orage added that he had paid Jean Walker's lawyers another $500 and that his debt was down to $3,000.

On the 26 October, Jessie's steamship docked in New York at 1 P.M. She went from the dock directly to Jane Heap's apartment to get news of the New York group to relay back to Orage. Then she went to meet Gorham Munson and Edith Taylor. The next morning, she met with Jean Toomer to relay Orage's instruction concerning the organization of the future Chicago group. Jean reminded her that he had been to

Chicago a year earlier and that he had contacts awaiting his arrival. Jean had also talked informally with some of the New York group to feel out their impressions of him as a future group leader, should Orage remain with Gurdjieff.

Meanwhile, to Jessie, he continued sending his daily reports: "G was here yesterday and now again today, with the result that I've not had much spare time! No more of the book is actually ready, but I've employed my time quite profitably. In fact, as you may say, I'm living the book, as if it were a conscious incarnation." The rest of his letter expresses his concern over the New York accounts, because Gurdjieff wanted to be assured of money on a continual basis for maintenance of the Institute. Orage had asked Jessie to represent him to the New York group to clarify the accounts. He also complained about Whitcomb's manners which seemed to bother Gurdjieff and to embarrass Orage, who had made it possible for Whitcomb to come to the Institute in the first place.

From "Château Gurdjieff" on 29 October, Orage wrote Sherman Manchester, next to Daly King his most trusted friend on the New York Group Committee:

> My dear Sherman, Jessie will have told you all the news, but I write this note, to wit, to thank you for all the good work you have done for the Institute and me this past season, and, secondly, to convey my earnest wish that you may continue in it and even more so. The completion of G's book is certainly still a monumental undertaking, and I am always appalled as I contemplate the labour still before him (and incidentally me) upon it. But you can realise for yourself what a world of difference it would make to our work to have the published book behind us, and hence the practical wisdom of helping its completion, by all the means in our powers. You know from Toomer and Munson about the amounts of the $5000 fund; and Toomer's pluck and generosity in undertaking the repayment of the loan to your fund himself. You can also be sure that your own drafts sent here are extremely welcome. (By the way, as G. has no previous bank account, you should make out checks to "Mme Olga de Hartmann"; his secretary). . . . I hope and am working like a horse to return to N.Y. at Xmas; and G. knows and approves. But there is some work! Only Whitcomb of all our band is now here; he will have much to say when he returns in December! Best wishes to you and Ilsa! Yours ever, A-R. Orage

Meanwhile, in New York on 30 October, Jessie had a long talk with Jean Toomer, who gave her his reckoning, and she reported in her diary that night: "very satisfactory talk which cleared up many things for us both."

But, things were not so easy for Jessie, because she felt that Jane Heap was presuming to represent Orage's interests in New York, and had contested the accounting. Jane had the confidence of members of the New York group, and Jessie was not, officially, a member of any group. So, on Halloween, she and Jean Toomer met at Jane's apartment and "thrashed things out," as she remarked in her diary. Nonetheless, by the next morning Jessie, as she looked at the newspaper reports of Houdini's tragic death the day before, wondered if things really were settled, so she cabled Orage at the Institute to complain that Miss Gordon and Jane were contesting the authority Orage had placed in her. Orage at once wrote both of them that Jessie was his agent in New York and to stop bickering.

That morning, Rita Romilly asked to see Jessie to get her side of the story. Jessie enlisted Jean Toomer's help and they met Rita at the Roma restaurant on McDougal Street. "I dreaded the meeting," Jessie wrote that night. "I don't think it went off too well on my part. I guess I was too scared. Jean was awfully good." Indeed, Jean Toomer was very good in the art of persuasion, with his deep strong voice and obvious sincerity in his deep dark eyes and smile.

Orage wrote Jessie to explain what he understood of Jane Heap's and Miss Gordon's position: "G knew they were going [to New York] in any case for their own affairs—and wished partly to give them standing re the institute, and partly to help you. He certainly thought calling them 1st and 2nd assistants was a sufficient hint of their status." At any rate, Jessie's mood lifted when she heard that Gorham Munson, the treasurer of the New York group, had gotten its members to subscribe help for the Institute to the amount of five thousand dollars. She happily relayed the news to Orage who, that moment, was writing his regular letter to her:

2 November, Tuesday. Yesterday being All Saints' Day, G and everybody went to the cemetery where a service was held over the graves of his mother and Mme Ostrowski [Gurdjieff's wife, Julia Ostrovska]. A special lunch was prepared for the Great Priest, and in the afternoon G and Hartmann gave a "concert." You know G's piano accordion. He made three quite marvellous noo moosics. Evening—at the café—G having been persuaded not to go to Paris. We sat in his room until about 3.30 A.M.

The "doctor" [de Stjernvall] is making the final revision with G of the Russian *texts, and these are now being handed to H and me. The Preface is really finished now, I think, and Miss Merston has been instructed to send you copies. I got very miserable today when G announced that he intended to add a complete chapter on "sport" à propos of England, But a chapter, it seemed, was only a "section" and he has gone to Paris this*

ingil me time rereading

evening to finish it. . . . For the moment I'm filling up my time rereading the 6th descent.[58]

I was interrupted just there by G and coffee-drink, and immediately on returning, Mme H, H and I went off to Paris. It was the usual thing— [Café de la] Paix, then dinner, then G's rooms and H and I returned by the 12.40. But we translated in the car, at the Paix, at G's flat, in the train and finished the lot on our return. Of course, I have now really to do it, but it's the 5th Descent and we are making progress.

G said today he wished to finish the first book in another week, and then go by car-trip to Dijon and to spend a few days there arranging for the printing.[59] *hope he does so and that he and Mme H etc make themselves responsible for all the details of paper, type, etc. We will guarantee the English text bill—but I shall be immensely relieved by the anticipated transfer of the detailed job.*

At this time, Orage assumed that Toomer was finally in Chicago and his groups operating. He was eager to get news, especially of Toomer's capacity to obtain subscriptions for the Institute. So, in his next letter to Jessie, he asked her for Toomer's Chicago address and anticipated "especially the prospect of money," adding: "I shall hope that the combined groups will keep up (after catching up) their guarantee fund. They have now paid $900 and the 2nd quarter ends Nov 30! I should leave here very lightheartedly if they were to send the balance due to date ($1700) before Xmas." His letter ends with resigned despair over Whitcomb's eccentric behavior, but adds, without conviction, that Whitcomb's wife, Lilian, thinks he is better.

On the 3rd, Jessie had lunch with Caesar Zwaska, writer and one-time "office boy" for Jane Heap and Margaret Anderson at *The Little Review*. Caesar had returned earlier from the Institute and was on his way to his native Chicago. He wanted news of the promised group there. Jessie was slightly embarrassed because she knew that her best friend, Edith, was the principal reason Jean was still in New York. Another was the World Series, in which the New York Yankees were playing. Jean had made a proposal of marriage to Edith and, though she refused, he was still content to remain close to her as long as he could, or else persuade her to come to Chicago with him. Jessie had no

---

58. The Sixth Descent, in the 1950 edition, is the third chapter of the second Book of *Beelzebub's Tales*.
59. Orage had connections with Darantière Press in Dijon that had published a good deal of English material.

assurances to give Caesar. Awaiting the effects of Orage's promised letters to Miss Gordon and Jane Heap, she found herself still embroiled in a misunderstanding of authority. In a letter to Orage dated the 4th, she repeated her complaints concerning Jane and Miss Gordon, and the next day went with Toomer to see Rita Romilly.

Orage was still busily occupied at the Institute with the translation, and wrote on Sunday the 7 November:

> *G hasn't been to Paris for two days, and he has been up and down, up and down, to Fontainebleau like a clock pendulum. Certainly it has been about the book, but I've had to scurry my translation in stolen intervals. However, I've just finished the last pages of the first section of 5 and Miss M[erston] has begun to type it. She has been busy all day with Mme S[alzmann] and Leely [Lily Chaverdian] revising the <u>Preface</u>! And the revised copy is to be sent to you . . . by G's express orders.*

Orage went on to describe the arrival of Georgette Leblanc (a famous actress and former mistress of Maurice Maeterlinck, Nobel Prize-winning poet in 1911) who had come by at Margaret Anderson's prompting to be introduced to Gurdjieff. Gurdjieff seemed not at all impressed by her importance, but he played music for her. As he closed his letter, Orage expressed concern that he had heard nothing of Toomer's whereabouts.

In fact, Toomer, Jessie, and Edith had become a mutually supportive threesome in New York. Edith, who also stayed clear of any "official" role in the Gurdjieff work, was a bird of the same feather as Jessie. The three were together throughout the week of 11 November, and both Edith and Jean took to dropping by Jessie's apartment to socialize. By this time, Orage had received Jessie's reports on her negotiations with Jane Heap and Miss Gordon, and of Jean's help, to which Orage replied from France on the 13th: "It was quite a good idea to use Jean. You know I always did myself—and, of course, because I felt him to be really serious. He could always be counted on to be serious in a serious situation. I have written him re his gift to the Institute." Orage was referring to his explanation to Gurdjieff that Toomer was giving separately "for policy." The day before, Orage had written Jean to say that Gurdjieff and Hartmann were still confused over the money sent. Orage himself assumed that Jean had authorized the use of the $2000 allocated to the publication fund for maintaining the château, and expected that Jean would replenish that fund out of his Chicago collections.

Orage had less leisure than Jean, Jessie, and Edith had in New York, but he thrived on pressure, and Gurdjieff had set him as a task to finish the translation before returning to New York. He was to translate with Hartmann everything done so far: that is, to catch up to Gurdjieff's almost frenetic pace of composition. He wrote a progress report to Jessie on the 9th:

> *After sitting up late, G took H and me to coffee early in the morning, and we worked there until 2, at which hour G suddenly decided not only to go to Paris hurriedly but to take me and H to translate en route. We scrambled down lunch, and then G said we would stay the night in Paris to translate more. Well, just as I was in the car, Fritz gave me your letters. . . . We translated, we had dinner, we translated again, and finally I was given a room at the neighbouring hotel. . . . We pottered about the Paix this morning and all came back this evening. I've a heap of translation and re-translation to do, and Leely is going over everything with Miss M[erston] and disputes are referred to me. And it's not really easy to do all this when I'm away with G most of every day. However, one must pay the postage, and though I cannot yet get "real hold" of the book, I'm a little nearer to sensing some of its ideas, and they are really earth-shattering. God knows if I'll be able to talk kindergarten again, but at the moment—once more—I feel too humble and stupid for anything.*
>
> *Jean is probably in Chicago by now; and, in fact, G thought he was already there and was half expecting a cheque from him. I didn't tell anybody that Jean was staying in NY for some days, and I was mildly amused at the thought of it. As for any wrong impression he can produce—well, it's not so very serious if he's not staying there. He'll learn a lot on his own in Chicago.*
>
> *Leely is pregnant, and I understand, is not at all pleased!*[60]

Responding to Jessie's continued concern with her role as his agent, Orage criticized Waldo Frank for addressing the New York group as if with "official sanction." Then, returning to his problems at the Institute, he wrote that he had had to talk "hard" with Whitcomb. The next day he added another chapter to his chronicle of ordeal working with Gurdjieff:

> *I nearly told G this evening that I was tired of being a dog, but I at once recollected that I've not sufficient force or understanding to be a master yet—and, of course, he knows that! He continues to be in general*

---

60. Lily Galumnian Chaverdian gave birth eventually to a boy, Sergei, and when she returned to the Soviet Union in the 1930s, she and her son were blocked there by the war. His present whereabouts are not known to any of my correspondents. All of Gurdjieff's other children to whom I have talked acknowledge that Sergei is Gurdjieff's son, and that seems to have been the unanimous opinion of residents of the Prieuré at that time. Fritz Peters, *Boyhood with Gurdjieff* (London: Victor Gollancz, 1964), p. 116, says that shortly after Mme Ostrovska's death, Gurdjieff was living with a married woman whom he made pregnant.

> *marvellously kind and considerate of me; and I'm quite certain that he really means my good.*
>
> *Tomorrow (the 11th) I go to Paris again with H to translate, but I hope to be back in the night at least. The book is going, and G is nearly up to the final chapter on "Art."[61] In fact, he said today that we should go to Dijon next week and arrange about printing, and as the big car is being got ready, I fancy he means it. By the way, he asked today if a cheque had yet come from America! He proposes to buy a new car, and says America must pay for it! If anybody, by the way, should talk of G's "extravagance," say what is true, that he spends less than tens of thousands of worthless people, and after all, he is writing (as I swear truly) a book of books for the world.*
>
> *Miss M[erston] is finishing to send off to you the <u>whole</u> of Chapter 1. G continues to be urgent about it. She goes to England, unfortunately tomorrow, and I shall have to "verify" with Leely and Mme S[alzmann] myself.*

With Miss Merston off to England for ten days, Orage had to look about for someone else to type his translation. Before she left, however, she said that she had received a letter from Miss Gordon in New York about Jessie's problems with Jane Heap.

Orage took pen in hand right away to prescribe some strategy of relief for Jessie:

> *You <u>might</u>. . . give the sections of the book over to Miss G and Jane, on condition that they make their own groups or read to a group for you. In other words, you might depute them to read at a group that you have got together or require them to collect groups themselves and be responsible to you for their conduct of them. You know, just what I let Toomer do with the coloured group. I started it and kept in touch with it—but he did the work and handed over the money to me.*
>
> *From 9 last evening to 2 this morning I sat in G's room with none but Russians, and except for about 2 words that G translated I understood nothing. At the same time, every attempt I made to go G checked. And it's the same always nowadays. I'm certainly swallowing a lot of impatience, and self-importance etc. Apparently kundabuffer consequences have to be "swallowed"—as we say we swallowed our pride. I've just put my foot in it about an hour ago. Having reams of work to do for Metz's typing and Leely's revision, I planned a long evening today with G in Paris. He suddenly asked me this morning if I wished to go to Paris, and I bluntly said 'No,' and he did not speak to me after that. I explained to H and the*

---

61. Chapter 30 on "Art" concludes the first Book of *Beelzebub's Tales*.

Dr my preoccupations, but they still thought I was wrong. Well, I do myself! After all, why should I care if the book is unfinished—more I mean, than G himself.? No, I lost a big point there. [And so Gurdjieff told him to stay and finish the translation started that morning, and Orage lamented that he missed out on a trip to Paris he would have appreciated.]

Georgette and Margaret [Anderson] were here for Sat evening and Sunday. G gave them hours of music at any rate, and I had a long talk with Margaret. G by the way said again yesterday that he hoped you were having enough of the book to read. "Very important," he said. But how the devil can I get on with no time to myself. Miss Merston away, and not a soul else who knows English!

Oh yes, I forgot Miss Gordon's question about "food." Air is taken in at the lungs, as food is taken in at the mouth, but just as the transformation of food begins only in the stomach, so the transformation of air begins only in the liver. The liver is the air's stomach!"

By now, Jessie had indeed gathered together three groups in New York and was scheduling readings of the material Orage was sending her. Daly King and Toomer helped her define topics for discussion. On Wednesday, 17 November, Orage wrote:

G has been away all day and I've gotten on a good deal. In fact, I'm close on his heels, and the plan now apparently is to go to Dijon on Sunday next and see the printers. It begins to look as if the book were coming out, but I confess I would like some competent person to revise my English. I've entirely lost the taste in a number of places. Metz typed for you and Toomer today the selections "Moon" and "Men" and I shall send them to you tomorrow, I hope. They cost me six hours with Mmes Galumnian and Salzmann. I pray for Miss Merston's return to relieve me of this horse-labour. I do occasionally however get a glimpse of some-thing wonderful. . . . You know my sticking capacity, and I'm determined to see this volume through as far as it depends upon me. By the way, I saw G after that little episode of yesterday and thinking, after what H had said, that G might have taken it wrongly. I began to explain, but he cut me short with "Bolda! You think I not know? I very pleased with you remember business!" So, that's that! He's back now and already we've been to coffee. It seems he has now begun the revision of the last chap-ter, that on Art. He'd better speed on.

Whitcomb has settled down a bit. G looked at him on Sat. evening and Whitcomb made some remarks, whereupon G said "I hate you, because you hate your mother." Whitcomb was absolutely bowled over. It seems he just realised it, and he afterwards sent a note to G that he hated himself!

The book is the current form of the old "movements," and it's as well to take it seriously. I cannot think what Meredith [Elizabeth Sage Hare, "Betty"] meant in saying that the NY groups were more important than the book. In my opinion—worth something if I am not mad—we shall have earned our existence from having contributed in our way to the production and publication of just this. Certainly it doesn't always appear to me in this light. After 16 hours of book—since 8 last evening—I'm seriously disposed to say that the book is just fancy.[62] But, at the same time, I know I am just tired, and my judgment is simply that of fatigue.

I never got back again and sat with G in his room until nearly 3 A.M. Today I have been translating steadily . . . and now it is Friday morning! G was going to Paris, and H and I have really to go. Well, we had something to finish, so I didn't object this time. Finished en route, went to the Paix, thence G's rooms and caught—I alone—the 12.40 P.M. and here I am.

That's just the itinerary, and as I said to G yesterday, everything is routine nowadays—outside. In another sense, I've been having the last few days some wonderful glimpses of the meaning of objective reason and morality. These glimpses fly off like blue sky in storm, but not having any purpose in deceiving myself, I can really say that they are real—as far as they come. The chance of having such a point of view <u>normal</u> to oneself seems so remote—but I see no other course open for me—apart from my craze about it.

Orage concluded by saying that Toomer had cabled him his Chicago address, and that he again asked that his group be allowed to give funds separately.

Monday, Nov 22. Yesterday G set off Vichy-wards on another of his trips, taking with him Bill, the Dr, Mme H and her sister, Mme Salzmann and Michel [de Salzmann, her son]. Dijon has been postponed to <u>next</u> week, since the last chapter of the book, viz. Art, is not yet finished by G himself. He not only, however, talks of having the MS entirely in printing before Xmas, but of immediately beginning on the second volume. I haven't told him myself yet that I intend coming to America at or about Xmas—because . . . even though it would be very very painful to be away from you at Xmas, I couldn't <u>conscientiously</u> leave the work <u>just</u> unfinished—but I mean to as soon as it is necessary. No doubt, as usual, you think this that or the other reason for my not telling him yet. But though

---

62. Anthony Storr, *Feet of Clay,* p. 233, pronounces that "The charisma of certainty is a snare which entraps the child who is latent in all of us."

*my reasons may be bad, I don't think so, of course, and I have quite a lot!
Anyhow, at the right moment I shall tell him and then hear what he has
to say.*

*In a recent letter I said that if the groups could send $1500 before
Xmas, it would be easier for me to leave with a good conscience. It might
be so—but also it might be not. After all, if you and Toomer don't send
money at once, somebody will have to get it! Really . . . I don't see how
you can get much. You must be disappointed, because what you are trying to do is really impossible. It is only possible to <u>try</u> as if it were possible. I cannot see why the Groups should be expected to pay for the
privilege of meeting each other, and as for the book-reading, I think you
are doing wonders to get more than a dozen in the absence of any accompanying lectures. . . . My idea would be to send G all the fees etc collected from <u>old</u> groups—which, of course, I would attend myself—<u>not</u> the
book readings, and to keep for <u>ourselves</u> the fees of the new groups. With
a hundred new people and some activities from Croly etc, it would, I
think, be possible to make the money we need and at the same time to
send G what is necessary.*

Orage then turned, in a stringent tone, to what he had understood from
letters about Jessie's tight relationship with Edith Taylor and Jean Toomer:

*I merely take note of the fact that in your desperation you <u>could</u> forget
all about Edith and "Jean" and the time and place and so on. If I
were to tell you that since you left me lonely here, I have found Jean (I
mean Salzmann) very disposed to be friendly, that I like her immensely,
that she is a tower of strength, that we have arrived at a perfect understanding after heart to heart talks, and that, as her rooms are next to
mine, we often have coffee together long after everyone else is in bed—
well, I shouldn't <u>write</u> this without feeling what you would at least
mechanically feel about it; and either I should <u>intend</u> that effect or I
should express the facts less suggestively. In fact, of course, there isn't
the shadow of truth in what I have just written about Mme Salzmann. I'm
more alone here and now than I've ever been in my life.*

Then, exploiting his play on name forms, he retraces "Jean" Walker's
demands to be paid off; and, with this passed, he lightens the tone of his
long letter with a scan of current Institute gossip, such as Rita Romilly's
predisposition to marry a certain "Bing," and Donald Whitcomb's bad
behavior that Gurdjieff, despite his discomfort, continued to tolerate. He
inserts a suggestion that, with Toomer in Chicago, Daly King might
consider expanding into Harlem, since his Orange group seemed to be
a success. He then returns to the question of the book's publication:

I'm working on the book at high pressure, even for me used to manu-
script. I still wonder if G will publish it. But at least we have it. Miss
Merston returned on Sat. and has been typing ever since. G left, as I said,
yesterday and I was to revise the translation from the beginning with
Leely and H. I suggested to Leely that she should first go over it with
Miss M so as not to delay our joint revision (with H) but she flatly told
Miss M she wouldn't do it—so I had to talk with her for the first time seri-
ously—and now she is translating with Miss M—but it's a trial now for
Miss M!

We were all pressed into Mme Ouspensky's for coffee last evening, G
having gone! I must say G is qualified of his titillation jibes. These
Russians spent the whole time in hilarious reminiscences of the
Constantinople Institute. But am I too damned serious about these ideas?
Anyhow, I didn't come here, and a thousand times no. . . to spend my
time so . . . . He is strange about money, but I think I see a method in
his madness. He certainly makes things adventurous—and therefore
always demanding initiative—for himself.

On 25 November, Thanksgiving Day, Orage sent Jessie a new progress
report:

G returns this evening and the battle will begin again. Not that there has
been none while he has been away. H[artmann], Miss M[erston], Leely
and I—with Metz occasionally—have put in at least 12 hours a day on
the book, and you will soon see some of the results. M[etz] and Miss M
are now typing three chapters for you, and as they have been revised by
Leely, H and Miss M and finally by me, they are really are the last word—
until G changes all the Russian again. At any rate, we are getting close
upon his heels with the fully revised translations, and if he has finished
the "Art" chapter at Vichy, he has only "Electricity" to finish the book.

On Saturday the 27th, after Orage announced to Gurdjieff his intention
to leave in time to be in New York for Christmas, he wrote Jessie to say:

G said yesterday that he was a desperate man now that he had <u>nobody</u> to
lose. . . . I've not yet found the right occasion for discussing America with
Gurdjieff, but it must be very soon now. I'll probably cable you as soon
as the decision is made. We haven't gotten on much with the book these
last two days because Leely has been in Paris, but with her co-operation
I could not finish all I can do on the first volume in about a week. I hope,
by the way, you approve of the final translations? It's the best I can do,
though after six months I could probably improve it a great deal . . . but
the book is too colossal! Suppose "God" were to begin observing him-
self, reviewing his past, and trying to put Himself normal—that is, what
Beelzebub seems to me to be doing. He is God—coldly, rationally,

reviewing himself—but, of course, his "past" extends back to creation. Beelzebub is a "brain-cell" of God, depicted, on the strength of his dislike of God, to make God's review of himself—seems to me to be rather an interesting idea and appears confirmed by many things G says of both B and himself. Also, there should be, as there are, many analogies in consequence between God's self-observation etc and any one person's.

On Sunday, he wrote of Gurdjieff's reaction to his desire to leave before Christmas:

After I finished writing you yesterday, G returned from Paris and sent for me to his room. He said he had a little plan for me. "You to America for 2 or 3 months and then come back, bring Miss Dwight, and we have ready second book [Meetings with Remarkable Men] to translate." Of course, it's a question of money—he doesn't see it coming from America without me. Also he has no intention of immediately printing the 1st volume—and the 2nd could go slowly, I am not needed here for a while. "Two months" is of course a time-whip, because he certainly will not have finished the 2nd book in that time. No, I imagine that about the same time as last year will be soon enough.

Orage then described to Jessie his plans for setting up new groups in January 1927, asked her to get applicants in order, and set a tentative schedule for readings from book:

After all, darling, G isn't a hoax! I can speak for his book as the most wonderful ever written, and you are a judge of his music. In other words, we need have no modesty about the value of the work we are trying to get money for. I'd almost steal it if it were that or nothing.

We are going off to Dijon tomorrow. Mr and Mrs H, Miss M and Mrs Galumian. G proposes to make enquiries only re the printing and talks of printing in 4 languages at once. Miss M and Mme H are to be in charge of the negotiations, so that one of them can always go to Dijon if necessary. That's a weight off my mind. I was afraid I might have to see the book through the press.

A weight still on Orage's mind, however, was Jessie's relations with Toomer. After he read her letter speaking of Toomer's charm and humor at a luncheon and meeting at Edith's to discuss the status of contributions that she and Jean were collecting for Gurdjieff from the Orage and Toomer groups, Orage wrote back with undisguised irritation:

Jean's situation . . . is quite different. The Obermann business is nothing—I shouldn't find it so—he has a nucleus of people before him and a book behind him, Also, as you say, he should have gone [to Chicago] before his feet cooled. However, in criticising "Jean" in these days, I know I'm risking your reaction. I always said you were fond of him, you know! And I was not in the least surprised, except by your surprise, to hear you had rung him up from Edith's to come there, and take you home to talk or that your heart to heart talk left you liking him "immensely" and in relations you are sure Gurdjieff would like. In fact, my darling Jessie, if "Jean" were only white, I should consciously advise you to go to Chicago and cooperate with him there.[63] *You would be a thousand times happier in equal association with a being of your own age. . . . I have not the least suspicion, darling, that your frank and heart to heart talk with "Jean" travelled outside Institute business to your personal relations; but I merely take note of the fact that in your desperation you could forget all about Edith and "Jean" and time and place and so on. . . . Well, so much for one unpleasant trifle. I shall only add that if "Jean" calls you "Dwight" again, I shall take the occasion "to kavatar."*

Coincidentally, Orage had earlier concluded his essay "On Love" (1924) with a denunciation of jealousy, that is "the dragon's . . . paradise; the hell of heaven; and the most bitter of the emotions because associated with the greatest."[64] Toomer's charm almost undid Orage and himself on this occasion. Fortunately, a few days later, after attending Brancusi's exhibition at the Brummer Gallery on East 57th Street, he was off to Chicago with Edith, who also wondered about the sudden intensity of Jean's and Jessie's relations. A few weeks later, Orage wrote coolly to Jean in Chicago to say that Gurdjieff expected money at any moment. Orage's earlier fears that Gurdjieff would coerce Toomer into promising more than he could deliver seem to have been justified. Since his return, Jean had been in contact with Mabel Dodge Luhan again, and was feeling buoyant about Taos for the establishing the Institute.[65] He probably mentioned this to Gurdjieff, who would have seized the occasion to ask for more Luhan money that Jean assumed he could deliver.

On 14 December, Orage finally cabled Jessie at 114 E. 56th Street the news she had been awaiting anxiously: "Leviathan, 14th." That evening, he wrote that "we were all at Dijon last week and our interviews with the printers (tell and thank Jane) were highly satisfactory. G is certainly putting up a good bluff (note my new English) but I still do

63. On the question of "color," see Toomer's 1938 *apologia*, titled *A Fiction and Some Facts*. For an excellent view of the problems of identifying skin color with literary authorship, see Henry Louis Gates, Jr.'s "Introduction: 'Tell me, Sir, . . . What is 'Black Literature?' " *PMLA* 105 (1990), pp. 11–22, and "White Like Me," *The New Yorker* 17 June 1996, pp. 66–68.
64. *On Love: With Aphorisms and Other Essays* (York Beach, ME: Samuel Weiser, 1998), p. 19.
65. Rudnick, *Mabel Dodge Luhan*, p. 229.

not see him publishing the book for years. However, I've had my first meal of it, and anybody can do as we have done. G has the 2nd and 3rd read to him now as if he were really preparing to continue."

As for his divorce proceedings, he noted that a new agreement would have him pay only $3000 to Jean Walker, and another $500 to the lawyers involved. He reiterated his eagerness to get to new groups in New York: "I have a kind of desperation now from having eaten a great deal of dog and it wouldn't be impossible for me to get up and leave a meeting without a word. Also money is our object."

On a bright Saturday on the 20th, Edith and Jessie met Orage's boat, and watched him descend the gangway with Margaret Naumberg at his side.

Chapter Six

1927–1929

NO AXE
BUT TRUTH TO GRIND[1]

Mysticism is democratic, initiation is aristocratic.
—Umberto Eco[2]

Perhaps I write not for me but for God.
—Orage[3]

Orage and Jessie settled into a happy social and working routine in New York, though they continued to live apart. Throughout January, they nurtured relations with Alfred Steiglitz, Glenway Westcott, Paul Robeson, and Lawrence Langner, Rita Romilly's associate in the Theater Guild. Orage began his classes that year with readings and commentary on the book.

1927: INDIVIDUALITY IS CONSCIOUSNESS OF WILL[4]

At his 4 January meeting, he set out a number of problems concerning reading procedures. He explained that the proper reading of Gurdjieff's book required a kind of reading capacity we have not yet attained.

---

1. Munson, *Aladdin's Lamp: The Wealth of the American People* (New York: Creative Age Press, 1949), dedicated to "A. R. Orage."
2. *Foucault's Pendulum,* William Weaver, trans. (New York: Ballantine Books,1990), p. 181.
3. "An Editor's Progress," *Commonweal* 3 (10 February 1926), pp. 376–379.
4. Orage, cited by James Webb, *The Harmonious Circle: G. I. Gurdjieff, P. D. Ouspensky, and Their Followers* (London: Thames & Hudson, 1980), p. 444. Ouspensky found the definition contrary to Gurdjieff's thought.

The opening is like an overture to an opera. The book is a series of
parables. Why a warning to the reader and not a Preface (will is heart,
wish is solar plexus)? It should put you on guard that it is not easily to
be understood. You must read it with both emotion and intellect. We
must understand and feel simultaneously. Consider this: If we went
into a squalid village and said, "before dinner it is customary to say
grace" our hosts would say "No, we do not know this custom."
Gurdjieff's introduction to his book is a custom from the Great
World—not on earth. We live in a squalid village—Earth. This book is
written in the name of the Holy Ghost. We have no Holy Ghost, only a
solar plexus. This book is written from the heart. Gurdjieff says, "I
have no wish" but proposes to write from the heart, from will.[5]

For the rest of this meeting and through his 11 January meeting (both of
which lasted until midnight), Orage proceeded to explicate in detail the
entire "Warning," beginning with an analysis of Gurdjieff's opening
statement: "I shall begin with a warning." He explained to his fifty
pupils in attendance that: "Art consists of conscious variations from
ordinary rules. All the art we see ordinarily in the world is just representation of nature as we see it. . . . Uniqueness is no merit. Consciously
unique is uniqueness according to art, not according to nature.
Conscious uniqueness will evoke conscious uniqueness."[6]

Orage had a double aim for concentrating on the book in his group
discussions, which continued well into 1929. Not only was he explaining the text of the book in terms that related and gave authority to what
he had been teaching of Gurdjieff's ideas, but, in carefully going
through the book with his pupils, he was discovering problems in his
own translation. For example, in contrasting "will" and "wish" in their
relationships to different organs of the body, he was able to perceive a
proper application of those terms in other contexts. So it was that his
early broad use of the term "voluntary suffering" in discussion led him
to suggest later to Gurdjieff another term: "Intentional Suffering."[7] He
told his pupils at his 7 February meeting that, despite "the help of
Gurdjieff in understanding an occasional sentence in the book, I later
found it difficult and often impossible to get any meaning from it, for it
needed exact context and continuity of the idea in the book for full com-
prehension. The book is an epic dialogue." [8]

---

5. Manchester Papers, p. 50.
6. Sherman Manchester's notes (Manchester Papers, pp. 50–56). Nott, *Teachings of Gurdjieff:*
Journal of a Pupil (London: Routledge & Kegan Paul, 1961), pp. 125–216, reproduces Orage's
commentary on *Beelzebub's Tales.*
7. Nonetheless, both terms were maintained, with distinctions carefully made.
8. Manchester Papers, p. 50.

Orage connected his reading of the book with continued discussions of self-observation as a mandatory activity. As he was wont to say, citing Sufi authority, "He is your worst enemy who tells you what you should learn by yourself." At his meeting on 18 January, he remarked that self-observation was a crucial step toward realizing the essential I that is a potentiality resident in us, the development of which will entitle us to say I. "To become a chicken, " he continued, "one must peck and break through the shell."[9] Wim Nyland intervened to say that we ought never to regret not having observed ourselves during a day. "Wrong!" shot back Orage.

If you don't treat yourself roughly you won't get anywhere. If you fail in a vow, stay up all night; don't give yourself that treat you had planned. Fine yourself! Set up a box at home and on those days when you fail in your vow, put in a dollar or a nickel or a hundred dollars. At the end of the month give the money to the Institute. We shall anticipate receiving some money, but with all our hearts hope that you adopt this suggestions and that we receive no money at all from this.[10]

Orage's point here is that a vow is what Gurdjieff calls a "will-task," a super effort to do and then redo a task. For Orage, the keeping of a vow is essential to self-observation and the recognition of one's chief feature, or chief weakness; that is, the pattern of undeveloped essence.

The American poet and scholar Allen Tate was brought by Gorham Munson to one or two of Orage's meetings, and he consulted with Orage about the possibility of visiting the Institute in the following summer. He wrote his favorable impressions of Orage to his friend Hart Crane, who had been a regular for a short time in Orage's group in 1924. Crane wrote back by return post on 7 January 1927, to say: "Your comments on Gorham's shrine and gland-totemism convince me that Orage talked as vaguely and arbitrarily in your presence as he did in mine on a similar occasion. Some great boob ought to be hired as a kind of heckler and suddenly burst out in one of those meetings held each year to attract converts—'Come on now, do your stuff—there's millions waiting!' or some such democratic phrase."[11] To Ivor Winters, he wrote on 29 May of that year:

9. Manchester Papers, p. 99.
10. Manchester Papers, p. 99. For Orage on vows, see C. Daly King, *The Oragean Version.* King Published the book himself.
11. *The Letters of Hart Crane and His Family,* T. S. W. Lewis, ed. (New York: Columbia University Press, 1974), p. 282.

> *The image of the "complete" or wished for ethical order is a good ideal-
> istic antidote for the hysteria for specialization that inhabits the modern
> world. . . . Munson, however, and a number of my other friends. . . being
> stricken with the same urge, and feeling that something must be done
> about it—rushed into the portals of the famous Gurdjieff Institute and
> have since put themselves through all sorts of Hindu antics, songs,
> dances, incantations, psychic sessions, etc. so that now, presumably the
> left lobes of their brains and their right lobes respectively function . . . in
> perfect unison."*[12]

Between February meetings, Jessie brought Orage to Albany to meet
her family, but Orage seemed less enthusiastic about their marital future
than was Jessie. His mind was still very much set on the book and on
the future of his own group work that he had renewed with rare intensity. He added to them addresses on Social Credit seconded by Gorham
Munson, whom he had converted to the cause. Further, Orage was
organizing work groups on the psychological exercises he had experi-
mented with even before going to Gurdjieff. Jessie noted in her diary on
7 February, just after their return from Albany: "Orage very depressed
. . . Orage and I then had a long quarreling argument. It's interesting that
my reactions should always be disagreeable." A long talk with Muriel
Draper the next day cheered her up, and Edith was back from Chicago;
apparently her relationship with Toomer had cooled. Jessie was glad to
have her as an escape valve from the pressure she was feeling.

One reason for Orage's depression was what Gurdjieff called the
"dirty dollar" question. Orage was doing his best to raise funds among
his groups, but not only was he unaware of what his group treasurer was
doing—Israel Solon had sent $500 to Gurdjieff without Orage's
approval—he was not aware of how much Toomer was sending from
Chicago. He was afraid that Toomer might be promising more than he
could deliver, and so wrote him in February with friendly advice: "G is
quite extraordinary about money, but not, unfortunately, unique . . .
Don't forget to keep me informed of anything you send."[13]

Jessie's and Orage's good moods were restored when they heard
that the divorce had been pronounced in London on the 22 February.
Now there was but a six-month waiting period to endure. They celebrated at a dinner given by Blanche Grant (later godmother to Orage's
daughter, Ann). After that, they met Muriel Draper and Edith, and

12. Crane, *Letters*, p. 298.
13. Toomer Collection, Box 6, Folder 205.

together they went up to Harlem to what Jessie described in her diary as "the big social event of the season . . . and I met Rebecca West and saw Paul Robeson and others. It was funny. We had a box and looked down on the dancing which was like nothing I've ever seen before. And they were all having such a good time—such clothes—some beautiful—others humorous." On 8 March, Jessie attended a meeting of the stockholders of the Sunwise Turn, and the dissolution of the bookshop was decided after Doubleday made a modest offer. A month later, Doubleday took over the property.

Jean Toomer wrote Orage in the spring to say that he would be going to the Institute for the coming summer. Orage, anxious again, wrote back at once to warn that he had better subtract the $2000 still owed him out of the funds he had raised in Chicago rather than ask the New York group to pay it out of the publication funds. The warning came too late. Jean had already sent the money to the Institute and, in return, had received a letter from Olga de Hartmann containing praises from Gurdjieff. Before this news got to Orage, he had written Toomer again to assure him that the Institute would accept all his students, quipping that they will be Gurdjieff's sole support for a while. Then, after he heard of the money Jean had sent, he wrote that the New York group itself had just sent $2500, adding: "Now you see why I urged you not to send before!"[14] Gorham Munson, as retiring treasurer of the New York group, consoled Orage with confirmation that Gurdjieff had been paid off in full, that more than half of the group's debt to Toomer had been paid, and the that remaining $500 had been pledged to him.

Jessmin Howarth was in New York in late April and early May and helped Orage with his movements class. Toomer, in April, came at Orage's invitation to his classes, which featured teaching the "psychological exercises." During his 18 April meeting, Orage stressed one of his favored themes, that what distinguishes humans from animals is not just the question of language, which animals have, of course, or the question of a sense of futurity, which animals act upon instinctively in the procreative act. "Dogs cannot do wrong," he indicated, "because they obey the law of their kind, or nature":

---

14. Jessie Orage told me that Orage felt obliged to look after Jean in relations with Gurdjieff. Eldridge and Kerman, *Lives of Jean Toomer* (Baton Rouge, LA: Louisiana State University Press, 1987), p. 190, mention demands placed upon Toomer at this time, mostly financial. It would seem that Gurdjieff would have the Chicago group match the New York group in support for the Prieuré.

Man has a choice, has doubts and the possibility of moving up or down on scales of being. Animals are a fixed note, but man is aware of potentials. Since man has choice, he can actualize higher series on the scale, but he lacks objective conscience to realize a cooperation with God. The planetary body we have inherited, our essence in the form of health and readiness, is potentially capable of any necessary accomplishment. Gurdjieff mastered fifty or sixty crafts to keep himself in a state of readiness. This is the first aim dictated by Objective Consciousness. This is why we have reason to feel contempt for the highly specialized skills of a gymnast, for example. We must aim to improve our selves and know more and more; but, the more a man knows, the less we find him to be. Our aim is to pay off as quickly as possible the debt incurred in becoming conscious responsible beings. This is the "terror of the situation," being both animal and conscious, but responsible for lightening the burden of our common father. We aim to move others up the scale of reason to the sacred degree of individuality. But, since the earth became split into essential and artificial things, we now produce sociological instead of essential values. This is the effect of Kundabuffer, and in its presence we have neither consciousness, individuality or will or cosmic consciousness."[15]

Orage reminded his pupils, as he usually did at the end of his teaching year, in preparing them for visits to the Institute, that lives in New York and at the Prieuré were both prisons. In their daily activities in New York, they were comparable to Lynceus imprisoned in a small cell, because they cannot see anything but still have power of vision. The Institute, a conscious prison, functions to release them from their prison of unconscious habit. Following Gurdjieff, he reminded them that, in order to escape from prison, they must have three elements: first, the realization that they *are* in prison; second, the tools to escape, and third, a guide who knows the way out. Nonetheless, Orage added, there is a fourth necessity—the will to escape, and this will necessarily involves voluntary suffering.[16] On 25 May—the day of his last meeting before the summer break and four days after Charles Lindbergh landed at Le

---

15. Manchester Papers, p. 42. King *The Oregean Version*, pp. 75–76, explains how the Buddhist *kundalini*, or the faculty inciting inspiration, is actually a diseased part of the faculty of imagination, and a buffer to reality, and so Gurdjieff gave the organ a proper name. For a detailed anatomical and physiological analysis of kundabuffer, see Keith Buzzell, "Kundabuffer," in *All and Everything '97*, pp. 80–103.
16. Lynceus is the sharp-eyed Argonaut who can see inner form beneath outer matter. He represents intellectual and moral perspicuity. Orage's *will* reflects Nietzsche's will as a power to struggle and overcome. It is an attribute of the Superman.

Bourget at the end of his solo flight across the Atlantic—Orage illustrated what he understood by "voluntary suffering." "It is suffering the
unpleasant manifestations of other beings, and it consists in controlling
your facial expressions and other forms of behavior, or in concealing
them, or in changing them. If a man enrages me, I want to strike him;
but, voluntary suffering requires that I respond as if he pleased me."[17]
Two days earlier, Orage had invited John Dos Passos and e. e. cummings to a last demonstration. Both were very impressed. After a discussion with him the next day, cummings said he should tell some
others about the work. Indeed he did, with significant consequences.
Cummings wrote to his good friend, the Blake and Milton scholar S.
Foster Damon (1893–1971). Damon contacted a number of Harvard
students, among whom were Payson Loomis, Lincoln Kirstein, Philip
Lasell, and a Hotchkiss school friend of Payson's, Nick Putnam. All
decided to go to the Institute together that summer after conferring with
Orage in New York. Jean Toomer also sent Chicago students through
New York before going to Fontainebleau, and Jessie and Orage gave a
party for them on 30 June, an occasion at which Gorham Munson gave
an introductory talk about Gurdjieff and the Institute.

Orage saw no good reason to go himself until he heard directly
from Gurdjieff what his mission might be. He hoped that Toomer would
take over some of the onus of editorial work on the translation and
responsibility for publishing the book. Besides, Jessie was very content
to be in New York alone with Orage in the summer with no hectic
schedule of lectures, readings, and movement classes. For a summer
vacation, Orage suggested a trip to Quebec, and told some of his New
York friends that he was scouting to see if the situation in Canada was
propitious for establishing new groups. The Orages set out in mid-July
with the Daly Kings and Sherman and Elsa Manchester in two cars.
In Montreal, they were among a large audience to meet the Prince of
Wales, whom Jessie described in her diary as "disappointing in appearance." They went on to Trois Rivières and then south toward New
England, but not before Daly bought a large quantity of whiskey that he
hid in his spare tire. They passed customs without a hitch on 1 August.

After their return to New York, Orage told Jessie that he had decided to go to Fontainebleau soon. On the 10th, he booked his passage.

---

17. Manchester Papers, p. 120. Orage did not have access to Ouspensky's voluminous notes on
Gurdjieff's teaching, but most of what he says is confirmed by Ouspensky's *In Search of the
Miraculous,* published twenty-five years after Orage's death (New York: Harcourt Brace and
World, 1949). Ouspensky, pp. 357–358, cites Gurdjieff on the necessity of suffering, but has
nothing to say of intentional suffering

Jessie asked him to stay, again on the grounds that Orage was giving too much of himself to Gurdjieff. After a long discussion between the two on the 12th, Jessie recorded in her diary: "[I am] very unhappy this morning because O says that when we are married, holding groups will be impossible and, as he is unhappy alone with me because he can't work, there doesn't seem to be much use of anything."

Orage sailed on the 17th, arrived in England on the 23rd—a day that Jessie marked in her diary with the "murder" of Sacco and Vanzetti—and immediately cabled Jessie their code word "love" to indicate safe arrival. He stayed in London awaiting the final divorce decree, which was pronounced on 2 September. Then, instead of going on to Fontainebleau as planned, he sailed back to New York on the 9th, arriving there on the 16th. In all haste, they filed the necessary papers, took their blood tests, and were married in a simple civil ceremony in Stamford, Connecticut on the 24th.

Meanwhile, at the Prieuré, Jean Toomer, Schuyler Jackson, Melville Cane, Edwin Wolfe, and the Munsons, as well as Gurdjieff, were awaiting Orage's arrival,[18] but Gurdjieff made signs neither of expectation nor irritation. For the moment he was showing favor to Toomer and said that Orage would arrive before the end of the year. Indeed, letters arrived at the Orages in late October requesting Orage's return as soon as possible. Jessie tried to persuade him against going, and wrote in her diary in early November: "Long argument concerning a return to the Institute in 2 months. . . . Got into a discussion concerning Fontainebleau which lasted until early morning. . . . More argument last night after the party until 6 A.M."

Orage remained calm and noncommittal while awaiting details from Gurdjieff on the need for his presence. In the interim, he was having great success with his teaching. The Swiss consul in New York, Robert Schwartzenbach, and his wife, Marguerite, were frequent visitors and almost the entire Swiss colony of bankers and businessmen in Westchester and Fairfield counties soon became enthusiastic visitors to

---

18. Munson, *Aladdin's Lamp*, p. 273, says Orage arrived at the Prieuré at the middle of his own stay in the summer of 1927, and Webb, *Harmonious Circle*, p. 361, locates him there in September for ten days. Nott, *Teachings*, p. 113, has Orage there all that summer, holding long talks with himself and Gurdjieff. Louise Welch, *Orage with Gurdjieff in America* (London: Routledge & Kegan Paul, 1982), p. 49, locates him there after telling Jessie he would return on 1 September. She adds that when Gurdjieff tried to trick him into staying to work on the book, Orage said: "I ran out of my first marriage. I will never do so again." It is, of course, possible that Orage, unbeknownst to Jessie, had made a quick trip to the Institute in the few days between the divorce and his return, but it would be unlike Orage not to mention the fact or to report the result. Moore, *Gurdjieff: The Anatomy of a Myth* (Boston: Element, 1991), typically cautious, does not mention Orage's presence in Fontainebleau in the summer of 1927.

Orage's lectures. The format of his meetings had changed since he had received material to translate from Gurdjieff. Now, group meetings consisted largely of reading and commentary on the chapter most recently translated. In his commentary on Gurdjieff's chapter on art, Orage spoke of the current absence of "objective art," which he defined as "the production of an effect or conveyance of a meaning by deliberately invented artificial means. . . . Self-expression has nothing to do with art, for there is seldom any self involved worth expressing."[19] Orage believed that the artist must also be a scientist. Art's function is to illuminate a truth by touching upon the experience of its receptor, not of the artist. For an example, he quoted what Katherine Mansfield had said to him concerning what she had learned at the Prieuré: "I have found my idea. . . . Katya understands something she never understood before . . . that of representing life not merely as it appears to a certain attitude, but as it appears to another and different attitude, a creative attitude."[20] What this meant to Orage was that Katherine had stripped back the "personality" of her art to find an objective stance emanating from her "essence." Orage told his group an illustrative story along these lines. He said that Gurdjieff once gave a dinner that included a bishop among a number of notables. Gurdjieff started telling stories. The guests were sometimes amused, sometimes shocked, but assumed he was kidding them. Later, the bishop became convinced that Gurdjieff really liked such stories, and so he told one himself, then another. Finally, Gurdjieff yawned and stopped the bishop, saying to the others, "See, he is not just priest inside. He was adopted by a priest, brought up to go to church, has no real priestliness in him."[21]

Besides his regular meetings and movements exercises, Orage was conducting "psychological exercises" with success, and had found a large audience for his ideas on Social Credit. In all, he had no good reason in the fall of 1927 to hurry back to the Institute. On the other side of the Atlantic, after having had a good summer's attendance at the Institute, Gurdjieff sent Toomer back to Chicago with the particular charge to prepare pupils for the Prieuré for the summer of 1928. Toomer, ardent baseball fan that he was, regretted not having seen Babe Ruth's historic 60th home run of the 1927 season on 30 September. Gurdjieff had not spent as much time with Toomer that summer as he

19. Cited by Munson, *Aladdin's Lamp*, p. 274.
20. Orage, "Conversations with Katherine Mansfield," *On Love* (York Beach, ME: Samuel Weiser, 1997), p. 41.
21. Cited by Sherman Manchester in notes to a meeting on May 23rd, 1927 (Manchester Papers, p. 141).

might have, because he had anticipated having Toomer and Orage together in discussions about the future of American groups. In October, speaking for Gurdjieff, Olga de Hartmann wrote Orage a stern letter requesting him to return to the Institute as soon as possible. Orage demurred. On 6 November 1927, according to his own words in the Prologue to the Third Series: *Life Is Real Only Then, When I Am,* Gurdjieff found himself in an uncomfortable situation and made a categorical decision:

> After working for almost three years with unimaginable difficulties and being ready to die happily . . . to mobilize all the capacities and possibilities in my common presence—to discover some possible means of satisfactorily emerging from such a situation. If this should in fact occur, then, in addition to everything else accomplished, I would be in possession of one or more excellent and extraordinary examples for a thoroughly practical proof of the law conformably arising consequences resulting from the fundamental cosmic law of "sevenfoldness," which law is theoretically explained by me in sufficient detail in my writings.[22]

He had explained earlier in his text that the crisis, in effect, concerned the written style of the first series, because:

> The form of the exposition of my thoughts in these writings could be understood exclusively by those readers who, in one way or another, were already acquainted with the peculiar form of my mentation. But every other reader . . . would understand nearly nothing. . . . I enlightened myself for the first time with regard to the particular form in which it would be necessary to write in order that it might be accessible to the understanding of everyone.[23]

Orage understood this problem well. Not only had he talked with Katherine Mansfield about "objective writings," but he had formulated for his pupils in New York something out of what that would consist: "sentences that will have, if read, a definite foreseen effect no matter what the state of the reader is, sentences as matrices, magic sentences."[24]

---

22. (New York: Dutton for Triangle Editions, 1975) pp. 33–34. Hippocrates said that "the number seven, through its hidden virtues, maintains everything in being."
23. Gurdjieff, *Life is Real*, p. 50.
24. Manchester notes on Orage's meeting on March 29th, 1926 (Manchester Papers, p. 3).

In effect, then, Gurdjieff was determined to have Orage at the Institute to restyle the first series as soon as possible. Toomer, busy in Chicago, need not be on hand, but he could get his instructions relayed by Orage. Accordingly, on 29 November, Miss Merston was dispatched to New York on the Mauretania to carry manuscripts for Orage to edit and to demand his immediate return. Orage complied, placed his groups under the responsibility of the New York Committee. He sailed with an unhappy and reluctant Jessie on New Year's Eve on the Mauretania. They arrived in Plymouth on the morning of the 6th, and went on to Cherbourg. At 1 A.M. on the 7th, they were in Paris, where Edith Taylor met them and drove them to the Prieuré.

1928: THE TERROR OF THE SITUATION

The next morning, Gurdjieff greeted the Orages with affection, gave Jessie a kiss and declared that she was now, as Orage's wife, half of him (or half of his). The day's activities were reduced, acquaintances and re-acquaintances made. Gurdjieff was in splendid form, and supper that night was at 1:30 A.M., with melons—Gurdjieff's favorite—for dessert, followed by music in Gurdjieff's room. Orage and Jessie were assigned to a large room in the Ritz, their first night together at the Prieuré.

At 10 o'clock the following morning, Gurdjieff had the Orages awakened (Jessie was a habitual late sleeper) and he led them, with Edith in tow, to the café Henri IV for coffee and talk. Gurdjieff went over the last chapter he had sent Orage with Mrs. Merston, then turned to Jessie and asked her what she had thought of it. "Not much," she replied, to which he just stared at her for a while, and then thanked her very much for her consideration, adding that he pitied her for her opinion. Gurdjieff left for Paris that afternoon and, the next day, Edith drove the Orages to meet him at the Café de la Paix at noon. Jane Heap was there as well, and they all discussed the manuscript. The Orages returned to the Institute by train, and Gurdjieff returned by car with Edith two days later.

January 13th was the Russian New Year and Gurdjieff's birthday. As usual, there were lavish festivities to enjoy. In all, there were sixty at the table that evening in formal wear. The children had their party the next day, presided over by Jessie and Edith. There was a continuous atmosphere of gaiety and, that evening, Gurdjieff announced that he would soon be taking a trip. On the morning of the 17th, the Orages and Gurdjieff, with Edith driving, went to Rouen. After visiting the cathedral and lunching, the Orages went to their room, where Jessie declared that she felt very much ill at ease in such close quarters with Gurdjieff. They walked alone through the city that evening, and rejoined the others for a quiet supper.

The second evening, Gurdjieff reminded them that this was a working trip. While Jessie went to her room and typed the pages Edith dictated to her, Orage and Gurdjieff talked together downstairs. On the 21th, they drove to Auxerre, arriving just in time for supper. Again, in their room, Jessie said that she had had enough of this and wanted some assurances that they would be soon on their way back to New York. As she noted the next day in her diary: "We went to bed at 11 and quarreled til 2:30. The usual complaint on my part. I am a damn fool and he is so dear to me." The usual complaint was that Orage put Gurdjieff's interests before hers.

In the days following, they drove to Autun to see the cathedral, then to Bourg and Bellegarde, before arriving on the 24th at one of Gurdjieff's favorite spots, the Col de la Faucille in the Jura, overlooking Geneva. They stayed there three nights, but on the second afternoon, there was a disturbing incident. At the picnic lunch overlooking the lake, Gurdjieff suddenly railed about Americans and their absurd lust for money, but no one seemed to know to whom he addressed himself. At dinner in the hotel, he turned to Edith and said that he had meant his anger for her, and then proceeded to insult her American ways in vicious terms. Jessie noted in her diary that "he was superb during the outburst. I sat very near him and stared. His eyes were never angry, obviously he was playing a role. Afterwards he came up to me and said he was sorry but he had drunk too much. I said 'don't apologize, you were delightful.'" Edith refused that evening to go to Gurdjieff's room with the others for a reading.

On the 27th, they arrived back at the Institute and, that night, Gurdjieff announced a new trip in a few days. It was on the 31st that the same group set off again for Rouen, just for the night, before proceeding on to Rennes on 1 February, then to Chartres to see the cathedral, and on to Orléans for the next night. Gurdjieff had ordered Jessie to bring along her portable typewriter and, between stops, while Edith drove with Orage beside her, Gurdjieff in the back seat dictated from Orage's translation, often suggesting changes. The pace was frenetic, and Jessie confided to Orage that she thought Gurdjieff seemed to be "blowing up a storm of some sort." Jessie took relief each evening in wine and armagnac. On 4 February, during their luncheon halt, Gurdjieff turned to her and said that, as long as she was the wife of the super-idiot, she should not touch alcohol.[25] If Jessie felt depressed by all this, Orage seemed to be pleased with Gurdjieff's remark, as well as with the progress of the work. He suggested to Jessie that they either stay at the Institute for a longer period or come back the following summer. Jessie wanted no part of either proposal.

On the 8th, they arrived in Vichy where Gurdjieff enjoyed taking the waters. A day later, they motored on to Grenoble. The next day, they turned south along the Route de Napoléon to Castellane in the Alps, where they stayed the night. On the evening of the 11th, they stopped at Cannes. Gurdjieff relaxed on the hotel terrace drinking and making notes, while the others went sightseeing. The next day, they drove to Nice for lunch and then on to Monte Carlo, where Gurdjieff gave each of the party 100 francs to lose at the casino while he stayed behind at the hotel. Edith and Jessie lost, but Orage won 150 francs, which put him in an ebullient mood. He remarked that Gurdjieff had sent them to the Casino to appreciate that life is a casino in which man is completely at the mercy of accident, but some win, for reasons Gurdjieff could explain. At the dinner table, Gurdjieff seemed unusually animated, spoke loudly with gestures, making English guests near them ill at ease, not to mention the maître d'hôtel, whose admonitions were ignored. Jessie and Edith found the situation both embarrassing and amusing, but Orage and Gurdjieff seemed oblivious to the comments that Jessie overheard.

They left on the 14th and drove to Avignon, where, at dinner, Jessie felt fortified enough with the wine to argue with Gurdjieff. When she laughed at something he said, Gurdjieff just stared at her. A day later, they stopped for the night at Thiers in the Massif Central. They regained Vichy once more on the 16th. During the stop, Edith argued with Gurdjieff and sulked for most of the evening. They stayed on another day in Vichy, while Gurdjieff and Orage took the waters and then consulted by themselves, leaving the women to find their own amusement. Back at the Institute, after Edith announced to Jessie that she was going back to Paris, perhaps never to return. Jessie, with nei-

---

25. Gurdjieff, who had an unusual capacity for drink, made a careful distinction between ordinary drinking and conscious drinking which could free the "I" to think, feel, talk and act; that is, to expose "essence." This is Orage's explanation to his group on the 30th of April 1928. (Manchester Papers, p. 65). See also King, *The Oragean Version*, p. 142.

ther Orage's knowledge or approval, told Gurdjieff that she and Orage were leaving the following week.

Nothing came of either woman's declaration. On the 21st, the same quartet, this time with Metz as well, were off to Rouen for two nights. Shortly after their return, Olga de Hartmann tried to calm down a complaining Jessie and have her understand the situation from Gurdjieff's point of view, but the discussion turned into a pointless argument. The same afternoon, Gurdjieff ordered the entire adult population of the Institute to come to his room and sow melon seeds in boxes. He said that he estimated that he could make thousands of francs from them.

The tension between Jessie and Gurdjieff came to a head the next day at Gurdjieff's flat in Paris. At lunch, Gurdjieff, whose patience with Jessie was waning, called her a "squirming idiot" and a candidate for a harmful one. He added that, if she kept Orage, his super-idiot, from being one of his inner circle—"because," he said, according to the diary entry for the day, "there must be one of each kind around him—the god of gods"—then Jessie would burn in hell.[26] Jessie was so taken aback she could hardly breathe, but she managed to look him in the eye and smile. That night, she decided that, if Gurdjieff had challenged her over the possession of Orage, she would surely win: "He is the biggest fool alive if he thinks he can make me do something by these methods," she wrote in her diary. "Also I am sorry to leave with the feeling I have about him now. Yesterday I felt very friendly and quite sorry to leave him—now, I hope I never see him again."

She spent much of the morning talking with Orage about her emotions. She declared that Gurdjieff was finished for her, though she regretted it. She refused to go back to his flat to eat, saying simply to Orage that she never wanted to see Gurdjieff again. Orage tried to appease her with his usual argument that Gurdjieff must not be considered as an ordinary man, and that she, herself, had seen and admired his self-control when he appeared to have lost his temper at Edith during their long trip. Furthermore, he said, this was to be their last meeting with Gurdjieff until the summer. So Jessie gave in and went with Orage to coffee with Gurdjieff at the Café de la Paix. Edith joined them there.

---

26. Webb, *Harmonious Circle*, p. 363, and Moore, *Gurdjieff: The Anatomy of a Myth*, p. 223, who cites Jessie herself as informant, both have "burn in boiling oil." Her diary has "Hell" in two different entries. One must question, however, Gurdjieff's intent here. Gurdjieff disdained the dualistic concept of heaven and hell in *All and Everything: Beelzebub's Tales to his Grandson* (London: Routledge & Kegan Paul, 1950), pp. 339–342, citing Babylonian error. At the end of *Tales*, Gurdjieff says that hell and paradise exist as earthly states for man.

That evening, they all had dinner at Gurdjieff's flat, after which they said goodbye. Gurdjieff's last words to Jessie on this occasion were "bring a little one back with you next time."

The date of their sailing from Cherbourg—amatory 29 February—can be read as an appropriate omen for Jessie that she had reclaimed her man from Gurdjieff's grasp. On 6 March, they disembarked in New York where, an ocean's breadth away from the Institute, Jessie felt free of Gurdjieff's influence on her husband. But Orage remained still faithful to his stewardship, however. The first draft of the book was about to be completed, and he felt committed to shaping it into publishable form in English.[27] They took a small flat on 28th Street, and Orage got back to work with his group. Zona Gale was visiting Muriel Draper, and both attended Orage's group meeting. Zona was still fascinated by the Gurdjieff work and, on Orage's recommendation, had decided to join Toomer's Chicago group. In mid-April, Payson Loomis returned from the Institute with news that all was well and that Gurdjieff had expectations of a good number of American pupils at the Institute in the coming summer.

Besides his other activities, Orage began holding private writing classes. Among his first students were Muriel Draper—who was writing of her European experiences before the first World War, published soon after by Harper and Brothers in 1929 as *Music at Midnight*—Tom Matthews—later editor of Time—and the labor union economist and writer Paul E. Anderson, who would serve several years later as Gurdjieff's secretary in the United States. Following a suggestion of Gurdjieff's that he should scan possibilities of new group locations, Orage decided to go to the West coast on a belated honeymoon. While he was making preliminary plans, Orage wrote Edith at the Prieuré to say that he was preparing some of his pupils to visit the Institute, including Tom Matthews' sister Peggy (later Flinsch). He reported on his money-raising efforts, noting that Mme de Hartmann had been writing for money from the New York group since their return. Orage had already sent $3000, and he asked Edith not to mention the fact to Jessie, because he was sending his *own* money, earned giving lectures on English literature at $250 each. He also made a pittance from his

---

27. Olga de Hartmann, *Our Life with Gurdjieff* (London: Penguin, 1972), p. 209, says the first draft of the book was completed in 1928, but she was not referring to the English text. Gurdjieff himself, in *Life is Real* (New York: Dutton for Triangle Editions, 1975), p. 4, at the Café de la Paix on 13 September 1932, writes that the first series was finished "today."

writing lessons. In the meantime, he was taking driving lessons in preparation for the trip west.

Shortly before leaving with Jessie, Orage wrote Edith again, saying that he had heard from Mme de Hartmann that Gurdjieff was not satisfied with what he had sent and was asking for $10,000 more within the next three months. He counted on Edith to mediate for him, "knowing how much Gurdjieff trusted her." All this while, in New York, Orage was working hard on revising the translation of the book he was, he said, in fact *reading* for the first time. "My only disgust with it," he wrote Edith, "is not that nobody can understand it, but that *I* cannot."[28] He told Edith that their plans for the West included finding support for the Institute. "You know," he wrote, "that I cannot forget the Institute or you who have been both its and my friend."[29]

The Orages left New York 5 June and drove through Washington to Charlottesville, where Orage visited acquaintances at the University of Virginia. They drove on the 22nd to Sparta, Georgia, to see the town that played a central role in Jean Toomer's *Cane*. From there, they went to Nashville, and, a few days later, to Fort Worth, Texas and Fort Sumner, New Mexico. They arrived on 30 June in Santa Fe, where Betty Hare had a house waiting for them. Betty introduced Orage to Senator Bronson Cutting, who was particularly interested in Orage's ideas on Social Credit, Governor H. W. Hockenhull, whom they saw often and with whom they developed a friendship, Mary Austin, Martha Mann, and Alice Corbin Henderson, the assistant editor of Harriet Monroe's *Poetry*. Over the next few weeks, they visited Pueblos with Tony and Mabel Luhan. They saw Los Alamos, Jemez Springs, where they took the baths, Cochiti, where they witnessed a corn dance, W. H. Lawrence's ranch, the Santuario de Chimayó, and Pueblo Bonito in Chaco Canyon. When Orage raised the issue with Mabel of the Gurdjieff work, she expressed her reluctance to renew an offer of her ranch for a Gurdjieff Institute on American soil, though she believed Orage's judgment that the Prieuré was insolvent and might close its doors at any time.

28. Letter to Edith Taylor 11 June, 1928, Taylor Papers. Orage and Toomer both sought the key to the book's code. Though his study has come to my attention too late to be taken into consideration here, Jon Woodson, *To Make a New Race* (Jackson, MS: University of Mississippi Press, 1999), claims that Gurdjieff's teaching led Toomer and other writers of the Harlem Renaissance to write in code.
29. Taylor Papers.

From Santa Fe, Orage wrote Edith at the Institute to say that he was bored and depressed in New Mexico, but that he hoped to give lectures and form groups in San Francisco between October and December. He said that he would sell the automobile in California and return to New York by train, unless Edith would come over to join them. He thought her own mission in Europe to raise money for Gurdjieff was futile, since the maintenance of the Prieuré was hopeless, even if the current debt on it were paid off. "I would return there," he wrote, "but the 'call' would have to be remarkably clear."[30] Near the end of the month, Jessie, not altogether pleased with their reception in some of the Pueblos, and Orage, disappointed with Mabel's intransigence, drove down to Albuquerque, then to the pueblo of Acoma and on to the Painted Desert and Holbrook, Arizona, where they spent the night. The next day they motored to the Grand Canyon, then south to Phoenix, and westward through Yuma, arriving in San Diego on 6 August. From there, they motored through Los Angeles, and up along the rugged coast to Big Sur to visit Lincoln Steffens and Robinson Jeffers, before settling into an apartment in San Francisco. A month later, they received a letter from Stanley Nott with the news that Edith was expecting Gurdjieff's child. Orage wrote her right away saying that he was "overjoyed."[31]

Three weeks later, Jessie experienced her own morning sickness, and a few days later, her pregnancy was confirmed. All this time, Orage was renewing literary acquaintances and making new ones in the Bay area. They lunched with Ansel Adams, who took a portrait photo of Orage in October. Then, having surveyed the terrain to their satisfaction, though failing to set up a structure for a future group, Orage and Jessie took the train down to Los Angeles and Hollywood, where they visited Charlie Chaplin before Orage gave a talk about Gurdjieff's work. The *Los Angeles Times* on 21 October, reported in humorous style the talk in Hollywood by this "fellow with wicked eyes and a dodgeful wit." As was customary for him, Orage spoke of people's neglect of their own potential, saying that, in this country of some 100,000,000 persons, perhaps only one hundred use anything near their mental capacity. He went on to give examples of what we can do by proper

---

30. To Edith Taylor, 14 July, 1928, Taylor Papers.
31. To Edith Taylor, 9 September, 1928, Taylor Papers. In the Fontainebleau town hall on August 31st, Edith was married to Caesar Zwaska, and gave birth in Rouen on November 13th to a daughter Eve.

training and concentration. The *Times* reported that the end of the talk, a young architect approached Orage angrily.

"How dare you say we can't think—that our minds need exercising? Now you repeat backwards what I have just said. Can you do it?"
"Certainly I can," Orage replied quietly.
"Do it then!"
"Certainly I won't."
"Well, what can you do with all your superior thinking that I can't?" the architect roared.
"I can keep my temper," Orage responded, whereupon his interrogator turned and fled the scene.[32]

From Los Angeles, they took the train back to New York, stopping off in Chicago for a few days to see Jean Toomer. Orage told Toomer that, in his opinion, the New York group could not possibly repay the outstanding debt on the Institute, and that his own summer had been a financial loss, despite the vacation it afforded him. Toomer said that Mme de Hartmann, along with her relays of Gurdjieff's demands for money, was keeping him posted on events at the Prieuré, but Orage suspected that her accounts were untrustworthy compared to Edith's. When, back in New York, friends asked Orage about his impression of California, he said simply: "Jesus Christ was not a Californian."[33]

1929: THE WORLD IS A SCHOOL IN WHICH THERE IS NO TEACHING, ONLY LEARNING[34]

On 7 January, Orage and Jessie were in a restaurant where they overheard a conversation between Edmund Wilson and Paul Rosenfeld at an adjacent table. Edmund remarked that Orage, whom he had not yet heard speak, was a master of nothing but spellbinding. He went on to say that Orage had an undue influence on Tom Matthews. Three days later, Bernard Metz arrived aboard the Majestic with news that Gurdjieff was just behind him. When the master arrived on the 23 January, Orage and Jessie, big with child, met him and the Hartmanns at the dock, and managed, with not unusual difficulty, to get Gurdjieff

---

32. The second exercise in Orage's *The Active Mind,* is "The Control of Temper."
33. Welch, *Orage,* p. 76.
34. Orage to his pupils, 25 April, 1927.

through customs.[35] The next evening, Muriel Draper gave a party in his honor with over a hundred guests. Gurdjieff was pleased and was unusually gracious throughout the long evening. A day later, Gurdjieff visited a group meeting and scheduled a demonstration for the 28th. Mabel Luhan was in New York and accepted an invitation to talk with Gurdjieff and Orage, but she demurred before their request to consider re-offering her Taos property.

On the same day the newspapers were vaunting Admiral Byrd's arrival in the Antarctic, Gurdjieff directed a demonstration at Carnegie Hall. Before it began, however, he stepped to the front of the stage and made a brief speech thanking Orage for his help in a crisis, and for having been a trusty steward during his absence. Then, looking down at Jessie in the audience, he said: "Orage wish very much have baby— now he very pleased. If boy I give him five books, if girl nothing." Jessie was visibly shocked, but Orage just smiled, and then the demonstration went ahead smoothly to a small audience of some 150 people.

On the 30th, Caesar Zwaska arrived from Chicago as Toomer's emissary and met with Orage and Gurdjieff to say that Toomer was too busy with his own groups at the moment, but would be in New York before the spring. Orage found his own groups in New York smaller than ever since his return. Gurdjieff advised him to hold meetings every night, but Jessie was especially vehement against such a commitment of time, especially when she was only a matter of weeks from giving birth. On the 9th, Gurdjieff held another demonstration at Carnegie Hall before a scant hundred in the audience. Orage went about the city looking up literary acquaintances to drum up interest. He even persuaded Theodore Dreiser to attend one of his meetings. Dreiser did so, but was not impressed, and Orage found him unimpressive. Jessie thought him a bore.

At a meeting of Orage with Gurdjieff and the New York Committee, Gurdjieff remarked on Jessie's condition and said that both Jessie and Edith Taylor were sterile until he put a potion in their glasses of armagnac. When Jessie heard this, she was furious, and when

---

35. In the afterword to *Beelzebub's Tales,* Gurdjieff says that this trip was made at Orage's insistence. I have found no hint of an invitation from Orage to Gurdjieff at this time, but there is evidence that Gurdjieff was thinking of moving the entire Institute organization to the United States, as the difficulty of managing the Prieuré increased. The only good reason for Orage to have insisted on Gurdjieff's visit in 1929 would have been to have Gurdjieff scan the possibilities Orage had uncovered in his western trip, though they seem to have been slight.

Orage returned from Gurdjieff's apartment at 2:30 A.M., Jessie argued with him until 4 A.M. The next day at lunchtime, Mme de Hartmann called Orage to relay Gurdjieff's invitation to Jessie for lunch. She refused. Later, when she and Rita were having a soda at a drugstore, Rita told her in all confidence that Gurdjieff had asked her to marry him, explaining that he hadn't married Edith because she was having an affair with Rosemary Nott.[36]

About this time, Gurdjieff was served in Child's regularly by a Ukrainian waitress from Brooklyn called Anna. Apparently no one knew her last name. She attached herself to Gurdjieff and protected him from the usual inconveniences of a bustling public venue. They spoke Russian or Ukrainian in their brief exchanges, and Gurdjieff learned that Anna earned money after work practicing the oldest profession. He was not shocked, but was interested in the story behind her vocation.[37] Day after day, she told him stories of her life which included taking the subway each day from Brooklyn to Manhattan and back. The manager of Child's soon complained about the time she spent with a customer who ordered very little and who was, he suspected, her pimp. Her salary was reduced to a single dollar a day, and she was reassigned to tables in the rear of the restaurant. So, Gurdjieff moved back there, away from his close view of the passing crowd, and more than made up her lost income with generous tips. Before he left, he had tutored her and given her instructions on how to make a more profitable career. He set her on her way by having her hired by Orage and members of his group as a house-help, telling her to observe how these very talented people went about their professions.[38]

On 8 March, Orage had lunch with Mabel and Tony Luhan. Mabel, now fifty years old, was still a fervent admirer and follower of Orage, but she felt that she had been deceived by Gurdjieff and Toomer when her $15,000 vanished into thin air.[39] Apparently, Mabel was all forgiving, but Tony thought his wife should not forget that she had been taken advantage of. By this time, all Orage could account for was the money

---

36. Rita, an actress, was fond of gossip, and it is very hard to give credence to this story. Webb, *Harmonious Circle,* p. 331, says that Gurdjieff asked the wife of the Swiss consul in New York, Marguerite Schwartzenbach, to marry him.

37. Fritz Peters, *Gurdjieff Remembered* (London: Victor Gallancz, 1969), p. 102, relates that Gurdjieff once told a prostitute that he was not from the Earth.

38. Anna is mentioned as a house-help regularly in Jessie's diary until September.

39. For the division and accounting of this amount, see Taylor *Shadows of Heaven* (York Beach, ME: Samuel Weiser, 1998), pp. 82–83.

he had directed to the New York Committee publication fund, but even this, apparently, had been liquidated when Munson resigned as treasurer. Sherman Manchester had taken over that office in his stead, and said all funds were accounted for.

On 16 March, Gurdjieff had Jessie join him and two other women for supper. Later, in the middle of the night, she became sick and remained so for two days, saying that Gurdjieff's food had poisoned her. Orage shrugged off the suggestion, and said it was her pregnancy, but Jessie insisted that she, like Orage a year earlier, had been poisoned. While she was still in her bed, Orage met again with Mabel and Tony. Mabel admitted that she still wanted to contribute to the work, and suggested that all three meet again as soon as Toomer arrived from Chicago.

A week later, on the 25th, Jean arrived and went straight to Gurdjieff's apartment, where he gave a detailed report of the activities of his Chicago group to Gurdjieff and Orage. Five days later, they met again. Gurdjieff was scheduled to return to France in a week, and he wanted assurances that the American operation was not only solid, which it wasn't, but that he could exercise certain control of the New York committee in the future. He was sensitive to a number of complications in New York. One, of course, was Orage's imminent fatherhood, which would necessarily reduce his commitment to the work and fund raising. Gurdjieff also knew that Orage was teaching material of his own—the psychological exercises—and having some success with them. This, too, threatened to limit Orage's work as his steward. Another consideration was Toomer's position. A year earlier, Gurdjieff had suggested that Orage remain at the Prieuré until the book was completed and in press, in order to cede to Toomer general direction over the work in the United States. The New York group could, in effect, operate by itself. It had a number of pupils besides Daly King capable of leading groups. What would be missing was the coherence Orage's presence gave the group.

On 4 April, Gurdjieff held his last meeting with the New York groups, after which he was given a supper attended by the Orages. After Gurdjieff sailed the next day on the Paris, Jessie was ecstatic and even Orage gave out a breath of relief. The pressure was off, and he felt free to concentrate for a while on his own interests. Nonetheless, Jessie admitted to him that she missed Gurdjieff, and wrote in her diary: "Whether one likes or dislikes G he leaves an empty place." The next morning, they heard that the Paris had run aground off Brooklyn. It was floated loose that afternoon at 3 P.M.

On 19 April, the child they had called "Jackie" in the womb was born. Orage, now fifty-six, finally a father, was enormously pleased with his handsome son, whom they baptized a few days later as Richard Dwight Orage, with Daly King and Amos Pinchot standing as godfathers, and Muriel Draper as godmother. With Gurdjieff gone and Jessie a happy mother, Orage turned his attention back to the book he was now "reading," rather than just translating. He expressed his frustration to Jessie and his close friends because, he confessed, he could not grasp the totality of the thing. The chapter "Purgatory," he proclaimed, was far superior to a thousand philosophical treatises he had read in his life, but it was the "whole" of the book, and certain elements in it, whose sense he could not fathom. Jessie said: "Poor darling. I wish I believed there was so much in it to understand."

In May, the terminal issue of *The Little Review* appeared in New York. It consisted of responses from a broad cross-section of the Western artistic population to a number of questions concerning views of self. The idea undoubtedly came to Margaret Anderson and Jane Heap from Orage's proposals to his pupils to respond to specific questions about themselves. Even the many refusals were published—some brusque, others insulting—and Orage's was brief. After writing "the public doesn't deserve my confession," he went on, as if in a self-reflective mode: "It's characteristic of world-reformers that they take themselves for granted. Under the pretense that they are too trivial a subject for question, they really mean they are above it. These ass-gods of reform!"[40]

The summer passed calmly. Edith Taylor was in New York much of the time, and she and Jessie, both recent mothers, spent a good deal of time together. Peggy Matthews, a mutual friend with whom Edith had nurtured friendship during the summer of 1928, invited both of them down to Princeton where she lived with her father, the Reverend Thomas Matthews, Bishop of New Jersey. In Princeton, Jessie first saw Edith's daughter, Eve, now six or seven months old, and remarked the striking resemblance to Gurdjieff. Edith explained that she had temporarily left Paris and had "escaped" the demands of the Institute. She recounted with humor to the Orages her multiple failures to raise money for the Prieuré. Her most important mission had been to her friend Bea Rothermere in Fribourg, Switzerland, to raise money. She enjoyed the

---

40. *The Little Review* (May 1927), p. 65.

stay, but came back with no promises, and suffered Gurdjieff's anger as a consequence.[41] Nonetheless, she was determined to return to the Prieuré, and left New York and the Orages in August with the promise that she would keep them informed about the summer activities

Later that summer, Jean Toomer arrived back at the Institute where Gurdjieff wanted to work closely with him. Toomer seemed to have more in mind a renewed effort in his writing career, having written a fictional account of his voyage over, entitled "Transatlantic," which he hoped the Compagnie Générale Transatlantique might subsidize. They didn't, and after a few days in Paris, he went down to the Institute. Gurdjieff was not pleased that he had sent few, if any, students that summer, and had arrived without any funds or subscriptions. What Gurdjieff did discuss with Toomer was his own early return in the autumn to the United States where, he promised, he would visit Chicago with expectations that some money for the Institute would be awaiting him.

In October, Toomer returned to Chicago with Gurdjieff's encouragement and contacted Orage from there to announce Gurdjieff's intentions. A few weeks later, Metz arrived in New York to make arrangements,[42] and spoke with both Orage and Toomer by telephone to urge them both to have money in hand. After an unhappy scene with Gurdjieff at the Prieuré, Edith had returned to New York at the end of September. She found a job with Fred Leighton, a Chicago friend of Toomer's, who had opened a New York branch of his "Trading Post," where he sold Mexican goods and Navajo and Pueblo Indian products. Fred joined one of Orage's groups, and all awaited Gurdjieff. Edith received a letter from Gurdjieff that he would arrive before the end of the year; nevertheless, Gurdjieff did not arrive, and no one seemed to know when he would. Without much concern, the Orages continued their social engagements.

---

41. Though Lady Rothermere had probably contributed a major share of the funds necessary to secure the Prieuré in 1922, she had shifted her financial attention to T. S. Eliot and the *Criterion*. Her adopted daughter, Dorothy Ireland, was a close friend of Edith's and an infrequent visitor to the Prieuré.

42. Olga de Hartmann, in her continuation to her husband's memoirs, *Our Life with Gurdjieff,* pp. 129–131, says that Gurdjieff was in New York in October, again at the urging of Orage, whom she places at the Institute that October. She also tells that story of the break she and her husband had with Gurdjieff at this time. Gurdjieff demanded that Olga accompany him to New York, but she said she had to stay with her ailing husband in Paris. Gurdjieff predicted something bad would happen to Thomas if Olga did not obey him. She refused, and neither of them ever saw Gurdjieff alive again. Olga places this scene in October, but she must be mistaking the year. Orage did not leave his family at any time during the summer and fall of 1929, and Gurdjieff did not leave France until the following year.

A new and active member of one of his groups in New York was Nick [Nicholas Herkimer] Putnam, who had visited the Institute the first time in the summer of 1927 with Payson Loomis. Nick was from an old Saratoga family that traced its line proudly back to General Israel Putnam, a popular hero of the War of Independence. According to Nick, his father, also Israel, was one of the first American officers to give his life in the Great War in 1917, on the Argonne.[43] Nick had an apartment in New York City and started to entertain group members that fall, but Nick's breezy manner and jocular style rubbed Orage the wrong way. Orage saw little serious purpose in Nick's conversion to Gurdjieffian ways. Caesar Zwaska was also in town from Chicago with news of Toomer, who was in the process of getting a collection of Gurdjieffian-like aphorisms published under the title *Essentials*. Nathaniel West was in New York and, at Dos Passos's urgings, he attended one of Orage's meetings and talked briefly with him afterward. A few days later he told his friend, the novelist and teacher I. J. Kapstein, that Orage's Socialism made more sense than Dos Passos's.[44]

The Stock Market crashed the day after Nick hosted a lavish party at the Sherry Netherlands Hotel for members of Orage's groups. Despite financial anxiety among many of Orage's circle, activities did not seem to wane, though receipts did.[45] The personal lives of the Orages seemed hardly touched by the sudden turn of events in America's economy. Meetings were still held at Muriel Draper's and Blanche Grant's. Rita Romilly still played the role of conveying gossip about Gurdjieff's "nefarious" activities; and all celebrated the end of the year at a lavish party given by Muriel Draper. Invitees included Carl Van Vechten, Elinor Wylie, Witter Brynner, and Mercedes de Costa, besides associates in the Gurdjieff work.

---

43. Nick's brother was Carleton Putnam, founder in 1935 of Chicago and Southern Airline that merged after WW II with Mississippi Delta and became, some years later, Delta Airlines. Shortly before his death, Lincoln Kirstein said that Gurdjieff and Nick Putnam were two of the most influential forces in his life.
44. Kapstein to the author.
45. For a firsthand account of the effects of the crash on Orage's groups, see Welch, *Orage*, pp. 77–78.

Orage, Big Sur, California, 1928.

Orage, 1910.

Orage, San Francisco, August 1928. Photo by Ansel Adams.

Back: Luba G, Jon, Peter. Front: Lida G, Nikolai de Stjernvall.
Summer, 1926.

Jean Toomer at Prieuré, 1926.

Jeanne de Salzmann, Summer, 1926.

Edith Taylor, Prieuré, Summer, 1926.

De Stjernvall, De Hartmann, Summer, 1926.

Dmitri Gurdjieff and Asta, 1926.

Gorham and Delza Munson, Prieuré, Summer, 1926.

Summer, 1924.

Summer, 1924.

Prieuré, Summer, 1924.

Orage, London, 1930.

Jessie and Richard, 1932.

Working on Baths, Jean Toomer, Summer, 1926.

Chapter Seven

1930–1931

ORAGE'S AGONY WITH GURDJIEFF

Man is a nerve of the cosmos, dislocated,
trying to quiver into place.

—Toomer [1]

He never waited for cats to leap.

—Pound [2]

1930: AMBASSADOR FROM HELL

The last year of the Roaring Twenties began for the Orages much as the previous year had closed. Jessmin Howarth was in New York in January and, when she wasn't helping with the dances for Orage's groups, she and her daughter, Dushka, now just over five years old, spent a great deal of time with Jessie and Edith and their children. On 22 January, Orage brought the poet Robert Frost to a demonstration, which intrigued him. The two dined that evening with the poet Edward Thomas while they discussed the moral structure of contemporary society. A week later, a visitor from Paris called on the Orages to say that Gurdjieff would arrive in early February. She then treated the Orages to stories of that "evil place, the Prieuré" and all the sinister doings there.

On the Ides of February, Rita Romilly called the Orages to read to them a telegram she had received from Gurdjieff, saying: "[Gurdjieff] Brings you 1000 kilos disillusion, 100 kilos monetary happiness and 10 lbs of retribution, signed 'Ambassador from Hell.'" [3] Orage received the

---

1. "As the Eagle Soars," *The Collected Poems of Jean Toomer*, Robert E. Jones and Margery Latimer, eds. (Chapel Hill, NC: University of North Carolina Press, 1988), p. 48. 2. Cited by Louise Welch, *Orage and Gurdjieff in America* (London: Routledge & Kegan Paul, 1982), p. 128.
3. One can read a number of meanings in the name on this salutation, but it would seem at the least that Gurdjieff is identifying himself with his protagonist Beelzebub, *out* of hell. The word *hell*, like the Greek *Hades*, signifies the "hidden place."

same day a cable from Gurdjieff, which read: "that if all his love for Gurdjieff had not been dissipated, he would arrange . . . for Friday nights and apple pie after at Child's, signed 'Grandson's unique phenomenal grandmother.'" While Orage just smiled, Jessie was perturbed by the inexplicable implications of these messages, though she had the consolation that Orage, having considered the future of his marriage and the raising of their son, had concluded definitive plans to return to England in May to renew his publishing career. Jessie, one of Orage's biographers observes, had "compelled" Orage to see the negative aspects of his relationship to Gurdjieff.[4] Orage had let Jessie know, nevertheless, that he was not renouncing either the work or his relationship with Gurdjieff, but simply moving it to another plane of participation. For one thing, he had no plans to hold groups again after his return, especially on English soil, where Ouspensky was enjoying great success. To one task for Gurdjieff he was irrevocably committed: to see the book finished and ready for press.

When Gurdjieff arrived on 18 February with twenty-five melons among his baggage, Edwin Wolfe and Louise Michel met him on the pier and succeeded in getting him through customs. They brought him directly to Muriel Draper's apartment, where Orage and sixty-five group members were waiting impatiently. Gurdjieff was impressed with the crowd, but to many there, he seemed to regard Orage with peculiar intensity. Perhaps he was displeased with the idea that Orage's decision to return to his literary career meant the end of his editorial work. It seems unlikely that Gurdjieff would have intended to precipitate a break between Jessie and Orage at this point in their relationship. True, a year earlier he had almost caused a breach in the marriage of Olga and Thomas de Hartmann when he insisted that Olga come with him to the United States while Thomas stay behind. Rather than separate, they left Gurdjieff, and their departure, perhaps, was Gurdjieff's intention.[5] Rather than drive wedges between people, Gurdjieff would "shock" them into observing themselves intently within their relationships. As for Orage, he had no intention of renouncing Gurdjieff or the work, but wanted to devote himself to his family, as well as continue to collaborate with Gurdjieff in the task of getting the book into print. Under all

---

4. Philip Mairet, *A. R. Orage: A Memoir* (New Hyde Park, NY: University Press, 1966), p. 98.
5. Olga de Hartmann, *Our Life with Gurdjieff* (London: Penguin, 1972), p. 131. In the preface, Olga writes: "A principle of Mr. Gurdjieff's method was to send his pupils, when they reached a certain stage of their work, back into the world. But not all pupils wished to leave him, so he was forced to invent such intolerable conditions for them that they were compelled to leave." This is a generous backward look, but Ouspenksy shared it, according to Tatania Savitsky Nagro. Louise Welch, *Orage*, p. 112, speculates that Gurdjieff pushed both Ouspensky and Orage out once they had gone as far as they could in the work.

these circumstances, it might well have been that Gurdjieff was preparing Orage for a "clean" break. To accomplish this, in keeping with his style, he would require Orage's complicity as much as Orage would require his.

Gurdjieff's regard for Jessie had been extremely considerate and affectionate since he had first met her in New York in January 1924 and when he had received her with particular attention at the Institute a few days before his accident that summer. One might speculate on a devious purpose behind his behavior toward her now, but there is little or no evidence of it at hand. Gurdjieff had been generous and considerate with almost everyone for whom he felt responsible in one way or another. When he provoked people with what sounded to witnesses like scorn and insult, the provocation was often, if not always, a psychological strategy intended to have its object assume what in the work is known as "intentional suffering."[6] At any rate, it seemed to Jessie, if not to Orage, that in February 1930, Gurdjieff was proving the strength of the bond between them with or without any conscious purpose to provoke either a rupture in their marriage or a rupture in the work relationship between Gurdjieff and Orage. Curious, however, is Jessie's diary entry recording that Rita Romilly—who had consulted with Gurdjieff soon after his arrival—announced that Gurdjieff "says I hate him outside, but inside love him—that is because I wished to live with him and he wouldn't have me—I influence O against him. Now because I hate him and he hate me—now he desire me very much. What a man!"[7]

Orage, on his side, was consulting regularly with Gurdjieff in the mornings at Child's, where Anna was no longer in attendance to pamper him. Most weekday evenings found Orage at Gurdjieff's apartment and, on Saturday evenings, he was at the baths with him. By the end of the month, Jessie lost her patience, and told Orage, as he was about to leave the apartment one morning, that if Orage went to Gurdjieff he

---

6. Anthony Storr, *Feet of Clay: Saints, Sinners, and Madmen* (New York: The Free Press, 1996), p. 28, is less charitable, asserting that "Gurdjieff was a dictator. He had the capacity to completely humiliate his disciples so that grown men would burst into tears . . . Those less infatuated are likely to think that, like other gurus, Gurdjieff enjoyed the exercise of power for its own sake."

7. Rita was a serious actress in her day, and later a noted teacher in Actor's Studio, but I felt, in the late 1930s and 1940s when I saw her often, that she was wont to perform roles of self-importance. She carried herself with an air of dignity, and always had a better story to tell than anyone else on any topic. I would not claim that anything she said was not true—Jessie seemed to believe her this time, though later became fed up with Rita for unexplained reasons—but my gut reaction to her stories was negative. Jessie admitted to me that she had always found Gurdjieff "fascinating" because of his bad manners and apparent utter disrespect for the feelings of others. She returned again and again to him as if to test her own feelings of repulsion. Long after Orage died, and shortly before Gurdjieff's death, Jessie went to Paris to see the old master, and he received her as old friend, and treated her with honor and deferential dignity. She was delighted when he addressed her softly as "Miss Jessie."

would never see her again. Orage shrugged his shoulders and stayed, but fate arranged it that they bumped into Gurdjieff later that day at Muriel's. Jessie muttered something rude, and Orage, normally tranquil under any conditions, turned to her and told her to shut up. Jessie reddened with anger, but held her tongue until they reached the street, where Orage resumed his normal tranquility before her fury. At Orage's next meeting with Gurdjieff, according to Jessie's diary, Gurdjieff observed: "Interesting thing Orage—whole group sheep, but Jessie not sheep—she dog. Sheep follow Orage because he too much like them— a bigger sheep."[8]

After one of the weekly meetings of Gurdjieff with Orage's group and other interested persons in Muriel Draper's apartment, where all meetings were taking place at this time, Gurdjieff asked Jessie to bring 1-year-old Dick with her next time. She did. Rita Romilly was there and, to Jessie's delight, Dick shied away from Gurdjieff's hand when he held out candy for him. After a short stay, as she was getting Dick ready to leave, Gurdjieff came to her and said: "This morning I think long time about you. I think you must come today or tomorrow you finished for me." Then, he looked at her in what Jessie described as "his most meaningful lewd fashion" and asked her in a whisper to come see him in his bedroom, that he wanted to talk to her for ten minutes, or if she had a phone, he would call. Then, at the door he nodded Rita out, pressed up to Jessie, took her hand and kissed it. Jessie recoiled from what she insisted later to Orage was an abject act of cruelty.

The most traumatic day in the sequence of Jessie's irritation over Gurdjieff was 31 March. Her diary entry for that date is the longest she had written since she started her entries in the fall of 1924. She described the day as beginning with Metz arriving at the door with a huge package of Turkish delight, dates, and candies. Jessie sent it back right away by messenger service. Angry and hurt, she turned to Orage to say that she thought he was too tolerant of Gurdjieff's outrageous behavior toward her. If he were a real man, she taunted, he would confront Gurdjieff and tell him to leave his wife alone. Orage replied coolly that he would react that way with any other man, but that he did not regard Gurdjieff as a man. Furthermore, he told Jessie, he felt he was pretty close to getting the key to knowledge that he felt Gurdjieff possessed, a key to the book that is a profound family secret that he wanted and needed in order to understand the book.

This exchange was interrupted by the arrival of Payson Loomis bringing a message from Gurdjieff for Orage to see him at once. Jessie

---

8. It is obvious here that Gurdjieff is chastising Orage for not exercising the kind of control over his wife that he had over his pupils.

put on a show of helplessness as Orage left. An hour or so later, he returned and said that Gurdjieff had asked him if he knew about the gift he had sent. Orage said that he did, and Gurdjieff demanded to know why it was returned. Orage replied that it was returned because Jessie felt insulted by it, and so was he. Gurdjieff then put on a look of innocent bewilderment and said there was a terrible misunderstanding. In fact, he explained, he liked the baby and felt that he and Orage's son had an essence agreement.[9] He recalled to Orage that Jessie had naïvely asked if he liked her son, and he said "no" jokingly, and then, to signal the joke, kissed her hand. Gurdjieff explained that she should have realized that he was teasing her, because she knew that he hardly ever kissed a woman's hand. In fact, Gurdjieff concluded, he had sent the candy to the baby and not to Jessie. In response to this report, Jessie just shook her head in disbelief, but Orage said he was quite satisfied.

On the next afternoon, April Fool's Day, Orage went to a meeting at Muriel's. He came back elated with the news that, midway in the meeting, Muriel had suddenly interrupted a reading and turned to Gurdjieff and asked: "Is this group so conscious that nothing else but hearing this book read is necessary?" Gurdjieff feigned great anger and directed insults at Muriel, but she replied by saying that she, too, was angry. His anger, however, did not answer her question. Gurdjieff looked sternly at her, and then gave an explanation why reading the book was important.

A week later at Muriel's, Gurdjieff had his last meeting with the New York group and announced his impending departure on 11 April. He had a last talk with Orage on the 9th, congratulated him for the fidelity of his pupils, and encouraged him to recruit more Americans for the Institute in the coming summer. Orage reminded him that this was not a favorable time for expensive foreign travel, considering the state of the economy. Two days later, Orage and several others saw him off at the pier.

On his first birthday, 19 April, Richard Dwight Orage, "Dickie," was baptized in Saint Mark's Episcopal Church, with Muriel Draper standing as godmother and Daly King as godfather.[10] The Orages now

---

9. In short, "essence" is the basic being or ego one is born with, but which is hidden in the course of life by layers of identities accumulated in social experience. "Essential" and "artificial" are antonyms. See the discussion in chapter 10 below on essence and soul. It is clear that many women to whom Gurdjieff paid attention could not read his intentions or, rather, read his gestures in conventional Western terms. Gurdjieff often drew attention to this problem. For example, in his New York talk in March, 1924, Gurdjieff called attention to sex education in Central Asia, saying that "there, sex education is part of the religious rites and the results are excellent. There are no sexual evils in that part of the world" *Views from the Real World* (London: Routledge & Kegan Paul,1976), pp. 126–127.
10. "Dickie" was the family name for Orage when he was a young boy.

had their sights set on England, and Orage spent a considerable time writing letters to his English contacts to prepare for his arrival. When John Cowper Powys heard that Orage might be returning to publishing in England, he sent a long letter to him in which he wrote: "You alone of all men of genius I have ever met seem totally to have conquered pride."[11] Orage had decided not to go back to *The New Age,* but to start a new journal that would emphasize a focus on Social Credit with a different slant. He felt that his nine years with Gurdjieff had given him fresh insights into socio-economic thought and its relations to philosophy and the arts.

Muriel Draper gave a grand party on the 14th for the Orages with over a hundred guests to pay tribute to the couple. Jean Toomer came to town from Chicago for the event, and took the occasion to see a ball game featuring his favorite Babe Ruth, who had signed a contract for the baseball season for the astronomical salary of $80,000. That evening, Orage spoke briefly to Muriel and her guests about his plans for the future, expressed his satisfaction with the work they had done together, then said that he and his family would leave in a week's time.[12] Almost ironically, considering Jessie's terminal antipathy to Gurdjieff's book, as she and Orage listened to a lecture two nights later by the Nobel Prize-winning physicist Robert Andrew Millikan, Jessie recognized Gurdjieff's Law of the Octave in the technical language pertaining to electrical gravitation.

On 22 April, the Orages embarked for Plymouth. They disembarked on 30 April. With friends who met them there, they drove to Stonehouse, Petersfield. Stanley and Rosemary Nott and their son Adam were nearby, Edith Taylor and her daughter arrived later, and the three families spent much time together. Orage spent most of the weekdays in London conferring with old associates from *The New Age* for his new publishing venture. He needed firm financial backing, but sponsors were scarce. Edith was pregnant again, and Orage found her a place to stay in Hampstead, where he located a place for his own family once he was back at work. He made contact with a number of people who had been at the Prieuré, including the French literary critic Denis Saurat— who had visited the Institute in February 1923—and encouraged them to write descriptions and impressions.[13] In October, he met with Noel Coward and Michael Arlen, whom he had known well in London in

---

11. Cited by Welch, *Orage,* p. 11.
12. Welch, p. 104, has Orage's last meeting on 13 May, at which he promised his pupils that he would return in January, 1931 for four months.
13. See Denis Saurat, "Visite à Gurdjieff," *Nouvelle revue française,* 1 November, 1933, pp. 286–298.

1916, to enlist them as contributors to *The New English Weekly,* which was set now for publication in early 1932. As for his work with Gurdjieff, on 11 June, he wrote Allan Brown in New York to say that he had told Gurdjieff that he was "growing chungaree [maize]" by himself. "Gurdjieff has ceased to teach me."[14]

After Orage was convinced that he had the means and the contributors to realize his project, he and Jessie made plans to return to New York to wrap up their affairs in the United States, particularly with Jessie's family in Albany. Meanwhile, Orage was being kept in touch with affairs at the Prieuré by Jean Toomer, who was relaying news sent to him by his best friend, Fred Leighton, who was at the Prieuré all that summer, and who had Gurdjieff's full confidence. What Orage heard with some regret, since he was no longer in a position to do anything about it, was Gurdjieff's increase in financial demands sent to the United States, and particularly to Toomer in Chicago. Gurdjieff needed $18,000 and, according to Leighton,[15] already had $15,000 from subscriptions Orage had obtained before he left New York. He expected the balance from Toomer. Leighton had also reported that Gurdjieff would return to New York in mid-November. About the same time, Metz informed New York and Chicago groups that Gurdjieff was intending to restructure the entire American organization. Orage began receiving letters from New York friends eager to have his counsel before Gurdjieff's arrival. In October, Sherman Manchester wrote Orage on behalf of the New York group to apologize for not having asked earlier for Orage's advice in preparing a response to Gurdjieff, for New York still considered Orage their group leader. Orage wrote back on All Hallows' Day:

> *My dear Sherman,*
>
> *Bless your soul, I'm quite incapable of any pique even supposing that I could dream you would willfully give me any reason for feeling it. The whole business in which we are engaged is so novel that from time to time every one of us will appear to each other in every possible light. But the chameleon remains the same creature; and I absolutely know, my dear Sherman, that you and I are friends and always will be, <u>any</u> damned thing to the contrary. About Gurdjieff—who really appears to be en route at last—I haven't wished to prescribe an attitude for the Group or for any individual, but only to acquaint them with certain facts and to <u>recommend</u> them to get from Gurdjieff something useful, if they can. Certainly and naturally, I shall be exceedingly interested in the outcome of G's*

---

14. Cited by Welch, *Orage,* pp. 108–109.
15. For the text of his letter to Toomer, see Taylor, *Shadows of Heaven* (York Beach, ME: Samuel Weiser, 1998), p. 146.

*visit. Equally, things cannot be unchanged by it. But my relations with G
on the one side and the Group on the other side is such that I shall not
blame either party if things do not turn out happy for me. What "personally happy for me" means concretely I'm not sure. I cannot be, for the
simple reason that it assumes that G would be starting something new, in
which the NY group and I can be enthusiastically interested. As I can
hope, but not forecast what that something may be, I can't exactly say
what I wish from G's visit. You can be sure, however and anyhow, that
anything you do, collectively or individually, I shall understand and sympathise with. Approval or disapproval is a matter of objective judgment
which, in any case, involves no personal attitude.*

*I'm sorry my letters to various members have confused your minds.
Perhaps had I written them all to one person to be read in meetings, my
views would have sounded simpler, as simple, in fact, as they are. As I've
said a score of times, they reduce to this: that I hope the Group will profit by G's visit as—in my opinion—it has not—at least directly—profited
before. Jessie sends her love, with mine, to you and Ilsa and the boys.
Our boy is ever so well. London agrees with him. I'm having a hectic time
re-arranging my old "New Age" colleagues; they've been scattered for
years both from me and each other. They would willingly re-unite, but I
haven't changed my intention of returning to N.Y. at the year's end . . .
And I wouldn't mind if it were tomorrow!*

Yours ever,
A. R. Orage[16]

To Israel Solon that autumn, Orage wrote that he had become too
attached to the group, and therefore had gone beyond Gurdjieff's understanding of what an agent's duty consisted. He went on to say that,
whatever Gurdjieff intended to do in New York, even if it was to take
over the group, it was fine with him. Orage had no further ambitions in
the work. "In truth," he confessed, "my belief is not absolute."[17]

Gurdjieff stepped back onto New York pavement on 13 November,
the second birthday of his youngest child. As soon as he was settled
in his apartment, he dictated a long letter to Toomer, accusing him of
being "partly the cause of the fact that I was compelled to come here to
America," and asking him to have $5000 on hand when he arrived in
Chicago in December.[18] Jean sent Orage a copy of the letter with a
request for advice, and a prompt response advised him not to commit
himself to anything. Busy in New York, Gurdjieff postponed his Chicago visit twice before finally going on 28 December, shortly after impos-

16. Orage Papers.
17. Welch, *Orage*, p. 115.
18. The partial text of the letter is reproduced in Taylor, *Shadows of Heaven*, pp. 147–149.

ing on the New York groups an oath to reveal neither anything of his work, himself, nor the Prieuré.[19] In Chicago on the 29th, Jean Toomer met him with an empty purse, but Gurdjieff sensed that the Midwest was still ripe for the picking and flattered Jean by attending his group meetings and making suggestions for reorganizing the Chicago group. He suggested that Jean train other group leaders for the greater Chicago area, as Orage had done for the New York and New Jersey area. Toomer assumed, in the absence of Orage, that Gurdjieff was thinking of using him and the Chicago groups to play a major role in a restructuring of all the teaching in America. He seemed to be offering Jean overall charge of operations in the United States outside of the New York City area, where Gurdjieff would assume direct control himself. The reason for this was evident. Since New York and Chicago were financing the Institute, a diminishing of the flow of funds that Orage's and Toomer's groups could assure would spell the doom of the Gurdjieff work on a school or Institute basis. In this regard, Gurdjieff was still considering the possibility of a move of the Institute to New York. Toomer set to work to found a group in Portage, Wisconsin, where Zona Gale was residing. He decided to inaugurate it with a summer "experiment" along the lines of the Prieuré summer sessions.[20]

By now, Gurdjieff had heard of Orage's plans to return to New York, and probably was planning the means by which he could "re-structure" relations with his formerly loyal "steward." At this time in England, the Orages were spending both Christmas Eve and Christmas day at 33 Buckland Crescent with Edith Taylor, who was in the eighth month of her pregnancy. On the 29th, she and Rosemary Nott saw the Orages off on the S.S. Washington for what was to prove a rough winter Atlantic crossing.

1931: FOOD FOR THE SUN AND THE MOON[21]

The Orages disembarked in New York on 8 January 1931, after a turbulent crossing that kept Jessie in her berth much of the way. Two years later, in *Life Is Real Only Then, When "I AM,"* the Third Series of *All*

---

19. Louise March, *The Gurdjieff Years 1929–1949: Recollections of Louise [Goepfert] March*, Beth McCorkle, ed. (Walworth, NY: The Work Study Association, 1990), p. 51, says the date of Gurdjieff's manifesto was 1 November 1930. It is unlikely that Gurdjieff had heard that Orage was encouraging a select few to write precisely about these things.
20. Toomer wrote of this experiment in yet unpublished "Portage Potential."
21. Orage used the following example to his pupils: "I say to a sheep, 'you are to provide mutton and wool.' But the sheep says, 'I don't understand.' So Beelzebub says, 'You are food for the sun and the moon.' But you reply, 'I don't understand.'" (February 7th, 1927, Manchester Papers, p. 102.) For Orage, the Moon, in this expression, can be understood psychologically as kundabuffer.

and Everything, Gurdjieff himself wrote an account of the events that involved him and Orage in the weeks that followed. It is worthwhile to trace it briefly, since Gurdjieff "de-constructed" historical fact in a story that would render his "truth."[22]

In *Life Is Real,* Gurdjieff writes that he arrived in New York on 13 November, 1930 to review "the financial question" and to "uproot . . . this evil occasioned by the misunderstanding of my ideas."[23] In the evening of that first day, he attended a general meeting of the New York group directed by Mr. [Israel] S[olon].[24] Not at all satisfied with what he heard, as the meeting was breaking up, from the doorway Gurdjieff turned and addressed the group as examples of "full-aged unfortunate people vegetating in American-scale organized 'lunatic asylums.'"[25]

Three days later, he met with Solon and five others (including Sherman Manchester and Muriel Draper) and proposed the formation of a committee to organize general meetings in his apartment to ascertain whether the group, in Gurdjieff's words, has either "become completely disappointed in my ideas or there should disappear the faith crystallized in their individuality during these years in regard to Mr. Orage and his authority."[26] Gurdjieff gave his First Talk to the group on 28 November.[27] After attacking the American culture of newspaper-reading, card-playing, and dancing—types of Babylon's "evil radiations"—he reorganized categories of pupils into three groups: an exoteric group for new pupils, a mesoteric group for those already initiated theoretically, and an esoteric group for those initiated both theoretically and practically. This transformation, says Gurdjieff, was the long-range effect of one of the "will tasks" of his thought in Montmartre three years earlier, 6 November 1927.

Anticipating a later excursus on the prolongation of life, Gurdjieff reminded his audience that the knowledge he dispersed had its source in the teachings of people aged two hundred years, some more than three hundred.[28] After reminding his audience of the circumstances under

22. I have published a version of this episode in "Gurdjieff's Deconstruction of History in the Third Series," (Proceedings of the Third Bognor Conference on *All and Eveything,* Bert Sharp and Seymour Ginsburg, eds. Bognor Regis, 1998), pp. 178–205.
23. *Life Is Real Only Then, When "I AM"* (New York: Dutton for Triangle Editions, 1975), p. 66.
24. Gurdjieff, *Life Is Real,* p. 67.
25. Gurdjieff, *Life Is Real,* p. 70.
26. Gurdjieff, *Life Is Real,* p. 72.
27. Gurdjieff, *Life Is Real,* p. 76.
28. Daly King, in his "Premises" to *The Oragean Version* (New York: privately published, 1951), p. 18, says that he thought the Third Series would contain ideas Gurdjieff had suppressed and hidden since his 1924 accident. Orage and Toomer had believed also that Gurdjieff had been withholding secrets from them, although Toomer came to believe that, during World War II, Gurdjieff began to teach a different matter. In his First Talk, Gurdjieff had said that after his accident he had been unable to finalize his teaching (see King, p. 80).

which he founded the Institute for Harmonious Development in France, he described the Prieuré, the Paradou, and the Study House. Then Gurdjieff offered a succinct summary of the purpose of his teaching, before turning to the immediate reason for his appearance before them.[29] Since his accident in 1924 had rendered him unable to return to form the "first fundamental branch of the Institute in America," he said, misunderstandings about his work flourished, and pupils remained blocked in the exoteric stage.[30] The Americans, he pointed out, have not yet advanced beyond the question of self-observation, while the English exhibit an *idée fixe* on self-remembering, and the Greeks on the Law of Seven and the "three existing aspects of every event"—a reflection of his own division of mental events into triads.

In the Second Talk, undated, but noted as having been delivered in the same place to a much larger audience,[31] Gurdjieff exposed the causes for the mistaken interpretation of his ideas. He reminded his audience that he had sent Orage to New York in 1923 as a translator and assistant to Dr. Stjernvall—who knew no English—in order to make arrangements for his own trip. Instead of "data of a higher level" formed in the New York group, Orage, in his presentation of Gurdjieff's ideas, produced "something quite contrary." He then stayed on in New York after Gurdjieff's departure to prepare a next trip; but more, insisted Gurdjieff, for romantic reasons. A week after his return to France, Gurdjieff suffered a near-fatal accident, after which he decided to close the Institute. But now, having realized how generously the New York group was funding the Institute through Orage, instead of closing it as announced, he had opened its doors to Americans.[32]

Between 1924 and 1930, Gurdjieff continued, Orage directed classes for the movements without his permission, and finally married the "young American pampered out of all proportions to her position." As for his teaching, Gurdjieff explained that Orage knew only "self-observation." So now, Gurdjieff proposed a "purification of undesirable elements from your group." For the reformed group, there would be

---

29. Gurdjieff, *Life Is Real*, p. 83.

30. Gurdjieff, *Life Is Real*, p. 85.

31. This statement rings off key, considering that Gurdjieff restricted the number of people in his apartment to fifty, with the understanding that those unable to attend could hear the substance of his words elsewhere. If he had fifty auditors for the first talk, where could he have placed more? The question is dilatory, of course, because the location of Gurdjieff's talk cannot be limited by reader expectations.

32. *Life Is Real*, pp. 89–94. Alexander de Salzmann was with Orage in New York throughout this period. Bennett, *Gurdjieff*, p. 164, observed that in 1924, Orage "was far too much of an individual to be able to play the role of second-in-command," and that Gurdjieff "could not accept Orage's undertaking as the natural development of what he himself had launched a few months earlier." It was thought generally by Orage's pupils, however, that the "launching" had been Orage's.

thirteen obligatory conditions for membership, seven of objective character for everyone, and six of subjective character for members of
Orage's old group.[33] He called his secretary, Louise Goepfert, in front
of the audience to dictate a "special oath for a newly formed exoteric
group," to the effect that no one was to have any relations with Orage
without the special permission of Gurdjieff or his substitute.[34] The talk
concluded with a deadline for compliance.

After an undated Third Talk outlining his aim of teaching and
explaining the three first impulses of the Law of Seven, Gurdjieff delivered a Fourth Talk to the new group on 12 December 1930 in the presence of Orage. He opened his address by summarizing general reactions
to the imposition of an oath upon the Orage group, but digressed from
his talk to interject the story of Orage's reaction to the sequence of
events that were taking place. He recalled that "two days before the
fourth general meeting reorganized by me on new principles, Mr. Orage
himself finally arrived in New York, already informed about everything
that had taken place here in his absence."[35] (That information would
have Orage in place by 10 December.)

The climax of his account of a dramatic encounter between two
"brothers in spirit" was at hand, but who was protagonist and who
antagonist in this scenario Gurdjieff does not pause to explain. His
interposed reflection notes that, upon arrival in New York, Orage
requested an interview. "Remembering the alarming news received by
me one hour ago [earlier?] of the bad turn of my material affairs," writes
Gurdjieff, "I decided to delay the answer." He had Metz write a formal
letter to Orage asking him to sign the "obligation I proposed to all the
members of the group you have directed." Orage arrived promptly at
Gurdjieff's apartment and signed while Gurdjieff was in the kitchen.
Orage explained calmly to the assembled people that he understood at
once what was hidden beneath the proposal, and confessed in his own
words "the maleficence of my verbal influence on people whom I guided so to say in accordance with his ideas" (p. 122). Recognizing that
there were deep thoughts beneath the superficial terms of the renunciation, he "decided therefore to begin by signing the obligation required by
Mr. Gurdjieff."[36] He resolved as well not to have anything to do with his
former self and asked to join the new group as an "ordinary member."

33. Gurdjieff, *Life Is Real*, pp. 95–99.
34. Gurdjieff, *Life Is Real*, p. 100.
35. Gurdjieff, *Life Is Real*, pp. 109–111, 120. The Introduction to *Life Is Real* says at least one
of the four talks was given at the beginning of 1931.
36. Gurdjieff, *Life Is Real*, pp. 122–123.

During this confession, Gurdjieff was in the kitchen, cooking a "gravity-center dish." The news he heard from the other room so distracted him that, in Chaplinesque fashion, instead of ginger he dumped a large amount of cayenne pepper into the casserole, then swung his right arm into the back of whomever was washing dishes, and flung himself into his room where he buried his head in half moth-eaten cushions and sobbed, to be consoled and relieved only by Dr. Stjernvall's prescription of an ample portion of Scotch whisky. He then returned to the main room to host a dinner consisting of "the dish I had so immoderately peppered."[37]

The next day, stirred by Orage's example, pupils besieged Gurdjieff with requests for membership, to which he replied positively on the condition that they all pay fines of either $3,648, $1,824, $912, $456, $228, $114, or $57, depending on their slowness and reluctance to sign. He then charged them for copies of his talks at rates of $10 for those who signed without hesitation, $40 for those who doubted him, and $20 for those who waited for Orage before deciding. The total gained from both fines and sales, he wrote, amounted to $113,000, of which one half he decided to keep for himself and the other half to go into a fund for the operation of the exoteric group.[38] That evening, after a musical demonstration, Gurdjieff delivered a talk whose text broke off at a crucial moment after "we . . . must know about that one [particularity] which since long ago has in the process of human life always been one of the chief secrets of all ranks of initiates of all epochs. This particularity is that . . . " [39] Gurdjieff's text abruptly stops.

This is an extraordinary essay, obviously set as a parable, whose intention and meaning baffle interpretation. It seems improbable that Gurdjieff, recalling important events in the history of the work, should get the month, year, and sequence of events wrong, just as the apartment in which he stayed should have been furnished with cushions "half moth-eaten." To break off the account of his recollection at the instant an essential secret is to be revealed is obviously not a manuscript lapse on his part, but a strategy for concealment.[40] No one who was there at

---

37. Gurdjieff, *Life Is Real,* pp. 124–125.
38. Gurdjieff, *Life Is Real,* p. 127. Sophia Wellbeloved of the University of London doctoral has analyzed all these sequences of numbers and concludes that they figure sequences of 3s and 7s, corresponding to Gurdjieff's laws of Three and Seven. It is doubtful that Gurdjieff raised anything near this figure. No one who has written of the incident, including Gorham Munson, Louise Welch and Daly King, admits to have paid anything.
39. Gurdjieff, *Life Is Real,* pp. 130.
40. It is rumored that there are other versions of the Third Series in the keeping of the Gurdjieff Foundation, but I have depended for my commentary entirely upon the extant published text. Gurdjieff's apartment was 10H, in the Parc Vendôme at 333 West 56 Street.

the talks, including Louise Michel [Welch]—who documented carefully the events of December 1930 and January 1931—Daly King, and Sherman Manchester, recalls the divulging of a secret particularity of initiates. The scene of reconciliation, in which Orage signs the paper of renunciation of self and in which Gurdjieff reacts by peppering his banquet, looks more high tragi-comedy than esoteric code. Gurdjieff's account reads like post-modernist fiction; and yet, what reason have we to believe that it is not a carefully woven design whose message is truncated and whose image is blurred only by our lack of insight? Circumstantial evidence of Gurdjieff's purposeful deconstruction of a chronology of events in the interests of an emblematic tale is the published testimony of others who were present at one or more of these events. However Gurdjieff's readers would understand in different fashion the purpose of this "misdated" chronicle, I have not met any satisfactory analysis of it.[41]

The "other" story of those who were in New York with Gurdjieff during the holiday season includes the fact that the New York group received a letter from Orage just before Christmas saying that he intended to sail from England on the S.S. Washington on 29 December.[42] Muriel Draper, Daly King, Rita Romilly, Israel Solon, Sherman Manchester, and Carl Zigrosser were among the many who met the Orages on the pier at 9:30 A.M. on 8 January, two days after newspapers the world over announced Malcolm Campbell's land-speed record of 245 miles per hour, set on the Utah salt flats. At Blanche Grant's apartment for an informal welcome reception, Orage heard that his group proposed to send an ultimatum to Gurdjieff by letter. He asked them to be patient, to wait and see what was to come.

The next morning, while Jessie went to look at an apartment at Grammercy Park, Orage composed a letter to Gurdjieff from their hotel room.

---

41. James Webb, *The Harmonious Circle* (London: Thames & Hudson, 1980), p. 368, has Orage arriving at the beginning of December, and remarks: "Despite the ever-present possibility that this story is one of Gurdjieff's mystifying parables, there is evidence that for once he is speaking of real events." Whitall N. Perry, *Gurdjieff In the Light of Tradition* (Bedfont, Middlesex: Perennial Books, 1978), p. 71, quotes Mme de Salzmann in a conversation with René Guénon shortly after Gurdjieff's death, saying her master "rarely spoke the truth." This should not be taken as an accusation of lying, but of reshaping "fact" into a "truth" comprehensible to others.
42. Welch, *Orage*, p. 165.

Irving Hotel
New York City
Fri. Jan 9, 1931

Mr. Gurdjieff!!

Dear and kind author of The Tales of Beelzebub, I have just returned from England and find to my pleasure the Christmas box you very patriarchally sent for my son Richard. I thank you for him and for myself.
Well, then . . .
I have been thinking while in London of what I could do to show my interest in the super-important question of the publication of your great work, the Objective Critique of Man. And I submit respectfully for your honorable consideration the following proposition:
I will undertake to revise completely the English text, with the help of anyone you name—Mr. Loomis, for example.
And to have the English text suitably printed and bound in any style you wish.
And to sell to students of your work one thousand copies at $10 per copy.
And to hand over the resulting $10,000 to you together with all printing plates and publishing rights for whatever use you wish to make of them.
And to complete the whole of this plan before December 31st of the present year.
If you should honor me by accepting this plan, a first $5000 could be paid to you on March 1st 1931, and the second $5000 on Dec 1st 1931.
Most unique and universal author, I beg to lay this humble proposal before you, and I await your impartial judgment.
Trusting soon to see you with my own eyes,

I remain,
Yours expectantly, ARO [43]

One need not read an intention of disrespect in the terms of this letter. The semi-satiric, semi-jocular tone might well be complicity in a strategic game Orage felt Gurdjieff was playing with him. Whether or not the tone of Orage's words was understood by Gurdjieff as frivolous, the substance is clear: Orage promises to complete the mission he had undertaken long ago, and which would be the end of his commitment of collaboration with Gurdjieff. No written answer came back, but the next day, Gurdjieff had an invitation for lunch sent to Orage. Before responding, on 11 January, Orage and Jessie met with Peggy Matthews and Marguerite Schwartzenbach, the wife of the Swiss Consul in New York, to get their accounts of what had passed, then called Gurdjieff. He was invited to join him for a midnight supper. What they talked about is not recorded, but the next day, he sent Orage an invitation to his birthday party, and added a request to have Jessie visit him, because he had "something to say to her that would make her day memorable."

Orage went to the party while Jessie stayed at home with their son, Richard. Whatever transpired that evening, she does not record, but on the 15th, a note came from Gurdjieff asking Orage to see him that evening to hear "how seven years ago he threw out Ouspensky, and now he will do the same to Orage for the same reasons." Orage chose to stay home, but Rita Romilly called the next morning to say there had been a great deal of excitement during the evening meeting. She reported that Gurdjieff had enumerated a number of reasons why Orage should be repudiated, one of which was the fact that "Orage had held groups without his knowledge—'Metz told him so'—so now anyone wishing to join his new group must sign a paper renouncing Orage and swear never to speak, telephone or have any communication with him" until released by Gurdjieff. He added that henceforth the Orage Group was to be called the "New York New Esoteric Group." [44] Gurdjieff's secretary, Miss Goepfert, then read the renunciation pact and asked all assembled to sign. Certain members, such as Daly King, argued that they had responsibilities toward Orage, and Miss Goepfert allowed them what she called "human relations."

Jessie and Orage were startled to hear that there had been little protest at the meeting raised by those whom they had considered loyal friends. Even Daly King had apologized to Gurdjieff for his contacts with Orage on the grounds of his status as Dick's godfather. Orage wondered "why didn't anyone have the guile or sense to sign and then do as they damn pleased? As G never honours his own signature, they should acquire some of his tactics by now." [45] To those who called him for counsel concerning the pact of renunciation—including Alan Brown,

---

44. Nikolai de Stjernvall, who was with the Gurdjieff party in New York, confirms the renaming of the Group in *Daddy Gurdjieff* (Geneva: Georg, 1997).
45. Much has been written about the incident of the renunciation pact. See Webb, *Harmonious Circle*, pp. 367–368. Moore, *Gurdjieff: The Anatomy of a Myth* (Boston: Element, 1991), pp. 238–289, reproduces the text.

and Carl Zigrosser—Orage said that they should do what they wished. Muriel Draper, who was absent from the meeting though it took place in her apartment, told everyone she saw over the next few days to sign and then ignore it.[46]

In effect, Orage had good reason to think that Gurdjieff was modeling a Beelzebub out of him. He was being exiled for presumption, but exiled with an obligation intact within the New York community of seekers. It is not surprising then that Orage would join the exoteric group as if to begin all over again. He was also playing unrepentant Prometheus to Gurdjieff's imperial Zeus. In this spirit, he decided to address his own point of view to Gurdjieff. Jessie recorded in her diary the following day, 18 January, the following account:

> Orage wrote G a letter yesterday explaining that Ouspensky and he are quite different—so Metz called up and told Orage he was invited to the meeting tonight if he would also sign the paper.[47] He refused, but went to see G at 6. . . . O told him he was resigning, holding no more groups or attending any.[48] G told him that his great fault was naiveté—that he had observed him for seven years and he had not yet gotten over it. "Therefore," O said, "why should he continue his association for another unprofitable period. It sounds to me like a man who goes to a doctor to be cured of an unknown illness. The doctor gives him exercises and at the end of seven years says "you have a weak heart—I've known it all along, but did not try to cure it—however, if you stay on with me perhaps I will tell you what to do."

Meanwhile, Rita Romilly fanned flames of scandal when she told the Orages "a shocking thing of what G had done to Lucy, his own niece (Lucia, the daughter of Sophia Kapadnadze). Lucy had threatened to tell unless he sent her home—so he did so—but the poor child is living in a

---

46. Welch, *Orage,* p. 119, says Orage was the first to sign the document, but she may be repeating a common understanding among the New York group. Daly King, *The Oragean Version,* p. 7, claims that the repudiation was a bluff. He denies that he himself signed it, and says that it seemed to him and others in the New York group that all continued as usual with Orage and Gurdjieff.

47. Storr, *Feet of Clay,* p. 41: "Orage, summoned back from England, demanded to see Gurdjieff, and, after remarking that he too repudiated the Orage created by Gurdjieff, signed the document denouncing his own teaching." He probably got this information from Webb, who, unfortunately, does not identify his sources. Moore, *Myth,* p. 239, without identifying his sources (though he had spoken with Jessie before her death) says that Gurdjieff in December [*sic*] said that Orage should sign, Orage did, and Gurdjieff broke into tears. Jessie's diary entry says that Orage refused to sign, but it is possible, if unlikely, that Orage, unknown to Jessie, did sign, realizing, as Gurdjieff's account has it, a deeper meaning beneath the demand.

48. Welch, *Orage,* pp. 114–117, records a letter Orage wrote to Israel Solon explaining his withdrawal from being "G's agent," and declaring that he put the New York group's interests before Gurdjieff's.

state of fear and I am afraid for her too." [49] The next day, Rita came up with another vicious piece of gossip to the effect that Gurdjieff had changed Peggy Matthews' name from "pig" to "sow," which had some people suspect she was carrying Gurdjieff's child, but Rita said it was not so. It was at this time that Jessie and Orage received the sad news that Jane Heap was suffering from diabetes.

January 22nd was Orage's birthday. After celebrating quietly with a few friends, he called a meeting of the New York group for the next evening. In an emotional address, he told them that they were nearly a real brotherhood, now well past the status of a group, and on the way toward a school. [50] Thereafter, Orage's former pupils defended him forcefully against any attack. Louise Welch recalls challenging Gurdjieff soon after with the argument that, if Orage had been teaching them wrong all along, after all, he was teaching them what Gurdjieff had taught *him*. [51]

Notwithstanding his status as pariah, in the course of the weeks following, Orage attended meetings of the esoteric group, during which Gurdjieff read a letter he had composed and would send to the press repudiating Orage. Orage's friends, particularly Muriel Draper, who had a will of steel and unlimited courage of conviction, said that public humiliation was senseless. Orage said to the group that Gurdjieff was to him a brother who had traveled to distant lands and learned other things, but that they were still brothers. From the other side, what Gurdjieff realized very soon was the fact that Orage's followers were more than disciples, they were devoted friends. Claude Bragdon recalled, in this context, that Orage "never let his devotion to an idea vitiate his human relationships or affect his feelings for his friends of an opposite persuasion. As partisan, devotee, disciple, he went the whole length and exerted all his strength, yet remained all the while appreciative, detached, open-minded." [52]

Orage resumed his lectures to groups all this time with Gurdjieff's knowledge and probable approval. Concerned with Toomer's situation as well, Orage cabled Jean in Chicago to warn him that Gurdjieff might well do the same with the Chicago group as he had done in New York, and suggested that Jean keep a low profile. Jean replied by telephone,

---

49. Nikolai de Stjernvall, who was twelve at the time, and Michel de Salzmann, six, accompanied Gurdjieff to New York on this momentous trip. Nikolai said to me that that the row Gurdjieff had with Lucy in his room was over a minor incident of misbehaval.
50. So Louise Welch reports in *Orage*, p. 111.
51. Welch, *Orage*, p. 115.
52. Claude Bragdon, *More Lives Than One* (New York: Knopf, 1938), p. 326.

saying that it was hard for him to believe the rumors circulating about Gurdjieff's treatment of Orage, and observed that when Gurdjieff was with him at the end of December, he had been very encouraging and expressed pleasure with the ways things were going there. He had made only a few suggestions about re-organizing the teaching to separate advanced and beginning pupils.

Meanwhile, Gurdjieff announced to the separate New York groups that he had booked passage for his return in early March, and so had much to do with them before then. When Isabel Rose interviewed him at his 59th Street apartment for the *New York Herald Tribune* edition of 28 January 1931, he used the occasion to promote his book. The *Tribune* headed the published article with: "Gurdjieff Seeks Literary Spice in City Rackets," and followed this with three sub-headings. Highest was "Whining Cult Chief Writing Beelzebub's Tales to his Grandson in 3 Volumes," followed lower by "Here Also to Shear Sheep," [53] and "21 Kinds of Idiots Says Ex-Forest Philosopher." In the main text, Gurdjieff was quoted as refusing to elaborate on his sheep-shearing project, but saying that he was in New York City "to give an authentic picture of American life."[54]

On the 29th, Orage called a meeting of the New York group, and was surprised to hear that Gurdjieff was having Metz write a letter to the newspapers renouncing him. The letter never appeared in print; yet, Gurdjieff did speak to the public when Paul E. Anderson arranged a meeting with a number of people of academic and intellectual standing, including the psychologist of Behaviorism, John B. Watson. To them, he read the chapter "America." At first, he bored his audience, then he charmed them when they remonstrated, and the meeting ended in the early hours of the next morning in a spirit of conviviality, somewhat abetted by spirits of alcohol.[55]

Throughout February, Orage met Gurdjieff regularly in private, held his own group meetings, and attended Gurdjieff's general meetings. Apparently, Jessie was not complaining, but she feared that the strain on her husband was beginning to depress him. She did not know the substance of Orage's daily consultations with Gurdjieff, but assumed that Gurdjieff was putting pressure on Orage to reconsider his decision to return to London. The Chicago group, according to Caesar

---

53. Toomer had remarked once that "Gurdjieff would charm a snake out of its skin if it had dollar-signs on it." The novelist James M. Cain, who was then reporting for the *World* and the *New Yorker*, interviewed Gurdjieff for the *New York World* in early February, but tore up his notes afterward without writing an article.
54. *New York Herald Tribune* (28 January 1931).
55. Moore, *Gurdjieff*, p. 139, following Welch, *Orage*, p. 93, who sets this scene in 1929.

Zwaska, who was visiting in New York, was loyal to Toomer and ready to resist any shift to Gurdjieff's control; but, for the time-being Gurdjieff's full attention was on the re-structuring of the New York operations. On St. Valentine's Day, Orage, Zwaska, and Loomis spent hours with Gurdjieff, after which Orage joined Jessie at Georgia O'Keeffe's exhibition. Whatever the upshot of Gurdjieff's talk, Zwaska called the next day to ask how Orage was, because both he and Loomis had had moments of blindness that they suspected was caused by the bootleg whisky Gurdjieff had offered them in honor of the Saint of Love. Orage felt fine. On the 21st, the Orages lunched with Jean Wick and Achmed Abdullah [Nadir Kahn], who confided to the Orages that the moment he saw Gurdjieff a week earlier, he knew he was Dordjieff, the tsarist agent at the court of the Dalai Lama.[56]

The curtain was rising on the last scene of Orage's active participation in the Gurdjieff work. Orage went to Gurdjieff's for a final meeting of the esoteric group on 5 March. Gurdjieff, repeating much of his second talk to the group before Orage's arrival, presented to his audience a long justification for his actions since November, the gist of which was that, because of his accident in July 1924, he had been forced to send Orage to New York to teach, though he had not sufficient instruction himself. Moreover, there were other things to be done along with self-observation that Gurdjieff had never been able to tell him because of his accident and strenuous work on the book. Because of these things, Gurdjieff concluded, Orage had had the New York group talk about and concentrate on self-observation instead of also "doing." Were this situation to continue, Gurdjieff explained, the members of the group would eventually become psychopathic.[57]

"So for seven years," said Gurdjieff according to Orage's own account to Jessie that night, "he, Orage, a conscious being, has allowed his followers and believers to become one-sided and entertain a misconception—not to mention those who have been made unhappy and desperate at the seeming futility of things and those who have given up

---

56. Ron Landau, *God is My Adventure* (London: Ivor Nicholson and Watson, 1935) gives credence to this identification. Webb, *The Harmonious Circle*, traces Abdullah's career carefully and fully. Both he and Moore, *Gurdjieff: The Anatomy of A Myth*, give ample evidence to prove that Dordjieff was *not* Gurdjieff. In fact, Achmed had seen and talked with Gurdjieff in 1924 during a dinner at the Colony Club (Bragdon, *More Lives*, p. 323). On the other hand, Webb, *Harmonious Circle*, pp. 68–72, makes a circumstantial case for Gurdjieff being the same man as Ushe Norzunoff, and, pp. 85–87, makes a case for his identification with Prince Ozay.
57. Orage had always emphasized to his group that he was not speaking in his own name. For an example, on 7 March 1927, he reiterated "Now I must try to correctly represent to you what the ideas of the school at Fontainebleau are—not what I know or believe—but faithfully transmitting" (Manchester Papers, p. 123). King, *Oragean Version*, p. 9, insists that Orage constantly confirmed that the source of all his teaching was Gurdjieff himself; and, he ventures, p. 11, that Gurdjieff was castigating a teaching that was learned at first hand *before* his accident.

the whole thing as hopeless. . . ." In light of these developments, Gurdjieff concluded that he was prepared, during his last few days in New York, "to give Orage the necessary instruction to carry everyone on." From his side, Orage assured Jessie that he would "carry everyone on for only the rest of the spring."

One member of that audience, Fred Leighton, wrote Toomer later of the events, saying: "There has been a great fight here over the question of Orage. Now I understand Orage has returned to the fold." [58] There is no record what Orage and Gurdjieff talked about after that, but Orage continued to meet with Gurdjieff every day. Their mortal eyes met for the last time 13 March as Gurdjieff looked down and waved to Orage on the pier from the deck railing of the steamship that carried him back to France. [59]

Throughout the spring, at any rate, Orage was back at his post as director of the newly formed groups, and was teaching the Gurdjieff method faithfully. Few of his friends saw any change in Orage's appreciation of the teachings of Gurdjieff. [60] Many assumed that Gurdjieff had undermined Orage's position of authority in order to cast him out—as he had forced breaks with Ouspensky and the de Hartmanns—for his own good; that is, because his work with him had come to a close, if not to a fulfillment. In effect, Orage wanted to finish this stage of his experience with Gurdjieff *en beauté*. His next and final stage was the completion of the book.

Despite the broad sweep of events the past two months, Orage continued to honor his commitment to the book, and soon after Gurdjieff left, he wrote Jean Toomer that he was looking for a publisher for "Beelzebub." "Knopf turned it down," he wrote, "I sent it to Doubleday. . . . I share your opinion that no publisher will accept it [in its present state]." In the same letter, he returned to the question of funds for the maintenance of the Prieuré, telling Toomer to "dream dollars." To encourage him, he noted that he was raising $5000 in subscriptions in New York, to which he would add $1000 out of his own pocket, and that Betty Hare had promised $2000. "Chicago for $2000?" he asked. "You and I have the job of *selling* a special edition. G says he talked it over with you, but he probably didn't." [61] Jessie noted in her diary for 7

58. 2 May 1931. Beineke Manuscript Library, Toomer Collection, Box 4, Folder 138.
59. Inexplicably, Webb, *Harmonious Circle,* p. 371, has Orage saying goodbye to Gurdjieff for the last time on 24 April 1931.
60. Gorham Munson, *The Awakening Twenties* (Baton Rouge, LA: Louisiana State University Press, 1985), p. 283, like King, believed that the apparent break between the two men "signified no dissent from the teaching of Gurdjieff" on the part of Orage. Mairet, *Orage,* p.124, says that Gurdjieff's actions in New York were to help Orage break away.
61. Beineke Library, Toomer Collection, Box 6, Folder 206.

May that she was too often audience to Orage's and his group's "usual disgusting [discussion] of how much money could be extracted for Gurdjieff."

Orage also took the occasion during this last sojourn in New York to advertise the Social Credit scheme he would shortly champion in the pages of *The New English Weekly*. He gave four lectures downtown at the School of the Theatre to large and interested audiences. The future head of Roosevelt's Department of Agriculture, Henry Agard Wallace was among them, and he spoke with enthusiasm of Orage's "solution" to the economic woes of the Depression. That spring, Orage wrote an article entitled "Economic Nationalism" that appeared in *Fortune* in November 1933. A number of Orage's pupils, headed by Gorham Munson, banded together to form the "New Economics Group of New York." In the summer of 1934, this group would publish the first number of *New Democracy,* a Social Credit review.

That final New York spring, Orage reinstituted his writing lessons that had always been a great success. Tom Matthews, poet, humorist, and later editor of *Time,* recalled that Orage taught him more about writing than anyone else had, because he had an unerring eye for a writer's potential.[62] Other writing pupils included the labor organizer Paul Ernest Anderson, who shifted his career to writing after his instruction by Orage, and the architect Hugh Ferris. The poetess Elinor Wylie sought out Orage's editorial aid in private consultations. Orage had an editorial gift of instruction in the art of the carefully chosen word, distinct from the casually spoken word. The oral performance, however, he insisted, remains the model for writing. "The art of the written word is an attempt to reproduce the life-model of perfected speech." [63]

To those aspiring to do critical writing, he advised: "The conversational tone is its proper medium, and it should be an absolute rule never to write in criticism what cannot be imagined as being easily said."[64] To the aspiring fiction writer, he advised keeping emotion out of art, and even evidence of his thought: "Thought is not only not art," he advised, "but the aim of art is to conceal thought." [65] On another occasion, he observed that "born writers tend to overpower, seize, and hold captive. . . . Such writing is irresistible, and its effects are permanent; for what is admired is more lasting than what is merely reason-

62. T. S. Matthews: *An Autobiography* (New York: Simon and Schuster, 1960), p. 214.
63. Cited by Welch, *Orage,* p. 58.
64. Cited by Hugh MacDiarmid, *The Company I've Kept* (Berkeley, CA: University of California Press, 1967), p. 67.
65. Cited by Margaret C. Anderson, *The Strange Necessities* (New York: Horizon, 1970), p. 112.

able." [66] Years earlier, he had written an extraordinary essay in *The Art of Reading* on Milton's *Paradise Lost,* where he pointed out the irresistible appeal of Satan's rhetorical voice, which contains "not sense but *supersense.*" [67] It is not the meaning in the words, but the power invested in their expression that has value. Such was eminently true of the persuasive voices of Gurdjieff, Toomer, and Orage himself.

Stanley Nott, who arrived in New York in May, left a few weeks later with Orage's instructions to publishing associates in England. In May, Orage gave his last talk to the New York group, an occasion at which Carl Zigrosser described Orage as "witty, subtle, ironic, sarcastic, noble. . . . It was a brilliant performance." [68] On 1 July, Muriel Draper gave the Orages a going-away party and then finally, on 3 July, they sailed from the United States, he never to see her shores again. Twenty years later, John Bennett assumed that Orage's decision to return to England was a consequence of Gurdjieff's actions in New York in January: "The truth is," he said, "that Gurdjieff made a demand of Orage which could, had he been able to respond to it, have set him free from his own central weakness. It was the inability to make the decision that made him return to London." [69] James Moore observes wryly that, once he left Gurdjieff, "it seemed he had never walked through the Prieuré gates." [70] Had he not walked through those gates, however, he would never have walked back out of his life with Gurdjieff the fuller man he had become. Nothing that happened in New York between Orage and Gurdjieff could unsettle the plans Orage had already made almost a year earlier. In essence, Gurdjieff had facilitated the keeping to them by releasing Orage from his New York ministry.

The Orages arrived in Cherbourg on the 11th and on the morning of 12th steamed up the Thames to London, from where they went on to Bovingdon, north of London. They were greeted there in the late afternoon by the Notts and Edith Taylor. Edith had spent the early summer

---

66. In "Orage in America," *Dynamic America* 10 (1940), pp. 12–16, Gorham Munson wrote an account of Orage's writing course, and included quotations. Orage himself published "How to Write a Short Story" and "How to Write an Article" in *Junior League Magazine* 18 (Oct. and Nov. 1931).
67. A. R. Orage, *The Art of Reading* (New York: Farrar & Rhinehart, 1930), p. 119.
68. Webb, *Harmonious Circle,* p. 37.
69. Bennett, *Gurdjieff: A Very Great Enigma* (York Beach, ME: Samuel Weiser, 1984), p. 235. He does not identify the "central weakness" in question, and Bennett hardly knew Orage at all. William P. Patterson, *Ladies of the Rope* (Fairfax, CA: Arete, 1998), p. 84, seems to expand on Bennett's thought when he says: "Gurdjieff returned in November and delivered a terrific shock to Orage, hoping it would shake him out of slavery to his chief feature—a weakness for women—but Orage sloughed it off." At this stage, with Orage a happily married husband and doting father, it would make little sense for Gurdjieff to shake loose what seemed no longer to be there.
70. James Moore, *Gurdjieff and Mansfield* (Routledge & Kegan Paul, 1980), p. 211.

there and was about to return with her two children to Paris, from where, throughout the rest of the summer, she wrote newsy letters to the Orages about the Institute. Robert McAlmon, the American poet, short-story writer and magazine publisher, was visiting Bovingdon as well, and he and Orage discussed the forthcoming *New English Weekly.* Before the end of the summer, the Orages moved to Keats Close at the bottom of Hampstead Heath.

Back in New York, Orage's group members continued their meetings at Muriel Draper's with Schuyler Jackson—Laura Riding's husband—as director, though some, Tom Matthews for one, quit following Gurdjieff's teachings after Orage left.[71] In September, Orage received a mimeographed announcement from the book committee of the New York Group, offering 100 mimeographed copies of *Beelzebub's Tales* for sale at $10, payable to Allan Brown, and deliverable by 15 September. The order to produce the copies, of course, had been from Orage, who had proposed the distribution in January of a thousand copies as a means of raising funds.[72] Whether Gurdjieff had given his permission or was pleased with this publicizing of the book, Orage did not know and appeared not to care. Jean Toomer's *Essentials,* a collection of aphorisms reflecting the Gurdjieff teaching, which he had printed privately, arrived at his door,[73] and Orage responded to Jean with praise, but wondered who his audience would be outside of people who knew him and the Gurdjieff work.

Before the end of 1931, Gurdjieff was back in New York. Shortly after his arrival, Blanche Grant, now Rossette, sent Orage a copy of a circular translated from Gurdjieff's Russian by Loomis and signed by Mme de Salzmann. It was dated 28 November 1931, and announced that Gurdjieff was in New York, finishing the third series and continuing the reorganization of the third group. The mimeographed circular announced general meetings in New York in order to obtain "dough."[74] The admission price per meeting was $5, but if one wanted to speak personally with Gurdjieff, the text read, he "must come equipped with twenty-five dollars, must put them on the table within the vision of Mr. Gurdjieff's right eye." A few days later, Orage heard from Gurdjieff directly.

---

71. *Under the Influence* (London: Cassell, 1977), pp. 167 and 315.
72. Bennett, *Gurdjieff,* p. 175, says that Paul Anderson had the idea.
73. Toomer had asked Gorham Munson to write an introduction to the collection, and Gorham did so, but Toomer left it out of the edition. Rudolph Byrd's recent edition (Athens: University of Georgia Press, 1993), reproduces it.
74. Payson Loomis was an accomplished linguist who worked several years as an interpreter at the United Nations. He mastered Russian and Arabic by self-instruction. He learned Japanese from his wife. The translation was awkward, probably because Loomis tried to translate Russian slang into English equivalents.

204 West 59th St., New York
December 3, 1931

Dear Orage,

Strange as it may seem to you, the fact is that I am now again in New York where, regulating the successive misunderstandings arisen thanks to the inevitable ordinary life, by means of all kinds of "combinations" and "cunning-devices," I am at the same time actualizing the task which has become during recent years the fundamental aim of my life.

I am now working on the third and last version of the third series of the books I had decided to write.

Just now, while deciding to write you this letter myself, as I am sitting in my usual place, known to you, in Child's, looking at the first chapter of the third series, which is lying on the table in from of me, and with only half of which you are acquainted, and occasionally at the bi-ped Americans moving like automatons in Columbus Circle, and am thinking how to dispose the fundamental ideas, already outlined in this chapter, so that in its last version it should correspond to the sum total of all my expositions and to my mental, i.e. theoretical, and organic, i.e. practical principles.

As I was thinking of this, in the aforesaid conditions, there gradually began completely to form in my thoughts two independent and, to me, satisfactory forms.

Continuing to think, already with less tenseness, of the details for both forms, and continuing at the same time to look over all the phrases flowing one from another in the said chapter, I suddenly, when I unexpectedly noticed your name in the text of this chapter, quite graphically and clearly constated, without the slightest "flaw," as clear as the "Sakro-oalnian-Cristal" mentioned by Mister Beelzebub, that one of these forms which I have thought out in almost the final form, and which moreover corresponds more to my aims, may for you and of course for your family—for you, namely, a man toward whom, owing to the life-circumstances, there has gradually been formed in my nature a "something" engendering in certain instances the sensation as toward my own brother—be almost in the literal sense of the word "death"; and the other, although "life," yet only a little better than, as is said, "vegetation."

When I constated this, then from that moment, the gravity-centre-initiating-factor in my thoughts, for the choice of the aforesaid forms, was "something" which may be formulated in words perhaps only as: "a prolonged-cinematographic-close-up-of-the-experiences-of-a-cameleon-in-motion."

Half an hour ago I had to stop writing this letter, as Loomis came to me with a report concerning a commission I had given him yesterday evening, relating to his meeting and talking with a certain man about publishing here in America the first book of my expositions.

I will now continue. Thanks to the conversation with Loomis, whom I cannot but call a "still-slobbery-boy," there has arisen in me quite another idea in connection with you, about which I shall not write at the moment, as I consider it necessary first to clear up a certain question connected with it. Therefore, taking into consideration both economy of time and also, of course, the dollars necessary for a telegram, I will send by post what I have already written, and when I have cleared up the aforesaid question, I shall send you a telegram.

When he finished reading this, Orage just shrugged and smiled, but Jessie was furious. She saw a death threat in the text, but Orage reassured her calmly. Somehow, the contents of the letter came to the attention of Orage's close friends in New York,[75] and they expressed a deep concern. Most recognized a strategic ploy on Gurdjieff's part, but no one could decipher its purpose, unless it was the unlikely one of persuading Orage to return to Gurdjieff's service. Jessie vented her own anger at Gurdjieff in an-end-of-the-year verse:

He calls himself, deluded man,
The Tiger of the Turkestan,
And greater he than God or Devil
Eschewing good and preaching evil.
His followers whom he does glut on
Are for him naught but wool and mutton,
And still they come and sit agape
With Tiger's rage and Tiger's rape.
Why not, they say, The man's a god;
We have it on the sacred word.
His book will set the world on fire.
He says so—can God be a liar?
But what is woman, says Gurdjieff,
Just nothing but man's handkerchief.[76]
I need a new one every day,
Let others for the washing pay.

---

75. Since all of Gurdjieff's letters in English were written by others from dictation, at this time either Metz, Jane Heap or Rita Romilly, all of whom were Gurdjieff's "secretaries," might have been the "leak."
76. Gurdjieff is often cited for his anti-feminism. In a talk in New York on February 13th, 1924, he explained, in keeping with conventional European lore, that men are A-types featuring an intellectual center, women are B-types featuring an emotional center, but that a merger of intellect with emotional produces a C-type human being. In other words, women and men have equal chances for development.

Chapter Eight

1932–1934

BETWEEN BEASTS AND GOD

Omni tempore diligit qui amicus est,
et frater in angustiis comprobatur.[1]
What should I do in Illyria?
My brother he is in Elysium.[2]
Be comforted. Our life is but one day of our life.

—Orage[3]

1932: THE NEW ENGLISH WEEKLY

The Orages were happily settled in Hampstead as the New Year began. Gurdjieff was again across the water in New York and Orage was in touch with events through his New York friends. He corresponded regularly with Israel Solon, the current director of the groups that Orage now styled a "brotherhood." Gurdjieff returned to France on 15 January, and was met in Cherbourg by Payson Loomis and Nick Putnam.[4] Shortly after, Edith Taylor wrote from the Prieuré that Gurdjieff was planning a trip to England in hopes of getting funds from the Ouspensky people. The Institute was on its last legs, with a debt still outstanding. Jessie would have nothing of Gurdjieff's arrival and threatened to write the Home Office, "anything to keep him out."

---

1. "He that is a friend loves through all time, and a brother is born for adversity" (Proverbs 17:17).
2. William Shakespeare, *Twelfth Night,* I, ii, 1–4.
3. "On Love,"from *On Love: With Some Aphorisms and Other Essays,* C. S. Nott, ed. (New York: Samuel Weiser, 1969), p. 19.
4. The date is Louise Goepfert March's in her memoirs, *The Gurdjieff Years,* Beth McCorkle, ed. (Walworth, NY: The Work Study Association, 1990). Webb, in *The Harmonious Circle: G. I. Gurdjieff, P .D. Ouspensky, and Their Followers* (London: Thames & Hudson, 1980), p. 419, says Gurdjieff sailed on the Bremen on January 16, after an amicable visit to Toomer in Chicago.

Gurdjieff did not come, and the news from the Prieuré was that Gurdjieff was contemplating, once again, the sale of the château. Orage was busy with the organization of his new journal and finding contributors. He promised writers that he would not edit their work if they would waive fees. Money was in short supply for Orage during this Depression year, but he succeeded in getting support from his New York friends.[5] Whereas Ouspensky and Maurice Nicoll had left Gurdjieff to establish their own teaching, Orage let his former pupils know that "I see no probability of my resumption of Gurdjieff groups or teaching for the rest of my life."[6]

His former associates, seeing him in editorial action once again, were pleased that the "old Orage" talent was still there.[7] Mairet, his new editorial assistant, noted that "Orage had returned from his wanderings a more integrated being."[8] Both those who anticipated that Orage's pen would be none the sharper for his ten-year absence, and those who feared that the new journal might turn out to be a forum for Gurdjieff's ideas, were happily mistaken.[9] T. S. Eliot was to say, in his *Criterion* memorial issue of April 1935, "I deprecate Orage's mysticism as much as anyone else"; though, considering Eliot's eclectic mysticism, the remark has to do more with the nature of Gurdjieff than with mysticism itself. "His greatest deception," Eliot lamented, "was to have been offered a magic when he was seeking a religion."[10]

In *The New English Weekly*, there was perhaps more of Social Credit than the *The New Age* had featured, but only because, in waiting for suitable material to include in the journal, Orage was writing a good deal himself about the economic problems of the Depression that held his interest. In this activity, it would seem that his work with Gurdjieff had given him a fresh structural view of Social Credit which he hoped to express to a broad audience. In short, Orage would do for society what Gurdjieff would do for individual man: establish a harmonious

5. Louise Welch, *Orage and Gurdjieff in Amercia* (London: Routledge & Kegan Paul, 1982), p. 122.
6. Letter to Israel Solon, 24 January 1932, cited by Welch, *Orage,* pp. 124–125.
7. Philip Mairet, *A. R. Orage: A Memoir* (New Hyde Park, NY: University Press, 1966), p. 107, says that a better Orage had returned to his work in London.
8. Mairet, *Orage*, p. 110.
9. Michael Coyle, "'A Profounder Didacticism': Ruskin, Orage and Pound's Reception of Social Credit," *Paideuma* 17 (1988), p. 18, cites Mairet to the effect that Orage had "kept alive his interest in [G's teaching] and was on the point of swinging over to advocating them openly when he died." I have not found the passage in my 1966 edition.
10. "A Commentary," *Criterion* 63, Jan. 1937, cited by Paul Murray, *T. S. Eliot and Mysticism* (London: Macmillan, 1991), p. 168.

relationship between parts. Social Credit had its own Law of Three. There was industrial production to begin with, consumption of produced goods on the other, and mediating the two forces was monetary distribution.

It was thought by many of those who saw a change of tactics, but misunderstood its base, that Orage had been attracted to Fascist economics. Nothing could be further from the truth for despite Pound's expressed admiration of Mussolini's economic reforms—or, perhaps, because of it—*The New English Weekly* featured a number of articles criticizing the economic programs of Mussolini and Hitler. On 16 March 1934, in Rapallo, Pound complained to Conte Ciano "I may frequently want to get a rock-drill in order to make Orage or Douglas SEE something, but I swear they are both honest, that you can't buy 'em."[11] Despite this reservation, Pound applauded Orage's return from Gurdjieff to journalism, and wrote to John Hargrave in January 1935 to say: "Last time I kussed at Orage for theosophy Which What, I was reminded that it was in America he got the wherewithal for new start (NEW)/he also planted the Soc/Cr seed over thaar. He fought 20 years in Eng/needed vacation."[12] Pound regretted that Orage wouldn't write for any journal but *The New Age* or *The New English Weekly*,[13] though he couldn't have been unaware of the wealth of Orage's literary production in New York. By 1933, as the American poet Theodore Roethke remarked to Dorothy Gordon, poets were lining up to get into *The New English Weekly,* and asked her anxiously in May 1934: "That piece 'Exhortation'? Has Orage seen that light piece?"[14]

One of the first issues of *The New English Weekly* featured a discussion of Munson's article in the *Saturday Review of Literature,* 24 August 1929, in which the author considered whether or not the American language could surpass the English. Orage, on 28 April 1932, wrote that the peculiarities distinguishing American from English literature were "much deeper than mere vocabulary-mannerisms."[15] The American poet, William Carlos Williams, who had read Ouspensky with enthusiasm, entered into the discussion in the 21 July issue, stand-

11. E. Fuller Torrey, *Roots of Treason: Ezra Pound and the Secret of St. Elizabeth's* (New York: McGraw-Hill, 1989), p. 328.
12. Pound Archives, Beineke Library, cited by Flory, *The American Ezra Pound* (New Haven: Yale University Press, 1989), p. 78.
13. Ralph J. Mills, Jr., *Selected Letters of Theodore Roethke* (Seattle: University of Washington Press, 1968), p. 14.
14. Mills, *Letters.* Pound contributed some 180 pieces to *NEW* between 1934 and 1939.
15. Orage Papers.

ing for the independence of American letters.[16] American reporting on *The New English Weekly* was very favorable. The *Santa Fe New Mexican* announced the forthcoming appearance of *The New English Weekly* on 16 March with a note about Orage's Santa Fe connections, and Gilbert Seldes wrote a positive account of Orage's Social Credit scheme in the 5 May number of the *New York Evening Journal.*

The Orages were happy with their move to Hampstead, where they enjoyed family life in common with the Notts and Edith Taylor, all with small children. Regent's Park was close enough for a daily walk with the children, while Orage labored as hard as ever to make a success of *The New English Weekly,* which got underway as scheduled in April 1932. It was hard going. Money was short. Friends, in particular Betty Hare, were trying to raise more in the United States,[17] but only a few persons interested in a magazine representing Social Credit gave anything, and very little at that. Something of Orage's predicament is revealed in his response to Sherman Manchester's offer of a piece for the journal in June in return for a modest author's fee.

My dear Sherman,

It grieves me to have to send your beautiful butterfly back dead, but the bare fact is that nobody is paid on the paper, least of all myself; and as for staff or correspondents or contributors, they are all voluntary and unpaid. Sherman, Sherman, try to realise that no such paper can even begin to pay, ever! You attack the Banks and at once and forever you are doomed. The press boycotts us, people daren't adventure in our pages, very silently, the news stands discourage sales; and without a miraculous recovery the paper wouldn't last a month. I myself not only do not derive a penny from it, but I pay all my own expenses and for books and tickets of my literary, dramatic and so on critics. I hope, my dear friend, you will try to realize all this as simple fact, and think of some other way of releasing yourself for a new task.

Yours and "yours" affectionately, A. R. Orage[18]

---

16. Mike Weaver, *William Carlos Williams: The American Background* (Cambridge: Cambridge University Press, 1971), p. 78. Orage's former pupil, the physicist John Riordan, wrote to Williams—who kept a photograph of Orage before him in his attic study—about the value of Gurdjieffian self-observation without analysis.

17. E. P. Walkiewicz and Hugh Witemeyer, *Ezra Pound and Senator Bronson Cutting* (Albuquerque: University of New Mexico Press, 1995), p. 245.

18. Manchester Papers.

Gurdjieff errupted into the satisfying routine of the Orage household in late August with a letter requesting that Orage to come to the Institute for at least one day to see him. He said that he had a very important thing to tell him. If he couldn't go, he was to send Jessie. Orage ignored the summons, but he was annoyed when a letter came the next day from Edith, back with Gurdjieff at the Prieuré, who reported that Gurdjieff had prophesied at the supper table that Adam Nott was to become a criminal and Dick Orage a savant, but soft.[19] And yet, of his own ten-year odyssey with Gurdjieff, Orage was heard to say: "I thank God every day of my life that I met Gurdjieff."[20]

Across the Atlantic, Orage's old group, probably incited by the series of lectures Orage had given on Social Credit before his departure, founded The New Economics Group of New York, and were launching a journal to propagate the principles of Social Credit. Orage was very pleased and, to add to his pleasure, he heard from Betty Hare that the governor of New Mexico, A. W. Hockenhull, and New Mexican Senator Bronson Cutting were advocating Social Credit publicly in Santa Fe and Washington. Elizabeth Holter had begun writing a book, *The ABC of Social Credit,* to bring its basic principles before the public eye. For his own part, Orage tried to make Social Credit a motivating force for the English Labor Party, but without success. Edwin Muir remarked, a year later, that Orage was "still leading an advanced army that has long since fallen into the rear; I don't think he feels quite at home. But he's a nice man."[21] Claude Bragdon quipped: "Orage without a cause was like Napoleon without an army."[22]

The nice man Orage had a nice life now that he was a father and devoted husband. The Orages toasted the end of a profitable year with the Notts and Edith Taylor. Jessie was particularly happy in England, having taken enthusiastically and energetically to English life, English ways, and even English speech habits. As for the Englishman Orage, who had fallen in love with, and then left, America, he felt he had been promoted to a stronger and more productive self, largely due, he told others, to his ten years in the service of Gurdjieff.

---

19. Someone identified with fantasy was, for Gurdjieff, a "criminal."
20. C. S. Nott, *Journey Through This World* (London: Routledge & Kegan Paul, 1969), p. 52. T. S. Matthews, *Name and Address: An Autobiography* (New York: Simon & Schuster, 1960), p. 207, recalls that "[Orage] once told me that he had never been able to make up his mind about Gurdjieff—whether he was a completely cynical charlatan, an inspired religious teacher, or a bit of both."
21. Letter to George Thornburn, November 11th, 1933, in Edwin Muir, *Selected Letters of Edwin Muir* (London: Hogarth, 1974), p. 80.
22. Claude Bragdon, *More Lives than One* (New York: Knopf, 1938), p. 325.

1933: ORAGE AGONISTES

Tous mes sourires venaient d'ailleurs,
heureuse ou malheureuse,
je demeurais entres les bêtes et Dieu.

—Georgette Leblanc[23]

Edith returned to Paris in early January 1933, and reported Orage's good mood to Gurdjieff.[24] Gurdjieff berated her for failing to mediate collaboration with Orage, and ordered her to return to England. What was on his mind now was a pamphlet he wanted to have printed, *The Herald of Coming Good,* that needed editing and brokerage with publishers. On 3 February, the Orages received a cable from Edith saying that she would arrive by air on the 6th. Orage was, unhappily, certain that she would arrive with Gurdjieff in tow, since her cable said that her business concerned Orage and was "secret." Neither Orage nor Jessie, however, wanted to believe that Edith would be disloyal to this extent, knowing well that they were not disposed to seeing Gurdjieff again. Apprehensively, Orage and Jessie, like Chaucer's Troilus and Pandarus

---

23. "All my smiles come from elsewhere, happy or sad, I live between beasts and God," "Epitaph," *Little Review,* May 1929, p. 44.
24. James Moore, *Gurdjieff, Anatomy of A Myth* (Boston: Element, 1991), p. 46, says that on 11 May 1932 the Prieuré folded and describes the events of the last days, but certain dates are elusive. Moore documents carefully a trip Gurdjieff took to the United States in late 1932 and his return to France "at the end of February 1933" (p. 248). His information comes from Fritz Peters (1965), who describes his own falling out with Gurdjieff during a trip with him to Chicago to visit Jean's group that winter. Nonetheless, Jean, whose wife, Margery Latimer (descended directly from the Puritan poetess Anne Bradstreet) had died a few months earlier, was either in Portage, Wisconsin, or in New York. He was not holding group meetings in Chicago. If Jean was not in Chicago, who was leading his group? How could Gurdjieff be in the United States when Edith, with both her children, was near him in Paris at the beginning of the month? Furthermore, if Gurdjieff had left the Prieuré for good before the middle of 1932, why did he locate his announcement to *The Herald* in Fontainebleau a year later? According to my sources, Gurdjieff and a few stayed on for a while, though no new pupils were admitted, and the Institute was formally closed. By this time, Gurdjieff had taken rooms in Paris, where he preferred now to work. Nonetheless, Jane Heap wrote from the Prieuré in May of 1933 and Rita Romilly was there with Gurdjieff in December 1933, from where she wrote letters for him. There were few of the old crowd still left in Fontainebleau. Some had no other place to go, and stayed on at Prieuré as long as they could. Gurdjieff's nephew, Valentin, in his original unpublished Preface to *Life Is Real,* 1973, says that Gurdjieff left the Prieuré in 1933 and moved into 14, rue Labia in Paris until his brother died, when he moved into Dmitri's flat in the rue Colonels Renard. Those who stayed the longest at the Prieuré property included the family of Dmitri and Asta, and Martin Benson, who married Rita Romilly. The story of how Gurdjieff let Prieuré go for a $40 debt, is recounted by Moore. Apparently Gurdjieff hoped to the last moment that he might save the Prieuré. The de Hartmanns had left in 1929, followed by the de Stjernvalls in late 1932, so that only the de Salzmanns and their children, of the original exodus group, remained with Gurdjieff. Gurdjieff was seen at the château on his saint's day in April, 1933. The last residents were, apparently, Benson and Metz, who moved out in the winter of 1933–1934. As fate would have it, the life of Gurdjieff's Prieuré and American Prohibition ended at the same time.

on the walls of Troy awaiting the return of Criseyde, waited through the long day for her, but, like Criseyde she never showed up. Edith appeared finally on 13 February, and explained with humor and obvious satisfaction that her flight, offered free of charge by an aviator friend of hers, had been endlessly postponed by weather conditions.[25] Jessie's expectations were not met. She had prepared herself to be angry with Edith and to resist the mission, but there was nothing very exciting in the urgent voyage, just a letter for Orage and a manuscript to be revised. The letter, which Gurdjieff dictated to Edith, read:

> *92, rue de Tocqueville.*
> *Paris XVII.*

My dear, dainty M. Orage,

If you imagine and are convinced that in the past I have vainly wasted my life upon you, you are greatly mistaken.

In the past, I partly instinctively, partly conscientiously "swallowed" the result of your various "unique-clever-manoeuvres" with the intention that when I should really want your help, as I do just now, I might with a clear conscience, tensed navel and entirely objective right, claim a strict fulfillment of the following six bequests of mine:

1) You will read in solitude my writings enclosed herewith with approximately translated into English and intended for publication as a sample, in the same way in which you are accustomed to read all your newspapers and magazines.

2) Having thus read my writings not later that 24 hours, you are to invite some friends of yours and read same aloud.

3) After another 24 hours, you will read my writings a third time, but now with the serious intention to grasp their contents and at the same time do not forget to meditate about what could be—of course in your opinion—the possible consequences of all this.

---

25. Webb, *Harmonious Circle,* p. 372, without mentioning the only source possible, Edith Taylor herself, recounts this journey, saying, "A pupil was sent. . . . G told her train and boat, she wanted to waste no time." Webb says Orage was furious that she had disobeyed Gurdjieff's (cont'd) instructions, and when she returned to deliver to Gurdjieff Orage's unwelcome refusal, she told him of Orage's anger, whereupon Gurdjieff smiled and said: "By this I know that Orage still friend." In explaining Gurdjieff's directions, Webb says that Gurdjieff did not like flying to begin with—itself a curious piece of information, since it is unlikely that Gurdjieff had ever flown—but Gurdjieff would have been right in assuming that travel by train and boat and train again would have been a much surer and almost always quicker way to cross the Channel in winter, since meteorological conditions in February would not often have been favorable for flight. Gurdjieff considered the mission too urgent to be entrusted to a frivolous adventure. Incidentally, there had been airline service between Paris and London since 1921, when the Goliath was put into passenger service.

*4) Next, having ordered a large cup of coffee and a large glass of scotch
whisky (of course not ersatz) to be brought to you every quarter of an hour,
you are to begin immediately to transform these my writings, in accordance with all our discussions, into good English, at the end of which work
you will immediately send me two copies, one for my files, and the other
for the typography, where the other languages are already in the press.
5) You will have the same printed in London for the time being in 1.000
copies and charge the amount to my financial minister.
6) And, finally, you will let me know if you can spare two days in the
course of the next month for a trip to Paris with purpose of making the
last correction of the English proof, of the first book of Mister Beelzebub.*

G. Gurdjieff

Gurdjieff's style, which Orage knew and read so well, did not persuade.
Edith stayed on for a week, then flew back to deliver to Gurdjieff another unwanted reply. She dreaded Gurdjieff's reaction to Orage's refusal
to edit the brochure. To ease her task, Orage took it upon himself to
reply directly to Gurdjieff. From his house, he sent a cablegram at once,
reading: "Once I crossed the Atlantic for you. Now I wouldn't even
cross the channel," and wrote the next day from his office:

*38, Cursitor Street,
London E. C. 4
February 15th, 1933*

Dear Mr. Gurdjieff,

*Two years ago when I suggested publishing "Beelzebub" complete for
you in America, and you refused, I came to the conclusion that you would
never publish it. I see no reason for changing my opinion, and I am therefore indisposed to do anything about your present proposal.*

*Yours sincerely,
A. R. Orage*

Gurdjieff's reaction was indeed dreadful, if not predictable. He
renounced Edith and ordered her out of his sight. With two children,
funds almost completely depleted by mismanagement, Edith took up
residence in a small apartment in Paris with a cook-housekeeper, sent
her children to Maria Jolas's school on the Rue d'Orleans, and wrote
friends for counsel and help. She had her eyes set now on the United
States where she eventually moved. It was Jean Toomer who helped her
by taking in her son to live with his own family in New York.

The New English Weekly, by now, was an established success with the critics, if not with the paying public. Some regretted that it was over-devoted to Social Credit propaganda, and it was rumored that Orage, who had left his continued interest in Gurdjieff's teachings alive, was "on the point of swinging over to advocating them openly."[26] At the same time, Orage's eye for promising literary talent brought the fruits of fresh talent into its pages. When he received an offer of a poem by an 18-year-old Welshman, he immediately accepted it with encouragment, and so Dylan Thomas had his first poem—"And Death Shall Have No Dominion"—published on 18 May 1933 in a national press. Though Thomas was upset that he received no fee for the poem, he continued to send Orage poems, including "Out of the Pit" (25 January 1934). He also sent Orage stories—"After the Fair" (15 March 1934) and "The End of the River" (23 November 1934), one of the last pieces Orage himself saw before his death. In the same year, Orage wrote a favorable review in *The New English Weekly* of W. H. Auden's Group Theatre's *Dance of Death,* in which he proclaimed that Auden had breathed new life into a moribund English drama.

In late May 1933, Orage received a copy of a letter written by Jane Heap, addressed from the Prieuré to Israel Solon. It asked the New York group to account for the $3000 Orage held and the $2000 Toomer retained from the old publication fund, and demanded that it be placed in escrow pending the publication of *Beelzebub's Tales.* Orage threw the letter away, but far away in Wisconsin, Toomer struggled once more to set the accounts straight by pointing out quite clearly that, far from being a debtor, he had not yet been repaid the $1000 the New York group owed *him.*

In September, Jessie gave birth to a daughter, Ann, and the Orages considered their ménage complete and their love well proved. Christmas with the Notts and Taylors was a happy celebration of family.

1934: BROTHER IN ELYSIUM

Throughout 1934, Orage kept hard at work with *The New English Weekly,* supported by faithful collaborators, including Philip Mairet, Ezra Pound, and T. S. Eliot. Good friends from New York found occa-

---

26. John L. Finlay, *Social Credit: The English Origins* (Montréal: McGill-Queen's University Press, 1972), p. 65. Moore, *Myth,* p. 212, says that Orage was about to shift *NEW* toward Gurdjieffian ideas, and John Bennett, *Gurdjieff: A Very Great Enigma* (York Beach, ME: Samuel Weiser, 1984), p. 235, says that Orage had let friends and associates know that "he [had] made up his mind to return to Gurdjieff at all costs." I cannot find the least evidence whatsoever of this intent in Orage's private papers.

sion to stop by. In March, they saw Paul Robeson, who was in London playing in Eugene O'Neill's *Emperor Jones.* Edith Wharton visited London and was invited to dinner by Orage. Mme De Hartmann, who had not seen Gurdjieff in five years, came by in March, and reported that Alexandre de Salzmann had died in Leysin, Switzerland on the 3rd. Blanche Grant stopped by and Orage persuaded her to commission a bust of Bernard Shaw by Jacob Epstein, since Shaw refused to sit unless the sculptor had a commission in hand. At the unveiling later in the year, there was mixed opinion about the style of the representation. Consequently, Mrs. Epstein wrote Shaw to complain that Orage was telling others that the playwright was displeased with the bust. Shaw wrote back kindly to say that only "Orage the Irresponsible" would transmit such rumors, but others had witnessed Shaw's own bewilderment before his stone face.[27] In the 2 February issue of *The New English Weekly,* Orage was pleased to quote Senator Bronson Cutting's speech in the Senate of the United States on 27 January, in which he presented and championed Orage's Social Credit scheme as a tool for Roosevelt's economic policies. In September of that year, Orage received a copy of Stanley Nott's edition of Elizabeth Sage Holter's *ABC Of Social Credit,* with an afterword by Allan Brown. In the spring, T. S. Eliot had pleased Orage by writing a letter to the Times urging "a thorough and public examination of the scheme of national credit."

Meanwhile, Gurdjieff intended to publish a new edition of *The Herald of Coming Good,* but he was satisfied with neither Metz, nor Payson Loomis, nor Nick Putnam as collaborators. So, in early August 1934, he sent Orage a copy of the text with a request for revision. Orage, exasperated by the request, wrote back a brusque response almost immediately, his last written words to Gurdjieff:

Aug 20.34

Dear Mr. Gurdjieff,

I've found very little to revise, in view of your unique style; but I have, at least, read every word with care. Unfortunately 10 pages were missing-from 22 to 32. With my good wishes for your work,

Yours sincerely, A. R. Orage

Later that month, Muriel Draper stayed a short time with the Orages on her way to the Soviet Union on a visit that would lead her into pro-Soviet

---

27. *Bernard Shaw: Collected Letters,* Dan H. Laurence, ed. (London: Max Reinhard, 1988), pp. 485–486. For Epstein's version of the story, see *Epstein: An Autobiography* (London: Hutton Press, 1955), pp. 81–83.

representation throughout and after World War II. In September, Orage and Dmitri Mitronovic issued the first number of *New Europe,* a journal ahead of its time in advocating a United Europe. In the latter part of October, Orage experienced an inexplicable pain in his thorax, but he kept up his work cycle. When he was asked to make a radio broadcast for a BBC series entitled "Poverty in Plenty," he accepted gladly, having been already convinced for some time that the radio had a future role that would eclipse the magazine article in communicating ideas.

On Monday, 5 November, the day set for his broadcast, the London Times carried Walt Disney's announcement of a plan to make a film cartoon version of the Grimms' folktale, Snow White. That evening, Maurice Evans played Benedick in the opening of a new version of Shakespeare's *Much Ado about Nothing,* and that night, in Germany, the last appeal of the accused killers of Horst Wessel was denied. Baron Edmond de Rothchild had died a few days earlier, but more ominous to Londonders was the death of the sculptor of the statue of Eros in Picadilly Circus.

Orage made his appearance before the microphone that evening, his first radio talk—though he had been interviewed briefly in Chicago ten years earlier—and with economy and eloquence he exposed a simplified version of Social Credit. His description was passionate and poetic, and many may have heard something of Gurdjieff's aspirations for humankind in it. Orage reviewed the economic chain in England, one end of which was the shop, behind which was a line of warehouses, "and, behind the line of warehouses, a line of factories and workshops; and behind those, quarries, and mines, and farms; and behind these, laboratories and research schools; and finally behind them all, the British people themselves, with their character, industry, genius and history." Then, as if referring to Gurdjieff's lifelong passion with machinery (contrasted with his negative view of a progressive degradation into the status of machinelike automaton), Orage proclaimed the extraordinarily hopeful view of future social profits for all in the application of scientific achievements beyond the ken of ordinary people. He said that "Applied Science seems to have made its mission in life to lift the curse laid on Adam and to transfer work from the backs of Men to the broader backs of Nature's other forces—steam, electricity, and ultimately, perhaps, to atomic energy."[28] He meant by this that the development

---

28. Quoted by Carswell, *Lives and Letters* (London: Faber, 1978), pp. 218–219. A synopsis of all the talks in the series is given in *The Burden of Plenty,* Graham Hutton, ed. (London: George Allen & Unwin, 1935). Orage's "Social Credit" covers pages 62–73. H. G. Wells, whom Orage admired for his scientific optimism, had foreseen years earlier the widespread possibilities of atomic energy, and had warned against the danger of an atomic chain reaction that might destroy life on Earth.

and control of inorganic machinery, along with conscientious use of scientific advances, would provide people with leisure and occasion to work on personal moral and intellectual development. Machines are good, but not mechanized people.

In Rapallo, Pound listened to the BBC broadcast from London and recalled that Orage's "voice came over the radio, curiously gentle and patient, without the fire I had known or the sharp snap and crack of the sentences, but very clear, as the transmission was mostly good, though the last sentence went with a crackle (thunder probably in the Alps)"[29] Pound recalled Orage's last words: "In the gap between Price-values and Income is enough gunpowder to blow up every democratic parliament." "*Adnuit*," exclaimed Pound, "that was a fine sentence to die on."[30] There was thunder over the Alps, a promised explosion in democratic economies to match what Guy Fawkes had plotted for England's Parliament, and rockets were bursting over the heath as Orage walked happily home that night.

He never saw the dozens of letters of congratulations that were posted to him the next day from all corners and walks of English life, for early in the morning of 6 November, he died of an exploding aneurysm in the left artery of his heart. Jean Toomer, now married since September to Marjorie Content, and settled in a house at 39 West 10th Street, heard the news of Orage's death that afternoon. He was overwhelmed with shock and sorrow, and sent Jessie a telegram of condolence immediately, saying that without Orage as his friend and counsel, he could not foresee any further role for himself in Gurdjieff's service.

The *London Times* carried his obituary on Wednesday the 7th, noting that Orage was the son of a clergyman [*sic*] and an Irish woman. His stance in favor of the Douglas Social Credit system was duly noted,[31] but his editorial activities drew the most praise: "Orage displayed not only the rare ability to detect new literary talent, but the power to keep a team of intellectual workers together." His career in the United States was referred to in guarded terms: "For the greater part of the next 10 years, Orage worked in the United States, mainly as a lecturer in litera-

---

29. William Cookson, ed., *Ezra Pound: Selected Prose 1909–1965* (New York: New Directions, 1973), p. 38.
30. Cookson, *Selected Prose,* p. 442.
31. In his autobiography, *The Company I've Kept,* pp. 104–136 (Berkeley, CA: University of California Press, 1967), Hugh MacDiarmid praises the Social Credit scheme and says that two decades after Orage's speech, the BBC allowed him to make a similar broadcast from their Manchester studios, after which he received overwhelming positive response from the public.

ture and psychology." Not a mention of Gurdjieff! The writer of the *Evening News* obituary said: "I do not suppose there has ever lived a man who was so great an influence on the famous men of his time, and was at the same time so little known to the general public." He went on to remark on Orage's career at the "highbrow semi-sanitarium at Fontainebleau." Far away in New Mexico, the *Santa Fe New Mexican* noted on the front page of its 7 November issue that "Orage, Former Visitor Here, Dies in London."[32]

Orage's final struggle with Gurdjieff which preceded his premature death, has features of a morality play in which the major actors— both of whom recognized the other as "his brother"—understood their roles as replications in kind of persons involved in the exile of Beelzebub in Gurdjieff's great tome. Beelzebub also viewed himself in relation to a brother. At the end of his book, Gurdjieff has Beelzebub released from exile to return home. Similarly, he may have tried to release Orage into an acute awareness of his own life in exile and, perhaps, to have him inquire into the means by which he could achieve a redemptive homecoming reconciliation with his own essence. There is a faint hint of this scenario in Gurdjieff's account in the last chapter of *Life Is Real* of his reaction to Orage's death. On the morning of 6 November 1934—a day that Gurdjieff notes as the first day of the "recommencement of my writing . . . on that very day on which, seven years before, I had decided once and for all to achieve without fail all the tasks required for my being"[33]—he was at Child's Restaurant in Manhattan. Late in the morning, while working on the Prologue to this last book and arguing with an American translator—probably Payson Loomis—over the distinction between the phrases "voluntary suffering" and "intentional suffering," he was called to the phone. A voice told him that a telegram had arrived announcing that Orage, "my close friend," had died that morning in London. The timing struck him, because exactly seven years earlier, at midnight in Montmartre (hill of martyrs), he had dictated a letter to Orage advising him to regulate his health by intentional suffering.[34]

32. Cited by Walkiewicz and Witemeyer. *Ezra Pound and Senator Bronson Cutting*, p. 245.
33. Gurdjieff, *Life Is Real*, p. 150.
34. Gurdjieff, *Life Is Real*, pp. 152–154. Louise Welch, who was with Gurdjieff when he heard of Orage's death, saw him "wiping the tears from his eyes with his fist, saying 'This man, my brother'" (*Orage*, p. 137). She locates the place, however, as a rented room on 57th Street.

The day of Orage's death is historical record, but one wonders at the coincidence of the discussion over the phrase "intentional suffering,"[35] a phrase that does not appear in the published version of the text on which he was working except at this point in his recollection. In other words, the phrase inserts itself into the text through the mediation of Orage's death an instant before his death is revealed! While the tragedy of Orage's premature death is real, the impact of it in Gurdjieff's account is of a different order of reality. Orage's death, in a crucial sense, is Gurdjieff's essence occasion for intentional suffering seven years to the day after he took an oath on certain will-tasks involving intentional suffering.[36] He himself had diagnosed Orage's situation and given a prognosis. When, years later, he wondered openly to others, "Why Orage let himself die?"[37] he was not interrogating himself; he was challenging his audience to contemplate reasons for and effects of death—a thematic concern at the core of *Life Is Real,* the text that encloses Orage's death and contains something of his life. Pound may have been close to the truth when he remarked simply: "Orage finally wore himself out."[38] Carl Bechhofer Roberts, one of Orage's first comrades in the work, thought back twelve years to Gurdjieff's opinion that Orage would realize his ambition to be one of the "elder brothers of the human race" only, as Gurdjieff had said, if he would "learn how to give, then you make other people free." Bechhofer Roberts thought he had, for Orage "was, without exception, the most generous man I have ever known."[39]

---

35. Marvelous coincidences abound here. The phrase "Voluntary Suffering" was the one Orage used in early drafts of *Beelzebub's Tales,* and continued using it in his group work and readings until late 1928. The definition he gave his pupils on 31 May 1927 was: "Voluntary Suffering is suffering the unpleasant manifestations of other beings . . . and consists in controlling your facial expressions and other forms of behavior or in concealing them—or in changing them. A man enrages me, I want to strike him, but voluntary suffering requires that I respond as if he pleased me." (Manchester Papers, p. 123).

36. Perhaps Gurdjieff would have the Law of Seven in operation here. Bennett, *Gurdjieff,* p. 235, says that Gurdjieff's particular grief came from the fact that he "had not allowed for his premature death," assuming Orage's return.

37. Tim Redman, *Ezra Pound and Italian Fascism* (Cambridge: Cambridge University Press, 1991), p. 158, cites a remark Pound made a few days later to Galeazzo Ciano: "I'm still not sure his death was by natural causes." In early 1939, when suffering from excruciating internal pains that resulted in 1940 in a kidney removal, Toomer suspected that Gurdjieff, who was in New York when the pains started, may have had some responsibility for his agony. Welch, *Orage,* p. 94, remarks that Rom Landau, during his interview with Gurdjieff in the spring of 1930, suffered discomfort that he attributed to Gurdjieff's magical spell. Landau, *God Is My Adventure* (London: Ivor Nicolson and Watson, 1935), p. 241, recalls that he had asked Orage for an introduction to Gurdjieff, but Orage refused.

38. *Criterion,* 4 January 1935.

39. Cited by Mairet, *Orage,* p. 115.

Chapter Nine

ORAGE'S LEGACY:
JOURNALISM, OCCULTISM, AND ECONOMY

The real never ceases to be.

—Orage[1]

What a man leaves after death in addition to his works is the dream his name inspires, which makes it a symbol of admiration, hate or indifference.

—Paul Valéry[2]

1934–1935: EULOGIES FOR THE MAN

Orage was buried in Hampstead. On the tombstone above his body, Eric Gill carved the Enneagram, Gurdjieff's geometric code for the Laws of Three and Seven. Immediately after his funeral, Ezra Pound, T. S. Eliot, and Herbert Read assured Jessie that they would continue *The New English Weekly,* with Philip Mairet as editor. The next issue, appearing on 15 November 1934, was devoted to a tribute to him from the literary world, with contributions from Shaw, Chesterton, T. S. Eliot, AE [George Russell],[3] H. G. Wells, J. C. Powys, Augustus John, Ezra Pound, Richard Aldington, and many others. On this occasion, Chesterton called Orage "the first fruits of a new sort of freedom."[4] Shaw asserted that Orage, "a desperado of genius, in whose capacities there was neither beginning, middle, nor end," was "interested in every-

---

1. Orage's epitaph, quoting Krishna to Arjuna.
2. Cited by René Zuber, *Qui êtes vous, Monsieur Gurdjieff?* (Paris: Courier du Livre, 1977), p. 79.
3. AE, somewhat deaf, had called at Orage's Cursitor Street office on the morning of the 6th to congratulate him for his talk, and had assumed from the tearful explanation of the secretaries that Jessie had died, whereupon he wrote a letter of condolence on the spot to Orage. The next day, having realized his error, he wrote to Jessie a tribute to her husband, saying that he "had the most luminous mind I met in this country" (*Letters from AE,* p. 216).
4. *NEW* (15 November 1934).

thing but vulgarity."[5] Edwin Muir wrote that Orage "gave out constantly an active and enlightened good-will such as I have never met in any one else." He had a "great endowment of negative capability," and "subjected all his beliefs to a 'trial by reason.'" Muir continued: "He was a charming companion, an enchanting talker, whether witty or serious or both, and a constant friend." He exercised "an incorruptible adherence to reason which was in him an objective passion." Orage's death was "a loss not only to civilisation but to the steady and informed good-will on which the hope for the future of society rests, and of which Orage was the purest and most disinterested representative of his age."[6] Mrs. J. S. Collis called Orage the only man she ever knew without egotism. AE wrote: "Wherever I looked into Orage's mind I found the long corridors lit."[7]

T. S. Eliot, who had, in a letter to Pound a year earlier, said that he, like Orage, believed in the priority of ethics over politics, spoke of the "inner order of the soul and the outer order of society" whose bond together was exemplified in Orage. Eliot called him the best of London's leader writers, "a man who could be both perfectly right and perfectly wrong," and then went on to speak of Orage's commitment to a humane economic system. Echoing Orage, he said: "Settle the problem of distribution," he wrote, "—of wheat, coffee, aspirin or wireless sets—and all the problem of evil will disappear."[8] In faraway Argentina, Ramiro de Maeztu wrote, in the Literary Supplement of *La Prensa:* "Alfred Richard Orage was one of the most influential spirits in England, although not one Englishman in ten thousand would know his name—because Orage only influenced influential people. He had no other public but writers."[9]

Perhaps the most moving testimonial to Orage in *The New England Weekly* special issue was penned by Pamela Travers, a confirmed follower of Orage and Gurdjieff. She offered this brief and eloquent poetic sentiment:

Now the Planets wheel away,
Leap and sap to roots are gone,
So unto his elements
Let him return

5. *NEW* (15 November 1934).
6. Cited by P. H. Butter, *Edwin Muir: Man and Poet* (Westport, CT: Greenwood Press, 1966), p. 74.
7. Cited by Louise Welch, *Orage and Gurdjieff in America* (London: Routledge & Kegan Paul, 1982), p. 55.
8. Russell Kirk, *Eliot and His Age* (New York: Random House, 1971), p. 232.
9. Cited by MacDiarmid, *The Company I've Kept* (Berkeley, CA: University of California Press), p. 75. De Maeztu was killed in the Spanish civil war defending Socialism.

That was a burning-glass
Glowing between
Darkness and light, that drew
Sun down into stone.[10]

Eliot put out a memorial issue of his journal *Criterion* on 4 January 1935, in which he and Pound added personal testimonials of appreciation for Orage. Pound's was entitled "In the Wounds," in which he summed up Orage as "that necessary and rare person, the moralist in criticism: not the inquisitor who tries to impose [his] morals upon literature, but the critic who perceives the moral of literature. . . . Then he took ten years' vacation. The trams of the Lord move slowly."[11] Eliot wrote, in his "Commentary," that Orage represented orthodoxy in bringing together "men of the most varied sorts . . . in loose but certain association, who otherwise would have no common ground."[12]

On 22 January, Orage's associates, collaborators, and admirers held the first of a succession of "Orage Club" memorial dinners that featured yet more plaudits. Though these are eloquent and well-deserved assessments, the extent and weight of influence that Orage's journalism had in the literary sphere of the English language is largely ignored today. Those who were associated with Orage in any one of his public endeavors were unlikely to forget him. The poet-critic Allen Tate, much Orage's junior, but someone whom Orage had invited to the Prieuré in the summer of 1927, declared a third of a century later that "within the memory of our time the great editors were Henley and Ford, the late A. R. Orage and T. S. Eliot."[13] If that legacy of Orage's is forgotten still fifty years after his death, as it was within a decade after his death, it is because Orage wrote with and for others who are remembered. Pertinent to Orage's case are the words of Harry Truman, thirty-third president of the United States, who said of teachers that they are to be judged the way one judges a Missouri bull, not by the number of hours put in on the job, but by the results. Orage, like the best of bulls, was one whose influence leaves no signature stamp on another's work. He preferred to free his pupils from the certainty of broad error rather than imprison them in a strait truth embroidered with his name. No one can count the number of writers in the English language whose works are indebted, more or less, to Orage's influence.

---

10. *NEW* (15 November 1934).
11. Ezra Pound, *Selected Prose*, William Cookson, ed. (New York: New Directions, 1973).
12. Cited by Jeffrey M. Perl, *Skepticism and Modern Enmity: Before and After Eliot* (Baltimore: The Johns Hopkins Press, 1989), pp. 99–100.
13. *Essays of Four Decades* (London: Oxford University Press, 1970), p. 54.

In Orage's beloved New York, his friends and members of the New
Economics Group of New York, inspired by Orage's talks on Economy
in 1931, launched a Social Credit Review entitled *New Democracy,*
which was edited by Gorham Munson and Larry Morris, and published
by Wim [Willem] Nyland. Its memorial to Orage appeared shortly after
he died and featured tributes by Munson, Mabel Dodge Luhan, former
New Mexican governor H. W. Hockenhull, and William Carlos
Williams.[14]

Five months earlier, on 15 December 1934, less than six weeks
after Orage's death, Jessie had returned with her two young children to
the United States to recuperate her morale close to her family. She had
vague plans to raise the children in New York but, disappointed and
depressed without the man she had fallen in love with there, she
returned to London on 9 January 1935, and took over, for a short time,
the general direction of *The New English Weekly.*[15]

1935–1999: LEGACIES

"Orage is unknown largely because Social Credit is unknown,"
announces one recent critic.[16] Like the literary legacy of Orage that is
largely forgotten, however, his economic legacy, though forgotten now,
was a crucial instrument in the development of theories of political
economy from the thirties into the seventies. Ezra Pound, who contributed some 180 articles to *The New English Weekly* between 1934
and 1939, penned many a tribute to Orage that allude to both his literary and his economic legacies. In the *Cantos,* he mentions Orage by
name six times,[17] most significantly in Canto XCVIII as a literary
example:

> But the lot of 'em, Yeats, Possum and Wyndham
>   Had no ground beneath 'em,
>   Orage had.[18]

---

14. Gorham Munson's *Aladdin's Lamp, The Wealth of the American People* (New York:
Creative Age Press, 1945), is an excellent statement of the Social Credit scheme in an American
context. I find no evidence that Toomer was invited to contribute to the issue. He made no effort,
apparently, to participate in the group, but planned his own teaching on a Bucks County property that he and Marjorie acquired soon after.
15. Jessie sailed back to New York on 6 July 1940, after France had fallen. She met with the
Notts in New York, then moved to Albany in late August. Finally in November, at the urging of
Betty Hare, she drove to Santa Fe, where she lived with her children until 1945, when she
returned to England to live until the end of her life in 1982.
16. W. S. Flory, *The American Ezra Pound* (New Haven: Yale University Press, 1989), p 44.
17. Cantos XLVI, LXXX, LXXXIX, XCVIII, CIV and CXI. For the citations, see Carroll F.
Terrell, *A Companion to the Cantos of Ezra Pound* (Berkeley: University of California Press,
1984).
18. "Possum" is T. S. Eliot, "Wyndham" is Wyndham Lewis. See also Canto CIV.

After the second line here Pound added the Chinese character *PU,* which signifies "No, not, absolutely not." Philosophically, *p'u* means "unwrought simplicity." It is a Taoist graph for man's natural state before his inborn powers, or essence, have been contaminated by mundane knowledge or morality.

A similar tribute appears in Canto LXXX as a retrospective view of literary influences: "Orage, Fordie, Crevel too quickly taken." He added a fittingly memorial to Orage's humanity in the notes for Canto CXI:

> A nice quiet paradise,
> > Orage held the basic was pity
> > > Compassione,
> > > > Amor[19]

"And that the truth is in kindness"—the last line of Canto CXIV— alludes to Orage's unstinting generosity as a benefactor of talent and truth.[20] The opening lines of Canto 52 have a typical Oragean sentiment:

> And the true base of credit, that is
> > the abundance of nature
> with the whole folk behind it.[21]

A week after the publication of the special issue of the *Criterion,* inspired by Orage's BBC broadcast, Pound gave a talk on EIAR (Italian Broadcasting Co.) to celebrate the economic triumph of Fascism. In a letter to Eric Mesterton in December 1936, he fumed: "The S. Acad. ought by now to get round to seeing that Douglas and Orage worked for peace, whereas dozens of soupeaters merely yodel about it in hope of his pence."[22] Pound was not alone in his sympathies. Almost all the writers who worked with Orage at one time or another were touched by his economic views. As Herbert Read reflected on his and Pound's common view: "From Orage we had both acquired similar ideas about politics and economics," including the idea that social revolution depends upon "its ability to deal with the monetary problem."[23] William Carlos Williams, considering Pound's rather Fascist version of Orage's eco-

19. This is in a "reconstruction" of the Canto. See Wendy Stallard Flory, *The American Ezra Pound* (New Haven: Yale University Press, 1989), p. 83.
20. J. J. Wilhelm, *Ezra Pound: The Tragic Years 1925–1972* (University Park: Pennsylvania State University Press, 1994), p. 352.
21. *Cantos.*
22. D. D. Paige, ed. *Ezra Pound: Selected Letters 1907–1941* (New York: New Directions, 1971), p. 283.
23. Quoted by Christine Brooke-Rose, *A ZBC of Ezra Pound* (London: Faber and Faber, 1982), p. 235.

nomics, wrote: "The things that made him [Orage] go," his essential message, "doubted it ever entered Pound's consciousness."[24]

Orage's influence on economic theory crossed the Channel as well as the Atlantic. In Germany, Max Weber (1864–1920), a political economist and psychologist of religion, was assuming heavy responsibilities in the Weimar government to stabilize the mark and balance a precarious economy. Weber had read Orage on Guild Socialism and Social Credit, and he looked for a way to apply these concepts to Marxist economics. Following Orage's example, he looked to India, China, and the Jews for the religious and social roots of capitalism. Orage's writings had convinced him that there was an ethical and religious factor in the Western world that was responsible for capitalism.

Gorham Munson's major writing on Social Credit, *Aladdin's Lamp, The Wealth of the American People,* is dedicated "To Orage"

> Who had no axe but truth to grind
> and with it struck at the root
> While thousands hacked only at the
> branches of economic evil.[25]

Whether one assumes that Gurdjieff understood or cared much for Orage's economic principles or not, curiously, Orage's broadcast of those ideas appeared close to saving the Institute a few months after Orage's death. Senator Bronson M. Cutting of New Mexico had heard of Gurdjieff through his close friends in Santa Fe and Taos, Betty Sage Hare and Mabel Dodge Luhan, but when he had received Orage and Jessie in Santa Fe in July 1928, he was persuaded by Orage's explanations of Social Credit. In subsequent correspondence with Ezra Pound between 1930 and 1935, Cutting became even more impressed by the Douglas scheme,[26] and Orage's name was imprinted like a watermark on their

24. Paul Mariani, *William Carlos Williams: A New World Naked* (New York: McGraw-Hill, 1981), p. 298.
25. Gorhan Munson, *Aladdin's Lamp: The Wealth of the American People* (New York: Creative age Press, 1945).
26. See Walkiewicz and Witemeyer, *Ezra Pound and Senator Bronson Cutting* (Albuquerque: University of New Mexico Press, 1995). Pound had even urged Cutting in 1931 to run for president on a Social Credit platform. Then, after Herbert Hoover lost to Roosevelt, Pound urged Cutting to run in 1936 as a Progressive Republican or Independent against Roosevelt. After Cutting's death, Pound turned to Huey Long of Louisiana as his Social Credit Presidential candidate (see Walkiewicz, and Witemeye, *Senator Bronson*, p. 94), but Long was assassinated four months later in September. Munson and others in New York kept alive *New Democracy* (1933–1936), to which Pound contributed. In these days of Roosevelt's "New Deal," as Earle Davis points out in *Vision Fugitive,* "Social Credit became mixed in the public mind with extreme and rabid panaceas: religious revivalism, professional rabble-rousing, populist revolution against the established community" (cited by Walkiewicz and Witemeyer, p. 245 n42). T. S. Eliot felt committed to the Social Credit scheme for a decade, though he claimed never to have really understood it.

paper. Senator William E. Borah of Idaho and other politicians of influence were being educated in Social Credit theory throughout the thirties.

A few days after Orage's death, Cutting won election to the Senate
seat he had held by appointment, and on 11 November, Mabel Dodge
Luhan hosted a celebration dinner for him.[27] Whatever he heard from
Mabel and Betty in the months that followed about Gurdjieff and his
hopes to reopen the Institute, he agreed to meet Gurdjieff in Washington
DC on 5 May 1935, six months to the day after Orage's BBC broadcast.
It has been assumed by scholars that Cutting was carrying an offer to
Gurdjieff for the work, either in the form of a New Mexico location for
a future Institute or in the form of a pledge of financial support. A
pledge would have been made in association with Betty Hare and Mabel
Dodge, both of whom wanted the work to continue in Orage's memory,
though both had refrained from investing themselves in a New Mexico
Institute. In the late winter of 1935, Gurdjieff had visited Taliesin in
Spring Green, Wisconsin, where he thought Frank Lloyd Wright might
host the Institute.[28] Olga Ivanovna, however, had plans for her own center there. So Gurdjieff, who had been staying in New York City with
Jean Toomer's best friend, Fred Leighton, went to Washington DC at
the end of April with Nick Putnam and Philip Lasell to make a proposition for Cutting. He waited ten days for the senator, but Cutting never
arrived. His plane went down in a field in Missouri.

Despite Cutting's untimely demise, Congressman T. Alan
Greenborough introduced a Social Credit Bill in Congress in 1935 that
had been drafted by Munson's New Economics Group. The bill was
tabled and reintroduced in 1937, but the effects of Roosevelt's New
Deal were beginning to take effect, and the bill, whose full text Munson
reproduces in *Aladdin's Lamp,* "died" on the floor of Congress. In the
Canadian province of Alberta in 1935, however, William Aberhart's
Social Credit Party won 57 of 63 seats in the Legislative Assembly, and
remained in power for thirty-six years, during which time Social Credit
provided the underpinning of the economy. In the nineteen eighties and
nineties in small towns in New England and the Midwest, Social Credit
operated unofficially as a means of keeping local money circulating
within communities rather than moving to large urban banking centers.

Another link between Orage, Gurdjieff, and the American economy in 1935 was Henry Agard Wallace, future Vice President of the
United States and candidate for the presidency in 1948 on a Socialist
platform. Wallace had listened appreciatively to Orage in the spring of

---

27. Richard Lowitt, *Bronson M. Cutting* (Albuquerque: University of New Mexico Press, 1992),
p. 270.
28. Brendan Gill, *Many Masks* (New York: Da Capo, 1998), pp. 226–227.

1931 in New York and had met Gurdjieff at the same time. He was named head of the Department of Agriculture in 1933 by Franklin Delano Roosevelt, and was on good terms with Senator Cutting. In early 1934, he appointed to his staff "Dr." Nikolai Konstantinovich Rerikh (Rerick, or, more commonly in the United States, Roerich [1874–1947]), a White Russian painter-designer-mystic who had arrived in New York in 1920. Orage might have known Roerich in London in 1918, where the Russian was working with Diaghilev. It is almost certain that Roerich attended at least one of Orage's talks in the autumn of 1924, and probably another in the spring of 1931. He may have met Gurdjieff at either time, or even earlier, in St. Petersburg before the Great War. It is improbable that he and Gurdjieff should have been unknown to each other, and it is possible that they were in contact over a period of years.[29] Roerich spent time in Tibet, Mongolia, Turkestan, and the Gobi Desert between 1923 and 1928. From the summer of 1934 to the autumn of 1935, Roerich, his wife, and his son George, the translator of the Tibetan *Blue Annals,* were in Central Asia on a mission for Wallace to search for drought-resistant grasses.[30] They were, however, more interested in identifying cultural objects to be preserved by treaty in case of war. They had convinced Wallace and Roosevelt that the Gobi desert was once grassed, and that cultural artifacts could be found to attest to ancient civilizations there and in Siberia, an historical "speculation" Gurdjieff' repeats in *Beelzebub's Tales* in the account of

---

29. Roerich, born in St. Petersburg in 1874, entered the Academy of Art there in 1893. His interest in theosophy brought him into contact with Ouspensky. His wife, Helena, was the first translator of the whole text of Blavatsky's *Secret Doctrine* into Russian. Roerich was also active in the world of music and dance, having worked with Stravinsky and Diaghilev in 1913 when he designed the décor and costumes for *Le Sacre du Printemps,* so he was probably known to De Hartmann as well. In 1920, the Roerichs moved to New York, and Nikolai traveled to New Mexico to make paintings of Indians. He met Mabel Dodge Luhan there, and back in New York was associated with Claude Bragdon in establishing an academy of the arts. He opened the Roerich Museum in New York City in 1928, and was nominated for the Nobel Peace Prize in 1929 for the Roerich Pact, or "Banner for Peace," a treaty to protect artifacts from the devastation of war (Frank Billings Kellogg, American Secretary of State, won the prize). The United States and twenty-one other countries signed the pact in the spring of 1935, when the Roerich family, with the exception of a son studying at Columbia University, were back in Central Asia. In 1936, they moved to India, where Nikolai died in 1947. According to a recent biographer, Jacqueline Decter, *Nicholas Roerich: The Life and Art of a Russian Master* (London: Thames & Hudson, 1989), his interest in mystical symbolism is represented by the Great Pyramid design on the one dollar bill, which he persuaded Franklin Delano Roosevelt to place there. She reproduces the map of the 1923–1928 expedition (p. 158) that resembles Webb's map of Gurdjieff's travels there thirty years earlier, described in *Meetings with Remarkable Men,* A. R. Orage, trans. (London Penguin, 1963), pp. 165–176. Whereas Gurdjieff arrived at the secret monastery of Sarmoung, Roerich was looking for the famed Shambhala, the earthly link to Heaven whose putative ruler was Rigden Djapo (Rig is the Indo-European root for "king").
30. In *Meetings,* p. 168, Gurdjieff speaks of the possible utilization of organic materials in and under the sands of the Gobi.

Beelzebub's second descent to Earth. Wallace, suspicious of a deeper purpose for the Roeriches' voyages, removed them from his department in 1936.[31]

Undeterred by the failure of the Greenborough Bill to pass Congress a year earlier, Munson founded the American Social Credit Movement in New York on 5 October 1938, and served as its General Secretary. Its manifesto included the statement: "We abominate anti-Semitism; the money question and Jewish question are not linked."[32] A majority of members were writers and former members of Orage's groups, including William Carlos Williams, who was a contributor to *New Democracy,* and Archibald MacLeish, who may not have been a formal member, but who spoke in favor of the Social Credit movement.

It may be that Orage's Social Credit, which was not looked upon favorably by the Labor Party in Britain, found its proper place in John Maynard Keynes' *General Theory of Employment, Interest and Money* (1936). Keynesian economics made famous the supply-and-demand equation. In the Depression, when demand diminished, there was a threat of productive overcapacity in industry. Keynes saw the necessity of government intervention to inject public debt into the economy, something Roosevelt later did with his WPA (Works Progress Administration). Since the Depression shrank consumer demand because of a lack of a broad base of buying power in the populace, the public needed money to consume production; and so, echoing Orage's general argument for Social Credit, Keynes called for the government to promote buying power by deficit circulation of money. National debt causes inflation, and inflation brings more money into public circulation. Soon European governments were consuming 50 percent of the gross domestic product, leading inexorably to the formation of welfare states in which the circulation and retention of monies is controlled by a central banking system.

After Cutting's tragic disappearance, Gurdjieff left the United States, but nothing seems to be known of his whereabouts until the fall of 1935, when he began teaching on a modest level from his brother Dmitri's Paris apartment. It is thought that he had returned to the Soviet

---

31. See Edward L. and Frederick H. Schapsmeier, *Henry A. Wallace of Iowa: The Agrarian Years, 1910–1940* (Ames: Iowa State University Press, 1968), and *The Price of Vision: The Diary of Henry A. Wallace 1942–1946,* John Morton Blum, ed. (Boston: Houghton Mifflin, 1973), p. 358. In an attempt to slander Wallace at the time he was running for president in 1948, the columnist Westbrook Pegler revealed Wallace's relationship with Roerich in the so-called "Guru Letters" that were to prove Wallace's dangerous mystical affinities.
32. Mike Weaver, *William Carlos Williams: The American Background* (Cambridge: Cambridge University Press, 1971), pp. 205–206.

Union with the idea of beginning again there, and many have speculated that he had gone to Central Asia, where the Roerichs were operating. He had said years earlier that what began in Russia would end there, and it is known that his secretary in the United States at that time, Paul Anderson, had inquired about visa possibilities at the Russian Embassy in Washington. Apparently, the Soviet authorities gave Gurdjieff permission to return, but not to teach. Aside from this restriction, the political climate in early 1935 was not favorable. Kirov had been assassinated in December 1934, and the full weight of Stalin's ethnic, linguistic, and political purges was crushing the morale of the people. Undiscouraged, back in Paris in Dmitri's apartment at 6 Rue des Colonels Renard just down the slope of Avenue Carnot from the Arc de Triomphe and to the left of the Rue d'Armaille, Gurdjieff, now almost alone, started a modest teaching to a small group that included a number of French pupils, as well as the members of the old "rope" group: Margaret Anderson, Jane Heap, Georgette Leblanc, Solita Solano—all of whom had begun their work earlier with Orage—and the former nun, Kathryn Hulme.[33] His earlier comrades on the exodus from Russia had dispersed since the closure of the Institute. The de Stjernvalls were in Normandy, the de Salzmanns by the shores of Lac Léman, and the de Hartmanns in a western suburb of Paris.

Gurdjieff took one last trip before World War II to the United States, in the spring of 1939. He may have had hopes of resetting the Institute on Jean Toomer's and Marjorie Content's large property in Bucks County, Pennsylvania, but Toomer, rather than see or talk with Gurdjieff, fled to Bermuda for a vacation. From New York, where he was staying with Fred Leighton, Gurdjieff visited Frank Lloyd Wright at Taliesin East in Spring Green, Wisconsin in June. The two got along well and one evening after Gurdjieff presumed upon Wright's hospitality to give a talk, the architect said: "'Well, Mr. Gurdjieff, this is very interesting. I think I'll send some of my young pupils to you in Paris. Then they can come back and I'll finish them off.' 'You finish! You are idiot,' said Gurdjieff. 'You finish! No! You begin, I finish.' 'You know,' said Olgivanna, 'Mr.Gurdjieff is right.'"[34] Gurdjieff returned to France in May, a few months before the outbreak of the war. When he came back on his last visit to the United States at the end of 1948, with the

---

33. Margaret Anderson traces this teaching in *The Unknowable Gurdjieff* (London: Routledge & Kegan Paul, 1962). Curiously, Gurdjieff's visiting card misspells the street name "6, rue du Colonel-Renard."

34. Nott, *Journey through this World*, p. 152. Secrest, *Wright*, p. 431, abbreviates the exchange. For a fresh account of Gurdjieff's relations with Wright, see Brendan Gill, *Many Masks*, pp. 226–227.

exception of Mme Ouspensky's pupils from Mendham, New Jersey, it was Orage's former pupils and friends who opened their arms, ears, and stores of admiration to Gurdjieff. This was palpable proof that Orage had performed a lasting service.

A year after Gurdjieff's death, Gorham Munson reviewed the thought of three "Black Sheep Philosophers, Gurdjieff, Ouspensky and Orage." He noted that Orage was more philosopher than psychologist, and that Gurdjieff had no religion whatsoever.[35] In the early fifties, Margaret Anderson revived some of Pound's dormant thoughts on Gurdjieff in her correspondence with him. For example, on 9 September 1953, Pound wrote to Anderson: "Gurdjieff I thot a man an a bruvver, but NO buddy is goin to swallow Ouspensky or the periphery, Lady R/etc."[36] When Anderson heard that Wyndham Lewis had gone blind, she wrote to Pound to suggest that Lewis had lost some of his physical powers and might now be more open than in the past to instruction in spiritual matters. She recommended Vera Daumal in Paris for Gurdjieff teaching. Pound wrote Lewis on 9 October 1953 to report that: "Marg Anderson wantin to git yr soul filled wiff sweetness and light via some gurdjieffite femme now in Paris. I have told her I am unable to promote the action."[37]

Through Orage's work in the arts, writers and painters were attracted to Gurdjieff's ideas. Lincoln Kirstein spoke favorably of Gurdjieff's ideas to many of his associates and friends, including W. H. Auden, George Balanchine, Paul Cadmus, and Pavel Tchelitcheff. Through the advice of Orage and Mairet in the early days of *The New Age,* the young Malcolm Lowry was sent to listen to Ouspensky lecture on Gurdjieffian ideas. In a June 1953 letter to Albert Erskine, his editor at Random House, Lowry grieved over his difficulty getting his contracted writings completed and admitted that he might "abandon writing altogether & in order to save my by then unsalvageable soul enter Gurdjieff's nursing home in company with the beneficent ghost (perhaps) of Katherine Mansfield."[38] Aldous Huxley reflects Gurdjieff's ideas in his novel *After Many a Summer Dies the Swan* (1939), as well as in his long essay, *The Doors of Perception* (1954). Works of Gerald Heard, John Cowper Powys, and Christopher Isherwood reveal

35. Cited in *Gurdjieff International Review* 1:3 (1998), p. 2.
36. Thomas L. Scott, *et al.,* eds., *Pound/The Little Review: The Letters of Ezra Pound to Margaret Anderson* (New York: New Directions, 1988), p. 314.
37 Timothy Materer, ed. *Pound/Lewis: The Letters of Ezra Pound and Wyndham Lewis* (New York: New Directions, 1985), pp. 276–277.
38. *Sursum Corda* (London: Jonathan Cape, 1996), p. 665.

Gurdjieffian influence,[39] and the figure of Orage appears in roman à clef novels by Bechhofer Roberts and Paul Selver. Either through Orage or directly from Gurdjieff, Brancusi sculpted forms that seem to reflect Gurdjieffian ideas in the eyes of Basarab Nicolescu.[40] The earliest direct influence of Gurdjieff, as well as indirectly through the intermediaries of Orage, Toomer, and Daly King, touched the movement in Harlem during the twenties and thirties know as the "Harlem Renaissance." Jon Woodson has traced carefully the line of development from Orage's and Toomer's writing and speaking to the appropriation of ideas from Gurdjieff's *Beezebub's Tales* in the works of Thurman, Fisher, Larsen, Schuyler, and Hurston, and considers *"Beezebub's Tales* as the urtext of the 'objective' tendency in Harlem."[41]

A half century later, the American poet James Merrill wrote questioningly in "The Changing Light at Sandover" (1983) about spiritualistic

> Popthink
> all this
> Warmed up Milton, Dante Genesis?
> This great tradition that has come to grief
> In volumes by Blavatsky and Gurdjieff?[42]

In his National Book Award-winning *Mirabell: Book of Numbers,* Merrill echoes Gurdjieff's cosmology with a character Bezelbob and Gods A and B, who are dim mirrors of Gurdjieff and Orage.

It would be impossible to trace Orage's and Gudjieff's indirect influence on American letters fully. It is known, however, that Witter Brynner became interested in Orage's ideas during his residence in New Mexico in the late 1920s, not only through contacts with the Santa Fe and Taos Orage connections, but due to his correspondence with Pound. Wallace Stevens, a good friend of James Merrill, echoed Orage's thought in an early volume of poems, *Ideas of Order* (1935). For one example, the line "Life is an old casino in a park" in his poem, "Academic Discourse in Havana" is a metaphor Orage used on occasion in

39. *The Oxford Companion to English Literature,* Margaret Drabble, ed. (Oxford: Oxford University Press, 1985), credits Gurdjieff with influence on Isherwood and Heard. Powys' *Wolf Solent* reflects a refutation of Gurdjieff's view of evil.
40. Personal correspondence to the author, 6 December, 1999 (Taylor papers).
41. Woodson's *To Make a New Race: Gurdjieff, Toomer and the Harlem Renaissance* (Jackson: University of Mississippi Press, 1999) reached my hands too late to be incorporated into this book. He places Ouspensky among the influential group.
42. Timothy Materer, *Modern Alchemy: Poetry and the Occult* (Ithaca: Cornell University Press, 1995), pp. 158–159.

his talks. Another poem in this volume, "A Fading of the Sun," has Gurd-jieffian resonance, and his sparse prose pronouncements on poetry as an "art of perception" could well have been taken from Orage's criticism.[43]

Though the direct influence of Gurdjieff's teaching is not my topic in this chapter, it is appropriate to acknowledge, if only briefly, the enormous effect Gurdjieff has had on literature, philosophy, and psychology, after his time as well as during his life, independent of Orage's mediation. His thought is currently reflected throughout New Age writing. One could cite many of the works of Colin Wilson as examples of New Age science drawing upon Gurdjieffian propositions.[44] Others include the recent flood of writings by Tony Schwartz, Oscar Ichazo, Claudio Naranjo, and Helen Palmer that base personality types and bio- and psycho-rhythms on the Enneagram. Directly or indirectly, Gurdjiffian thought finds its way into fiction as well. The Norwegian Jostein Gaarder's 1997 novel, *Solitaire Mystery,* extends the simple Gurdjieffian axiom that "man is more alive than conscious."[45] Gaarder illustrates this in a fable about a world populated by playing cards that cannot escape their prescribed roles, and thus exemplify existence as habit. Gaarder even includes a counterpart to Gurdjieff's kundabuffer in a "rainbow fizzy" beverage that removes the drinker's awareness of his own essence.

More recently, the biography of the Amercian boxer, "Hurricane" Carter, imprisoned unjustly, reveals how the once militant Black, after reading Ouspensky's *In Search of the Miraculous* and *A New Model of the Universe,* disdained his personality in a successful quest to redis- cover his essence.[46]

Gurdjieff's influence on his former English and American pupils is recorded elsewhere in detail. Perhaps not enough is recorded in French records of his influence on the essayist-poet René Daumal and the novelist Luc Dietrich, both of whom worked with Gurdjieff and Jeanne de Salzmann until their untimely deaths during the German occupation. René Zuber and Louis Pauwels (whose ambivalent attitude toward Gurdjieff wavered between admiration, fascination, and disdain) are other examples.

---

43. "A Collect of Philosophy," *Wallace Stevens Collected Poetry and Prose* (New York: Library of America, 1996), p. 858.
44. For a complete scan of publications on Gurdjieff, see J. Walter Driscoll *Gurdjieff: An Annotated Bibliography,* intro. Michel de Salzmann. Garland Reference Library 225. New York: Garland, 1985, and *Gurdjieff: An Interim Bibliography* (Los Altos, CA: Gurdjieff Electronic Publishing, 1999).
45. *Solitaire Mystery* (London: Phoenix, 1997), p. 138.
46. James S. Hirsch, *Hurricane: The Miraculous Quest of Rubin Carter* (Boston: Houghton Mifflin, 2000), pp. 171–177.

It is axiomatic that esoteric schools do not survive more than a season after the death of their founders. Would Christianity have flourished, or even survived in the form of a slight historical footnote, without a Paul? After Gurdjieff's passage from the Earth, few saw a Paul, and many despaired for the future of Gurdjieff's teaching. Others had seen Orage as Gurdjieff's Peter and his Paul, and Orage was enormously successful in transmitting, or transforming, if you will, "the message" to others. Ouspensky may have had a larger following during his life, but, at the end of Gurdjieff's life in 1949, the exposition of his ideas was advanced principally by those who were introduced to Gurdjieff's world by Orage. In her account of Orage with Gurdjieff, Louise Welch writes; "Owing to Orage's luminous exposition of Gurdjieff's subtle thought, there are more people in America engaged in the study of his teaching than in any other country."[47] His stewardship has produced an enduring legacy in the cultural milieu he engaged on Gurdjieff's behalf.

---

47. Welch, *Orage*, p. xii. For a general overview of the work in America, see Kathleen Riordan Speeth, *The Gurdjieff Work* (Los Angeles: J. P. Tarcher, 1989).

Chapter Ten

GURDJIEFF AND ORAGE
ON BEING, KNOWING, AND LOVING

The Universe is a machine for the making of God.

—Henri Bergson[1]

To seek a sun of fuller fire.

—Wallace Stevens[2]

The people of the West have a devil proper to themselves which no one envies them. Let them negotiate with them as they will and can, but let them stop engaging us in stories that do not concern us at all.

—René Guénon[3]

One problem the biographer-critic faces in setting Gurdjieff and Orage in an historical context of ideas is identifying the philosophical schools of thought they drew upon, or that their ideas seem to echo. To begin with, the 20th-century boundaries between the disciplines of religion, philosophy, psychology, and theology are blurred. It is curious to some observers that entries under Gurdjieff's and Ouspensky's names appear in Mircea Eliade's monumental *Encyclopedia of Religion,*[4] but neither have entries in Paul Edwards' *Encyclopedia of Philosophy.* Gurdjieff never claimed to have founded a religion. In fact, in *Tales to his Grandson,* Beelzebub castigates current religions as "hasnamusses," ungainly spiritual gestures distinct from the teaching of genuine "messengers from above" such as Buddha, Lama, Moses, Mohammed, and Christ, whose messages have been diluted and diverted in the swirls of the historical flow of civilizations. Orage explained that this is what happens when genuine truth is accessible to common people, for gen-

---

1. *The Two Sources of Morality and Religion* (Notre Dame, IN: University of Notre Dame Press, 1977).
2. "How To Live, What To Do," *Ideas of Order* (New York: Library of America, 1996), p. 103.
3. *Études sur la franc-maçonnerie et le compagnonnage* (Paris: Seuil, 1964).
4. Above the name of Michel de Salzmann.

uine truth is understood only by the initiated, such as Christ. Beelzebub, who compares contemporary Christianity with one-and-one-half-day lentil soup, castigates occultism, theosophy, psychoanalysis, and other current doctrine. "There is no religion," explained Orage, echoing Gurdjieff, "there is only one God."[5] The point is not irrelevant here, because Orage insisted early in his group teaching that his pupils investigate the etymology of the word *religion*. He wanted them to appreciate that Latin *re-ligare* means to "re-bind" or "tie back."

If a religion is simply a shared recognition of a sacred or transcendental reality, as distinct from secular and profane reality, then Gurdjieff represented a religious movement.[6] Nonetheless, as far as I know, Gurdjieff never spoke of his teaching within the framework of any particular religious or philosophical stance, though his teaching and his writings can be measured against any number of philosophical positions of the day. The affinities of the material in *Beelzebub's Tales* to tendencies in the history of philosophy have been traced often. "The Holy Planet Purgatory," for example, displays aspects of Pythagorism, Platonism, Neoplatonism, Agnosticism, Stoicism, Origenism, and Sufism, just to suggest a few segments in the arc of its classical learning.[7] In his teaching of Gurdjieff's ideas, Orage formulated carefully ontological and epistemological contents carefully, in terms recognizable by his pupils. As Paul systematized Christ's teaching, Orage did so with Gurdjieff's in his own teaching. Orage drew upon an extraordinary erudition and an ability to measure Gurdjieff's teaching against current ideologies. His erudition did not noticeably influence Gurdjieff's thought, but Gurdjieff's ideas had an extraordinary influence on Orage, principally because Gurdjieff represented for Orage what he had long sought: an integration of Eastern esotericism with Western science. Furthermore, *Beelzebub's Tales* outlines a psychology of myth in Eastern terms. More importantly, Orage's basic beliefs, no matter how much they seemed to shift radically in the course of his career, were

5. Gurdjieff, *Tales of Beelzebub*, in *All and Everything* (London: Routledge & Kegan Paul, 1950), pp. 708, 249, 233. The invention of religious doctrines is attributed to King Konuzion of Maralpleicie (p. 216). In his chapter "Religion," pp. 694–743, Gurdjieff traces the fall of religions from their primal purpose to free people from the consequences of kundabuffer (pp. 715 and 732), and notes that only the Essenes have preserved an original force. Theosophy, Beelzebub laments, is mental perversity (p. 734). In *Search*, p. 286, Ouspensky quotes Gurdjieff to the effect that "Theosophy and Occultism bear grains of truth."
6. Emile Durkheim (1858–1917, *The Elementary Form of the Religious Life* (Chicago: University of Chicago Press, 1963), p. 47, defines a religion as "a unified system of beliefs and practices relative to sacred things"; and Mircea Eliade, *Encyclopedia of Religion*, p. xv, associates religion simply with "the element of the sacred."
7. Raphael Lefort, *The Teachers of Gurdjieff* (London: Victor Gollancz, 1966), was the first to trace Gurdjieff's acquisition of knowledge in the East.

always inclined toward Gurdjieff's thought, even when the expression of that thought seemed to others to contain significant contradictions. In the pages that follow, I will draw attention to ideas that seem to me to have some Gurdjieffian and Oragean resonance, even where formal philosophic positions stand opposed to what can be considered the mainline of Gurdjieff's thought. My purpose is simply to open lines of inquiry, not to set rigid categories of thought into which I can squeeze Orage's or Gurdjieff's teaching.

Orage himself identified a number of categories in which he would have placed himself at the time he entered into intellectual contact with Gurdjieff. Early in his career, Orage was an avid Nietzschean and knew well the works of Plato, Aristotle, Kant, and Hegel that Nietzsche drew upon. Long before he left London for Paris and Fontainebleau, he had become familiar with the major Western philosophical writings of his day. He would have easily reconciled Gurdjieff's triad of positive, negative, and neutralizing forces with the Hegelian method of thesis, antithesis, and synthesis, and with Plato's triad whose *tertium quid* mediates between any two numbers, objects, or poles of thought. Orage's 1907 lectures on consciousness have a distinct Nietzschean bias in Platonic terms.[8] In his first lecture, he pointed to the Norse mythological world-tree Yggdrasill as an image of creation comparable to Plato's chain of love that links the *haut* of the First Mover with the *bas* of the Earth. In his second lecture, he put into question the "native dualizing" habit of Western thought, arguing that all of life is a *tertium quid* between poles. Orage suggested that there is, in the world, a universal psychology that resists the vagaries of cultures, in contrast with simple reflections and opinions that differ in place and time.

By the time he held classes in New York, Orage was sensitive to the affinities and distinctions between Gurdjieff's thought and current philosophy, and in his own teaching he often rephrased Gurdjieff's ideas in identifiable philosophical terms that would be familiar to many, if not most, of his own pupils. A caveat is in order here, for the term "philosophical" is both too broad and too narrow to describe Gurdjieff's and Orage's thought. Though Gurdjieff has been called a mystic, and though mysticism has been promoted toward philosophical status through the influence of Evelyne Underhill (*Mysticism,* 1911), Rufus Jones (*Studies in Mystical Religion,* 1909), Friedrich von Hügel (*The Mystical Element of Religion,* 1908), René Guénon, William Ralph Inge, F. H. Bradley, and others, mysticism is more widely categorized

8. Published with an introduction by Louise Welch as *Consciousness: Animal, Human, and Superman* (London: Pembridge Design Studio, 1954).

today as a domain of religious thought and parapsychology. A mystic is one initiated into the esoteric knowledge of divine things, one reborn into eternity. Mysticism (from Greek *mysto* "to close [lips or eyes]" and *mustes* "closed mouthed") is a term used to replace the earlier *contemplatio,* a withdrawal from the world. Underhill defines mysticism as "an art of union with Reality" referring to three things: a type of experience, a way of knowing, and a state of consciousness.[9] An essential aspect of Gurdjieff that distinguishes him from most mystics is his activity in the public arena that requires pupils, or disciples, whereas the strict mystic tends to limit or exclude contact with other people. Since his earliest associations with the Seekers after Truth, Gurdjieff believed that a group, brotherhood, and school could accomplish far more than one person alone.[10] Jiddu Krishnamurti (1895–1986) was a "mystic." If Gurdjieff was one, it was of a different order. Both had access to higher being, Krishnamurti through the awakening of kundalini, Gurdjieff through the elimination of its kundabuffer effects.

One can locate Gurdjieff's and Orage's thought somewhere in philosophical contexts between finalism and mechanism, materialism and Platonism, existentialism and idealism, aestheticism and utilitarianism and, in matters of language, between realism and nominalism. The logical and analytical philosophy of Alfred North Whitehead (1861–1947) and Bertrand Russell (1872–1970), both of whom Orage knew personally,[11] was gaining popularity in both England and the United States. So were the phenomenological schools of thought derived from the basic assertion of Edmund Husserl (1859–1938) that phenomena are the sole source of knowledge. Both of these tendencies interested Orage, and he applied some of Russell's and Whitehead's logic (*Process and Reality,* 1929) to his own *Psychological Exercises;* but, neither movement spoke to his esoteric interests. Neither did the positivism or biological evolution of Darwin and Thomas Huxley that Gurdjieff's Beelzebub disdains in the story of his fourth descent.[12] Orage rejected the Darwinian mechanistic scheme of evolution with its theory of accidental variation under influence of exterior forces. For Orage, as well as for Gurdjieff, man's environment need not be altered to effect his psychophysical development. They would both agree with Saint

---

9. Cited by F. C. Harrold, *Mysticism* (London: Penguin, 1963), p. 38.
10. Colin Wilson, "Two Russian Mages," *A History of Magic and the Occult,* Kurt Seligman, ed. (New York: Random House, 1997), p. 404.
11. Orage wrote on Russell in *NA* 23, 2 May 1918, pp. 9–10. He used a Russell text as an object for discussion with his group on 15 December 1927. He discussed Whitehead along with John Dewey with his group on 7 March 1927.
12. Gurdjieff, *Tales,* p. 273.

Augustine's argument that different reactions to the same stimulus result from differences, not of nature, but of will, with the reservation that the will be consciously and not involuntarily exercised.[13] The argument that individual development in the human is a function of internal and psychological principles is axiomatic in neo-Lamarkian philosophy. As early as the late 18th century, the German Johann Gottlieb Fichte (1762–1814) introduced psychological considerations into philosophic discourse in terms that sound familiar to the student of Gurdjieff. Fichte argued that consciousness is a product of an ultimate cause in the universe, and that the world of each person is his own, brought into being through the creative agency of the Ultimate. Man's ego can be located at the point where creative activity of the Absolute emerges in individual consciousness. Fichte reasoned that the purpose of the world is to give man the occasion for realizing the ends of his existence. The world is the material for the fulfilling of his duty—an idea foreshadowing Gurdjieff's assertion that the world is man's arena for developing an objective consciousness that qualifies him to repay the Ultimate for the gift of life.[14]

In the late 19th century, Herbert Spencer (1820–1903) was the most influential of a group of philosophers who incorporated the relatively fresh sciences of psychology and sociology into philosophical discourse. Building upon Darwinian theory, Spencer advanced the idea that evolution moves from homogeneity toward heterogeneity, or from simple to complex forms of matter, motion, and force. His *Study of Sociology* (1873) argued against socialism and in favor of cooperatism within a positivistic argument that evolution was progress. Deviating somewhat from Darwin was Spencer's view that complexity, in its manifestations in individualism, comprises distinct rather than general adaptations. Man's mind and matter swing between evolution and dissolution, and between integration and diffusion.[15] Spencer's *Principles of Biology* (1910) was based on the premise that life is the continuous adjustment of internal relations to external relations, whereas Edmund Husserl's phenomenology, with its Platonic slant, argued that evolutionary movement was toward universalistic forms. Essence is not individual in character, but universal, partaking of pure being. Each of these thinkers was influenced, more or less, by Eastern

---

13. Augustine, *Confessions* from *Great Books of the Western World,* vol. 18, Morton J. Adler, ed. (Chicago: Encyclopædia Britannica, 1952), p. 12.
14. So, St. Thomas Aquinas argued that man's life in this world is occasion for him to qualify himself to receive God's gift of grace.
15. See Orage's "French Spencerianism," *Theosophical Review* 39 (September, 1906).

religions, particularly Hinduism, in which myth and religion are laminated within a single belief pattern. In 1922, the axial year in Orage's
adventure of the spirit, Herman Hesse's *Siddhartha* represented the
quest for essence in fictional form, foreshadowing in kind Gurdjieff's
Beelzebub's Tales.

It is clear that the causal theories imbedded within the psychological movements associated with the names of Sigmund Freud
(1856–1939), Carl Gustav Jung (1875–1951), and John Watson (1878–
1958) attracted the attention of Orage. It was Orage who introduced
Freud and the young science of psychoanalysis to general English readers of *The New Age.* It is beyond my scope and capacities to display here
the extent of the influences of psychoanalysis on Orage's thought, or to
compare psychoanalytic studies of human behavior with Gurdjieff's
teaching. Gurdjieff had little use for psychoanalytic procedures himself,
though he had used hypnotism in his own medical practice. He had no
use at all for the theory of psychological determinism. What Orage
found positive in their works, however, was a conscientious effort to
locate and describe the qualities of human consciousness.[16] Freud's *The
Unconscious* (1915), for example, argues, as Gurdjieff did, that "only a
small content is embraced by consciousness at any given moment, so
that the greater part of what we call *conscious knowledge* must in any
case exist for very considerable periods of time in a condition of latency . . . of not being apprehended by the mind."[17] In his Vienna lectures
from 1915 to 1917 (translated into English in 1920 as *General Introduction to Psycho-Analysis*), Freud examined a range of neuroses and
psychoses. In "Anxiety," the twenty-fifth lecture in the series, Freud
associated anxiety with a neurosis in the vagal nerve,[18] and declared that
anxiety is acquired, not innate. The effort of psychoanalysis to reveal
the essence beneath personality traits could not but appeal to Orage, but
he felt that the deterministic assumptions behind analysis were misleading. To illustrate a danger in Freudian readings of the psyche, Orage
told his pupils to imagine the patient's mind in a psychoanalytic process
as a box of children's letter blocks. When the analyst spills them on the
floor and they spell "pig," what is the significance?[19] Nonetheless,
Orage remarked that Feud's triadic consciousness—ego, super ego,
and mediating id—corresponded to Gurdjieff's positive, negative, and
mediating neutralizing forces.

---

16. See "Psychoanalysis," *NA* 22, 25 April 1918, pp. 501–502, and *NA* 25, 19 June 1919, p. 134.
17. Sigmund Freud,*The Complete Psychological Works*, vol. 14, James Strachey, ed. (London:
Hogarth Press, 1974), p. 167.
18. Robert Hohenberger reminds me that the left vagal nerve connects higher with lower emotional centers.
19. Manchester Notes for June 1927 (Manchester Papers, p. 3).

Jung, best known for his theory of archetypal mental patterns in thought, argued, in *Modern Man in Search of a Soul,* that spiritual consciousness was necessary to live in the present world. "To be wholly of the present," he writes, "means to be fully conscious of one's existence as a man." Like Gurdjieff, Jung recognized that man with reason must turn his attention from material things to his own subjective processes.[20] Both Maurice Nicoll and James Carruthers Young, among the first of Gurdjieff's pupils at the Institute, were Jungian in their direction, a fact that amused Freud, who said of them: "Ah, you see what happens to Jung's disciples."[21] Jung's elements of man's triadic mind—a positive consciousness, a negative unconsciousness, and a neutralizing ego[22]—correspond to Gurdjieffian categories, as does Jung's characterization of the unconscious as habit and reflex. Gurdjieff's four centers—moving, instinctive, feeling, and thought—find counterparts in Jung's hierarchical scale of sensation, feeling, intuition, and thought.[23]

John Watson's Behaviorism, based on the theory that consciousness can be structured and adapted to whatever particular mundane task the psychologist determines, fascinated Orage, and he had his pupils read Watson's *Behavior: An Introduction to Comparative Psychology* (1914). Watson, in turn, was impressed in New York by Orage's teaching. Orage saw initially that Watson was like Gurdjieff in his belief that essential being was influenced by impulses from outside. Watson argued that thinking is implicit behavior, and that human reflexes could be fully conditioned in a stimulus-response pattern. Similarly, Gurdjieff and Orage saw people as too often controlled by conditioned reflexes, or habit, but neither could agree with Watson's intransigent conviction that all human material can be determined for a fixed mentalistic end. Daly King, himself a trained psychologist, reproduced Orage's view in his study, *Beyond Behavorism.*[24]

Orage had always been interested in developments in psychology, though more with the functional and analytic than with the clinical or structural. His own position leaned toward psychological empiricism, perhaps influenced by the utilitarian empiricism of John Stuart Mill (1806–1873) and Hermann Ludwig Ferdinand de Helmholz (1821–

20. "The Spiritual Problem of Modern Man" (London: Kegan Paul, Trench, Trubner, 1933), pp. 227–237. This text could well stand as a commentary on Gurdjieff's thought.
21. *Century*, 1924, cited by Moore, *Gurdjieff: Anatomy of a Myth* (Boston: Element, 1991), p. 178.
22. Jolande Jacobi, *The Psychology of C. G. Jung* (London: Routledge & Kegan Paul, 1942), p. 21.
23. Jacobi, *C. G. Jung,* pp. 25–26.
24. In a group meeting on 30 April 1928, Orage faulted Watson for his teaching that the *whole* body is subject to conditioning.

1894), who denied the doctrine of innate ideas in arguing that all knowledge is based on experience transmitted hereditarily. Like Spencer and Helmholz, whose interests in the role of psychology in philosophical investigations go back to Berkeley, Hume, Condillac, and Kant, all of whom recognized that human perception of space and time depend upon sense impressions. Orage was attracted toward the study of the reaction of individual entities to environmental conditions, and agreed with the observation that such reaction was, on the whole, mechanical. He deviated in his belief that man could resist, even escape, the influences of exterior forces and circumstances that incite mechanical or habitual reactions. He also criticized contemporary psychologists and psychoanalysts for their lack of investigation into the central problem of the nature of consciousness.[25] They are limited in charting the actual of behavior, but fail to see the potential. Ontologically, for Orage, consciousness may reveal reality, but does not distort it, even if human consciousness is not a universal whole, but individual. Matter is, for the majority of us, Orage taught, independent of our consciousness, but a developed consciousness may affect matter. Orage would have found more to his interest in the later school of existential psychoanalysis.[26]

Contemporary English philosophers within Orage's ken included Francis Herbert Bradley (1846–1924), Alfred North Whitehead (1863–1947) and G[eorge] E[dward] Moore (1873–1958), whose early works Orage knew. In *Appearance and Reality* (1893), a study that proclaimed itself as having been written from a higher common sense, Bradley takes an idealist stand against the phenomenologist and empiricist associations of ideas as a logic for psychologism. He argued that cause, time, and space are merely appearances, as are all distinctions between primary and secondary qualities; that is, such things can only be conceived of in relation to other things. What is *real* must be consistent, harmonious, and all-inclusive. Bradley insisted on the spiritual nature of the universe and the superior reality of the soul. His Platonic mysticism, or absolute idealism, defined reality as a harmonious system of experience, a spiritual unity in diversity. These ideas, and Bradley's conception of his own philosophic role as a proponent of skepticism—compatible with much of Orage's thought—had a direct influence on Whitehead and G. E. Moore.

Whitehead, in later stages of his work, turned toward metaphysical considerations that have correspondences with the thought of Orage and Gurdjieff. His *Religion in the Making* (1926) proposed a relative

25. King, *Oragean Version* (privately published), p. 41.
26. Jacob Needleman, "Existential Psychoanalysis," *Encyclopedia of Philosophy,* Paul Edwards, ed. (New York: Macmillan, 1967).

metaphysics that held that there was no reality beyond the experience of subjects; that is, of any actual entities or spatial-temporal unites. All things, he argued, are sensitive to the existence of other things. The relation between these entities is *feeling*, which is a positive force distinct from abstractions, which are negative. When a unity dies, Whitehead posited, it is preserved in its relations to other things.

Moore agreed in general with Bradley on the non-existence of time, and he defined reality as a condition of absence of contradiction. He differed from Bradley in his empiricist approach by insisting on a sensory apprehension of the real. This is an approach that Orage and Gurdjieff described as a *desideratum* for harmonious development, in which the real is the true, though Gurdjieff would argue that sensory apprehension is but a single, if necessary, step toward a consciousness of reality.[27]

Orage was acquainted with the works of the French philosophers Henri Poincaré (1854–1912) and Gaston Milhaud (1852–1918). Both of whom, as did Orage and Gurdjieff, countered the evolutionary positivists like Darwin and Spencer who had argued that the physical sciences are the only valid sources of knowledge and facts the only valid objects of knowledge. For positivists, philosophy was tantamount to science. Poincaré and Milhaud demonstrated that the human equation cannot be subtracted from knowledge, and that scientific concepts are enclosed within the limits of human thought.

Orage was also interested in philosophic existentialism, a movement that exemplifies many aspects of Gurdjieff's teaching. Its basic tenet is that the source and elements of knowledge are sensations as they exist in human consciousness, and that there is no difference between the internal and the external world. Only phenomena that can be examined psychologically have existence in the states of mind. Therefore, the mind-body state is epiphenomenal in relation to neural processes.[28] The existentialist *Psychologie der Weltanschauungen* (Psychology of the World-view) of Karl Jaspers (1883–1969) was not published until 1922, but its ideas had already been disseminated a decade earlier. What attracted Orage initially to Jaspers was the promotion of psychology in philosophic discourse. In large, Jaspers promulgated a philosophic description of human existence. He sought to establish bounds to the human psychic life in order to understand what we are. Like Gurdjieff, he believed that existential antinomies, like death, accident, and guilt could be controlled to some extent by the psyche (the American tran-

---

27. See *NA* 25, 5 June 1919, p. 102.
28. Epiphenomena are secondary or by-products of phenomena.

222 GURDJIEFF AND ORAGE: BROTHERS IN ELYSIUM

scendentalist, Ralph Waldo Emerson, in his essay, "Fate," argues that the more we grow ourselves, the further and longer we keep fate from our door). Like Gurdjieff, Jaspers saw both good and ill in modern technology. The good is the power it affords us in our collaboration with natural forces; the ill is the *gestell,* or framing of ourselves in material uses that reduce the psyche. Jaspers would elucidate existence by a cognitive probe into reality on the basis of the deepest inner decisions experienced by an individual to satisfy the deepest demands of human nature. If the mind-body relationship is governed by neural processes, then consciousness must be epiphenomenal, rather than phenomenal.

The existential figure whose works seem most to place Orage's and Gurdjieff's thought within the parameters of existentialism is Martin Heidegger (1889–1976). Like Orage, Heidegger adopted, early in his career, a Nietzschean perspective toward the Aristotelian question: "What is being?" (*Metaphysics* VI, 1.1026a). He enumerated four properties of our sense of self: essential and non-essential, the true (propositions, mathematics, judgments), potentiality and actuality, and the senses. For being in time, Heidegger, as did Husserl in his *Phenomenology* in 1910, referred to an internal consciousness. Being in the abstract sense, Heidegger agreed with his master Husserl and Nietzsche (*Will to Power*), is simply a necessary fiction. More importantly for Orage, Heidegger's *The Doctrine of Judgment in Psychologism* (1913) reduces logic to psychological processes. Psychologism is a philosophical system based on a psychological self-observation that insists that truth is a subjective element of self-observation, a concept not foreign to Gurdjieff's teaching (Daly King associated it with panpsychism). Heidegger's phenomenology rejects authority by directing attention to the thing itself, which he identified as "the presence of what is present in unconcealment,"[29] a term that Gurdjieff seems to reflect in his writings as "manifestation," or even, in many contexts, "actualization" or "crystallization." In *Sein und Zeit (Being and Time),* published in February 1927, Heidegger questions being in a phenomenological concrete manner. To grasp what being is requires a questioning of the question and an inquisition into the being of the questioner.[30]

An English proponent of Husserl's phenomenology whose work Orage knew was Shadworth Hodgson (1852–1913), whose materialist

---

29. *Basic Writings,* David F. Krell, ed. (New York: Harper and Row, 1997), p. 13.
30. It is a curious coincidence that a few months later, in November 1927, Gurdjieff inquired directly into the question of his own being within the question his *Tales* present: "The form of the exposition of my thoughts in these writings could be understood exclusively by those readers who, in one way or another, were already acquainted with the peculiar form of my mentation. But every other reader . . . would understand nearly nothing. . . . I enlightened myself for the first time with regard to the particular form in which it would be necessary to write in order that it might be accessible to the understanding of everyone" (*Life Is Real,* p. 5).

approach to reality in *The Metaphysics of Experience* (1898) acknowledges that an unseen world could be recognized by moral compulsion rather than by speculative conviction. Hodgson contended that consciousness gives us knowledge of a reality independent of cosciousness itself. Thus, knowledge is not a product of observation of phenomena, but of epiphenomena, or the secondary effects of phenomena.

Orage's personal psycho-philosophical stance seems to be aligned particularly with the ideas of a few thinkers whom he knew personally. The most direct influence on his thought came from the American William James (1842–1910), the Frenchman Henri Bergson (1839–1941), the Italian Benedetto Croce (1866–1952), and the Hispano-American George Santayana (1863–1952). It may be that James, whom Orage met for the first time with G. K. Chesterton in 1908, was most influential, although it is also possible that his empirical concepts were simply similar to Orage's reactions to the mechanism of Darwinian evolution. Their common interests in psychic phenomena are also marked, and both seem to have been influenced by Hodgson's relations between material and non-material worlds. In 1884, James founded the American Society for Psychical Research, and in 1901, he gave the Gifford Lectures in Edinburgh, published a year later as *The Varieties of Religious Experience.* The influence of these lectures in England must have touched Orage in his most formative years, particularly the eighth lecture entitled "The Divided Self," and the last lecture, "Philosophy," which promoted pragmatism over dogmatic theology. An early lecture on the "Power of Ideas" in the same series argued for the capacity of suggestion to concentrate consciousness. Though James' "suggestion" includes hypnosis, a practice Gurdjieff turned away from using at the Institute, he was thinking of the conditions under which one could marshal energies of will and mental influence over physiological processes. Such a concept is at the heart of Gurdjieff's physical training in general, and the dances and movements in particular.

On 28 December 1906, James gave the Presidential Address before the American Philosophical Society titled "The Energies of Men." A central concern in his talk was pyschasthenia: the distortion of relationships between the self and the world that Orage was to call "Chief Feature," or the relation between essence and personality. The general topic of the talk was "the amount of energy available for running one's mental and moral operations," in which James argued that people, compared to what they ought to be, are only half awake.[31] This issue and the author's hypothetical stance resemble Gurdjieff's. James

---

31. *William James Writings 1902–1910* (New York: Library of America, 1987), p. 1225.

went on to identify forms of imperfect vitality, and spoke of suggestive therapeutics for it, including hypnotism (the subject of another essay). He noted that a crisis in our affairs and love, among other factors, increases our energy, but James does not, as Orage later would, speak of interior forces inciting energy flow.

In a January 1910 article in the *Journal of Philosophic Psychology and Scientific Method*, comparing the philosophies of Bradley and Bergson, James wrote that "the way to know reality intimately is to . . . get *our sympathetic imagination to enlarge bounds*," of the data of perception.[32] In the fourth chapter of his massive study, *The Principles of Psychology*, James speaks of the debilitating force of habit that diminishes human attention, and the positive force of will that can increase it,[33] as if he had in mind Orage's psychological exercises. Habit, lamented James in a well-chosen metaphor, is the enormous fly-wheel of society.[34] In all of this, James, as did Orage and Gurdjieff, represented the influenced of Eastern thought. Both James and Orage refer often to the authority of the three yoga (literally, "restraints" of self)—karma, bhakti, and jnana—controlling act, emotion, and spirit, or thought. Orage approved of James' shift away from materialism and the pragmatism of Charles Sanders Peirce (1839–1914) toward Platonism and the cosmic form behind organized material.[35] Daly King recognizes the importance both Orage and James accord the *gestalt* importance of the whole of being in contrast to the relationship of individual parts to the whole. King finds this appropriate to pan-psychism in which "every unit of matter is associated with a unit of consciousness."[36]

The works of Henri Bergson introduced Orage to vitalism, the doctrine stipulating that to exist is to change, and that the time frame in which we bring about change in ourselves is a subjective measure of existence, rather than a scientific measure of duration. Vitalism is anti-Kantian in its premise that knowledge is gained from experience, and that knowledge of the relation between things is a matter of direct experience. It is anti-Spencerian in its dismissal of materialism. Like James' empiricism, Bergson's vitalism is anti-deterministic, and counter to Whitehead's conception of evolution as a patterned process of events in

---

32. James, *Writings*, p. 1267.
33. *Great Books of the Western World*, vol. 53, Morton J. Adler, ed. (Chicago: Encyclopædia Britannica,1952), pp. 68–71.
34. Op. cit., p. 79.
35. Steele, *Orage and the Leeds Art Club 1893–1923* (Aldershot: Scolar Press, 1990), p. 108.
36. See *The Psychology of Consciousness* (London: Kegan Paul, Trench and Trubner, 1932), pp. 30–46. In his *State of Human Consciousness* (New York: University Books, 1963), King identifies Orage as a Jamesian.

a world that has an actuality distinct from individual perception of it. In his *Creative Evolution*—which defines an empirical stance toward Darwinian determinism—Bergson argues that variation in species is not simply a biological adaptation or variation in living things, but is effected by consciousness and will. Bergson situated his own thought somewhere between the mechanistic theory of the influence of exterior forces and circumstances and the finalistic concept that evolution moves toward a fixed end.[37] Similarly, Gurdjieff rejected the imperative influence of exterior forces and circumstances on human development, and brought into question the finalistic and teleological Christian doctrine of salvation, the spiritual reward given in a pre-determined program of creation.

In this respect, Gurdjieff's and Orage's thought seem close to that of Samuel Alexander (1859–1958), who promulgated a radical empirical metaphysics that conceives of the mind as a nervous system that can be developed into awareness. Orage knew Alexander in 1920, when the latter gave the Gifford Lectures on "Space, Time, and Deity," in which he defined his position by saying that "the act of mind and the object as they are in the experience, are distinct existences united by the relation of 'comperience.' Experience is a piece of the world consisting of these two existences in their togetherness."[38] Alexander was best known to the general public for his view that space and time pertain to a single space-time continuum, out of whose proto-form life emerges, an idea not incompatible with Gurdjieff's cosmology. Orage was fond of Alexander's pronouncement that space is the mother of time.[39]

George Santayana, as Orage had, investigated the East-West confluence of thought. Orage approved of Santayana's "natural religion" that reflects the Buddha's sacred prana, or pranayama "vital breath"—a form of Gurdjieff's conscious reason. For Santayana, consciousness reveals, rather than distorts, reality, which is an infinity of essences or Platonic ideas. Matter is external to consciousness, unevenly distributed, but capable of becoming conscious. The concepts of knowledge and reality are by-products of the mind's interaction with phenomena. In this, Santayana seems to have been influenced by Baron Friedrich von Hügel (1852–1925), whose *Essays and Addresses on the*

37. John Gross, *The Rise and Fall of the Man of Letters* (London: Weidenfeld and Nicolson, 1969), p. 229, draws attention to Orage's Bergsonism. For Orage's remarks on Bergson, see "The Popularity of Bergson," *NA*, 22, 7 May, 1914, p. 12 and 28 May 1914, pp. 85–86.
38. *Encyclopædia Britannica*, vol. 1, Harry S. Ashmore, ed. (New York, 1961).
39. 17 May 1927 (Manchester Papers, p. 137). He elaborated on Alexander's ideas in his 14 March meeting.

Philosophy of Religion (1921) must have appealed to Orage as well. Von Hügel opposed both positivism and idealism, arguing instead that reality is perceived according to the nature of our own minds, and therefore phenomenological content must be excluded from consideration—hence—the importance of mystical experience.

Orage's announced choice of a "Philosopher of the *New Age*" was Benedetto Croce, whom he probably met for the first time in 1933 when Croce gave a series of lectures at Oxford, though Orage knew of him through his *Philosophy of the Practical,* which appeared in English in 1913.[40] Like Orage, Croce, influenced by Moore's neorealism, believed that the activities of the spirit move from aesthetic perception to logical or reasoning perception. The order of the spirit's practical activities issues from economic or utilitarian consciousness, to ethic or moral consciousness, and they together comprehend the will. Croce, like Orage, was a student of literature and of the influence upon it of literary criticism.[41] Croce argues that art is the first formulating force in civilization. Logic, or the recognition of universals, is consequent. Croce propounds a vitalistic belief that concrete reality is linked to history, a thought Beelzebub instills carefully in Hassein through his account of world history in *Tales.* History, Croce asserts, is the work of one omnipresent spirit whose emanations have four grades: aesthetic, logical, economic, and ethical. In his studies of the philosophy of conduct, economics, and ethics, Croce argues that the task of abstract philosophy is to formulate a methodology of history. He conceives of economy as an autonomous moment of spirit, and history as the work of one spirit. Like Orage, he emphasizes utility as a function of art in harmony with beauty and truth.

Another philosopher of art whose work Orage knew was the French-born American Curt John Ducasse (1881–1969). With his Brown University colleague Foster Damon, Ducasse listened carefully to Orage and Gurdjieff in Boston in the spring of 1924. He spoke with Orage later in New York and exchanged ideas on paranormal psychological phenomena, a topic about which Ducasse was later to write a seminal study. As Orage does in his writing, Ducasse argues for an objectification of art so that it might evoke in its audience the same emotional consciousness as in the artist. This consciousness is what Orage calls "supersense." Objective art, Orage explained often to his

---

40. Wallace Martin, *Orage as Critic* (London: Routledge & Kegan Paul, 1974), p. 43.
41. Orage wrote extensively about Croce (*NA* 14, 11 December, 1913, pp. 176–177 and 18 December, 1913, pp. 208–211; *NA* 15, 27 August, 1914, p. 392; *NA* 17, 14 October, 1915, pp. 573–574; *NA* 19, 13 September, 1916, pp. 278–280.)

pupils, accomplishes an "illumination of truth through the emotional experience of the *recipient,* not the artist. An ancient example is the Great Pyramid, but current examples are rare," he noted, outside the architecture of the Gothic cathedrals.[42] It is no surprise, then, that Gurdjieff was particularly drawn to the cathedrals at Sens, Rouen, Rheims, Chartres, and Mont St. Michel. Gurdjieff himself referred to Orpheus's music as "objective," having defined objective art as distinct from subjective art, by its power to render an intended emotional response.[43] Literary texts that contain aspects of objectivity include scripture that relates individuals to the universe, and major works of prose that evoke a one-on-one relationsip. At the bottom of the literary scale is journalism that, at best, relates facts.

In 1927, Orage came across Oswald Spengler's *Decline of the West* (1922, translated into English in 1927), and could not but agree with the general thesis that modern life had fallen away from the creativity imbued in earlier civilizations. Spengler (1880–1936), an historian of philosophy whose formal training was in classical literatures, contrasts the material culture of the present with the creative culture of Greece and Rome to which he would have us return. So far so good, though Orage would have the reflection go further back and further abroad in its exposition of creativity. What Orage found lamentable in Spengler was his negative attitude toward ethical economics, sociology, and, particularly, psychology. Neither Orage nor Gurdjieff could approve of the Spencerian castigation of psychology as "the shallowest and most worthless of the disciplines of philosophy, a field so empty that it has been left entirely to mediocre minds and barren systematists."[44] His particular target is clinical psychology, but his view covers the entire field. He writes that psychology fails to define the will and cannot approach the soul as a *numen* or experience. In brief, psychologists cannot go beyond descriptions of thinking, feeling and willing.[45] Of particular interest to Orage and Gurdjieff might have been Spengler's attack on Russian thinkers, and his charge that "Russians look after their 'I' as they do after their fingernails."[46]

---

42. For a full exposition of Orage's views on art, see King, *Oragean Version,* pp. 194–199. Recently, William Segal, "Inviting Hell into Heaven," *Parabola* 24:2 (1999), p. 65, quotes Gurdjieff to the effect that if one is sufficiently aware, one can receive an energy that has been deposited throughout the ages there by people in prayer.
43. P. D. Ouspensky, *In Search of the Miraculous* (New York: Harcourt Brace and World, 1949), pp. 295–297.
44. Oswald Spengler, *Decline of the West* (London: George Allen & Unwin, 1927), p. 299.
45. Spengler, *Decline,* p. 304.
46. Spengler, *Decline,* p. 309.

Gurdjieff's and Orage's natural philosophy (physics) complements their moral philosophies. At the turn of the century, Albert Einstein's general theory of relativity and Max Planck's quantum mechanics were changing the way physicists looked at the material and temporal structure of the universe.[47] Like psychology, physics constitutes a philosophy in its own right. First of all, Planck's insistence on the materialism of the entire universe matches Gurdjieff's description of cosmic content; that is, that all space contains physical matter and all physical matter has its proper space.[48] The similarity of humans, nature, and the cosmos— that all universal matter is found in the individual, or that the individual is indeed a microcosm—is also Gurdjieffian. Life can neither exist without the universe nor the universe exist without life, and so, as Gurdjieff insists, life is not an accident, but a cosmic necessity, an idea more advanced now by science than philosophy. Gurdjieff's conception of the *autoegocratic* is matched by the scientist's anthropic, or auto-created and maintained universe. The view that discontinuity, acceleration, and deceleration describe energy flows in the universe fits Gurdjieff's stance on physical and temporal change. The Earth as a living organism, an idea upon which Gurdjieff insists, reflects not only indigenous American thought—a fact appreciated by Orage in his contacts with New Mexican Pueblo Indians with Tony Luhan—but what is known currently by ecologists as the Gaïa hypothesis. Basarab Nicolescu has demonstrated clearly how Gurdjieff's Laws of Three and Seven are reflected in current scientific thought about the fundamental physical laws of the universe, particularly in the vertical and horizontal exchanges of energy within and between systems.[49] Appropriately, both Einstein and Planck demonstrated that time has no objective signification.

Though Orage identified his own thought in both writing and teaching in terms of a number of 19th- and 20th-century philosophies, one should be especially wary of categorizing Gurdjieff's thought in terms of any of the positions outlined above. Undoubtedly, Gurdjieff knew well the major tenets of the mainline philosophical developments in the West, from the pre-Socratics to his own time, but one must look at the esoteric periphery of these movements to reveal something of the extent of his learning. There are at least five groups that can be readily

---

47. On Gurdjieff and Einstein, see Kenneth Walker, *The Making of Man* (Routledge & Kegan Paul, 1963), p. 153.
48. This proposition was known in the Middle Ages as the Principle of Plenitude.
49. "Le Philosophie de la Nature de Gurdjieff," *Dossiers 14*, Bruno de Panafieu, ed. p. 272. Nicolescu's summary of Gurdjieff's science is concise and clear.

identified as distant sources for Gurdjieff's thought, whether major or minor. Many who have come to Gurdjieff's teachings after his death claim precedence for Sufi doctrines as a major influence. One recent writer argues that Gurdjieff was most influenced by Sufism and identifies the Sarmoung Brotherhood as an Islamic Sufi group.[50] Neither Gurdjieff nor Orage, however, spoke specifically of Sufism, though both spoke often of the Dervish offshoot of Sufism, and both cited Dervish traditions in connection with the work. In *Meetings,* Gurdjieff associates the Sarmoung monastery with the Dervish (*darwish* "spiritual paupers"), whose name was an honorific title for a mystical fraternity considered by most Western historians of religion as distinct from the mainstream Sufi hierarchy. The trance-like state into which the Dervish transform themselves in dance is a means of manifesting God's omnipotence and omniscience.[51] In *Beelzebub's Tales,* Gurdjieff castigates the Turks for closing Dervish monasteries and identifies Dervishism as the "last spark" upon which Saint Mohammed counted and for which he had hoped.[52] In the chapter titled "The Bokharian Dervish," Beelzebub cites the Dervish Hadji-Asvatz-Troov as a preserver of ancient science, the last great sage of the Earth. He is, Beelzebub remarks, "a three-brained being of that planet with whom it is not forbidden us from Above to be frank."[53] What is particularly noticeable in Dervish practice in some fraternities that recalls Gurdjieffian organization is the strict master-pupil relationship that, nonetheless, permits the return of the pupil to the secular world after his religious instruction is concluded.

In the larger Sufi mystical hierarchy are God-appointed saints, both visible and invisible, who instruct, reflecting "messengers from above" like Ashiata Shiemash in Beelzebub's account to his grandson. Besides this, there are general and vague correspondences that can be drawn between Sufi and Gurdjieff teaching. For example, the Sufi proposition that the world was created, or ignited, by love, is a basic Platonic idea that corresponds with Gurdjieff's conception of cosmic love. Sufism preaches the annihilation of self in order to join God. The Sufi mystic Farid al-din 'Attar characterized the process of annihilation of self for union with God as a journey of seven stages,[54] similar to the

50. Tony Schwartz, *What Really Matters* (New York: Bantam, 1995), p. 379.
51. Murat Yagan, "Sufism and the Source," *Gnosis* 30 (Winter, 1994), p. 44.
52. *Tales,* pp. 707–711.
53. Gurdjieff, *Tales* p. 901. Gurdjieff notes that his book *Opiumists* (not extant) has more on these ideas (p. 917).
54. F. C. Harrold, *Mysticism,* p. 56.

seven steps of the Buddhist. A basic Sufi dictum is "He who knows his essential self knows God," and another holds that we are responsible for the restoration of our souls to consciousness. The Sufi also distinguish between our essence and our personality, but this distinction is hardly exclusive to Sufism. The mystic, ascetic, and quietist qualities of Sufism are attributed to Mohammed, one of God's messengers. Furthermore, in later Turkish and Persian Sufi thought, the distinction between good and evil is abolished, but the Sufi stations in the process of purgation of self, which include voluntary abstinence and poverty, are irrelevant to Gurdjieff. In brief, it would be more accurate to assign to Gurdjieff a Dervish influence than a Sufi one.

Sufism is the youngest of major ancient influences that can be easily traced behind Gurdjieff's work, and much in Sufism has been shaped by earlier esoteric teachings. One of these is Pythagorism, which had both a scientific and a religious component. At the core of the former was a dualistic concept of thought and sense, in which the soul is an opposing force to the physical body, ideas derived most likely from the Indo-Iranian and Babylonian dualism that Gurdjieff's Beelzebub castigates consistently.[55] Pythagoras (Diogenes Laertius, 572–c. 500 B.C.E.) also taught the immortality and transmigration of the soul, neither of which are Gurdjieffian tenets, but his theory that there is a natural affinity of the soul to the sky and the stars does find echoes in Gurdjieff's cosmology. For Pythagoras (or those who report his teaching, since we have no direct record of his work), all things in the universe share kinship and partake of a universal harmony. Attributed to Pythagoras are communities of learning including *akousmatikoi,* oral performers like the trans-Caucasian *ashokh* of Gurdjieff's day, and *akousmata,* or oral instructions. The Neopythagoreans, from the time of Plato to the second century C.E., thought of Pythagoras as a revealer of esoteric cosmic secrets.

More interesting in relation to Gurdjieff's work is Pythagorean science, which is linked to religious thought by the concept that all phenomena are sensuous expressions of the mathematical ratios that describe the harmonious relations of all things in the universe. The harmony of sound, he taught, is associated with the philosophy of number.[56] Number, Pythagoras preached, is the key to the order of the universe. He postulated that the distances between the orbits of the

---

55. The Hindu *Siva Sutra,* a yoga text, was revealed to man by Siva to counter the effects of dualism.
56. Tobias Danzig, *Number: The Language of Science* (New York: Macmillan, 1970), p. 101.

seven planetary bodies visible to the naked eye duplicate the Greek musical scale, so that their motions perform what is commonly called "the music of the spheres." Based on those distances, he described the musical intervals in arithmetic ratios. Gurdjieff's cosmology, similarly, is created and maintained according to what can be loosely called the musical octave that Pythagoras saw as replicating the structure of the cosmos.

In Gurdjieff's *Tales,* Beelzebub refers to a later esoteric and mystical movement when he asserts that traditional esoteric lore has been lost except among the Essenes.[57] The wisdom of the Essenes is preserved in the monastery at Sarmoung where Gurdjieff achieved his ultimate knowledge, according to *Meetings.* The Essenes—perhaps more properly known by the Greek term *essenoi*—are a pharisaical Pythagorean sect that was most active between 150 B.C.E. and 75 C.E., and seems to have been a forerunner of contemporary *Hasidim.* Though Essene manuscripts have been uncovered in Qumran in recent years— still under scholarly scrutiny—there is little scholars have been able to retrieve of its esoteric lore besides what is extant in *midrash* commentary. More is available of its practices. The Essenes are known for their strict asceticism and disciplined observance of virtuous ritual behaviors. They teach community of property, charity in relations, and ritual pursuit of virtue. Josephus (c. 75 C.E.), the historian of the early Jews, places their origins in Egypt, but their affinities with the Pythagoreans and Alexandrians suggest origins in Greek religious practices. Philo Judaeus (before 50 C.E.) calls them *therapeutae.* They believed in absolute predestination and the immortality of the soul, a concept probably borrowed from Hellenic beliefs. The most notable Gurdjieffian practices that recall the Essenes are self-sufficiency in manual labors and ritual feasts spiced with philosophical discourse. Orage said that Christianity is a broadcasting of the teachings of the Essenes of which Christ was a high initiate.[58]

A fourth ancient source of Gurdjieff's teaching and writing are traditional hermetic writings that, in their turn, may have influenced Essenic lore. These are so named after Hermes Trismegistos (thrice great), an emanation of the Egyptian god Thoth. He is known as a patron of music and a god of eloquence. He is associated with Apollo, the Sun and the *logos,* whose adherents appropriated hermetic cult features. Hermes is renowned in Greek lore for having "remembered him-

57. Gurdjieff, *Tales,* p. 704.
58. King, *Oragean Version,* pp. 40 and 196.

self"; that is, for having been reborn into sacred wisdom. In the *Pimander,* the first volume of the *Corpus Hermeticum,* Hermes addresses his son with a number of aphorisms, many of which look like distant replications of some Gurdjieffian cosmological precepts. For example, in the first of its seventeen books, one reads the following aphorisms: "Every living thing is not mortal," "not every living thing is immortal," "the world for man, man for God," "of the soul, that part which is sensible is mortal, but that which is reasonable is immortal," "every essence is unchangeable," "good is voluntary, or of its own accord," "and evil is involuntary or against its will."[59] Hermetism comprises three principal branches—astrology, alchemy and magic. Its earliest Greek texts date from the second century B.C.E. Hermetic geometry maps the cosmos in six- or eight-sided figures. Gurdjieff would have known these through his reading in Blavatsky's *Secret Doctrine.* Orage had read both Blavatsky and G. R. S. Mead's *Thrice Greatest Hermes* (1906), and was acquainted in the 1890s with the Hermetic Order of the Golden Dawn and Liddel Mathers' "The Hermetic Students."

A fifth and yet more ancient source of esoteric materials for Gurdjieff is Orphism, a traditional lore with origins at least as early as the sixth century B.C.E., Orphism probably infiltrated Egyptian hermetism. Gurdjieff's teachings reflect much of the Orphic models of mythic, poetic, and ethical strains. The first two strains comprise the power of voice and a vocabulary of separation, or *diakrisis.* In the mythic records, Orpheus is son of Apollo (the Sun) and the Muse Calliope (καλλι "beautiful" and οπ "voice"). He is a figure of the *logos,* or the reified word. It is Orpheus's voice that gives him power to pass between Scylla and Charybdis. The Orphic mythic figure abhors blood and seeks to rule with bloodless sacrifice, though Orpheus and other figures of peace are inevitably destroyed by that which they preach against. The Orphic figure is sacrificial, willing to give up its self to rescue the world from loss. In brief, Orpheus is an emblem of order.

The poetic strain refigures mythic origins in insisting upon bloodless fashions. Orphic writing is dedicated to representing the force of voice. In *Laws,* Plato describes the duties of Orphism to write a cosmogony, to abhor blood, and to heal (762c). For the Orphic sage, the book is a cultural arm to reconceive human duty, recast creation, and establish a new genealogy of the gods. In Orphic thought, whose written form has two topics—creation and bloodless sacrifice—the Sun is

---

59. *The Pymander,* W. Wynn Westcott, ed. (London: Theosophical Society, 1894). Eliade, op. cit., p. x, draws attention to the important role of Hermetic esoterism in Western religions. For Gurdjieff on evil, see Ouspensky, *Search,* p. 158.

the source of the new blood strain. Orpheus himself, like the later Plato who journeyed to Egypt to obtain ancient wisdom, is a figure of the seeker for knowledge, a model humankind—partly divine and partly wicked. Our goal, like Orpheus's, is to rid ourselves of wickedness by a life of purity and ritual discipline. Having done so, our soul, are incarnated and freed from karma-like reincarnations to join with the divine.

It is not difficult to see striking similarities between esoteric Orphism and Gurdjieff's work. Foremost is the power of voice, or performance, to communicate essential ideas. Associated with the role of voice for Gurdjieff is music, whose mythological source is Orpheus's matrix. The father of Orpheus, the Sun, is represented in Gurdjieff's cosmogony by the Sun Absolute, the space-time matrix of his endlessness. The Orphic voice is resounded by Gurdjieff's *theomertmalogos,* or Word-God. The Orphic ethical command to renounce blood sacrifice is heard throughout Gurdjieff's writings (though the Orphic command demands vegetarianism, an extreme that Gurdjieff disdained). The Orphic duty of refiguring creation is re-enacted in Gurdjieff's mythology of creation in "The Holy Planet Purgatory," and a new genealogy of the gods is reflected in the succession of "messengers from above" who labor to bring and maintain truth among successions of civilizations. The followers of Orphism strive for saintliness and triumph over death.

The importance of the book for Orphism is reflected in Gurdjieff's "legominism," defined by Beelzebub to Hassein as a body of codes, including sacred dances and other "means of transmitting information."[60] In this respect, Ashiata Shiemash, the first legominist, is comparable to Orpheus. Gurdjieff, like the renunciant Orphics, eschewed political activism. Overall, the most pertinent link between Orphism and Gurdjieffian thought is the emphasis on a self-discipline that creates order within the disordered consciousness. Nonetheless, where the Orphic sage withdraws from the world to achieve his mission, Gurdjieff embraces the world.

A major feature in Gurdjieff's teaching that has no obvious relation to known religious or scientific sources is the geometric symbol known as the Enneagram. It is beyond the space available and my capacities to scan the complexities of this symbol, but, in short, the Enneagram, as Gurdjieff explained, is a universal symbol, a fundamental hieroglyph of a universal language that contains all knowledge.[61]

---

60. Gurdjieff, *Tales,* pp. 349, 519.
61. Ouspensky, *Search,* p. 294.

Gurdjieff referred to it in order to illustrate the inter-workings of the Laws of Three and Seven in the musical octave with its "shocks" and in the anatomy of the physical universe, including the seven planets visible to the naked eye and the nine months of human gestation. Its sources are disputed, but there are no clear precedents in known traditional literatures, though its arithmetic complexities are well known to every mathematician. One can assume that the Enneagram was accessible to Gurdjieff in Babylonian astronomical treatises, but they were not explicated for the Western world until Joseph Epping published his *Astronomisches aus Babylon* in 1889. I have scanned Otto Neugebauer's magisterial three volume *History of Ancient Astronomical Mathematics* (1975) in vain pursuit of some astronomical theory or practice based on the number nine, but have found only random insignificant appearances of planetary degrees that should not be forced into such a theory.

For the Pythagorean "sieve of Eratosthenes" (a numerical representation by dots), nine is a square number whose triangular predecessors are six and three. As the product of 3^2, nine is the *nomen* of the square of four. Despite the limitations of Greek number symbols, Pythagoras knew proofs by the rule of nine, and he recognized the unique combinations of the addends of nine that identify multiples of the number. So, in the Enneagram, $1 + 8 = 9$, and $18 = 9 \times 2$; $2 + 7 = 9$, and $27 = 9 \times 3$, etc. If one places the number values at the end points of the connecting lines of the Enneagram in numerical order, even more combinations can be construed that have cosmic relevance. Platonic philosophical writings illustrate the structure of the universe in concentric circles representing planetary orbits and outer-directing forces. If one adds to the number of the orbits of the planets (seven) the *stellatum* or sphere of the fixed stars (thought by many ancients to be equidistant from the Earth) and the crystalline sphere, or empyrean, we arrive at nine concentric circles.[62]

Since Gurdjieff's Enneagram consists of one equilateral triangle and one irregular hexagon (where a regular nine-sided polyhedron would comprise three intersecting equilateral triangles), even greater number combinations can be generated. Further, the points of the hexagon and the apex of the triangle are identified as the seven notes of the octave. The pseudo-Platonic *Epinomis,* a discussion of wisdom paralleling the *Timaeus,* identifies a core science without which no essential knowledge would be available, and attributes it to Ouranus, the cosmos

---

62. Medieval Astrology, following Ptolemy, preferred the number ten, situating the First Mover, or God, beyond the nine spheres.

(976e), a figure mirrored by Gurdjieff's Endlessness. The Athenian in the dialogue refers to eight sister powers in heaven of which the first three are the Sun, the Moon, and the fixed stars (986b).[63] The neo-Platonist Plotinus entitled his reflection of Plato's thought *Ennead* to allude three triads of One, Noys (intelligence), and Soul.

There is a traditional association between the number nine and music that foreshadows Gurdjieff's Enneagram octave. I refer to the nine Greek Muses that Hesiod describes in his *Theogony* (8th century B.C.E.) as the nine daughters of Mnemosyne (Memory) and Zeus. The Muses give their name to music, and one of them, Calliope—wife of Apollo (Sun) and mother of Orpheus—is identified by medieval commentators as *optima vox* (best voice) and *armonia celestis* (celestial harmony). The Pythagoreans were the first to identify the Muses with the music of the spheres—that is, cosmic music. Consequently, Ambrosius Theodosius Macrobius, in his 4th-century *Commentarorium in Somniun Scipionis* (Commentary on the Cicero's *Dream of Scipio Africanus*), says that the eight Muses represent eight celestial bodies and their harmonious modulation. On the island of Lesbos, the Muses were counted as seven, while the Pythagoreans, as did Macrobius, counted eight. The addition of Uranus (Macrobius's harmonious modulation) makes up the conventional nine. It is likely that the ultimate source of Gurdjieff's Enneagram is associated with the origin of the Muses.

A relatively modern reflection of the Enneagram is the geometry of Nordic myth. In the early 13th-century *Edda,* the cosmogonic myth of the Norse identifies nine roots beneath the world-tree Yggdrasill, and nine worlds. In his talks, Orage referred frequently to this tree as an emblem of being. On the world's surface, there are three concentric circles of three worlds. The center world of the gods represents mentality, the middle world of humans represents feeling or emotion, and the outer world of giants and elves represents the world of matter.

As obvious as all this seems to be, the sources of the Enneagram, as well as the full scope of its cryptic sense, remain obscure. Analogies in psychology are perhaps more pertinent. Jung's mandalas, almost always marked by eight divisions, illustrate spheres of consciousness that suggest a system of psychological types that Gurdjieff called idiots (idiosyncrasies). Current lay commentators, as I have remarked earlier, read the Enneagram as an astrological typology of chief features, nine

---

63. Plato, *Collected Dialogues*, Edith Hamilton and Huntington Cairns, eds. (New York: Pantheon Books. Bollingen Series 71, 1961), pp. 1517–1533.

in all, akin to, if exceeding in number, the Catholic Church's seven deadly sins.[64]

While James, Bergson, and Croce were kindred philosophic spirits for Orage, Gurdjieff had foils in the German mystic Helena [Rottenstein-Hahn] Petrovna Blavatsky (1831–1891) and the contemporary French occultist and esoterist, René Guénon (1886–1951). Gurdjieff found the names of both Orpheus and Hermes Trismegistos in Blavatsky's *Secret Doctrine* (1888), of which he had read exerpts before starting out on his own quest for esoteric knowledge in Central Asia.[65] Madame Blavatsky had gained access to Tibet as early as 1856, before traveling extensively in the United States, where she founded the Theosophical Society in New York in 1875. In 1879, she moved her activities to India, where she died in 1891. During her stay in India she dedicated herself to forming a nucleus of a universal brotherhood of humanity, promoting the study of comparative religion, philosophy, and science, and investigating the unexplained laws of nature, including the latent powers of humans. Gurdjieff told Orage that he had followed Madame Blavatsky's references in the *Secret Doctrine* and found, in a colossal waste of time and energy, nine out of ten of them in error. At any rate, Blavatsky's three major premises—that there is an omnipotent, ubiquitous reality of which matter and spirit are aspects, that there is a universal periodicity, or cycle, of existence, and that all souls are identical to one oversoul—seem rather conventional beside Gurdjieff's complex epistemic system. Blavatsky's influence derives rather from her amazing parapsychological gifts and indomitable spirit.

Guénon—whose name, unfortunately, echoes the French word for a species of monkey and a derogatory allusion to an ugly woman—was an avowed rival of Gurdjieff in the dissemination of oriental ideas in France. To this day, he enjoys a scholarly reputation among philosophers and historians of religion in France that eclipses Gurdjieff's. One of the latter's biographers judges that Guénon and Gurdjieff are "preposterously contrasted,"[66] but there is much to compare. Guénon, given

---

64. Richard Smoley, "Why the Enneagram?," *Gnosis* 30 (Summer, 1994), pp. 18–24, consists of an interview with Helen Palmer, author of *The Enneagram* (San Francisco: HarperSanFrancisco, 1988). The best informed discussion of the Enneagram that I know of is in Sophia Well-beloved's 1999 unpublished doctoral dissertation, pp. 54 ff. that I have seen too late for consideration here. Webb, *Harmonious Circle*, p. 506 locates the three triangle design of the Enne- agram from the early fourteenth century in Ramon Lull's *Ars Generalis Ultima*.
65. If Gurdjieff read Blavatsky first in Russian exerpts in the late 1880s, then he would not have seen the name of Roerich's wife, Helena, who made the first full translation. Wellbeloved compares Gurdjieff and Blavatsky in detail, pp. 49–53 and 66–69, pointing particularly to similar content.
66. Moore, *Gurdjieff: The Anatomy of a Myth*, pp. 228–229, citing Jean-Pierre Laurant, *Le sens caché selon René Guénon* (Lausanne: L'Age d'Homme, 1975).

birth by Blois, nurtured by Catholicism and Free Masonry (of which he never fully rid himself), and adopted by Paris, wrote twenty-nine books and over five hundred articles, many of which were dedicated to investigating the esoteric doctrines of the East integrated into Western Christianity. Best-known among these is *l'Orient et l'occident* (1924), written as Gurdjieff was coming into prominence in the Parisian cultural scene. In his mature writings, such as *L'État de l'être* (1932), Guénon, an advocate of the conviction that there is a universal nature of traditional truth at the heart of all religious forms, advances four fundamental hypotheses for his work. First is the idea that modern Western civilizations might well disappear just as ancient civilizations and their wisdom disappeared. Second is the hypothesis that the knowledge preserved in the East could be used in the West to retrieve an essential intellectuality. Third, the Orient could and would collaborate with the West in this endeavor. Finally, study groups immune from socio-political issues of their cultures might obtain the necessary results, though, overall, Guénon remained pessimistic.[67]

Guénon contested the authenticity of current so-called occultism in the West and the capacity of occidentals to constitute an authentic esoterism. Since Gurdjieff was a living text of the East, a teacher of esoteric knowledge, founder of a school, and leader of a large number of adepts—none of which Guénon could claim, nor could he aspire to the charisma of Gurdjieff's character—Guénon was characteristically wont to castigate Gurdjieff's authenticity. To the disinterested observer, however, the two had a good deal in common. Like Gurdjieff, Guénon believed that in order to appreciate esoteric doctrines, it was necessary first to clear away the cultural debris and mistaken dogma of the West. As Gurdjieff did, he posited the universal nature of traditional truth. In this spirit, he scanned the thought of the Rosicrucians and Free Masons, in which he found vestiges of authentic traditional knowledge. Where Gurdjieff had traced the descent of human knowledge and wisdom through a number of worldly catastrophes and diversions from truth— the most prominent of which was Babylonian science—Guénon traced modern decadence along a fault line from superior spirituality (knowledge) to inferior spirituality (physical power) that Gurdjieff would call mechanicalness.[68]

---

67. Jean Bies, "René Guénon, hérault de la dernière chance," *René Guénon,* Laurant and Barbanegra, eds. (Paris: l'Herne, 1985), pp. 29–36.
68. This contrast is well illustrated in Henry Adam's autobiographical essay, "The Dynamo and the Virgin," in *The Education of Henry Adams* (1907).

In 1912, Guénon was initiated into Sufism and embraced Islam (which Beelzebub castigates as the religion most perverted from its sacred source). In the 1930s, he moved to Cairo, where he remained until his death. In view of Guénon's apparent competition with Gurdjieff in his quest for esoteric wisdom, it is not surprising that he spoke disparagingly of Gurdjieff, not only calling him a charlatan, but questioning whether he "was really initiated into timeless mysteries in the Gobi."[69] Guénon cast doubt on the accounts of Gurdjieff's appearance in 1900 in India with news of the discovery of a monastery that kept alive the Pythagorean doctrines of the Jewish Essenes.

In *Tales,* Gurdjieff mentions a German doctor, Steiner, with strange conceptions, and it is reasonable to suppose he is referring to the Austrian Rudolf Steiner (1861–1925), author of *Philosophie der Freiheit* (1894). Steiner propounded a science of knowledge produced by a higher self that he called anthroposophy, disdained by Beelzebub in *Tales.* Anthroposophy asserts the existence of a spiritual world comprehensible to pure thinking, and Steiner hoped, by it, to enhance consciousness to perceive spiritual reality. Beelzebub speaks with admiration of Franz Anton Mesmer (1734–1815), who posited animal magnetism in the universe available for human use.[70]

Although Orphism is, perhaps, the major example of classical wisdom reflected in the teachings of Gurdjieff, to recent observers, he seems to have been acquainted in one way or another with the contents of all the major philosophical and psychological scientific currents of the 19th and early 20th centuries that had a prominent place in Orage's large repository of learning. Neither Gurdjieff nor Orage, however, seem to have preferred any single movement of modern philosophical speculation. Like Guénon, both saw Eastern roots beneath the growth of Western philosophy. Like Croce, they were vitalistic, and like Heidegger, existential, but I would qualify both terms with "contingent," since Gurdjieff and Orage alike believed that positive development is *contingent* upon individual as well as universal forces. Contingent vitalism is, effectively, an existential challenge to self-development and control.[71] For one example, Gurdjieff and Orage seem to agree with Bergson's and Heidegger's position that tenses—past, present, and future—are arbitrary temporal boundaries, and that full

---

69. De Wendel, Sylvain, "Vive la Résistance," *René Guénon* (Planète Plus, 1970), p. 51.
70. Gurdjieff, *Tales,* pp. 576, 562.
71. Robert Hohenberger, who has made a careful study of the philosophical implications of Gurdjieff's teaching, tells me that he would place him in the category of a "Evolutionary Existentialist."

knowledge cancels time.[72] In knowledge, time is realized as wholly subjective, or the "unique subjective," as both Orage and Gurdjieff postulated,[73] though there is a physical objective time.

It is understandable, then, that Orage insisted emphatically that the reality we call "actual" is an abstraction with no measure, because it is a function of a perception of the present in terms of the past. Since the present perceived is always past, therefore, reality must include the future; and, the future must be an extension of the past. Thus, in the human organism, conscious memory (not the instinctive memory that has us place one foot in front of the other without a thought) is the basis upon which we can move beyond passive reaction to exterior forces toward positive action. Orage called this basis "potentiality," by which he meant the inherent capacity of an individual to create itself. We are what we do consciously. The principle that a potential is activated by will and memory seems to collide with Ouspensky's concept of recurrence, illustrated so dramatically in his novel *Ivan Osokin*. Memory would obviate recurrence of existence, and if not memory, will; but Ouspensky's hero is victim of an impotent will, until—made clear at the end of the novel—he accepts a teacher as guide. Gurdjieff said often that we cannot essentially change without the aid of another's will.[74] The teacher is one, like Beelzebub instructing Hassein, who remembers the sources of creation and maintenance of the world. One is reminded of Heidegger's *seinfrage,* which involves instructed memory in an attempt to recover hidden sources of being.

Though all of the modern philosophical tendencies I have touched upon can be located in the background of Gurdjieff's work, there are areas of the foreground of Gurdjieffian thought that seem to be allied with traditions peripheral to the mainstream of Western Christian thought. One is a disdain for the Christian doctrine of eternal rewards: the soul's bliss in heaven and punishment in hell. This is true simply because, like Nietzsche, Gurdjieff denied an ontology of evil. Nietzsche

---

72. *Creative Evolution* (New York: Random House Modern Library, 1944), pp. 43–44. It has been readily assumed in academic discourse that T. E. Hulme was the early promoter of Bergson in England, but it was Orage who first introduced Bergson to both Hulme and Ezra Pound, and promoted him for his English audience. Hulme's "invention" of Imagism is based on Bergson's work.

73. A. R. Orage, *On Love: With Some Aphorisms and Other Essays,* C. S. Nott , ed. (York Beach, ME: Samuel Weiser, 1998), p. 56, and *Tales,* p. 124. King, *The Oragean Version,* pp. 234–256, reviews Gurdjieff and Orage on time.

74. *Search,* p. 348. The implication in *Ivan Osokin* is that the teacher can instruct him to move backward in time to correct errors. Ouspensky's concept of eternal recurrence, though it differs, seems to have been derived from Nietzsche's assertion in *Thus Spake Zarathrustra* that, after the superman, comes eternal recurrence.

had argued that humans had invented hell in order to contemplate the eternal suffering of oppressors.[75] Orage reminded his pupils insistently that one purpose of *All and Everything* is to destroy the idea of evil.[76]Another purpose of the book is to redefine, or relocate, the soul. For the Catholic, the soul of an individual is eternal. After its brief sojourn on Earth, it is rewarded either with eternal bliss in heaven, eternal pain in damnation in hell, or penitential residence in purgatory. Purgatory may be but a temporary dwelling place before ascension to Heaven, though it may remain a permanent residence in a moral limbo, for in Catholic doctrine, as Dante's *Comedia* reveals, the soul cannot descend from purgatory to hell. God's chain of order reaches only as far as purgatory. Gurdjieff's denial of the immortality of the soul reflects the mortalism of Aristotle, Lucretius and the 17th-century English Puritans. "Mortalism is the belief that human souls are physical elements that die with their bodies."

Gurdjieff flatly denied the existence of the Christian's hell and reformulated the human triad of potential afterlives. To the general concept of a life after death, Gurdjieff said that our lives, like wisps of vapor, do not survive, because there is nothing in them to survive.[77] Instead, he divided our posthumous fate into three principle categorical possibilities. The planetary bodies of those who have not developed themselves beyond their physical status, affirms Beelzebub, decompose and returns into the Earth. Their astral, or *kesdjan,* bodies—their higher emotional "coating"—decompose into the cosmos. The higher-being bodies of those who have achieved objective reason during their mortal residence on Earth take residence with Endlessness on Absolute Sun. Those who have not completed the perfection of their higher-being body in objective reason are appointed to the holy planet Purgatory until they do so. So, for Gurdjieff, destiny is something earned by those with essence, while others are subject to the law of accident.

At the core of this thought is Gurdjieff's contention that *soul* is a lazy human fantasy. We have no innate soul or higher-being body, though we can develop it by nurturing consciousness toward perfect objectivity. One recalls Nietzsche in *Beyond Good and Evil* observing that internalization is the first form of soul. Gurdjieff's commonsense

75. *The Works of Friedrich Nietzsche* (New York: Tudor, 1931), p. 177.
76. Manchester notes for May 27, 1928 (Manchester Papers, p. 75). In his chapter on "Religion" in *Tales,* p. 695, Gurdjieff has his hero reject the "Babylonian" maleficent idea of good and evil. Nietzsche had announced that: "He who must be a creator in good and evil— verily, he must first be a destroyer, and break values into pieces" (*Works*, p. 162).
77. Cited by Colin Wilson, "Two Russian Mages," in *A History of Magic and the Occult,* Kurt Seligman, ed. (New York: Random House, 1997), p. 405.

explanation of selective soul bodies is simply that, were all living things to possess souls, there would be an overpopulation of souls just as there would be a continuous diminution of the source from which souls arise. As Gurdjieff has remarked: "Blessed is he who has a soul. Blessed is he who has none; but woe and grief to him that has it in embryo."[78]

The location and material identification of the soul is a long and complex chapter in the history of human thought. Pythagoras taught that the soul is a force distinct from physical being. For Plato, the individual soul is but an emanation of a universal soul, or an *anima mundi.* Aristotle declared the soul a term for the principle of life. To live is to have a soul, so all living things possess one. Lucretius assumed that the soul shares the physical properties of any other human organ. In the 18th century, Bishop Berkeley argued that we do not have a soul, but *are* soul. It is the body, he asserted, that has no reality. William James brings the question of the soul's provenance close to Gurdjieff's view by considering the idea of soul necessary, neither for personal identity, nor for moral responsibility. Evoking the idea of "soul" is futile in verifying the facts of conscious experience, he argues, but one can cite the soul as a term for personal identity, one's empirical and transcendental ego. Ego can achieve transcendence in the sense that the true soul, as the *Upanishads* and *Sutras* indicate, can remain unconditioned by material or mental changes of world shape.

In this respect, Gurdjieff indicated that there are, basically, negative and positive egos. The former is the ego of habit, a feature of the personality that is coated by one's experience in a social, educational, and religious environment. The latter is the conscious ego, or "I," that controls a person's relationship with the external world and mediates the interests of the soul. Jung argued that the psyche is not always to be found within man, but remains outside at those times when psychic life is ignored.[79] The connection between humans and the cosmos outside them is an image for Orage of what Gurdjieff called Chief Feature. So, Orage explained to his pupils, consider that Gurdjieff's grandmother— who in *Meetings with Remarkable Men* advises her grandson not to do what others do—embodies Chief Feature.

---

78. Cited by Moore, *Gurdjieff: The Anatomy of a Myth,* p. 341. Orage wrote a four-part series on the soul in *NA* between November 7 and December 19, 1912, concluding with an assertion of the soul's existence. In Celtic mythology, the "ancestor" sends his creatures into the world and permits them to die, at which time their souls return to him.
79. Carl Gustav Jung, *Modern Man in Search of a Soul* (London: Kegan Paul, Trench, Tubner & Co., 1933), p. 231.

Just as there are grades of reality—an exterior one toward which we tend to be passive, and an interior one which gives force for us to act positively—there are concomitant levels of thought. One is habitual and integrative. Habitual thought integrates individuals in the habitual actions of their kind. Integrative thought is conscious and idiosyncratic; that is, conscious thought creates a discrete existence. So memory may be factual, a repository of material events, or it may be subjective, a recreating of an event into significant form. The latter is meta-memory, plastic and creative, like the memory of a true artist, rather than brittle and static, like the memory of the chronicler of "fact."

Similarly, love may be passive and instinctive, or active and creative. For Orage, the word *philosophy* must mean both "love of knowledge" and "knowledge of love," and perhaps here the views of the mentor may be distinguished from the pupil. Both thought alike of love as a creative principle and a positive emotion, but seemed to hold different views on love in conscious psycho-sociological practice. To insist on differences, however, risks inciting misunderstandings. I suspect that Orage and Gurdjieff shared the same general view on love between the sexes, but they manifested it to others in diverse ways. For both, cosmic love was a divine emanation, a force implicit in the creative word identical to the Apostle John's *logos,* that which the Alexandrine philosophers at the beginning of the second century called *spermatologos* ("seed word"), comparable to Gurdjieff's *theomertmalogos,* or Word-God.[80] As a biological, or instinctive drive—what Orage explained to his pupils as the law of one's being,[81] that is, the Law of Kind—they agreed on the necessity of an instinctive drive to propagate the human species. The apparent difference in their conceptions of love concerns the intermediary form of love between the spiritual and the biological: that is, the emotional form of love that since the 18th century has become inextricably confused in the Western world with sentiment and romance.

On the one hand, Gurdjieff immunized himself against the manifestations of sentimental love that feature the verbal commitment of one's own emotions to those of someone of the opposite sex. On the other hand, he disdained the artifice of sentimental language in amatory contexts, as he disdained both verbal and moral "dalliance," or the waste of language and atrophy of emotion. Love was, for him, a unified

---

80. "The Holy Planet Purgatory," *Tales,* p. 756.
81. Manchester notes for April 1927 (Manchester Papers), p. 43.

force, not a role to play in order to satisfy an instinctive urge. He taught that "to love, one must forget all about love. . . . As we are we cannot possible love."[82] As best we can learn to love, we nurture and strengthen positive emotions. To escape its biological limits and exercise its full powers, Gurdjieff taught, love must be de-subjectivized and de-anthropomorphized. As such, love has three positive thrusts: toward unification and return of force, away from and separation of force, and around, or remaining in an orbit of fidelity.[83] In these terms, Gurdjieff sending Orage from him in 1931 was an act of love.

I suspect Gurdjieff would have agreed in spirit with Santayana's view for the population at large that love is an emotional bond that holds two persons together long enough for them to become friends. A man, says Santayana, "is polygamous by instinct, although kept faithful by habit,"[84] and Gurdjieff disdained the constraints of habit. What makes it difficult to seize firmly Gurdjieff's view of love, as Santayana's, is the apparent judgment that women are ontologically inferior to men. This was certainly the view of Schopenhauer and Nietzsche. In *Thus Spake Zarathrustra,* the latter said: "In woman's love there is injustice and blindness to all she does not love. . . . Woman is not capable of friendship; women are still cats and birds. Or at the least, cows."[85] Gurdjieff remarked to Orage that "the cause of every anomaly can be found in woman."[86] Nonetheless, probably the more numerous of his followers were women; and, he encouraged women to commit themselves to his work. At his life's end, he turned his own teaching mission over to Jeanne de Salzmann to perpetuate. Perhaps it is safe to say that Gurdjieff felt that women were more likely to allow their essential beings to be influenced by exterior considerations, so that women faced a more difficult task than men in ascending the scale of development from sensuous to emotional to intellectual to objective consciousness. Before the New York group on 13 February 1924, Gurdjieff explained that intellect is a predominant trait in "A" men, and emotion is predom-

82. Kenneth Walker, *A Study of Gurdjieff's Teaching,* cited in *Gurdjieff Home Page,* p. 4. For Orage on love, see King, *The Oragean Version,* pp. 192–195.
83. See Keith Buzzell, "The Biological Foundations of the Sacred Impulses," *All & Everything '99.* In Christian thought, as in many systems of belief, death is a return, and life is a sending away.
84. "Love," *The Life of Reason* (New York: Charles Scribner's Sons, 1955), p. 96. Beelzebub attributes to Christ the aura of "resplendent love" in *Tales,* p. 702.
85. *The Works,* I, 14.
86. Orage Papers, but the thought is repeated often. For a positive view of women, see Gurdjieff's *Meetings,* p. 56.

inant in "B" women. Conjoin these gender features and the product is an integrated "C" person. So, he reasoned, women and men have equal possibilities of development.[87]

Gurdjieff often spoke about love publicly, particularly in the first years of his European sojourn and in the lectures of his first American tour in 1924.[88] He characterized love as a commutative force between humans (both sexes) and the totality of their organic environment. In relations between the sexes, love is a generator of positive emotions. When love is but a "mood" alternating with "hate" as contexts vary, it is a negative emotion. Love must have *direction*, he and Orage insisted. They both distinguished love from sexual activity quite clearly, although neither excluded love from sexual relations and *vice versa*. It would seem that, in his personal experience, love and sexual activities were kept distinct, quite consciously, the latter pertaining to instinct and the former pertaining to objective reason. In Orage's terms, sex is either procreative or creative.

That Gurdjieff loved his mother and his wife profoundly is beyond question, but to "outsiders" the manifestations of his filial and espousal love were mystifying. What can one make of the inscription he had engraved on his mother's tombstone?[89] Or of the fact that on the evening his wife died he hosted a vodka party, reassigned her room to Jessie Dwight, and did not, to all appearances, display any emotion? Why, again, was Julia Ostrovska never referred to as Madame Gurdjieff? It is on his own record, however, that he cried on two occasions over Orage, first when Orage signed the pact renouncing his self, and later, when he heard of Orage's death.

It is easy to assume that Gurdjieff felt the bond between two men who share essential characteristics as being stronger than the instinctive and emotional bond between man and woman. Orage and Toomer alike felt that men and women could forge relationships coordinating the three centers of being. Yet, both Orage and Toomer held the male gender higher in possibilities of progress toward objective consciousness, conscience, and reason. As Orage writes: "The procreation of children is the particular function of instinctive love" and, "there is no necessary relation between love and children; but there is a necessary relation

---

87. *Views from the Real World* (London: Routledge & Kegan Paul, 1976), p. 84. In Christian doctrine, there is no gender privilege for Grace.

88. C. S. Nott, *Teachings of Gurdjieff: Journal of a Pupil* (London: Routledge & Kegan Paul, 1961), pp. 22–23.

89. "Ici Repose/La Mère de Celui/Qui se Vit par/Cette Mort Forcé/D'Ecrire Le Livre/Intitulé/ Les Opiumistes." (Translation: "Here Lies/The Mother of The One/ Who Found Himself/By Her Death Forced/To Write The Book/ Entitled/ The Opiumistes.")

between love and creation. . . .The aim of Conscious love is to bring about rebirth, or spiritual children."[90] Gurdjieff's "doctrine" of love is well known. Love is one of a triad of sacred-being impulses that include faith and hope. Love of consciousness engenders the same in return; love of feelings evokes the opposite, and physical love depends upon type.[91] Santayana, who spoke with Orage in the early twenties in London, before he moved to Rome in 1925, held love to be "a true natural religion. . . . It sanctifies a natural mystery; and, finally, when understood, it recognises that what is worshipped under a figure was truly the principle of all good."[92] It was clear to Orage and others that Gurdjieff's sexual practices were controlled coordinately by all his centers. Neither instinct nor emotion nor reason dominated his ego to the exclusion of the others.

When Toomer told Orage in the spring of 1926 that he was entering into an amatory relationship, Orage offered him this brief piece of advice: "The only type of sexual relations possible are with someone who is as advanced and capable as oneself. In either case there will be no feeling of responsibility in regard to progress in the work to interfere. Such a feeling of responsibility should not cut across a sexual relationship. Real sex is impossible if it does. We are not permitted to entertain ideas of development or reform for another person."[93] Gurdjieff told Ouspensky that "sex which exists by itself and is not dependent on anything else is already a great achievement . . . Evil is not in sex, but in the abuse of sex."[94] Ouspensky defined *normal* sex as that which exists without discord with other functions, emotional and intellectual.[95] When Gurdjieff was asked once about a higher sexual function, he stopped the discussion with a blunt reference to Buddha and Christ.

There are two points to be underscored here. First, the "work" should be neither an impediment to a sexual relationship, nor be negatively affected by it. Second and most important, the responsibility for an individual's development toward objective consciousness is the individual him- or herself. The role of the teacher is to awaken that sense of

---

90. *On Love*, p. 13. Nott, *Teachings*, p. 101, says that Orage "pours out love on people."
91. *Tales*, p. 361. Orage rephrased the series to have "conscious love" and "emotional love," the latter evoking hate.
92. George Santayana, *The Life of Reason* (New York: Charles Scribner's Sons, 1955), p. 101.
93. Toomer Collection, Beineke Manuscript Library, Box 68, Folder 1544. Nott, *Teachings*, p. 119, describes Gurdjieff's favorable ideas about husband-and-wife relations. He recalls that Gurdjieff was pleased with his decision to marry Rosemary Lillard.
94. Ouspensky, *Search*, pp. 255–257.
95. *A New Model of the Universe* (London: Routledge & Kegan Paul, 1938), pp. 526–527.

responsibility and to furnish tools for self-development. In the work, there are no schools and no teachers, Gurdjieff was wont to say in castigating the Western notion of education as pedagogical imperialism and cultural cloning. In an early talk, he explained: "I never teach directly, or my pupils would not learn. If I want a pupil to change, I begin from afar, or speak to someone else, and so he learns. For, if something is told to a child directly, he is being educated mechanically and later manifests himself equally mechanically."[96]

Orage's counsel to Toomer to the effect that neither man nor woman should feel responsible to the other in the context of a sexual relationship seems to reflect Gurdjieff's view in general terms. Gurdjieff himself said, as far as sex is concerned, it is a matter of type. Gurdjieff and Orage would both agree with the Orphic tenet that sexual union can precede marriage or take place without it, and both acted as if love can not or must not be constrained by the administrative fetters of law in the social institution of marriage. Both wanted children and both were pleased with fatherhood, though each acted out the role differently. Gurdjieff spoke fondly of his parents and his family life as a boy, but had no intention of duplicating that domesticity in his own carefully controlled environment. He discovered in his travels other models, and ultimately constructed his own.

---

96. Gurdjieff, *Views from the Real World* (London: Routledge & Kegan Paul, 1976), p. 127.

Epilogue

MENTORS AND STEWARDS

*[The dimension of stillness is] an initiate's
participation in a higher state of being.*
—Ouspensky[1]

Deus ad omnia indifferens est.
—Descartes[2]

Though Orage had a confident and sure sense of his own capacities and individual strengths as a writer and teacher, he acknowledged openly, clearly, and repeatedly that Gurdjieff was his mentor, one who showed him a new path to knowledge. Orage was perceptive enough, as he had learned from Gurdjieff, to understand that he should have others learn as much as possible from the mentor, if not directly, then through his agent. One cannot teach Gurdjieff very well with a glossary and blackboard diagrams. One can diagram concepts out of *Beelzebub's Tales,* but the lesson will touch our intellectual acuity only shallowly. A comprehensive grasp of Gurdjieff's ideas requires a collaborative probe into all three centers: intellectual, emotional, and physical (i.e. the moving, or instinctive, center).

A complication in the process of teaching pupils in the work is Gurdjieff's cautionary warning in his introduction to *Life is Real* to the effect that no one could understand his work who did not know his style of thought, that is unless he knew *him.* In this regard, one can only teach Gurdjieff by achieving a certain acquaintance with his being and by replicating his pedagogy without necessarily duplicating his style. That style is activated by a pedagogical philosophy that features the principle of shocking people out of habitual ways of viewing and doing. He would shock people loose from locked views of themselves—all the fictions of self and the identity one constructs to feel safe in the world—and he would shake people loose from stereotypical views of the world.

---

1. Cited by Demeter P. Tryphonopoulis, "'The Fourth; the Dimension of Stillness': D. P. [*sic*] Ouspensky and Fourth Dimensionalism in Canto 49," *Paideuma* 19 (1990), p. 121.
2. *Discourse on Method,* Laurence J. Lafleur, trans. (New York: Liberal Arts Press, 1950), p. 25. I have restored the original Latin.

He would strip off the "coating" of personality that one unconsciously acquires from social, educational, and religious experience. To accomplish these ends, he had to "step on people's corns." In brief, he would have his pupils "suffer intentionally," since comfort is counterproductive to conscious development. Hence, in *Life Is Real,* Gurdjieff asks that he be spared from those who make his life "too comfortable." Gurdjieff's "ideas," in and of themselves, in literary context, may be found distracting, confusing, and soporific; in proper performance— that is, in a direct oral presentation by a competent teacher—they are dynamic, astounding, and penetrating. One remarkable quality that Gurdjieff, Orage, and Toomer shared is the resonance of their voices. Their voices commanded attention, and all three had imposing physical features, particularly eyes. Orage's were bright and playful, Toomer's and Gurdjieff's were deep and hypnotic. The eyes of all three men spoke a language of engagement.

The voice and gesture performing Gurdjieff's ideas should be one's own, but a guide is necessary for acquiring the necessary tools to develop one's self and to direct others toward personal development. An important early step in one's development toward a harmonious collaboration of the three centers is instruction and training in laying bare one's "essence," or idiosyncratic "entity" of being. Identity, on the other hand, is a scarecrow in a deadend lane where no corn grows. An identity is a dependent association with an exterior value, while an entity is a personal and idiosyncratic formation, which is termed in Christian dogma, "a gift of nature," distinct from personality—which Gurdjieff identified with acquired social, educational, and religious values—in conventional Christian terms, a "gift of fortune." Dostoievsky's "idiot" (Prince Myushkin) and Yeats' "saint and hunchback" are beings close to nature and to "essence"—that is, relatively free of laminations, or coatings of socio-cultural debris. As Orage wrote: "Truth before God is essence; 'truth' before man is personality."[3] To his pupils, he explained that "essence knows why we are alive, what we wish to be and do."[4] This conception reflects the Buddhist "essence," which is the unchanging "real" person. In this respect, Orage often told his pupils of the Indian fetus in the womb that prays that it will not lose its essence after birth. The unchanged center is the soul. Thus, when Orage referred to himself in the third person, as distinct from the first person, he was echoing the Vedanta distinction between Átman "I" and Parusha "it."

---

3. *On Love: With Some Aphorisms and Other Essays* (New York: Samuel Weiser, 1969), p. 51.
4. Sherman Manchester's notes for May 17th, 1927 (Manchester Papers, p. 139). The contrary to essential consciousness is "grafted" consciousness. Since man is pervaded by the effects of kundabuffer, Orage said, he is never fully essential (Manchester, p. 6). Echoing an Ouspenkian pun, Orage differentiated "real" man from "reel" man.

Orage refused to play "guru" to his pupils, and he disdained adulation as much as he cherished friendship. He would learn from others, while giving them the means to learn for themselves. As his letters to Jessie about the Institute demonstrate, he felt and needed to feel a certain discomfort with himself in order to build a "new" Orage, and he wished to inculcate such sensitivity of being into his pupils. Orage had a talent for accomplishing this with a crowd, while another teacher, Toomer for example, preferred to work "one on one." Orage, like Toomer, "humanized" his contacts with students, but it was not easy for either of them to avoid moral entanglements. Gurdjieff, on the other hand, was very adept in keeping his pupils, friends, women dear to him, and even his kin at a measured distance. He exemplified intensive concern manifested in enlightened disinterest.[5]

Gurdjieff had the trickster's talent to deconstruct and reconstruct people's emotional sensibilities, to train their bodies to adopt nonhabitual postures and movements, and to challenge their epistemological grasp of realities. Orage was most forceful irritating *intellectual* corns. He worked diligently on the movements with his pupils, but lacked Gurdjieff's extraordinary choreography talents. Orage, in the urban landscape of New York, did not have the possibility of duplicating the conditions at the Institute where it was possible to effect a balance of physical, emotional, and intellectual travail.

Orage was self-conscious of his role as mediator for Gurdjieff, and he played the part faithfully. He denied being at the top of any catena of knowing, and fully acknowledged that his role was as Gurdjieff's steward, or God's "deputy steward."[6] Even when that role was put into doubt strategically by Gurdjieff at the beginning of 1931, Orage remained committed to the task Gurdjieff had assigned him as early as 1925: to edit the book that Gurdjieff hoped would sound his voice after his death. When, at the end, Orage confided to others that he only "half-believed" Gurdjieff, he was referring to a secret of life in the esoteric lore Gurdjieff held out like a carrot toward him. Never for an instant did he lose an iota of belief or confidence in the value of the work of the Institute. That Gurdjieff was his proper mentor was never a doubt in Orage's mind. Orage was not ready, however, to close off other avenues to his growth as a full human being. He had been transformed emotion-

---

5. Louise Welch, *Orage and Gurdjieff in America* (London: Routledge & Kegan Paul, 1982), pp. 111–112, sees a fundamental difference between the unconditioned minds of Ouspensky and Orage and the mind of Gurdjieff that represented a balance of three centers. King, *Oragean Version,* p. 14, distinguishes between Orage's rationality and Gurdjieff's inspiration.
6. Robert de Ropp, *Self-Completion* (Nevada City, CA: Gateways, 1988), p. 87, offers a neat definition for deputy steward.

ally by Gurdjieff, and had gained knowledge of and confidence in the being or the "I" that Gurdjieff revealed to him.

What he wanted yet from Gurdjieff, and felt he never got, was the key to Gurdjieff's knowledge—that is, its source and deepest core substance. He believed fully in the efficacy of Gurdjieff's psychological methods. He was in awe of the book, and supposed that it contained timeless secrets of life in coded form. All he needed was the key. Even when he felt that key had been withheld from him, however, he remained loyal to his task to see the text finished in good English form. Orage's loyalty to his stewardship never wavered. Orage believed to the end that the book was a door to perception of an esoteric lore, or "secret of life," and that Gurdjieff had hidden its key. Toomer had also thought Gurdjieff was withholding something crucial, wittingly or no. Where Orage thought the key was the book, Toomer thought it was the teaching. One might reply to these suppositions by arguing that the teaching is the book, but this would beg the question. Gurdjieff himself was the book, and now the book *is Gurdjieff.*

The term "steward" is Gurdjieff's, though it was probably Orage's English choice to render a particular Russian denomination, perhaps *oupravlyayushchego* (from *oupravl* "control, manage, govern"). Gurdjieff explained that, when God sees the necessity to retrieve control over a situation become chaotic, he must appoint a steward to mediate his interests. Before the steward can be chosen and trained for the job, however, a deputy steward (Russian *deputar*) must secure the ground. Reflecting this parable for the human condition, Orage was Gurdjieff's steward and God's deputy steward. He was Gurdjieff's most enduring steward during his lifetime. Ouspensky played the role in England in 1921 and 1922, plowing the terrain for the seeds Gurdjieff would plant when he arrived in February of that year. Ouspensky went to Paris to be with Gurdjieff and remained in his service until late 1923, when he returned to England, discontent with the direction of Gurdjieff's teaching.[7] He never returned to the Institute. At this critical juncture, and for the seven years following Ouspensky's defection, Orage filled the office of steward.

The appellation in its English form has particular relevance in this context. *Steward* is the modern development of Old English *stig-weard,* literally "guardian of the enclosed place." As a simplex, *stig* can refer to either a hall (*Stig-wita* designates "a hall wiseman or counselor") or a pen for animals, most often a pigsty. For Gurdjieff, the worldhall that

7. The final pages of Ouspensky's *In Search of the Miraculous* document his reasons for departure.

God had created had become a pigsty, an asylum enclosing the mentally and morally denatured. His own deputation was dedicated to awaking its inhabitants and redressing their situation, and so Orage was sent ahead to the United States to open the gates. What Orage was ably fit to do was to provide an analysis of the terrain and clear the cultural debris out of ears to which Gurdjieff would address his message.

In his critique of modern society in the form of a memoir, Waldo Frank, one of the many whose ears were cleansed by Orage for Gurdjieff's tonic message, Gurdjieff's emphasis on the isolated ego, "I," is characterized as a dangerous usurpation of cosmic and group energies.[8] Frank had been long estranged from the Gurdjieff work, in anger over what he took as a personal insult from Gurdjieff in the summer of 1926 or 1927,[9] though he remained in touch with his teaching afterward through an increasingly waning participation in Orage's group in New York. After Orage's death, Frank expressed little but disrespect for the Gurdjieff work and Orage's participation in it. He was scandalized by the renewed interest in Gurdjieff by so many of his acquaintances in 1948 and 1949.

In the context of a discussion in his memoirs of the necessity to unburden oneself of the barrier to truth that ego constitutes, Frank acknowledges the fundamental value of isolating the ego by self-observation. He observes that "the method, as a simple exercise in detachment, was a kind of dynamo from which power could be sluiced into the stresses of one's life."[10] Beneficial result from such a practice, he assumes, however, is unattainable in the Western social milieu to which Gurdjieff pointed his teaching; and so, the exercise is almost always one of vanity. He recalls that Orage in New York and Toomer in Chicago expatiated upon the method, and says:

> So far as I could tell from my contacts with Gurdjieff in France and with Orage, the value axioms of the original method were never discussed. . . . Whether they knew it or no, [the pupils] were all products of an age of ego power. . . . By submission to him, they blindly hoped for power. . . . But, as with bastard theosophical schools of the previous generation, a method aimed at freeing the self from its ego center became an instrument for *developing* the ego. . . . The "I" that observes the body and the world remains unchallengedly ego.[11]

---

8. *The Rediscovery of Man* (New York: Braziller, 1958), p. 425.
9. At a luncheon at the Prieuré, Gurdjieff had criticized Frank's choice of a new wife in racial terms. The episode is related in full in Taylor, *Shadows of Heaven* (York Beach, ME: Samuel Weiser, 1998), p. 90.
10. Frank, *Rediscovery,* p. 425.
11. Frank, *Rediscovery,* pp. 425–426 (emphasis mine). Frank associates Gurdjieff's with Mussolini's power-ego.

Frank goes on to contrast Gurdjieff's practice of self-observation unfavorably with Buddha's progressive detachment of ego from body, feeling, thought, idea, and the realm of value.

Surely this is a skewed vision of the teaching of Gurdjieff and Orage. For both, the goal of self-observation (Frank's ego detachment) is to recognize oneself, or one's "I," clearly in relation to the world and the cosmos as a function of a human being with individual particularities or idiosyncrasies of being distinct from the mass social machine. The goal is ego self-control, not ego mastery over others. Exercises in self-control are dedicated to the reassumption of essential humanness. Rather than exercise what Frank calls a "demonic" power over others, Gurdjieff and Orage isolated egos as a means of immunizing the total being from such power exercised by others or by society as a total organism. Essence is the child-father of the individual, and, as such has no desire to dominate, because it is primal and not political, human and not artificial.[12]

Gurdjieff was the most human of human beings I have ever known, perhaps because his essence, or his "I," was always viewable, no matter what guise he assumed in order to display or hide it. He was a trickster whose many roles challenged the reading of a single nucleate center beneath them. If he was misread more often than not, the reading itself was a lesson for others in becoming aware of their own habitually locked perspectives and perceptions. Gurdjieff would both display and hide the child in himself. He believed that children's games and their verbal play exhibit essence, whereas education and social exposure "coat" them over. Gurdjieff played games unabashedly. So did Toomer. He would do so artificially as well as naturally, but it would seem that Orage rarely could or would play in the same comic and cosmic spirit, except perhaps with Gurdjieff and with his own family.

Orage yearned for his own family, with children to rear and with whom to play children's games. Besides this, he felt a need for a mundane occupation to exercise his intellectual energies; and, he wanted a woman to love and by whom to be loved. He would bring love, work, and fatherhood into a harmonious collaboration with his unyielding quest for knowledge of his place and purpose in the world. The sincerity of his endeavor held the admiration of everyone who knew him. His detractors are ghosts. Gurdjieff was Orage's All-Father; Orage was Gurdjieff's Everyman.

---

12. See Matthew 18:3: "Truly I tell you, unless you change and become like children, you will never enter the kingdom of heaven."

Selected Bibliography

Ackroyd, Peter. *T. S. Eliot.* London: Hamish Hamilton, 1984.

AE [George Russell]. *Letters from AE.* Alan Denson, ed. London: Abelard Schuman, 1961.

All & Everything. Proceedings of the International Humanities Conference. H. J. Sharp and Seymour B. Ginsburg, *et al.,* eds. Bognor Regis: Privately published, 1996, 1997, 1998.

Alpers, Anthony. *The Life of Katherine Mansfield.* London: Jonathan Cape, 1980.

Anderson, Margaret. *The Fiery Fountain.* London: Rider, 1953.

———. *The Strange Necessities,* New York: Horizon, 1970.

———. *The Unknowable Gurdjieff.* London: Routledge & Kegan Paul, 1962.

Anonymous [under the name Armagnac]. "The Strange Cult of Gurdjieff," *Psychology Today,* Dec. 1926, 21–31.

Auden, W[ystan] H[ugh]. *Dance of Death.* London: Faber & Faber, 1933.

Baker, Rob. "No Harem: Gurdjieff and the Women of the Rope," *Gurdjieff International Review,* 1:2 (1997/1998).

Baldwin, James. *The Fire Next Time.* London: Michael Joseph, 1963.

Bartlett, John. *Familiar Quotations.* Garden City, NJ: Permabooks, 1953.

Bechhofer Roberts, Carl E. "What Was Seen by Outsiders," in *Gurdjieff.* Louis Pauwels, ed. Douglas, Isle of Man: Time Press, pp. 142–167. Reprinted from *Century,* 1924.

Bennett, Elizabeth and John G. *Des Idiots à Paris.* Genève: Georg, 1991. First published as *Idiots in Paris,* York Beach, ME: Samuel Weiser, 1991.

Bennett, John G. *Gurdjieff: A Very Great Enigma.* York Beach, ME: Samuel Weiser, 1984.

———. *Gurdjieff: Making a New World.* London: Turnstone, 1962.

Bergson, Henri. *Creative Evolution.* New York: Random House Modern Library, 1944.

———. *The Two Sources of Morality and Religion.* Notre Dame, IN: Notre Dame University Press, 1977.

Bies, Jean. "René Guénon, hérault de la dernière chance." In *René Guénon.* Jean-Pierre Laurant and Paul Baronegra, eds. Paris: Editions de l'Herne, 1985.

Blavatsky, Helena [Hahn-Hahn] Petrovna. *The Secret Doctrine.* London: Rider, 1888.

Blum, John Morton, ed. *The Price of Vision: The Diary of Henry A. Wallace 1942–1946.* Boston: Houghton Mifflin, 1973.

Bragdon, Claude. *More Lives Than One.* New York: Knopf, 1938.

Brennecke, Ernest. "Behind the Scenes at Gurdjieff's Weird Château of Mysteries, in *New York World.* 25 November 1923.

Brooke-Rose, Christine. *A ZBC of Ezra Pound.* Berkeley, CA: University of California Press, 1971.

Butkovsky-Hewitt, Anna. *With Gurdjieff in St. Petersburg and Paris.* London: Routledge & Kegan Paul, 1978.

Butter, P. H. *Edwin Muir: Man and Poet.* Westport, CT: Greenwood Press, 1966.

Buzzell, Keith. "The Biological Foundations of the Sacred Impulses," *All & Everything '99.*

———. "Kundabuffer," *All and Everything '97.*

Byrd, Rudolph. *Toomer's Years With Gurdjieff.* Athens: University of Georgia Press, 1989.

Carroll, Raymond G. "Gurdjieff Heads Newest Cult, Which Harkens Back to Ancient Day," in *New York Evening Post.* January 26, 1924.

Carswell, John. *Lives and Letters.* London: Faber, 1978

Cookson, William, ed. *Pound, Ezra: Selected Prose 1909–1965.* New York: New Directions, 1973.

Cowley, Malcolm. *Exiles Return: A Literary Odyssey of the 1920s.* New York: Penguin, 1976.

Coyle, Michael. *Ezra Pound, Popular Genres and the Discourse of Culture.* University Park: Pennsylvania State University Press, 1995.

———. "'A Profounder Didacticism': Ruskin, Orage, and Pound's Reception of Social Credit," *Paideuma* 17 (1988), 7–28.

Crane, Hart. *Letter of Hart Crane and his Family.* Thomas S. W. Lewis, ed. New York: Columbia University Press, 1974.

Croce, Benedetto. *Philosophy of the Practical, Economic and Ethic.* London: Macmillan, 1913.

Cumberland, Gerald. *Set Down in Malice.* London: Grant Richards, 1920.

Curle, Richard. *Caravansary and Conversation.* Freeport, NY: Books for Library Press, 1971.

Dampierre, Pauline. "Les mouvements." In *Panafieu,* 129–134.

Danzig, Tobias. *Number: The Language of Science.* New York: Doubleday Anchor, 1956.

Daumal, René. *Correspondance.* 3 vols. Paris: Gallimard, 1996.

Davis, Earle. *Vision Fugitive: Ezra Pound and Economics.* Lawrence, KS: University of Kansas Press, 1968.

Decter, Jacqueline. *Nicholas Roerich: The Life and Art of a Russian Master.* London: Thames & Hudson, 1989.

De Jong, H. M. E. *Atalanta Fugiens: Sources of an Alchemical Book of Emblems.* Leiden, Netherlands: E. J. Brill, 1969.

De Stjernuall, Nikolai. *Daddy Gurdjieff.* Genere: Georg, 1917.

Descartes, René. *Discourse on Method.* New York: Liberal Arts Press. 1950.

Dinnage, Rosemary. "The Great Mystifier," review of Webb's *The Harmonious Circle,* in *The New York Review,* 23 October, 1980, 20–24.

Draper, Muriel. *Music at Midnight.* New York: Harper & Brothers, 1929.

Driscoll, J. Walter. *Gurdjieff: An Annotated Bibliography.* Introduction by Michel de Salzmann. Garland Reference Library 225. New York: Garland, 1985.

———. *Gurdjieff: An Interim Bibliography.* Gurdjieff Electronic Publishing. Los Altos, CA: Gregory M. Loy, 1999.

Douglas, C. H. *Credit Power and Democracy.* London: Cecil Palmer, 1920. With commentary by A. R. Orage, 153–212.

Ducasse, Curt John. *Philosophy of Art.* London: Allen & Unwin, 1930.

Durkheim, Émile. *The Elementary Forms of the Religious Life.* Rodney Needham, trans. Chicago: Chicago University Press, 1963.

Eco, Umberto. *Foucault's Pendulum.* William Weaver, trans. New York: Ballantine Books, 1990.

Edwards, Paul, gen. ed. *Encyclopedia of Philosophy.* New York: Macmillan, 1967.

Eliade, Mircea, gen. ed. *Encyclopedia of Religion.* New York: Macmillan, 1987.

Eliot, Valerie. *The Letters of T. S. Eliot, Vol I, 1898–1922.* London: Faber & Faber, 1988.

Ellis, David. *D. H. Lawrence: Dying Game 1922–1930.* Cambridge: Cambridge University Press, 1998.

Ellman, Richard. *Oscar Wilde.* London: Hamish Hamilton, 1987.

Epstein, Jacob. *Epstein: An Autobiography.* London: Hulton Press, 1955.

Evola, Julius. *Masques et visages du spiritualisme contemporain.* Phillippe Baillet, trans. Paris: Paidès, 1991. (Mascero e volto dello spiritualismo contemporaneo Roma: Mediterranee. 1971)

Field, Andrew. *Djuna.* New York: G. P. Putnam's Sons, 1983.

Finlay, John L. *Social Credit: The English Origins.* Montreal: McGill-Queens University Press, 1972.

Flory, Wendy Stallard. *The American Ezra Pound.* New Haven: Yale University Press, 1989.

Forster, R. F. *W. B. Yeats: A Life.* Oxford: Oxford University Press, 1997.

Frank, Waldo. *The Rediscovery of Man: A Memoir and a Methodology.* New York: Brazillier, 1958.

———. [Search-Light]. *Time Exposures.* New York: Boni and Liveright, 1926.

Fremantle, Anne. "Travels with a Searcher," review of *Meetings with Remarkable Men* in *The New York Times Book Review,* 8 September 1963.

Freud, Sigmund. *The Complete Psychological Works.* 24 vols. James Strachey, ed. London: Hogarth Press, 1974.

Gaarder, Jostein. *Solitaire Mystery.* London: Phoenix, 1997.

Gagneron, Marthe. "Danses sacrés," *Dossiers H.* Bruno de Panafieu, ed. Paris: L'Age d'homme, 1952. pp. 152–156.

Gates, Henry Louis, Jr. "Introduction: 'Tell me, Sir, . . . What is 'Black Literature?'", *PMLA* 105 (1990), pp. 11–22.

———. "White Like Me," *The New Yorker* 17 June 1996, pp. 66–68.

Gansthorpe, Mary. *Up Hill to Holloway.* Penobscott, ME: Traversity Press, 1962.

Gibbons, Tom. *Rooms in the Darwin Hotel: Studies in English Literature, Art, and Ideas 1880–1920.* Nedlands: University of Western Australia Press, 1973.

Gill, Brendan. *Many Masks.* New York: Da Capo, 1998.

Gross, John. *The Rise and Fall of the Man of Letters.* London: Weidenfeld and Nicolson, 1969.

Guilleminault, Gilbert, ed. *Les années folles.* Paris: Denoël, 1968.

Gurdjieff, G[eorgii] I[vanovich]. *All and Everything.* London: Routledge & Kegan Paul, 1950.

———. *The Herald of Coming Good.* Edmonds, WA: Sure Fire Press, 1988 (reprint of 1933 Paris edition).

———. *Life is Real Only Then, When "I AM."* New York: Dutton for Triangle Editions, 1975.

———. *Meetings with Remarkable Men.* A. R. Orage, trans. London: Penguin, 1963.

———. *Views From the Real World: Early Talks of Gurdjieff.* London: Routledge & Kegan Paul, 1976.

Gurdjieff, Luba [Everitt] with Marina C. Bear. *Luba Gurdjieff: A Memoir with Recipes.* Berkeley, CA: Ten Speed Press, 1993.

Hahn. Emily. *Mabel: A Biography of Mabel Dodge Luhan.* Boston: Houghton Mifflin, 1977.

Harrold, F. C. *Mysticism.* London: Penguin, 1963.

Hartmann, Thomas de. *Musique pour les mouvements de G. I. Gurdjieff.* Paris: Janus, 1950.

Hartmann, Thomas de and Olga de Hartmann. *Our Life with Gurdjieff.* London: Penguin, 1972 (translated from the French *Notre vie avec Gurdjieff.* Paris: Planète, 1968).

Hastings, Beatrice. *The Old "New Age": Orage and Others.* London: Blue Moon Press, 1936.

Heideggar, Martin. *Basic Writings.* David Farrell Krell, ed. New York: HarperCollins, 1997.

[Hermes Trismegistos]. *The Pymander.* W. Wynn Westcott, ed. London: Theosophical Society, 1894.

Heyman, C. David. *Ezra Pound: The Last Rower: A Political Profile.* New York: Viking, 1976.

Hirsch, James S. *Hurricane: The Miraculous Quest of Rubin Carter.* Boston: Houghton Mifflin, 2000.

Hodgson, Samuel G. *National Guilds.* A. R. Orage, ed. London: G. Bell & Sons, 1914.

Hoffman, Maud. "Taking the Cure in Gurdjieff's School," *New York Times,* 10 Feb. 1924, Arts Section, p. 12.

Holroyd, Michael. *Augustus John.* New York: Holt Rinehart Winston, 1974.

Holter, Elizabeth Sage. *The ABC of Social Credit.* New York: Coward, McCann, 1934.

Homberger, Eric. *Ezra Pound: The Critical Heritage.* London: Routledge & Kegan Paul, 1972.

Howarth, Jessmin. "Wise Woman," *A Journal of Our Time.* Toronto: Traditional Studies Press, 1979.

Hughes, Langston. *The Big Sea: An Autobiography.* New York: Hill and Wang, 1963.

Hulme, Kathryn. *Undiscovered Country.* Little Brown, 1966.

Hutchins, Patricia. *Ezra Pound's Kensington: An Exploration 1885–1913.* London: Faber & Faber, 1965.

Hutton, Graham. *The Burden of Plenty.* London: George Allen & Unwin, 1935.

Hynes, Samuel. *Edwardian Occasion.* London: Routledge & Kegan Paul, 1972.

———. *The Edwardian Turn of Mind.* Princeton: Princeton University Press: 1968.

Jacobi, Jolande. *The Psychology of C. G. Jung.* London: Routledge & Kegan Paul, 1942.

James, William. *The Principles of Psychology.* Chicago: Encylopædia Britannica Great Books of the Western World, vol. 53, 1952.

———. *The Varieties of Religious Experience: A Study in Human Nature.* New York: Random House Modern Library, 1929.

———. *Writings 1902–1910.* New York: Library of America, 1987.

Jaspers, Karl. *Psychologie der Weltanschauugen.* Berlin: J. Springer, 1922.

Jung, Carl Gustav. *Modern Man in Search of a Soul.* London: Kegan Paul, Trench, Trubner & Co., 1933.

———. *The Psychology of Kundalini Yoga.* Sonu Shamdasani, ed. Princeton: Princeton University Press, 1999.

Kerman, Cynthia Earl, and Richard Eldridge, *The Lives of Jean Toomer.* Baton Rouge: Louisiana State University Press, 1987.

Keynes, John Maynard. *General Theory of Employment, Interest and Money.* London: Macmillan, 1935.

King, C. Daly. *The Oragean Version.* New York: Privately published, 1951.

———. *The Psychology of Consciousness.* London: Kegan Paul, Trench, Trubner & Co., 1932.

———. *The State of Human Consciousness.* New Hyde Park, New York: University Books, 1963.

Kirk, Russell. *Eliot and His Age.* New York: Random House, 1971.

Kirstein, Lincoln. "A Memoir: At the Prieuré des Basses Loges, Fontainebleau," *Raritan 2* (Fall, 1982), pp. 35–50.

———. *Mosaic.* New York: Farrar, Straus & Giroux, 1994.

Landau, Rom. *God is My Adventure.* London: Ivor Nicolson and Watson, 1935.

Lanoux, Armand. "Les Belles du Montparno," in *Les Années Folles.* Gilbert Guilleminault, ed. Paris: Denoël. 1968. pp. 267–307.

Larson, Charles R. *Invincible Darkness: Jean Toomer and Nella Larsen.* Iowa City: University of Iowa Press, 1993.

Laughlin, James. *Pound as Wuz.* Saint Paul: Graywolf Press, 1987.

Laurant, Jean-Pierre. *Le sens caché selon René Guénon.* Lausanne: L'Age d'homme, 1975.

Laurant, Jean-Pierre, and Paul Barbanegra, eds. *René Guénon.* Paris: Editions de l'Herne, 1985.

Lefort, Raphael. *The Teachers of Gurdjieff.* London: Victor Gollancz, 1966; New York: Samuel Weiser, 1966.

Loeb, Harold. *The Way it Was.* New York: Criterion Books, 1959.

Lowry, Malcolm. *Sursum Corda! The Collected Letters, Vol II: 1947–1957.* Shervill E. Grace, ed. London: Jonathan Cape, 1996.

Lowitt, Richard. *Bronson M. Cutting.* Albuquerque: University of New Mexico Press, 1992.

McAlmon, Robert, and Kay Boyle. *Being Geniuses Together 1920–1930.* Garden City, NY: Doubleday, 1968.

MacDiarmid, Hugh [Christopher Murray Grieve]. *The Company I've Kept.* Berkeley: University of California Press, 1967.

Mairet, Philip. *A. R. Orage: A Memoir.* New Hyde Park, NY: University Press,1966.

———. *Autobiographical and Other Pages.* Manchester: Carcanet Press, 1981.

Mansfield, Katherine. *The Journal of Katherine Mansfield.* John Middleton Murry, ed. New York: Knopf, 1927.

March, Louise. *The Gurdjieff Years 1929–1949: Recollections of Louise [Goepfert] March.* Beth McCorkle, ed. Walworth, NY: The Work Study Association, 1990.

Mariani, Paul. *William Carlos Williams: A New World Naked.* New York: McGraw-Hill, 1981.

Martin, Wallace. *The New Age Under Orage: Chapters in English Cultural History.* Manchester: University of Manchester Press, 1967.

———. *Orage as Critic.* London: Routledge & Kegan Paul, 1974.

Materer, Timothy. *Modern Alchemy: Poetry and the Occult.* Ithaca: Cornell University Press, 1995.

———, ed. *Pound/Lewis: The Letters of Ezra Pound and Wyndham Lewis.* New York: New Directions, 1985.

Matthews, T. S. *Name and Address: An Autobiography.* New York: Simon and Schuster, 1960.

————. *Under the Influence.* London: Cassell, 1977.

Merrill, James. *The Changing Light at Sandover, Mirabell: Book of Numbers.* New York: Atheneum, 1978.

Meyers, Jeffrey. *D. H. Lawrence: A Biography.* New York: Alfred A. Knopf, 1990.

Mills, Ralph J., Jr. *Selected Letters of Theodore Roethke.* Seattle: University of Washington Press, 1968.

Moore, James. *Gurdjieff and Mansfield.* London: Routledge & Kegan Paul, 1980.

————. *Gurdjieff: The Anatomy of a Myth.* Boston: Element, 1991.

————. "Moveable Feasts: The Gurdjieff Work," *Religion Today* 9.2 (1994), pp. 11–16.

Mouravieff, Boris. *Ouspensky, Gurdjieff et les fragments d'un enseignement inconnu.* Bruxelles: Synthèse, 1957.

Muir, Edwin. *Selected Letters of Edwin Muir.* P. H. Butter, ed. London: Hogarth, 1974.

Munson, Gorham B[ert]. *Aladdin's Lamp: The Wealth of the American People.* New York: Creative Age Press, 1945.

————. *The Awakening Twenties: A Memoir–History of a Literary Period.* Baton Rouge: Louisiana State University Press, 1985.

————. "Black Sheep Philosophers: Gurdjieff, Ouspensky, Orage," *Tomorrow* 9 (1950), pp. 20–25.

————. "Orage in America," *Dynamic America* 10 (1940), pp. 12–16.

Murray, Paul. *T. S. Eliot and Mysticism.* London: Macmillan, 1991.

Murry, John Middleton, ed. *Journal of Katherine Mansfield.* New York: Alfred A. Knopf, 1927.

Needleman, Jacob. "Existential Psychoanalysis," in Edwards, *Encyclopedia of Philosophy.* vol 3. New York: Macmillan, 1967.

Neugebauer, Otto. *A History of Ancient Mathematical Astronomy.* Berlin: Springer-Verlag, 1975.

Nicolescu, Baserab. "La Philosophie de la Nature de Gurdjieff," in *Dossiers H.* Bruno de Panafieu, ed. Paris: L'Age d'homme, 1952, pp. 267–294.

Nicoll, Maurice. *Psychological Commentaries.* vol. I. London: Vincent Stuart, 1952.

Nietzsche, Friedrich. *The Works.* New York: Tudor, 1931.

Norman, Charles. *The Case of Ezra Pound.* New York: Funk and Wagnall's, 1968.

Nott, C[harles] S[tanley]. *Journey Through this World.* London: Routledge & Kegan Paul, 1969.

————. *Teachings of Gurdjieff: Journal of a Pupil.* London: Routledge & Kegan Paul, 1961.

Orage. A[lfred] R[ichard]. *The Active Mind: Adventures in Awareness.* New York: Hermitage House, 1954.

————. *An Alphabet of Economics.* London: T. Fisher Unwin, 1917.

————. "An Editor's Progress," *Commonweal* 3 (10 February 1926), pp. 376–379.

————. "American Literature," *New Republic* 39 (20 Aug. 1924), pp. 357–358.

————. *The Art of Reading.* New York: Farrar & Rinehart, 1930.

————. *Consciousness: Animal, Human and Superhuman.* London: Pembridge Design Studio, 1907.

————. "The Fear of Leisure," *Social Credit and the Fear of Leisure.* Vancouver, BC: Institute of Economic Democracy, 1977.

————. "Henry James and the Ghostly," *Little Review* 5 (Aug 1918), pp. 41–43.

————. "Literature in America," *New Republic* 39 (6 Aug 1924), pp. 299–300.

———. "New Standards in Art and Literature," *Atlantic Monthly* 135 (Feb. 1925), pp. 204–207.

———. *Nietzsche in Outline and Aphorism.* London: T. N. Foulis, 1907.

———. *On Love: With Some Aphorisms and Other Essays.* C. S. Nott, ed. York Beach, ME: Samuel Weiser, 1969. First published in the *New Republic,* Dec. 3, 1924, pp. 36–39, and in *Essays of 1925,* Odel Shepard, ed. (Hartford, CT: Edwin Valentine Mitchell, 1926). Reprint York Beach, ME: Samuel Weiser, as *On Love & Psychological Exercises,* 1998.

———. "The Mystical Value of Literature," Theosophical Review 31 (1903), pp. 428–434.

———. *Psychological Exercises.* New York: Farrar & Rinehart, 1930.

———. *Selected Essays and Critical Writings.* Sir Herbert Read and Denis Saurat, eds. London: Stanley Nott, 1935.

———. "Talks with Katherine Mansfield," *Century* 109 (Nov. 1924), pp. 36–40, and *The New English Weekly* 1 (19 May 1932), pp. 109–111 (Reprinted in *On Love*).

———. "A Theatre For Us," *The Little Review.* Winter, 1926, pp. 30–32.

———. "Unedited Opinions III: Religion in America," *New Republic,* Dec. 31, 1924, pp. 141–142.

Ouspensky, P. D. "Autobiographical Fragment," *Remembering Pyotr Demianovich Ouspensky.* New Haven: Yale University Library, 1978, pp. 9–13.

———. *A New Model of the Universe.* London: Routledge & Kegan Paul, 1938.

———. *In Search of the Miraculous.* New York: Harcourt Brace and World, 1949.

———. *The Fourth Way.* London: Routledge & Kegan Paul, 1957.

———. *The Strange Life of Ivan Osokin.* London: Penguin, 1960.

Paige, D. D. *Ezra Pound: Selected Letters 1907–1941.* New York: New Directions, 1971.

Palmer, Helen. *The Enneagram.* San Francisco: HarperSanFrancisco, 1988.

Panafieu, Bruno de. *Les Dossiers H.: Georges Ivanovitch Gurdjieff.* Paris. L'Age d'homme, 1992.

Pankhurst, E. Sylvia. *The Suffragette Movement.* London: Longmans, Green, 1931.

Patterson, William Patrick. "The Kanari Papers," I & II, *Telos* 2 & 3 (1996, 1997).

———. *Ladies of the Rope.* Fairfax, CA: Arete, 1998.

———. *Struggle of the Magicians.* Fairfax, CA: Arete, 1995.

Pauwels, Louis, ed. *Gurdjieff.* Douglas: Times Press. Translated from *Monsieur Gurdjieff,* Paris: Seuil, 1954.

Perl, Jeffrey M. *Skepticism and Modern Enmity: Before and After Eliot.* Baltimore: The Johns Hopkins University Press, 1989.

Perry, Whitall N. *Gurdjieff in the Light of Tradition.* Bedfont: Perennial Books, 1978.

Peters, Fritz. *Boyhood with Gurdjieff.* London: Victor Gollancz, 1964.

———. *Gurdjieff Remembered.* London: Victor Gollancz, 1969.

Plato, *Collected Dialogues,* Edith Hamilton and Huntington Cairns, eds. New York: Pantheon Books. Bollingen Series 71, 1961.

Pound, Ezra. *Autobiography.* London: Picadon, 1967.

———. *The Cantos.* London: Faber & Faber, 1964.

———. *Guide to Kultur.* New York: New Directions, 1938.

———. "In the Wounds." *Criterion.* 4 January 1935.

———. *Selected Letters 1907–1941.* D. D. Paige, ed. New York: New Directions, 1971.

————. *Selected Prose 1909–1965.* William Cookson, ed. New York: New Directions, 1973.

Powys, John Cowper. *Autobiography.* London: Picador, 1967.

Rawlinson, Andrew. *The Book of Enlightened Masters: Western Teachers in Eastern Traditions.* N. P.: Open Court Publishers, 1977

Read, Forest. *76: One World and the Cantos of Ezra Pound.* Chapel Hill: University North Carolina Press. 1981.

Reckitt, Maurice B. *As It Happened.* London: J. C. Dent & Sons, 1941.

Redman, Tim. *Ezra Pound and Italian Fascism.* Cambridge: Cambridge University Press, 1991.

Robinson, Roxanne. *Georgia O'Keeffe: A Life.* New York: HarperCollins, 1989.

Ropp, Robert S. de. *Self-Completion: Keys to the Meaningful Life.* Nevada City, CA: Gateways, 1988.

Rudnick, Lois Palken. *Mabel Dodge Luhan: New Woman, New Worlds.* Albuquerque: University of New Mexico Press, 1984.

Salzmann, Michel de. "Gurdjieff." *Encyclopedia of Religion.* Mircea Eliade, ed. New York: Macmillan, 1987.

Santayana, George. *The Life of Reason.* New York: Charles Scribner's Sons, 1955.

Saurat, Denis. "Visite à Gurdjieff," *Nouvelle Revue Française,* 1 Nov. 1933, pp. 686–698.

Schapsmeier, Edward L. and Frederick H. *Henry A. Wallace of Iowa: The Agrarian Years, 1910–1940.* Ames: Iowa State University Press, 1968.

Schwartz, Tony. *What Really Matters: Searching For Wisdom in America.* New York: Bantam, 1995.

Scott, Thomas L., *et al. Pound/The Little Review: The Letters of Ezra Pound to Margaret Anderson.* New York: New Directions, 1988.

Secrest, Meryle. *Frank Lloyd Wright.* New York: Knopf, 1992.

Segal, William. "Inviting Hell into Heaven," *Parabola* 24:2 (1999), pp. 58–65.

Seldes, Gilbert. *The Seven Lively Arts.* New York: Sagamor Press, 1924, 1957.

Selver, Paul. *Orage and the New Age Circle.* London: Allen & Unwin, 1959.

Seymour Smith, Martin. *The 100 Most Influential Books Ever Written.* Secaucus, NJ: Carol Publishing Group, 1998.

Sharpe, Clifford. "The Forest Philosophers," *New Statesman,* 3 and 17 March, 1923.

Shaw, George Bernard. *Collected Letters.* Dan H. Laurence, ed. London: Max Reinhardt, 1988.

————. *Collected Letters 1898–1910.* Dan H. Laurence, ed. London: Max Reinhardt, 1972.

Smith, Russell. *Cosmic Secrets.* Sanger, TX: privately published, 1993.

Smoley, Richard. "Why the Enneagram: An Interview with Helen Palmer," *Gnosis* 30 (Summer, 1994), pp. 18–24.

Speeth, Kathleen Riordan. *The Gurdjieff Work.* Los Angeles: J. P. Tarcher, 1989.

Spengler, Oswald. *The Decline of the West.* Charles Francis Atkinson, trans. London: George Allen & Unwin, 1926.

Steele, Tom. *Alfred Orage and the Leeds Arts Club 1893–1923.* Aldershot: Scolar Press, 1990.

Stevens, Wallace. *Collected Poems and Prose.* New York: Library of America, 1996.

Stock, Noel. *The Life of Ezra Pound.* New York: Pantheon, 1970.

Storr, Anthony. *Feet of Clay: Saints, Sinners, and Madmen.* New York: The Free Press, 1996.

Surette, Leon. *The Birth of Modernism*. Montréal: Queen's University Press, 1993.
———. *A Light for Eleusis: A Study of Ezra Pound's Cantos*. Oxford: Clarendon Press, 1979.
Sutton, Walter, ed. *Pound, Thayer, Watson and The Dial*. Gainesville: University Press of Florida, 1994.
Tate, Allen. *Essays of Four Decades*. London: Oxford University Press, 1970.
Taylor, Paul Beekman. "Gurdjieff's Deconstruction of History in the Third Series." Proceedings of the Third Bognor Conference on *All and Eveything*. Bert Sharp and Seymour Ginsburg, Bognor Regis, eds., 1998, pp. 178–205.
———. *Shadows of Heaven: Gurdjieff and Toomer*. York Beach, ME: Samuel Weiser, 1998.
Terrell, Caroll F. *A Companion to the Cantos of Ezra Pound*. Berkeley: University of California Press, 1984.
Thatcher, David S. *Nietzsche in England, 1890–1914*. Toronto: University of Toronto Press, 1970.
Thistlewood, David. *Herbert Read: Formlessness and Form*. London: Routledge & Kegan Paul, 1984.
Tomalin, Claire. *Katherine Mansfield: A Secret Life*. London: Penguin, 1988.
Toomer, Nathan Jean. *A Fiction and Some Facts*. Doylestown: privately published, n.d. (1938?)
———. *Cane*. New York: Boni and Liveright, 1922.
———. *Essentials*. Chicago: Lakeside Press, 1931. Reprinted, with introduction by Rudolph Byrd. Athens: University of Georgia Press, 1993.
———. *The Collected Poems of Jean Toomer*, Robert B. Jones and Margery Latimer Toomer, eds. Chapel Hill: University of North Carolina Press, 1988.
———. *The Wayward and the Seeking*. Darwin T. Turner, ed. Washington DC: Howard University Press, 1980.
Torrey, E. Fuller. *The Roots of Treason: Ezra Pound and the Secret of St. Elizabeth's*. New York: McGraw-Hill, 1989.
Tryphonopoulis, Demeter P. " 'The Fourth; the Dimension of Stillness': D. P. [*sic*] Ouspensky and Fourth Dimensionalism in Canto 49," *Paideuma* 19 (1990), pp. 117–122.
Upward, Allen. *The Divine Mystery: A Reading of the History of Christianity Down to the Time of Christ*. Boston: Houghton Mifflin, 1915.
Val, Nicholas de [Nikolai de Stjernvall]. *Daddy Gurdjieff*. Genève: Georg, 1997.
Walkiewicz, E. P., and Hugh Witemeyer. *Ezra Pound and Senator Bronson Cutting: A Political Correspondence 1930–1935*. Albuquerque: University of New Mexico Press, 1995.
Walker, Kenneth. *A Study of Gurdjieff's Teaching*. London: Fletcher and Son, 1957.
———. *The Making of Man*. London: Routledge & Kegan Paul, 1963.
Washington, Peter. *Madame Blavatsky's Monkey*. London: Secker and Warburg, 1995.
Weaver, Mike. *William Carlos Williams: The American Background*. Cambridge: Cambridge University Press, 1971.
Webb, James. *The Harmonious Circle: The Lives and Works of G. I. Gurdjieff, P. D. Ouspensky, and Their Followers*. London: Thames & Hudson, 1980.
Weber, Brom, ed. *The Letters of Hart Crane*. Berkeley: University of California Press, 1952.
Weintraub, Stanley. *The London Yankees*. New York: Harcourt Brace Jovanovich, 1979.

Welch, Louise. *Orage with Gurdjieff in America*. London: Routledge & Kegan Paul, 1982.

Welch, William J. *What Happened In Between*. New York: George Brazillier, 1972

Wellbeloved, S[ophia] A. L. "Gurdjieff, Astrology and Beelzebub's Tales: An Analysis of G. I. Gurdjieff's Beelzebub's Tales to His Grandson in Terms of Astrological Correspondences." University of London, unpublished thesis, 1999.

———. "G. I. Gurdjieff: Some References to Love," *Journal of Contemporary Religion* 13 (1998), pp. 321–332.

Wendel, Sylvain de. "Vive la Résistance," *René Guénon. Planète Plus*, 1970. pp. 39–53.

Wilhelm, J. J. *Ezra Pound: London and Paris 1908–1925*. University Park: The Pennsylvania State University Press, 1990.

———. *Ezra Pound: The Tragic Years 1925–1972*. University Park: The Pennsylvania State University Press, 1994.

Wilson, Colin. "Two Russian Mages," in *A History of Magic and the Occult*. Kurt Seligman, ed. New York: Random House, 1997.

———. *The War Against Sleep: The Philosophy of Gurdjieff*. London: Aquarian Press, 1980,

Wilson, Edmund. *The Twenties*. New York: Farrar Straus & Giroux, 1975.

Wineapple, Brenda. *Genêt: A Biography of Janet Flanner*. New York: Ticknor and Fields, 1989.

Woodson, Jon. *To Make a New Race: Gurdjieff, Toomer and the Harlem Renaissance*. Jackson, MS: University of Mississippi Press, 1999.

Wright, Frank Lloyd. *Collected Writings of Frank Lloyd Wright*. Bruce Brooks Pfeiffer, ed. 5 vols. New York: Rizzoli International Publications, 1992–1993.

Yagan, Murat. "Sufism and the Source," *Gnosis* 30 (Winter 1994), pp. 40–47.

Zigrosser, Carl. "Gurdjieff," *The New Republic*, 5 June 1929, pp. 66–69.

Zuber, René. *Qui êtes vous, Monsieur Gurdjieff?* Paris: Courier du livre, 1977.

Index

Goefert Louise. *See* March,
Louise
Gordon, Dorothy, 187
Gordon, Elizabeth, 53, 75,
116–117, 122, 124,
127
Grant, Blanche [Rosette],
93, 101, 109, 138,
158, 172, 182, 194
Greenborough, T. Alan, 205
Greenborough, Bill, 207
Gross, John, 4n, 19, 225n
Guénon, René, 172n. 213,
215, 236, 238
Guggenhein, Peggy, 24
Guild Socialism, 4
Gurdjieff, Georgii
Ivanovich,
Early life, x, xi; 1924
accident, 67, 80; cri-
sis with Jessie
Orage, 148, 162;
break with Orage,
169 ff; Chicago
demonstrations,
57–59, Paris demon-
stration, 35;
Family Gurdjieff,
Giorgias Georgiades
(father), x; as
ashokh, 31; mother,
x; Julia Ostrovska
(wife) dies, 111–112;
Dmitri, 112, 113,
119n; Dmitri's wife,
Asta, 190; Dmitri's
daughter, Luba, xn;
Sister Sophia
Kapanadze and
niece Lucia
Kapanadze, 175; On
Blavatsky, 30, 210;
Frank's criticism,
251–252; Guénon's
criticism, 236, 238;
Landau's view,
178n; Lawrence's
criticism, 12, 39, 47;
Anti-feminism, 243; Art
(objective), 107,
226–227; Love,
242–246; Religion,
213–214
Essenes, 231–232;
Orphism, 232–233,
246;

Pythagoreanism,
230–231, 234;
Sufism, 229–230;
Essence and person-
ality, 140
Legominism, 233
Sex, 244–245
"Stop" exercises, 47
Suffering, intentional
and voluntary, 136,
197– 198
Works:
*All and Everything:
Beelzebub's Tales to
His Grandson,*
beginning, 97, 107
et passim; method of
composition,
101–102, Orage's
interpretation, 136 *et
passim;*
*Meetings With
Remarkable Men,* x,
106, 229;
*Life is Real Only
Then, When I Am,*
144, 222, 168 *et
passim,* 198, 247;
*Herald of Coming
Good,* 191–194;
*Views From the Real
World,* 222n.
Hanfstängli, Putzi Hitler's
"Clown Prince," 22
Hare Elizabeth Meredith
Sage "Betty," 29,
74, 93, 99, 101–102,
128, 150, 189, 204
Hare, Lawrence "Larry," 60,
69, 74, 93, 99
Hargrave, John, 187
Hartmann, Olga, 25, 53–58,
60, 72, 77, 86, 88,
105, 112–113, 115,
121, 123, 139, 144,
148–150, 154, 160,
179, 190n, 194
Hartmann, Thomas de, x,
25, 58, 78–79, 81,
89, 113, 116, 123,
125, 160, 179, 190n
Hasnamuss, 213
Hastings, Beatrice (Emily
Alice Haigh), viii,
xii, 3, 16, 45, 53n,
70n

Heap, Jane, viii, ix, 22, 24,
34, 60, 71–86, 94,
99, 112–116, 120,
122, 123–126, 145,
156, 176, 208
Heard, Gerald, 209
Hegel, George Wilhelm, 215
Heideggger, Martin, 222,
238–239
Helmholz, Ludwig
Ferdinand de, 219
Hemingway, Ernest, 22–24
Henderson, Alice Corbin,
150
Henley, William Ernest, 201
Herbert, Victor, 42
Hermes and Hermetism,
230–231, 236
Hesiod, *Theogony,* 235
Hesse, Herman, *Siddharta,*
218
Hewitt, Anna Butkovsky,
113n
Hinduism, 82n, 218
Hippocrates, 144n
Hitler, Adolph, 187
Hobson, Samuel G., 3
Hockenhull, Governor H.
W., 150, 189, 202
Hodgson, Shadworth,
222–223
Hoffman, Maud, 37, 47
Hohenberger, Robert, xvii,
238n
Holter, Elizabeth Sage, 11n,
189, 194
Hoover, Herbert, 204n
Houdini, Harry [Erich
Weiss], 122
Howarth, Dushka (Sophia),
xvi, 92, 159
Howarth, Jessmin, ix, xvi,
92, 103, 111n, 139,
159
Howells, William Dean, 2
Hügel, Friedrich von, 215,
225–226
Hughes, Langston, 23, 91
Hulme, Kathryn, 208
Hulme, T[homas] E[rnest],
10, 239n
Hume, David, 220
Hunt, Violet, xin
Hurst, Fanny, 46
Hurston, Zora Neale, 92,
210

About the Author

Paul Beekman Taylor was born in London, lived at the Prieuré with Gurdjieff, and studied with him from 1948–1949. He was a Fulbright Scholar and then a Fulbright Lecturer before becoming a Professor of Medieval English Languages and Literatures at the University of Geneva. He has published many works and papers, including *Shadows of Heaven: Gurdjieff and Toomer* (Weiser, 1998). He is also a member of the Planning Committee and Advisory Board of the Bognor *All and Everything*. Taylor lives in Geneva, Switzerland.